SAMUEL PHELPS AND SADLER'S WELLS THEATRE

SAMUEL PHELPS
and
Sadler's Wells Theatre

By

SHIRLEY S. ALLEN

Wesleyan University Press

MIDDLETOWN, CONNECTICUT

ISBN: 0-8195-4029-3
Library of Congress Catalog Card Number: 72-120259
Manufactured in the United States of America
First edition

To Anne, John, and Elizabeth

Contents

List of Illustrations

Preface

THIS book is an attempt to reverse the verdict of history on the merits and accomplishments of Samuel Phelps, an English actor and theatrical manager of the nineteenth century. His name is almost forgotten today, and the place accorded him by theatrical historians is a minor one. Yet in his own time critics ranked him with Garrick, Kemble, Kean, and Macready. His management of Sadler's Wells Theatre was one of the few successful managements of the Victorian period, surviving the years of economic depression known as the "hungry 'forties" and flourishing during two decades that saw the virtual disappearance of English drama from London theatres.

Many aspects of Phelp's management are noteworthy. He produced thirty-one Shakespearean plays, some of which had not been acted since Shakespeare's time. In a number of them he replaced the acting versions, used for a hundred and fifty years as improvements upon Shakespeare's work, with the original Shakespearean text. He discarded the star system of acting Shakespeare, bringing back to the stage the complete parts of minor characters and giving a new emphasis to the total effect of the play. He applied to his Shakespearean productions the methods of directing which have become standard in the twentieth-century theatre, imposing his own conception of a play and supervising both acting and staging to carry out his intention. At the same time he made his theatre a training school for actors, providing both instruction and the opportunity to progress from the lowest ranks of a repertory company to a position of importance. He developed a new theory of stage decoration, using it as a means of dramatic interpretation, which anticipated by fifty years the principles accepted today. He used new techniques of staging that

achieved illusion without the excessive realism which had already begun
to dominate the theatre. He taught managers the use of darkness by his
Macbeth and the use of suggestive simplicity by his *Lear*. He showed
them how to make ghosts vanish in his *Hamlet* and how to create a
fairyland in his *Midsummer Night's Dream*.

Although these achievements of Phelps's management make it worthy
of a prominent place in the history of the English theatre, his most important accomplishment was the reintroduction of poetic drama to a
popular audience. From the closing of the theatres by the Puritans in
1642 until Phelps's opening of Sadler's Wells, play-acting had been carefully restricted. After the Restoration exclusive royal patents gave the
right of acting plays to a few theatres patronized by the upper classes. In
London patents belonged to Covent Garden and Drury Lane, and later
for summer seasons to the Little Theatre in the Haymarket. Provincial
towns had their legitimate or royal theatre with the same exclusive rights.
The prices charged at the two great national theatres—double those of
the minor houses—and their location in the West End of London removed
them from the patronage of the middle and working classes who lived
in suburban districts. Indeed, a major purpose of the theatrical monopoly
had been to safeguard public morality by restricting dramatic performances to audiences drawn from the educated and wealthy classes.

Minor theatres were licensed for forms of entertainment not restricted
by the monopoly law: acrobats, dancers, performing animals, concerts,
pantomime, burletta, and musical dramas. The gradual development in
the early nineteenth century of plays with spoken dialogue accompanied
by a tinkling piano, or melodrama, was officially tolerated because it
offered no competition to the patent theatres. It was considered a variation
of the type of entertainment traditionally offered at minor theatres,
characterized by its ephemeral nature and its suitability to the taste of
the lower classes.

Although the monopoly was at last repealed in 1843, the conviction
that only the upper classes could appreciate tragedy and comedy was still
generally held by actors, managers, and critics. Repeal came not as a
result of the claim long pressed by the minors, that all theatres should be
equally free to present plays, but rather because the patent theatres had
suffered such a series of financial losses that they could no longer be
maintained as playhouses. After the repeal there was no immediate change
in the status of the minor theatres. Legal sanction did not confer equality.

A year later the only attempt to produce Shakespeare at a minor theatre was the one made at the suburban Sadler's Wells.

The success of Phelps's management, from 1844 until 1862, demonstrated for the first time that the classic repertory of the English stage could attract and hold a popular audience. Clerks, shopkeepers, and wage earners of many types who lived in the surrounding area poured into Sadler's Wells to see the plays which had formed the repertory of the great national theatres. After a few seasons, this inexperienced audience became known for discriminating appreciation and for a remarkable acquaintance with poetic drama. When the reputation of Sadler's Wells became established, the local audience was joined by playgoers from all parts of London and by many of the most distinguished literary men of the time, who found themselves at home there as at no other theatre in London. But these patrons followed rather than led the taste of the inhabitants of Islington who formed the bulk of the audience and the main support of the theatre.

Among all classes of society, only the aristocracy was never attracted to Sadler's Wells. Queen Victoria, despite occasional goads from *Punch,* did not visit the theatre during the eighteen years of Phelps's management. Members of the highest circles of society found Islington too far from fashionable London to be taken seriously as the dramatic center of the city. And they were perhaps unwilling to recognize the existence of a theatre which seemed to proclaim the equality of all classes in the appreciation of drama.

The absence of royal patronage and the lack of interest shown by the social class which traditionally had been the chief support of the English stage prevented Sadler's Wells from achieving full recognition. Samuel Phelps's career as an actor and his important management of Sadler's Wells have both suffered an undeserved obscurity, largely from this cause.

The early part of Phelps's career on the London stage suffered from theatrical conditions during the last years of the monopoly and particularly from the tyranny of William Charles Macready. The story of these years, 1837 to 1844, is important not only for evaluating Phelps's abilities as an actor and for explaining the conditions which led to his experiment at Sadler's Wells, but also for understanding the collapse of the traditional English theatre, which left the early Victorian period almost without serious acted drama. Theatrical historians have dealt with this period primarily from Macready's point of view, taking their materials from his own diary and from the writings of his friends. The tendency to look at the theatre of his time through Macready's own eyes has been continued in the most recent biography, Professor Alan S. Downer's *The Eminent Tragedian, William Charles Macready* (Cambridge, Massachusetts, 1966). The effect of the inherited attitude upon Phelps's reputation is nowhere more evident than in Professor Downer's references to Phelps as a *protégé* of Macready. In order to rescue Phelps from the obscurity in which Macready tried to bury him I have portrayed Macready as many of his contemporaries saw him. Fairness to the actors and authors whose work and reputations suffered because of Macready's influence and the support of his articulate friends demands a reappraisal of the long-accepted view.

Another reason for the obscurity of Phelps's reputation can be found in the subsequent changes in the English theatre. While he was still at Sadler's Wells, the managers of West End theatres began to adopt practices radically different from the traditions of the previous century. A new interest in realistic stage setting, which led to spectacular productions that were far too expensive for the repertory system, helped to establish the "long run." Concurrently, the influence of the French theatre and of English melodrama fostered a new style of acting suitable to the everyday speech of domestic plays and far removed from the traditional elevated style used in poetic drama. By the end of Phelps's career in 1878 there had been a revolution in the English theatre that made his kind of management and his style of acting seem to belong to the remote past.

Interest in repertory theatres, and particularly in theatres devoted to the production of serious drama at popular prices, has recently appeared on both sides of the Atlantic. In spite of the radical changes that have affected the theatre in the past hundred years, we now face many of the same problems faced by the London theatre of 1840. We also are concerned with the restriction of drama to a limited audience, with the absence of the classic poetic drama from our commercial theatre, with the lack of opportunity for playwrights, and with the overwhelming popularity of musicals. The following history of Phelps's successful experiment at Sadler's Wells may serve a useful purpose as a guide for popular repertory theatres. Many of the principles of his management are still applicable today, and the very uniqueness of his achievement makes it worthy of serious consideration as a model for a popular theatre.

Acknowledgments

MEMORIES of Phelps were retained long after his death by some actors, critics, and playgoers, but in recent years knowledge of his achievement has been limited to a few discerning theatrical historians, and it is to one of the most distinguished of these, Professor Arthur Colby Sprague, that I owe my interest in this subject. His conviction that an injustice had been done Phelps by stage historians led me to undertake this study. He guided me to the Phelps materials in the Harvard Theatre Collection, and he directed my work on Phelps's management of Sadler's Wells, which appeared as a doctoral dissertation at Bryn Mawr College in 1949. Although Professor Sprague has not read this book and is not responsible for any of its errors, his work has served as both model and inspiration for mine.

I am indebted to the late William Van Lennep, former curator of the Harvard Theatre Collection, for giving me free access to the manuscript letters of Samuel Phelps and for making available the many resources of the Theatre Collection. I am grateful to Helen Willard, present curator, for her help and to the trustees of the Harvard College Library for permission to use quotations from these manuscript materials.

I am also indebted to the directors of the Folger Memorial Shakespeare Library for access to the collection of Phelps prompt books and several manuscript letters, and to the British Museum Newspaper Library for use of London and provincial newspapers of the nineteenth century. I owe special thanks to Wyman Parker, librarian of the Olin Library at Wesleyan University, for allowing me to use the Howard Moulton

xv

Theatre Collection before it had been catalogued, and to Linda Polsby for her careful reading of the early chapters, many thoughtful suggestions. and encouraging approval at a time when the end was not yet in sight.

For help in gathering material, for twenty years of patient listening, careful criticism, and constant encouragement I thank Archibald Allen.

SAMUEL PHELPS AND SADLER'S WELLS THEATRE

The Training of an Actor

SAMUEL PHELPS was born in Devonport on February 13, 1804. His family held a position of some social importance, and his father was a successful merchant, who was able to provide him not only with good schooling but also with opportunities to visit London, where a cousin who was a dramatic critic frequently took him to the theatre. When he was nine years old, his family spent several months in London, so that during the season of 1814–1815 he saw John Kemble, Charles Young, Mrs. Faucit, and Miss O'Neill at Covent Garden and the newly discovered genius Edmund Kean at Drury Lane. The following season he saw the Kemble production of *Cymbeline* and Kean's unforgettable performance of Sir Giles Overreach in Massinger's *A New Way To Pay Old Debts*. In the history of the English theatre there has been no period more exciting for the variety and individual genius of its actors. The experience made a lasting impression on Phelps and formed the basis of a life-long devotion to the theatre.

When he came home to Devonport, he spent his free time at the Devonport Theatre making himself useful backstage. While he was still a schoolboy he was given walk-on parts in the afterpieces (the farce, short comedy, or musical piece which customarily followed the tragedy or comedy of an evening's performance). Suddenly, when he was sixteen, the circumstances of his life completely changed. He was left an orphan and was sent to live with an older brother, who was a wine merchant in Plymouth. This brother, having a family of his own to support, told Phelps to give up his boyish dreams of becoming an actor and settle down to the serious business of earning his own living as soon as possible. Young Samuel obediently took a position as a junior reader on the local newspaper, but secretly he kept up his attachment to the theatre. Whenever he found an opportunity, he slipped out of the house in the evening and went to Devonport in time to be backstage for the afterpiece.

It was an unhappy year for him. After losing his parents and his home, he seemed also to have lost all hope for a career on the stage. And in addition he was made to feel that he was a burden to his brother's family. At last he decided to go to London, take up his own career, and support himself without help from anyone. When he was seventeen he left Plymouth, not telling the family of his plans, and arrived in London without money, friends, or sure hope of employment. The strength of his determination to make his own way is indicated by the fact that, except for a brief note sent immediately after his arrival in London, he did not write his brother again until he had established his reputation as an actor, nearly sixteen years later.

He soon found that no theatre would hire an untrained boy of seventeen, even as a "utility man" for afterpieces. Hunger finally forced him to look for work on a newspaper. He was given a trial by the *Globe* as a temporary junior reader and after proving his competence was hired as a permanent member of the staff. He began at once to look for an opportunity to learn the art of acting and eventually found a small private theatre in Rawstone Street, Islington, where a company of amateur actors put on performances several times a week. For the next five years he devoted his official working hours to journalism and his evenings to the theatre, advancing to the position of senior reader on the newspaper and becoming the leading actor of the amateur company.

In the spring of 1826 a professional actor of the Olympic Theatre saw one of Phelp's performances and was sufficiently impressed to ask for his services as guest star for his own benefit performance. Although an actor was not paid for contributing his services on a benefit night, Phelps regarded this invitation as his first professional appearance and decided to make it a test of his readiness for entering upon an acting career.

The Olympic was forbidden by the monopoly law to present plays, but like other minor theatres it regularly circumvented the law by disguising its performances as musical entertainments. The theatre was famous for melodrama, and it was in two typical specimens of this popular genre that Phelps, announced on the bills as "a gentleman amateur," played the leading roles. He was Eustache de St. Pierre in *The Surrender of Calais* and the Count de Valmount in *Foundling of the Forest*. The young actor was well received by the audience, and with the applause echoing in his ears he decided to make the stage his only profession.

The next morning his friend Douglas Jerrold, a colleague on the newspaper and a prominent member of the amateur group at the Rawstone Street Theatre, tried to point out the rashness of his decision. He had watched Phelps's performance at the Olympic, but he could not encourage a friend to give up the steady income of 4 pounds a week, which he earned as a head reader, for the uncertainties of a career on the stage. "If you persevere," he predicted, "you *may* eventually make a good Walking Gentleman, and get your five-and-twenty shillings a week; but you must stick to it, remember." [1] This discouraging warning from the future dramatic critic of *Punch* did not, however, deter Phelps, who spent the summer looking for a position in a stock company. He finally heard of an opening on the York circuit and obtained a contract for 18 shillings a week for the autumn of 1826. On the strength of this engagement he resigned his position on the newspaper.

Courage was needed, for he had fallen in love and was married on August 11 at St. George's Church in Queen's Square. His wife, Sarah Cooper, was only sixteen years old, and they had no money aside from his scanty salary. Although this marriage may have appeared at the time to be unwise, neither of them ever regretted it.

They went to York, where Phelps left his young wife in the care of her aunt and uncle while he traveled from one theatre to another with a Yorkshire company under the management of an actor named Downe. His first engagement is reported to have been at Pontefract and his first appearance in *Macbeth* as six characters: the Third Witch, Duncan, the First Murderer, Ross, one of the apparitions, and the servant whom Macbeth addresses as "thou cream-fac'd loon." Such an assignment would seem to give more opportunity for learning the art of quick change than that of acting, but it was not an unusual assignment for a Walking Gentleman in the days of traveling stock companies.

During the next season, the winter of 1827–1828, Phelps began to advance from the lowest rung in the professional ladder, playing roles in the category of Light Comedian and occasionally Jeune Premier. He sang the part of Sir Frederick Vernon in a musical version of *Rob Roy*, played Malcolm in *Macbeth*, Benvolio in *Romeo and Juliet*, Careless in *The School for Scandal*, and in one performance the Ghost to Charles Kemble's Hamlet. Toward the end of their stay at the Hull Theatre he was allowed the leading roles in two tragedies, *Pizarro* and *George Barn-*

well. His ability to sing and his versatility in acting obviously made him a valuable member of the company.

Physically he was well suited to play a variety of roles, since both his face and figure possessed a rare plasticity. He was of medium height (5 feet, 9 inches) and slender build. Off stage he held himself erect and moved with a stiffness that suggested military training; but he could transform his gait and bearing to imitate courtly grace, sidling hypocrisy, or faltering age. He had a high forehead, a straight, strong nose, and a broad square jaw. His mouth was wide, thin-lipped, and resolute, but extremely flexible in expression. Although his eyes were small, set close together, and pale in color, the brows above them were well marked and mobile. In repose his face seemed rigid and inexpressive, but on stage it could convey subtle shades of emotion across the footlights and could be changed like a mask from one character to another. His voice was powerful, with unusual range and resonance and a clear, almost musical, tone. He learned to control it to any desired expression, and he freed his speech from all provincialisms.

The company practiced a true repertory system, with a different feature every night and few repetitions during their stay at any one theatre. Besides the featured play or opera there was always an afterpiece, and Phelps often played in both. It was a demanding profession with the constant study of new roles, daily rehearsals, and a long evening program. The salary was too small to provide for a wife, so Sarah remained at her uncle's house in York, where her husband could see her on Sundays by walking from the town where he was playing and returning at night in time for Monday morning's rehearsal. He went on foot because he could not afford travel by coach even when Sunday schedules offered the opportunity. In June, 1828, when their first child was born, Phelps was acting in Leeds, thirty miles away.

These years of apprenticeship in the theatres of Yorkshire were probably worth the privations he suffered. He thoroughly learned his trade in the excellent school of a repertory company, where versatility and quick mastery of new parts were demanded. He learned from experienced actors the traditional interpretation of important roles and the stage business handed down from previous generations. He spent his lonely afternoons in voice training, practice in reading poetry, and the study of plays. Gradually he developed his own style and become sufficiently experienced in stage practice to qualify for leading roles.

By the season of 1828–1829 he had attained the rank of Second Lead, playing Macduff, King Claudius, and Julius Caesar to Calvert's Macbeth, Hamlet, and Brutus. He also sang Ottocar in *Der Freischutz.* At the end of the season H. W. Butler took over the management of the Hull Theatre, replacing Cummins, who only a year before had replaced Downe. Hard times had set in for provincial theatres, and managerial failures were so frequent that many theatres were closed the greater part of the year. Towns which formerly had supported both a royal theatre and a minor house could now scarcely support one.

During most of the summer Phelps played in Hull, and in the following winter Butler took the company to Sheffield, where the opening performance was *Othello* with Butler and Phelps in the leading roles. During the winter of 1829–1830 he played the title role in *King John* with such a mastery of his art that the two Sheffield newspapers began to predict for him a distinguished career on the London stage.

The characteristics of Phelps's acting are described in reviews of the *Sheffield Independent,* whose theatrical critic possessed a knowledge of the theatre and a precision in writing not commonly found in provincial newspapers. He notes Phelps's "intellectuality," remarking that "he thinks for himself and will take no man's conception secondhand." He comments on Phelps's success with his audiences, who indicated approval by enthusiastic applause and increased patronage. He also mentions, though as a fault, his "cold and precise mode of speaking." All three of these attributes—the well-studied conception of a role, the ability to move the sympathy of the audience, and the precise, distinct diction—remained characteristic of Phelps's acting through the fifty years of his career on the stage.

In spite of Phelps's popularity and the general competence of Butler's management, audiences were not large enough to meet expenses. In February Butler tried to fill the theatre by announcing the first appearance in Sheffield of Charles Kean, son of the famous Edmund Kean. The great name aroused interest, but it also conferred upon a young and inexperienced actor the privilege of playing leading roles far beyond his abilities. His performances of Sir Edward Mortimer in *The Iron Chest* (one of his father's most successful roles) and of Othello, with Butler as Iago, were disappointing. The *Sheffield Courant* of February 12 declared that Kean would never be more than "an excellent second-rate performer." Phelps, who had been reduced to minor roles during Kean's engagement, was preferred by audience and critics. The *Independent* of March 6, in summing up the season, found little to praise in Kean's performances and pronounced Phelps one of the most promising young actors of the provincial stage.

Whatever satisfaction Phelps derived from these opinions must necessarily have been tempered by the realization that the failure of Kean's engagement meant the end of Butler's management of the Sheffield Theatre. Phelps was now twenty-six years old and ready to assume the position of leading actor in a good provincial theatre, but he found almost no opportunity to act. Butler's company went next to Wakefield but closed after one week. Then they tried York, where a two-month season proved a financial failure. In the meantime, Cummins had closed the Hull Theatre, announcing the loss of 2,300 pounds in eighteen months, not including remuneration for his own services or those of his wife. Commenting upon this state of affairs in the provincial theatre, the *Wakefield and Halifax Journal* of March 12, 1830, remarked, "In many places it is dying away."

While managers of provincial theatres often worked without salary, at the same time risking imprisonment for debt, London stars who toured the provinces continued to demand high salaries. In the spring of 1830, Fanny Kemble, whose name placed her in the first rank of actresses, was reported by the *York Chronicle* to have refused an offer of 50 pounds a night from the Bath Theatre and demanded instead 1,000 pounds for twelve nights. Edmund Kean was still commanding a large amount for his engagements, although "the decline of physical power and intellectual energy" in his acting was noted by the *Manchester Guardian* of November 19, 1831.

In the autumn of 1830, the Sheffield Theatre was opened by H. Beverly, but he was even less successful than Butler had been and was forced to close before January. On January 22 he offered the scenery and costumes of the Sheffield Theatre for sale, and for the rest of the year the theatre was empty. In January, 1831, Beverly opened the Theatre Royal, Manchester, where the companies of Liverpool and Manchester had combined, and announced a season of legitimate drama with Phelps as leading actor. The "season" lasted only three weeks.

Manchester newspapers for 1830 and 1831 contain frequent announcements of the closing of the Theatre Royal and of its reopening under new management. Neither the strength of the combined companies nor the starring engagements of Edmund Kean attracted sufficient audiences to support the theatre. The Minor Theatre of Manchester had no better success with lighter forms of entertainment. It also frequently closed without notice and after a recess opened under new management, with some new attraction prominently advertised. A manager named Neville attempted tragedy at the Minor, although the consistent failure of drama at the Royal would seem to have offered small inducement to risk infringement of its patent. The proprietors of the Royal, themselves in financial difficulties, demanded enforcement of their patent rights. When Neville in the spring of 1831 again violated the monopoly—this time by producing an Italian opera—he was arrested and sent to prison, where he might have remained indefinitely, burdened by debt in addition to his sentence, had not public opinion been shocked into effective action.

Amid such conditions Phelps searched the theatres of northern England for any engagement. It is not surprising that he had almost no success. During most of the year 1831 he was without employment, and his second child, a daughter, was born in a wretched Sheffield tenement. Thirty-five years later when he visited the place he wrote his wife: "There are no pleasant recollections connected with it." [2] Finally in the spring of 1832 he obtained an engagement with the actor Tom Ryder, who managed a company playing in Perth, Dundee, Aberdeen, and Inverness. Economic conditions in Scotland were slightly better than in the industrial belt of northern England. The *Edinburgh Observer* of September 25, 1832, commenting upon the beginning of the dramatic season in Edinburgh, remarked that "almost every large theatrical establishment in the three kingdoms has been overtaken by ruin, except our own." With his engagement in Scotland Phelps had some reason to hope that his worst trials were over, but he had hardly begun to win a reputation in Ryder's company during the spring of 1832 when the serious illness of his wife and son forced him to abandon his engagement in order to hurry back to York.

After he was assured of his wife's recovery, he obtained an engagement for the summer with Watkins Burroughs, manager of the Preston Theatre. It was a fairly good position with the chance of playing secondary leads. He played Isaac the Jew in a dramatic adaptation of *Ivanhoe* which featured Burroughs and his wife in the principal roles. Houses were small even though the company was described, by a reviewer in the *Preston Pilot,* as "rather above the ordinary level." The same reviewer commented that "theatricals are not much in fashion anywhere just now."

The *Preston Chronicle* of August 18 asserted that small attention could be paid to the theatre amid the more important political discussions of the times. Burroughs was able to keep the theatre open only by reducing prices of admission "in consequence of the general depression of the times." The season ran until the end of September.

Phelps then left Burroughs's company because he had obtained a second engagement with Tom Ryder in Scotland. It was fortunate for him that he did so, since the company came to grief soon afterward in Blackburn. In the middle of November bailiffs confiscated the properties of the Blackburn Theatre as security for Burroughs's debts. Burroughs disappeared, and his stranded company staged two benefit performances on their own behalf to recover part of their unpaid salaries. The theatrical properties belonging to Burroughs were then sold at auction for 5 pounds, a small fraction of their value.

Phelps in the meantime had returned to York to prepare for his move to Scotland, where Ryder's offer promised sufficient security to provide a home for his wife and children. On October 21, 1832, before leaving York, he wrote to an acquaintance named Cleneshaw in Northallerton, Yorkshire, asking him to redeem a trunk and send it to him:

> When I was at Northallerton 2 years ago with Mr. Herbert, necessity compelled me to leave in the possession of Mrs. Walbrun, ironmonger, a trunk as security for £1—which I stood indebted to her. Since that time I have been overwhelmed by misfortune—in fact during the last 2½ years I have not been in a situation more than eight months, so that trifling as the sum of 1 £ may appear I have never been able to send it her.[3]

After six years as a professional actor Phelps did not have enough money to pay this small debt.

Under Ryder's management he at last had a full season's engagement and the opportunity to play Lear, Macbeth, Othello, and Shylock. When he found that Scottish plays were particularly successful with local audiences, he studied the dialect until he had mastered it. He then played the Dougal Creature to Ryder's popular Rob Roy and Sir Archy MacSarcasm in *Love à la Mode,* developing his talent for eccentric comic characters which had already brought him some fame as an actor in afterpieces.

After a year in Scotland he took an engagement at the Theatre Royal, Belfast, for the winter season of 1833–1834. The theatre, after being closed for several seasons, had reopened in October under the management of

Watkins Burroughs (identified in newspaper advertisements as former manager of the Royal Coburg and Surrey Theatres of London, but surely the same Watkins Burroughs who had escaped the bailiffs in Blackburn a year earlier). For the next three years Phelps played alternately in Scotland under Ryder's management and in Belfast under Burroughs's, earning a solid reputation as a tragedian during a period of hard times and small audiences. Prices of admission were cut in half at Belfast in May of 1835, a few weeks after Phelps's third child was born; and the theatrical fare for the rest of the season catered to the taste of the gallery patrons, who preferred topical melodramas to tragedy. Phelps made a hit as Daniel O'Carolan, the peasant hero of *Ireland as It Is; or, the Peasant, the Middleman, and the Absentee.*

After another winter in Scotland Phelps decided that it was time for him to look toward London and his debut on the stage of one of the patent theatres. His first step was an engagement for the summer of 1836 at Worthing, the summer resort of many Londoners, where he played a variety of leading roles including a number of comic parts suitable to the holiday mood of the audience. He was well liked and became known almost at once. Reports of his success reached the comedian Hay, manager of the Exeter and Plymouth theatres, who offered him the position of leading actor at the Exeter Theatre from November 9 to Passion Week, the entire winter season of 1836–1837.

This engagement, which Phelps accepted, was in some ways preferable to an immediate London debut. It offered an assured income while giving him the chance to win a reputation in a theatre under the eye of London managers. Since Edmund Kean's triumphant entry into London by way of Exeter and Dorchester in 1814, the doings of these theatres had been a matter of interest in the metropolitan theatre.

Phelps opened in Exeter on November 23, 1836, as Eleazar in *The Jewess* (Planché's translation of Scribe's romantic drama, which had been a hit in London the previous season) and as Nicholas Flam in Buckstone's farce, the afterpiece of the evening. His second performance was the title role of John Howard Payne's *Brutus,* a role so completely identified with Edmund Kean that few actors had dared to attempt it. Phelps's success was immediate, and his reception in Exeter must have equaled his most optimistic hopes. A review in *Trewman's Exeter Flying Post* (November 30, 1836) reported that his performance was greeted by "applause never exceeded by anything we have witnessed," and pronounced him "beyond all question superior to anyone [seen in Exeter] since the days of the late Edmund Kean." Speaking of his Brutus the reviewer said, "We remember the elder Kean in this character, and it is no disparagement to his memory to say, that while throughout not inferior, in the counterfeited idiocy, Mr. Phelps was superior to that great actor." The *Western Luminary* (December 5, 1836) also remarked upon the "repeated plaudits of a numerous and fashionable audience" and called Phelps's Brutus "as fine a specimen of tragic acting as we have ever witnessed," preferring it to Kean's because the transitions from idiocy to sanity were "not so marked or abrupt as used to be evidenced by Mr. Kean, but more in keeping with the dignity of the character." *Featherstone's Exeter Times* (November 29, 1836) asserted, "Never since the days of *Kean* have we had on our boards a local actor whose histrionic powers could come at all in competition with those of *Mr. Phelps.*" *Woolmer's Exeter and Plymouth Gazette* spoke of the crowded house that gathered to witness Phelps's second appearance although the weather was bad enough to have deterred most audiences.

Phelps went on to provoke further comparison with Kean by playing three of the great tragedian's most celebrated roles: Shylock, Sir Edward Mortimer (in *The Iron Chest*), and Richard the Third. He also acted Hamlet—by custom the test of a tragedian's maturity and in this case especially challenging because Charles Kean had recently made a good impression in Exeter with his Hamlet.

His Shylock was well received, although it puzzled many reviewers because of its new conception of the character. Touches of irony in the early scenes and a manly strength of character were shockingly different from the cringing and intense malignity of Kean's Shylock. One critic remarked, "We were at first rather startled by his originalities, but we remain for the most part convinced by their truth." [4]

On the night that *The Iron Chest* was played he had to contend with a more unusual deterrent than bad weather. It was the night of the mayor's bespeak, and because a new Reform mayor had recently taken office the Tories stayed away. Nevertheless, the house was full and Phelps's attraction undiminished by political controversy. The *Western Times* of December 9 described the response of this audience to his Sir Edward Mortimer:

> He carried the house with him, the applause gathering strength as he proceeded, till in the end it was almost overwhelming; and when the curtain

fell, it pleased the house to demand his re-appearance. . . . We are no admirers of this new custom, though it is difficult to resist its influence. . . . Mr. Phelps, however, made his appearance with much modesty, he merely crossed the stage bowing in acknowledgement of the plaudits which were still showered on him.

The "new custom" of curtain calls, which had recently come to England from France and had been adopted by Edmund Kean and Macready, was still generally condemned by critics, and Phelps himself was embarrassed by it. His modesty, noted by this reviewer, was not feigned but an essential aspect of the man.

His own style of acting, however, was in part responsible for the audience's insistence upon his reappearance after the fall of the curtain. Audiences had long been accustomed to the practice of applauding frequently during the course of a play—as we still do for operatic performances. Actors measured their success by the amount of applause that followed immediately upon their most effective "points," and without stepping out of character they encouraged such response by emphasis, gesture, pause, or other dramatic device. This special designation of certain passages was expected by audiences and was not considered detrimental to theatrical illusion. Phelps, however, attempted a more complete and consistent identification with the character and discouraged applause by avoiding abrupt transitions and minimizing the set speeches that were traditionally used to display an actor's art. The audience became absorbed in the character and, not being reminded by any sign from the actor of the points customarily marked for a round of applause, they allowed a scene to flow on uninterrupted, until Phelps's departure from the stage suddenly made them aware of their omission. As if to atone for it, they registered approval with increased volume at the end of the play, often demanding his reappearance after the final curtain.

This reaction of the audience to Phelps's obvious intention is indicated in reviews of his first Hamlet in Exeter. The *Devonshire Chronicle and Exeter News* of December 10 said:

The audience several times would have testified their approbation, but they were too deeply engaged in catching the tones and manner of the performer to allow them to interfere with the current of his vivid declamation, and a single "hush" repressed what all were most willing to award, but for the fear of interrupting the object of their admiration.

The *Flying Post* (December 7, 1836) made a similar observation:

> The audience were awed into silence, which was not permitted to be broken until the instant that Mr. Phelps, in the several parts of the play, was about to quit the stage.

These comments hint at the quality in Phelps's acting that stirred the Exeter audience into almost unprecedented enthusiasm. His submergence of the actor in the character brought a new sense of reality to the stage and increased the emotional response of the spectator. In the involvement of the audience with the passions and sufferings of the hero—the quality called "pathos" in the nineteenth-century criticism—Phelps's acting differed from that of the great actors known to his generation. After the "classical" school of the Kembles, with its emphasis on the beauty of external form, Edmund Kean had thrilled audiences by the brilliance and intensity of his acting expressing depth of emotion in certain unforgettable passages. William Macready had impressed audiences by the subtle intelligence of his reading, which brought out the meaning of well-known lines, and by the consistency of interpretation, which gave new insight into character. But none of these actors had sought anonymity in a role. They preferred to have artistic details recognized and applauded. Even Macready, who frequently refers in his diary to his attempts at identification with a character, needed the stimulus of frequent applause. Phelps, on the contrary, lost himself in the character, preserving a consistent interpretation that was not laid aside for an instant during the course of the play. The audience perceived his new approach and responded with silence where they normally would have applauded.

Phelps's departure from traditional point making was most remarkable in *Richard the Third* because the version of Shakespeare's play universally used on the stage since 1700 was that of Colley Cibber, who had turned the text into a series of points for the leading actor. Phelps surprisingly achieved a triumph in this role without using its most obvious theatrical asset—strong emphasis upon dramatically effective lines. According to the *Western Times* (December 16, 1836):

> A crowded and enraptured house followed him through every scene of the tragedy with a deep and intense interest, which though partaken by ourselves in common with everyone who witnessed it—absolutely astonished us at the effect it produced on the house. . . . The spectators were constantly turning and greeting each other with exclamations of wonder and delight. . . . There was nothing of Kean, nothing of Macready, noth-

ing like a following after old "points," nothing like a desire to make new. The chief beauty of the delineation consisted in its evenness.

That this evenness was something more than the absence of points is made clear in a review written by the discerning critic of the *Plymouth Herald* (May 6, 1837):

> The manner in which his *Richard* drew from personal defect a privilege for moral deformity, and triumphed in the all-conquering subtleties of his tongue was most felicitous. . . . We shall not be consulting either Mr. Phelps's interest or our own critical principles in dwelling on isolated particulars. We desire to be understood as eulogists of a performance, illumined by the steady light of a pervading intelligence, and not by the flickerings of occasional intelligence. . . . Breaking, as he does, through all the commonplaces of precedent,—not with an idle aim at novelty, but with the simple impulse of an original and energetic mind—he throws himself at once upon the chance of finding an unprejudiced recipient in his critic, and being measured solely by the standard of the poet's meaning.

Such an unprejudiced reception was granted Phelps's Richard by the audience in Exeter, who seemed not to regret the absence of the brilliant theatrical effects almost demanded by Cibber's version and used with overpowering force by Kean. They accepted with enthusiastic applause Phelps's new and more nearly Shakespearean interpretation of the character, although it was comparatively untheatrical and much more subtle. After the curtain had fallen on his first performance of the part, the audience cheered and called until he reappeared to receive their applause. After seeing his second performance, the critic of the *Western Times* (December 30, 1836) pronounced him "decidedly the first Richard of the day."

Having established his reputation as a successor to Kean, Phelps undertook the more difficult task of challenging comparison with Macready, then at the height of his career, by playing Macbeth, Othello, Lear, and Virginius (in the tragedy of that name by Sheridan Knowles). In these roles he was placing his abilities alongside those of a living actor and one whose experience on the stage and careful study of his characters combined with unusual intelligence and a polished manner to achieve a mastery of his art that might well discourage any provincial actor. In Macbeth especially, Phelps's performance was compared at every important speech with Macready's accomplished reading of the same lines. Both the *Flying Post* and the *Western Luminary* found his delivery of the dagger scene inferior to Macready's. He was also criticized for his reading of "My way of life is fallen into the sear . . . ." The difference between Phelps and Macready is concisely summarized by the *Western Luminary* (January 30, 1837):

> Wherever energy and strength of passion is required, Mr. Phelps is at home, but he does not equal Macready in giving due emphasis to those declamatory parts so deeply tinged with philosophy and true poetry.

This dictum is echoed by critics in London during the following decade.

In Othello and Lear Phelps's "strength of passion" and his identification with the character carried critics beyond comparison with Macready's declamation. The *Flying Post* (January 11, 1837) praised both the correctness of his interpretation and its compelling reality on the stage:

> Mr. Phelps, in his strong and nervous acting, proved that he has a mind capable of entering into the very spirit of the author, and possesses powers of such surpassing splendor as enable him to give this with a faithfulness conveying with it the stamp of reality and truth, to the audience.

A week later the same critic noted the freshness of Phelps's interpretation in several roles: "His manner is his own, and we are warranted in ranking him among the best living commentators on Shakespeare which this country possesses." The *Western Times* (January 13, 1837) pronounced his Lear "one of the highest achievements of histrionic art in the present day" and commented on the remarkable impression it left upon the minds of the spectators.

Achievement of reality of emotion on the stage also made his Virginius impressive. The suffering of the famous Roman who chose to kill his daughter rather than allow her to be dishonored found a sympathetic response in nineteenth-century audiences, and Phelps's gift for pathos made it unusually moving. His performance was called a masterpiece, and after his third appearance as Virginius the *Western Times* said that although Macready had first acted the role, Phelps had made it his own.

During January and February the attraction of Phelps's performances continued to fill the Exeter Theatre night after night, making the season a highly profitable one for the manager, Hay. His popularity was remarkable both for its long duration and for its extension to all parts of the audience. Applause was general, critics noted, and not restricted to enthusiastic partisans in gallery and pit. The boxes were full for the first time in many seasons. His Shakespearean roles were generally preferred, although during the last weeks of the season he introduced a number of tragedies from the early years of the century: Sheridan's *Pizarro,* Maturin's *Bertram,* Banim and Sheil's *Damon and Pythias,* and Knowles's *William Tell.* For his benefit performance on February 20, he decided to show his versatility, which had been somewhat eclipsed by his concentration on tragedy, by playing Sir Giles Overreach in *A New Way To Pay Old Debts* and the leading roles in both comic afterpieces. The house was crammed for this performance, bringing in 90 pounds instead of the usual 30 pounds to 50 pounds.[5] Because of the unusually successful season, Hay generously allowed Phelps the total profits for the evening without deducting the usual percentage for the manager's expenses.

During the spring of 1837 Phelps played at the Plymouth Theatre, returning in triumph to his home town and his family, whom he had not seen in sixteen years. They greeted him warmly in the theatre and sought his company off the stage. Local actors, critics, and playgoers found him accessible, though rather shy, and more concerned with his profession than with his own importance. Among those who gathered in his dressing room after performances was George Wightwick, an architect who was also a theatrical critic and reviewer for the *Plymouth Herald.* The Mordaunt sisters, who had been acting with Phelps, introduced him to Mrs. Nisbett, a third sister, who had already made her name on the London stage.

London was now uppermost in Phelps's thoughts. His success in Exeter had provoked comment in the newspapers, including his former employer, the *Globe,* which reported on December 11 that "a Mr. Phelps, a tragedian, has been creating a sensation at Exeter." In April he received a tentative offer from Alfred Bunn, manager of Drury Lane, for the winter season of 1837–1838, but he hesitated to sign with Bunn for two reasons. The first was his hope of appearing in London during the summer, and the other was Bunn's reputation for driving hard bargains with his actors. Everyone knew of Macready's quarrels with him, which had erupted into physical violence the previous spring; and John Vandenhoff, a tragedian of provincial celebrity recently come to London, had also left Drury Lane because of an argument with Bunn. On the other hand Phelps worried that Bunn's offer might be his only chance to get to London, since the other two legitimate theatres, Covent Garden and the Haymarket, had not yet been leased for the coming season.

While he was acting in Plymouth, he learned from the Mordaunts that Benjamin Webster, a comedian in the Covent Garden company, had become manager of the Haymarket and had already engaged Mrs. Nisbett for his company. Phelps decided to go to London for interviews with Webster and Bunn before making any commitment. He set out for London on May 23, taking with him his brother's oldest son (who later recorded the events of the trip in his biography of Phelps). On the evening of their arrival, he tried to see Bunn at Drury Lane but was refused admittance and had to be content with a seat in the dress circle for Taglioni's performance in *La Sylphide*. The next day, after obtaining a letter of introduction from Mrs. Nisbett to Webster, he went to the stage door of Covent Garden well before the opening curtain, in the hope of seeing Webster before the performance of *Henry the Eighth*.

Webster surprised Phelps by the cordiality of his reception. He said that he already knew of Phelps's reputation and showed him a clipping from the *Plymouth Herald* of George Wightwick's review of his Richard the Third (quoted above). He agreed at once to introduce Phelps to London on the stage of the Haymarket during the summer, provided that a definite commitment about the date of the debut could be postponed until the length of Macready's engagement there was determined. He promised that Phelps should appear, in any character he wished, immediately after Macready's departure. Phelps, who had been discouraged by Bunn's inaccessibility, the obvious preference for opera and ballet at Drury Lane, and the absence of other opportunities in London, was so delighted by the prospect of an early debut that he agreed to this rather indefinite arrangement. Even Webster's airy assurance that the length of Phelps's engagement and the amount of his salary could be determined later by letter was accepted without question by the hopeful provincial actor, taken off his guard by the warmth of Webster's manner. He then escorted his nephew to the front of the house, where they both saw Macready for the first time, in the role of Cardinal Wolsey, with Helen Faucit as Queen Katherine and Webster in the minor role of Lord Sands.

After he returned to Devonshire, early in June, 1837, Phelps filled a short engagement at the Devonport Theatre, where as a boy he had acted minor parts. He settled his wife and family in lodgings there and waited with increasing uneasiness for Webster's promised letter. He suddenly realized that, although he was under contract to Webster, Webster had made no definite commitment to him beyond an initial performance. Should his debut be judged unsuccessful, he might well have no engagement for the rest of the season. His misgivings increased when Webster's terms finally arrived—nearly a month after their interview—proposing that Phelps play three roles at the Haymarket and allow his subsequent salary to be decided by the degree of his success. Webster also said that he could not yet fix a date for the debut but suggested that it might be early August.

The effect of this letter upon Phelps can be deduced from a page of rough notes in Phelps's handwriting, preserved in the Harvard Theatre Collection. This page evidently contains notes for two letters written at the same time, one to a friend who had recommended him to the manager of the Southampton Theater for a summer engagement and the other to Webster in reply to his proposal. To his friend he wrote that he did not feel free to go to Southampton because the season there began too late to allow him time for a rest before the tentative date of his London debut. Although the season in Southampton was scheduled to begin on July 18, that was also the date of the opening of the races, and Phelps thought that "acting tragedy during that week would be out of the question." Declining the engagement in Southampton, he told his friend what he proposed to do during July:

> I have written to Mr. Webster by this post to ask him for a *certain engagement* for the remainder of the Haymarket season, which if he gives me I mean to spend 6 weeks in a little cottage on the coast of Cornwall not many miles hence, where I shall have a delightful garden, fields, etc. on one side of me, and the ocean on the other so that I shall be able to spout "Hamlet" to the flowers and howl "Richard" to the waves.

The remainder of the page is filled with jottings for the letter to Webster —not an easy one to phrase.

> It is the opinion of several of my friends, and that opinion is echoed by [my] own feelings on the subject, that the anxiety attendant upon acting for an engagement would render me incapable of displaying whatever talent in its full extent I may possess in any thing like a vigorous or efficient manner. I wish to know if you feel inclined to speculate by giving me an engagement (after the 5th of August) for any stated period and thereby render my success of mutual consequence—under such circumstances I should have no fear. You will oblige me by an *immediate* reply as the passage to America tho' still open will remain so but a few days longer.

The reference to a proposed trip to America seems to have been invented as a means of putting some pressure on Webster, since there is no other indication of definite arrangements for an American tour, although the possibility of such an alternative had probably come to Phelps's mind. The actual letter he sent to Webster on June 24, 1837 (which is now in the Folger Shakespeare Library) was more mildly stated:

> The only objection I have to "playing three parts and allowing my emolu-ment to be decided by my success"—is that the anxiety attendant upon such a proceeding (suffering as I do from *excessive nervousness*) will probably mar my efforts.

The statement that he suffered from excessive nervousness was no exag-geration. From the beginning of his career he had fought against an unusual susceptibility to stage fright, which in fact sixty years of acting did not cure. Before an opening curtain he needed a long period of solitude. Whenever possible he preferred to have his wife serve as his dresser. First nights were always an agony for him, and frequently his voice was so tense on the first night of a new role that it sounded harsh and unmanageable. In order to control his voice on such occasions, he made a practice of underplaying, to lessen the risk of losing, under the stress of emotion, all ability to manage it. He had learned from experience that reviews of his first-night performances were likely to be only mildly approving, whereas the same critics were often moved to high praise after seeing him a second time in the same role. In later years many London critics became aware of this acute first-night nervousness and made allowance for it whenever they were unable to postpone judgment until after a second performance. It is not surprising that Phelps was worried as early as June 24 about his opening night at the Haymarket, especially if his whole season's engagement, and therefore his future in London, were to depend upon the result.

Webster, however, was so little concerned about Phelps's worries that he did not answer the letter until July 5, and then he wrote only to set the date of his first performance for either August 28 or September 4. Phelps was bitterly disappointed by this response. The news that he would not get to London until the end of the summer gave him new cause for worry. He would have to make his debut at the end of the Haymarket season and after Macready's unusually long run in a new play, since it was the success of Sheridan Knowles's *The Bridal* which had postponed Phelps's appearance. Presumably the important actors of the Haymarket company would be taking their benefits during the week of

Phelps's three performances, and therefore his chances of attracting large houses would be much diminished. And should his debut be successful in spite of these difficulties, he could not hope for much of a contract from Webster so late in the season—only a few weeks before the two winter theatres opened.

He was so depressed by these prospects that he delayed writing Webster until he could talk the matter over with friends who knew more about managerial practices in London than he did. In the meantime he arranged to take the summer engagement in Southampton, stipulating only that the season should begin after the first week of races. He also agreed to act in Exeter during the last week of July, when the assizes would be in session. His hopes of a holiday by the sea were evidently given up.

Webster wrote him a curt note on July 20, demanding to know what three parts he wished to open in. Phelps answered from Exeter, where he was acting Werner (in Byron's tragedy) and Shylock on alternate nights. The letter, dated July 25, tells quite frankly and specifically the reason for his reluctance to accept Webster's terms, adding rather humbly, "I would feel obliged by your *candid* opinion on the above view of the case." He was not bold enough to break the contract or refuse to name the parts he wished to play, although his words reveal an effort to withhold full consent:

> In the event of my coming to town, I would wish to avoid touching (at present) any of Macready's well-known and all-recognized parts. I have been most successful in some parts of the late Kean's which Macready, I think, has not played much, especially Shylock and Richard, with Sir Edward Mortimer, etc., though my way of acting them is *wholly* and *totally* different from Kean's or any other person's. I should like to open in *Shylock*.[6]

Webster's answer made clear that he would hold Phelps to their agreement, referring to Phelps's earlier letter as if he had given his consent, and brusquely dismissing any objections:

T. R. Haymarket
July 26th, 1837

My Dear Sir,

        On the faith of your letter I have underlined you for more than a week past. As regards playing you in the midst of benefits or bringing you up at the end of my season is not my mode of acting and whoever informed you so was not in any way warranted in making such an assertion considering I can continue my season to the 15th January 1838 & commence again on the 15th March following. I shall announce you tomorrow for Shylock & wishing you every success, I remain,

Yours truly,

B. Webster

Phelps would have been surprised to learn that while he was being forced into a disadvantageous contract with Webster, another London manager was showing particular interest in his abilities. Macready had written the following letter to his friend George Wightwick, the Plymouth architect whose interest in the theatre has already been mentioned:

London, July 18th, 1837

My Dear Wightwick,

Will you excuse the trouble I am seeking to impose on you, and the hurried manner in which I do it? Some time since I received a Plymouth paper with a criticism upon the performance of a gentleman who rejoices in the name of Phelps; other accounts that I have had represent him very favourably. As it is not improbable I may have some concern in the direction of one of the Winter Theatres next season, I should very much wish to concentrate all the talent that can be brought together, and I am very desirous of having your opinion, which I so highly value, upon the merits of this gentleman. . . .

W. C. Macready

P.S.—Mr. Phelps is going to act at the Haymarket, when I shall see him; but I am anxious for your opinion.[7]

The tone of this letter indicates that Macready did not know of Wightwick's friendship with Phelps. Evidently he was surprised by the warmth of Wightwick's reply, which not only praised Phelps's acting but begged Macready to look after him in London, as a friend. Macready's second letter to Wightwick, dated July 30, reveals that his characteristic touchiness on the subject of rival actors had been roused by Wightwick's letter:

Mr. Phelps is engaged to make his appearance at the Haymarket—to act three characters, and upon his success to receive an engagement there. I am much interested in the event, and shall be truly happy to foster and watch over the development of his talent, should he need such a professional friend; but I hope he is moderate in his expectations of *remuneration,* for ours is now a *struggle for existence,* not for profit, and every salary on our establishment is largely but willingly reduced. I should like very much to know what is his aim in coming to town: whether he has the "aut Caesar, aut nullus" views of young Kean, or a resolution, in the love of his art, to study and toil for perfection in it. If I have the pleasure of any dealings with him, you may be sure that I shall be more than just to his deserts from the interest that you have evinced in him. Most cordially do I wish him success, and that he may add another actor to our scanty muster-roll.[8]

The day after writing this Macready commissioned his manager, George Bartley, to write Phelps. When Phelps received Bartley's note and learned that Macready intended to take over Covent Garden—a decision that had not yet been publicly announced—he must have regretted his eager acceptance of Webster's first offer. He replied to Bartley that he was already under contract to Webster at the Haymarket, knowing from Webster's most recent letter that the Haymarket season might overlap the opening of the winter season at Covent Garden.

On August 3, Bartley wrote Phelps a second letter, assuring him that "although Mr. Macready hopes to have the advantage of your services here next season—you are not in any way to consider that it will interfere with your understanding or arrangement with Mr. Webster at the Haymarket." [9] He also said that he hoped Phelps would act on the following Monday at Southampton "a character you consider yourself strong in—as I have no doubt but a principal of Mr. Macready's will be present on that evening."

This letter brought Phelps a sudden new hope. It seemed to promise that if Macready's agent thought well of Phelps's acting in Southampton, an engagement at Covent Garden would be offered that would neither conflict with his contract with Webster nor depend upon the success of his debut. He spent an anxious ten days waiting for the evening of August 14, when an unknown spectator would decide whether Macready would engage him or not. What happened that evening is described in a letter from Phelps to his wife:

Southampton
Tuesday, August 15

My dearest Sarah,

    As I know you will be anxious to hear how I got on last night, I lose no time in writing to you. Being here by myself, and having nothing to do last week I fretted myself ill—yesterday all day I was in such a state that I scarcely knew what to do with myself. I played as well as I could, but I thought very badly. I did not know if any person was in the house from London; but at the end of the "Iron Chest" a note was sent

round to me from *Macready,* who had been there all the time *himself.*
I was with him last night for upwards of an hour, and the result was
that I go to Covent Garden on the 16th of October. He wanted me to
name my salary, which I declined doing until I have played in London;
but at last I agreed to take the same salary that I may agree for at the
Haymarket—which, if I succeed I will take care shall be a good one, or
I will not agree at all. . . . My success here last night was very great, and
Macready said he thought I should succeed in London. . . .

> Your most affectionate husband,
> S. Phelps[10]

Macready's impression of Phelps, which is recorded in his diary,[11] was
decidedly higher than of any rival actor described in those pages. In
comparison with his remarks on Edmund Kean, Charles Kemble, John
Vandenhoff, Charles Kean, and many lesser actors, this grudging approval
of Phelps as an actor and a man is indeed high praise:

Southampton, August 14th.—Saw the play of the *Iron Chest*; what a
thing it is. I was disgusted with the patches of sentiment and claptraps
upon national privileges, humanity, and all the other virtues in which G.
Colman was so rich—on paper. Mr. Phelps in Sir Edward Mortimer displayed intelligence, occasionally great energy, some imagination—not much;
want of finish, of experience, of logic in the working out the character—
(to lay violent hands on the term)—of *depth* in all the great parts. His
best scene decidedly was his death, but even there was a want of method.
His level speaking is often very pleasing—always sensible. I expected from
his opening more than he achieved. There was no *absorbing* feeling
through the great scenes, no evidence of the "slow fire" "wearing his vitals";
this was particularly manifest in the last act, where he was direct and
straightforward even to commonplaceness. I think he will improve, and
run both Warde and Elton hard, and very likely do much more. I left
my note for him. He called at the Dolphin, and I offered him either the
salary he might take from Mr. Webster, or to give him now a salary, if
he would name one, that I could meet. He preferred waiting for Mr.
Webster, and we interchanged agreements to that effect. I liked his tone
and manner.

Neither account explains why Phelps agreed to a contract that was to
begin on October 16, when he knew from Webster that he might not
be released from his commitment at the Haymarket until long after that
date. Phelps's letter to his wife reveals no uneasiness about this aspect of

the agreement, although one would expect, because of their unusually close relationship, some mention of any subject which troubled him. Macready must have given him assurances that his Covent Garden engagement would not interfere with the Haymarket one. Phelps's nephew says, in his biography, that Macready claimed to have Webster's sanction for the new contract and asserted that Webster himself was engaged to appear at Covent Garden under Macready's management, since the Haymarket would be closed at the end of September.[12]

Certainly Macready had arranged matters in a way most beneficial to himself. After seeing Phelps's performance at Southampton, he felt confident that the new actor would not be a failure in London and therefore took no risk in offering him a season's contract. At the same time, by transferring Phelps early in October from the Haymarket to his own theatre, he would prevent Webster from reaping any great benefits from Phelps's debut, should it be extremely successful. As a theatrical manager, he could congratulate himself on an arrangement that weakened a rival theatre and strengthened his own. As an actor, jealous for his position as first tragedian on the English stage, he could be equally satisfied with an arrangement that placed a possible rival under his own control, while at the same time alienating him from the one manager in London who might have advanced his career at Macready's expense. Macready, who was a man capable of a high degree of self-deception, quite possibly did not think of his actions as dishonest, although he surely knew how Webster would regard the stealing of a promising actor from the Haymarket company. He may even have persuaded himself that he was keeping his promise to Wightwick and looking after Phelps's own interests in engaging him for Covent Garden.

Phelps was naive rather than dishonest in accepting Macready's offer. As in the case of the interview with Webster, he liked the man and took him at his word. Macready's outward appearance of integrity and gentlemanly reserve concealed his egotism and ambition from many a more experienced man than Phelps. One important advantage Phelps gained from his contract with Macready: a relaxation of tension about the success of his debut. With the assurance of a contract for the winter season, he no longer felt that his whole career depended upon three performances. This advantage, although minor in comparison to the severe damage the contract eventually inflicted upon his career, was important to Phelps.

He opened at the Haymarket on August 28, 1837, in the role of Shylock. Webster's announcements and reports of Phelps's success at Exeter had drawn a large audience, who greeted him with great applause. That this reception, which would have encouraged most actors, disconcerted Phelps is clear from the report of an honest and observant playgoer named Charles Rice, who kept detailed criticisms of the performances he attended in a notebook entitled "Dramatic Register":

> So far as patronage and encouragement were concerned, Mr. Phelps came in last night for a very good share, and, I must say, whatever applause he received seemed to arise out of the giver's opinion, and not from bribery; this was rare and meritorious. . . . Mr. Phelps's reception was most gratifying, the clapping of hands and waving of handkerchiefs, hats, playbills, &c. lasting for some minutes, and when he commenced the dialogue of his part, it was obvious that this flattering greeting had tended to make him considerably nervous, as some of his first sentences were very tremulously uttered; but still his conception was visible.[13]

Because of his nervousness Phelps played with restraint, afraid to risk the full power of his voice, depending upon his carefully studied interpretation of the character and his training in the art of acting to carry him through the first night. The audience applauded enthusiastically, responding to the intensity of emotion and loss of self which Phelps was able to convey. There was no doubt about the success of his debut.

Reviews the next morning were favorable, although without the enthusiasm shown by the audience. The *Times,* the *Chronicle,* and the *Post* agreed that he was a practiced actor, that his interpretation of Shylock was correct and judicious, that his declamation was often powerful, and that he fired the audience into sympathetic reaction, but that his performance was pitched too low throughout. They missed Kean's "flashes of lightning," although the *Herald* found in Phelps a "warm and undisguised passionateness, which was far from commonplace." In choosing Shylock rather than Macbeth or Lear, Phelps had deliberately put himself in comparison with the great Kean and had risked censure for not making the famous "points" Kean had used. Charles Rice and the critic of the *Sunday Times* complained that Phelps had missed every point in the part, but most critics recognized a basic difference in interpretation and hesitated to condemn him. Wightwick's review of Phelps's Shylock in the *Plymouth Herald* of April 29 had discussed this problem with unusual frankness:

Critics should put on a qualified bearing when they have such a man as Mr. Phelps to deal with. Actors often commit such obvious errors as come within the just censure of ordinary criticism, but they occasionally appear before us with such evident proofs of native intelligence as to induce inquiries of a more self-mistrusting nature; and we feel such a diffidence in alluding to the *Shylock* of Mr. Phelps. . . . Accustomed, as we have been, to the more deliberate—yet deeply earnest manner in which the deceased Kean went through the opening scenes of the Jew, we naturally require a little self-persuasion as to the more buoyant dialogue of Mr. Phelps; and, vitiated as we may possibly have been, by the "point-making" school of actors, we felt that an effort of judgement is necessary to give up our regard for the peculiar manner in which certain brief passages were "struck out" by the great master to whom we have alluded. At the same time we feel that Mr. Phelps, as an artist of genius, and as a critic of judgement, has positive claims on our submission; nor shall we suffer *our* prejudices to interfere with the free exercise of *his* discretion. . . . We are grateful for what he has taught us.

Such humility could not be expected of London critics; and yet, most of them were favorably impressed by his first performance, which was decidedly inferior to those Wightwick had seen—marred, as it was, by underplaying as a result of Phelps's nervousness.

Macready, who was acting in Bristol at the end of August, anxiously waited to hear the result of Phelps's debut. His diary for August 29 records his reaction:

Sent for the "Morning Herald," and read the account of Mr. Phelps appearance, which seems to me a decided success. It depressed my spirits, though perhaps it should not do so. If he is greatly successful, I shall reap the profits; if moderately, he will strengthen my company. But an actor's fame and his dependent income is so precarious, that we start at every shadow of an actor.[14]

For his second performance Phelps played Sir Edward Mortimer in *The Iron Chest* on September 1. The house was full, and the pit crowded. Phelps was evidently less nervous and acted with more abandon. Reviews were more enthusiastic and recognized that the character was Phelps's own creation, not merely an imitation of Kean's famous original. The *Times,* noting that he had "a good figure, expressive features, and a splendid voice," said that "his performance, though not absolutely perfect, was of a very superior order, and of that peculiarly impressive character which carries an audience forcibly along." The *Morning Herald* also spoke of the emotional force of his acting and praised the physical power of his voice.

The announcement of his appearance in Hamlet on September 8 drew a large audience even though he was now "playing in the midst" of benefits, despite Webster's assertion that this was not his mode of doing things. His Hamlet appealed to those critics who were willing to set aside the traditional emphasis upon particular passages. The *Morning Herald* praised his "naturalness" in the Ghost scenes, where he deviated from customary practices, and declared that the whole performance avoided rant without sinking into tameness. Charles Rice, on the other hand, found his Hamlet lacking in points and therefore deficient in force and interest, although he admits that the performance "raised him a few degrees higher in my estimation." [15] The basis of his objections to Phelps's style of acting is indicated by his comment on the delivery of Hamlet's advice to the players, which he (quite properly) asserts ought to demonstrate an actor's ability in his own art:

> His "advice" was spoken with a rapidity of utterance, and sparingness of action, which gave a most perverse construction to the words of his speech.

Most critics felt that Phelps had successfully passed the severe test of acting Hamlet. The *Morning Herald* summarized the performance:

> That he has maturely studied the character is evident, from the perfect ease and self-possession which his representation throughout evinced; and if in some cases he did not quite carry out his conceptions, a repetition of the performance will enable him to do so, backed as the present was by the general approbation of a well-filled house. . . . In person, deportment, and action, Mr. Phelps will bear comparison with any whom we have seen assume the royal Dane. . . . His features are handsome and flexible; his voice is of good quality, of various tone, and of considerable compass; and what is most remarkable, without being at all a copy of any, he occasionally reminds you, either in voice or feature, of Macready, Vandenhoff, Kean, etc.

His first appearance as Othello, on September 14, was less assured. The *Morning Post* found him too harsh and rugged in the first three scenes—an indication that he had been unable to keep the tenseness out of his voice. The reviewer praised him for an intelligent and convincing conception of the character but said that "only in the fourth and fifth acts did the actor seem to bring his full powers into play." The *Sunday Times* called it one of the most inefficient performances ever seen, but added that his delivery of the soliloquy in Act Four beginning "Had it pleased Heaven" was marked by "the decided impress of genius." After this fourth new role, reviewers became aware of his unusual ability to submerge his own personality in the part he played. The *Morning Post* remarked, "In each character in which we have had the opportunity of seeing him, he has appeared a different man: he loses his identity, in fact, in the character he for the time portrays."

During his six weeks at the Haymarket, Phelps acted Shylock, Sir Edward Mortimer, Hamlet, and Othello each twice and Richard the Third four times. His popularity with audiences increased, and he drew good houses during a normally slow season. Webster featured his performances in tragedy in alternation with the usual productions of comedy for which the Haymarket company had special talent. During this autumn they had a triumphant success with a new comedy by Sheridan Knowles called *The Love-Chase,* which was performed fifty times, beginning shortly after Phelps's debut. Even though Phelps was competing with the attraction of this play, his performances were profitable to Webster, who was displeased when Phelps left the Haymarket to join Macready's company.

II

From Actor to Manager

Macready's management of Covent Garden Theatre, which had begun on September 30, 1837, was hailed by a sizable group of playgoers, dramatic critics, and writers as a great step forward in reviving legitimate drama. A number of prominent and influential men were committed to aid his management in the hope that he would be successful in restoring the drama to a place in the center of English cultural life. Although financial problems had been the chief concern of the managers of the patent theatres ever since their enlargement at the beginning of the century, the public had only recently become aware that legitimate drama was losing its vitality. The years of John Philip Kemble and Mrs. Siddons were now remembered as "the palmy days" of the theatre although even they had not been able to produce Shakespeare profitably in their vast and expensive new Covent Garden. For a few years after 1814 the genius of Edmund Kean, by attracting thousands of spectators to Drury Lane, had postponed the financial collapse which constantly threatened the theatre and had for a time obscured signs of the death of legitimate drama.

After Kean's powers faded, although Macready had already established his reputation and was highly admired as a Shakespearean actor, the patent theatres were seldom filled. Increasingly the managers resorted to opera, ballet, and pantomime, which seemed to have a wider appeal than poetic drama. This dominance of spectacle in the two London theatres dedicated to drama had awakened general concern for the survival of the classic English drama. Macready, supported by some critics and writers, openly expressed his opinion that managerial policies had caused the decline in interest among playgoers, and he specifically blamed Alfred

Bunn, the manager of Drury Lane, for degrading drama through incompetent management and irresponsible pandering to the taste of the lower classes.

Macready began his management with the strong support of two influential reviewers: Fox of the *Morning Chronicle* and Forster of the *Examiner*. He also had the backing of the proprietors of Covent Garden, who had been generous in the terms of his lesseeship, and the active interest of cultured society. He was assured, through high-placed friends, of the young Queen Victoria's patronage. These advantages, combined with his own great abilities as an actor and his intelligent grasp of poetic drama, promised hope of success even in the face of public apathy toward plays.

Certain disadvantages which Macready brought with him to the management were better known to the professional theatrical world than to the literary and social coterie which supported him. Among his fellow actors he was famous for his overbearing manner, violent temper, jealous fear of rivals, and insistence upon plays that concentrated attention upon his own role. During the years before he became a manager he had used his position as the first actor of the day to dominate the legitimate theatre, employing a variety of methods to impose his will upon Charles Kemble, Alfred Bunn, and most recently Benjamin Webster, the managers who had engaged him.

One of his most effective tools against rival actors was the dramatic criticism of John Forster, his most intimate friend and in Macready's own opinion an incorrigible sycophant. Forster's loyal support of Macready extended beyond frequent and favorable reviews to violent dispraise of rival actors. His slashing criticism of Edwin Forrest helped drive the American tragedian out of London.[1] Fear of his intemperate partisanship kept Charles Kean from making his London debut until he had come to a private understanding with Forster.[2]

Macready's domination of playwrights was another drawback to his competence as manager of a patent theatre. His penchant for revising plays to magnify his own part was so well known that it was the subject of a farce produced at Covent Garden in 1826, with Tyrone Power as Macready and Charles Kemble in the role of the unfortunate author.[3] The artificial conditions caused by the theatrical monopoly gave Macready a privileged position in dealing with playwrights, since in most cases his opinion of the play as a vehicle for his own talents was the only tribunal available. Bulwer-Lytton learned to tailor a play to suit Macready, as a contemporary critic noted:

> When Mr. Macready put on Sir Edward's "Claude Melnotte," not a crease nor a wrinkle was to be observed by the most critical eye; and this is no small praise to any author, who *descends* to the task, as Mr. Macready is considered amongst the dramatic fashioners as a very difficult customer to measure, and a misfit always ensures "condemnation," as many of our writers know to their sorrow.[4]

Such a reputation was not likely to attract professional dramatic writers to support Macready's management.

When Phelps reported to Macready at Covent Garden on October 16, 1837, he came with an attitude of respectful admiration for the great tragedian. Although he may have heard disparaging comments about him in the green room of the Haymarket, where he had met William Farren and other actors well acquainted with Macready, his own impression of the man from their meeting at Southampton had been good. There had been a current of sympathy between them; agreement had been reached quickly; and Phelps had looked forward to joining his company. He regretted the embarrassment that his contract with Macready caused at the Haymarket, but he did not believe that Macready had deliberately misled him into conflicting engagements.

He found Macready harassed with the problems of management. Ever since the opening night houses had been poor in spite of a variety of offerings. The financial deficit of the second week had totaled 300 pounds. Reviews, except for the *Morning Chronicle* and the *Examiner,* had been unenthusiastic. Daily entries in Macready's diary reveal his worries. He was concerned about his own performance of Othello; he was distressed about the inadequacy of his supporting actors, George Vining, James Anderson, and Mary Huddart; and he was disgusted by uncooperative singers, who were paid three times the salary of the actors in the company and yet refused to act in afterpieces when asked. He had tried to spark public interest by having Forster's laudatory review of *The Bridal* reprinted in pamphlet form, but there was no discernible improvement in audiences. He was discouraged and utterly weary. On October 16, he noted in his diary, "Mr. Phelps called, but I did not see him."[5]

By October 23, when he found time to see Phelps, he had received two encouraging pieces of news. Clarkson Stanfield, the distinguished painter, had indicated a willingness to paint scenery for the Christmas pantomime, and Queen Victoria's spokesman had promised a royal visit to the theatre in November. Heartened by the prospect of help from these important persons, Macready could talk to Phelps in a more cheerful frame of mind. They settled upon a salary of 12 pounds a week, which was 2 pounds more than Webster had been paying and double that of other prominent actors in the company. Only Helen Faucit, the leading actress, had a higher salary. To be sure, 12 pounds a week was low compared with the 16 pounds Macready had commanded at Covent Garden when he first came to London in 1816, but the desperate condition of the legitimate theatres could be blamed for the difference. In signing up his company Macready had obtained every actor (except Helen Faucit, whose engagements were arranged by William Farren, her guardian) at a reduced salary and under contract to play whatever roles might be assigned, on the grounds that all actors of legitimate drama must cooperate in the effort to rescue the theatre from total collapse.

Macready also arranged with Phelps his initial roles at Covent Garden. For his first night he offered Phelps the choice of either leading role in Otway's *Venice Preserved,* agreeing himself to play the other. Phelps chose Jaffier, the role usually played by the older actor when a young aspirant was being introduced as Pierre. Macready says in his diary that he was surprised and tried to dissuade him from this unusual choice, but Phelps was firm. For his second appearance Phelps was to play Othello, with Macready as Iago. These two excellent opportunities gave Phelps hope of a great increase in his reputation and promised more than sufficient recompense for leaving the Haymarket.

On October 27 Phelps and Macready appeared as Jaffier and Pierre in *Venice Preserved,* with Helen Faucit as Belvidera. The performance was almost as great a test of Phelps's ability as his London debut, since he was appearing for the first time on the stage of one of the large national theatres and playing opposite the leading tragedian of the day. In spite of his nervousness Phelps acted with assurance. The audience responded with enthusiastic applause which left no doubt of their approval. Macready, who had gone through a distressing day with his managerial problems, rather sourly commented in his diary: "I acted indifferently; was called for—on account of Mr. Phelps, I suppose." Reviews confirmed the success of Phelps's first appearance. The *Sunday Times* (October 29) commented upon the significance of the occasion and remarked that Phelps had come out well in close comparison with Macready.

As a manager Macready might have rejoiced in the success of his new actor. The warmth of the applause and the interest of reviewers could have given him hope for some improvement in attendance and critical opinion. Instead he reacted with jealousy for his own position as leading actor. When *Venice Preserved* was performed a second time, he substituted Warde for himself as Pierre. After that the play was withdrawn.

Their second appearance together, which took place the following week, increased Macready's fears. His own performances of Othello earlier in the season had not been well received, whereas Phelps carried the house with the force and compelling reality of his performance. Unrestrained applause was clearly directed toward the new actor, ignoring for a time the excellence of Macready's Iago. This triumph was the cause of the blighting of Phelps's career, since from that night on Macready limited him to roles which gave him no opportunity to increase his reputation or win popularity with the audience.

Although the published portions of Macready's diary contain no reference to Phelps during this week of October 29 to November 6, there is evidence that he was burning with jealousy and resentment. On November 3 he began rehearsals of *Macbeth,* taking up his favorite and most admired Shakespearean role and casting Phelps as Macduff. On the opening night, November 6, he lost control of his temper during the sword fight with Macduff in the last act and attacked Phelps with violence:

> I had drunk much wine, and was very vehement, swearing rather loudly (unwise, ungentlemanly and dangerous passion!) at Mr. Phelps in the fight. . . . I went to bed very late, but *could not sleep* all night.

The "unwise, ungentlemanly and dangerous passion" must certainly refer to his jealousy of Phelps, which may have been mentioned in passages of his diary withheld from publication. The admission that passion had influenced his treatment of another actor is, I think, unique in Macready's diaries, although the subject of his using violence on the stage is frequently mentioned. An entry for October 10, 1836, is typical of these cases:

> Mr. Pritchard came into my room to try over the fight and asked me not to "strike so hard." . . . He was disposed to be very absurd, and said

that I had "damned him" on the previous night. This I declare to be a shameful *falsehood*.

The denial is characteristic, though on several occasions actors threatened suit for damages after his maulings, and more than one actress feared to play Desdemona to his Othello. Careful reading of the diary reveals the fact that these instances of violence on the stage usually occurred with persons against whom Macready had already expressed resentment, as in the case of Pritchard and Fanny Kemble. Invariably Macready claims that his actions were no more violent than what was required by the role he was playing. In Phelps's case, however, he clearly felt that he was at fault, adding that he could not sleep. On the following day, November 7, he wrote:

> Arose wearied and with headache: went to theatre, when much of the morning was talked away; my spirits and body were equally wearied. Had a long conversation with Mr. Phelps, to whom I sent in order to excuse myself for my last night's violence. He did not take offence at it. *I was very much to blame.*

Macready's feelings of remorse were not, however, sufficiently strong to induce him to alter his decision about Phelps's future roles. During the month of November he kept Phelps entirely off the stage, except for his weekly appearance as Macduff.

Although his policy successfully preserved Macready's position as leading actor, it cost him much as a manager. He was paying Phelps 12 pounds a week to be idle, while he paid Miss Huddart, the Lady Macbeth, only 9 pounds and Anderson, the Jeune Premier of the company, only 5. Moreover, his company lacked strength in secondary roles. Warde was back in debtors' prison after Macready had once bailed him out. Elton had annoyed Macready by his incompetence as well as by his "unfair" tactics on the stage. Vining's bad acting had, in the manager's opinion, caused the failure of the one new play of the season. He felt that George Bennett needed instruction. From a managerial point of view Phelps's success on the stage could have helped Macready. A new star would have been an attraction, and a suggestion of rivalry might have sparked interest among playgoers. A judiciously controlled use of Phelps's ability to draw audiences would certainly have recommended itself to a manager less jealous of his own position on the stage.

November was a difficult month for the overworked manager of Covent Garden. In order to increase attendance at the theatre he had compromised his principles and commissioned an opera, adopting the course he had formerly condemned in Bunn. But the composer had been late in fulfilling his commission, and the opera had to be hurried on to the stage, where it was condemned by the audience. The custom of allowing a first-night audience to decide the merit of a new production was taken seriously in the early nineteenth century: when a work was hissed and booed on its first performance, it could not be performed a second time. The only new addition to the repertory during November was *Macbeth,* and although Macready's portrayal of the leading role was a distinguished piece of acting, it was too well known to arouse much interest among playgoers. Competition from Drury Lane irked Macready, who was galled by any indication of Bunn's success. When he discovered that Bunn was rehearsing a new opera by Balfe on the subject of Joan of Arc, he commissioned Thomas Serle, hack writer for his company, to work up a lavish spectacle on the same subject, which he brought out at Covent Garden just three days before the first performance of Balfe's opera at Drury Lane. This seeming defection from the high cause of English drama was excused by Macready's champion on the *Morning Chronicle* (Nov. 29, 1837):

> Mr. Macready, determining very wisely not to adhere too rigidly to his chivalric purpose of restoring the legitimate drama, brought out last night a spectacle more in accordance with the taste of the town, and more likely to fill the coffers of his treasury than the fine old plays which are the admiration of critics.

Although the tactic of anticipating a rival theatre's production was not unknown, this case was sufficiently blatant to provoke derisive comments in the Drury Lane playbills and unfavorable reviews in some newspapers. Macready, who was very sensitive to criticism, reacted strongly, neglecting his work at the theatre in order to pursue his quarrels with the press. On December 7, the day of the Queen's second visit to Covent Garden, when he normally would have been concerned about the evening's performance, he was talking to his solicitor about legal action against the editor of the *Age* and complaining to the editor of the *Morning Herald* about the theatrical reviewer of his newspaper. By December 16, expenses of the theatre had run 2,200 pounds ahead of receipts, despite two visits from the Queen, which had attracted full houses. Macready was working feverishly on the Christmas pantomime, hoping that the attraction of a beautiful spectacle would bring large attendance.

Among those who questioned Macready's "chivalric purpose" could now be numbered Phelps, whose hopes had been thwarted by Macready's decision to keep him in the background. Macready had not concealed his change of policy. He is reported to have told Phelps quite frankly that he intended to hold him back as he felt he had been held back by Edmund Kean.[6] As early as November 19 rumors had reached the columns of the *Sunday Times,* where it was reported that Phelps had been objecting to Macready's casting. The reviewer commented that "Mr. Phelps would be a serious loss to Covent Garden." Phelps protested his treatment directly to Macready, recalling the terms of their agreement. Macready then showed him that the contract contained no specific provision about the type of role Phelps was to play. Their understanding had been verbal, later reinforced by the amount of the salary agreed upon. When Phelps understood his position, he asked to be released from his engagement, but Macready refused except on the condition that Phelps leave London.[7] Phelps then engaged an attorney to advise him about his legal rights in the dispute.

The stunning effect of Macready's actions upon Phelps's hopes can be seen in a letter he wrote to his friend Thomas Latimer of the *Western Times,* Exeter:

> I am sorry to tell you I am not so happy, or even comfortable, as I expected—and ought to be. Macready is using me infamously. I have been now at Covent Garden since the 16th October, and have only acted four parts. I opened in Jaffier (Venice Preserved), and my reception was enthusiastic in the highest degree—the triumph being greater because Macready played Pierre with me. I then acted Othello, with the same degree of success. Venice Preserved was so highly spoken of and inquired for that he was obliged to do it a second time, but would not play in the piece himself—so weak a man is he that he cannot bear the idea of sharing the honor of a night with any one.
>
> During the last month I have acted only once a week,—Macduff, on the Monday nights, and on one occasion Rob Roy. He had made several attempts to force me into subordinate characters, which I have resisted. I wonder you have seen nothing in the papers (Sunday). Several of them have taken up my cause very warmly: *The News, Satirist, Sunday Times,* &c., have had very long articles relative to his treatment of me. So convinced am I that, had I been properly treated, I should by this time have

stood on a pinnacle, that I have been employing an attorney to see if there was any legal way of getting off my engagement, and last night we took Sir William Follett's opinion on the subject, which I regret to say was unfavourable. The only alternative Macready will allow me is entering into a bond *not to act in London during the present Covent Garden season,* or to fulfil my engagement with him,—which if he pursues his present treatment (and he will do so), will bend my spirit downwards to such a degree that its elasticity will be lost, and it will never spring into place again. I have expended about £150 on costumes, but I am afraid I must for some time hang 'em up at home—to look at.[8]

In his desperation Phelps tried "walking through" his part of Macduff, hoping to force Macready to release him from his contract; but he soon realized that a new actor could not afford to risk his reputation with bad performances. Eventually he set out to distinguish himself within the limited scope allowed him, and he was rewarded by favorable notice from reviewers on the perfection of his Macduff. During the rest of the season of 1837–1838, he was excluded from the cast of every important production at Covent Garden. In *Coriolanus,* Byron's *The Two Foscari,* and Bulwer-Lytton's *The Lady of Lyons* (the hit of the season), the prominent roles after Macready's were given to Anderson, Elton, and Bennett. After the run of *Macbeth,* Phelps seldom appeared on the stage.

When the theatre closed for the summer on July 6, 1838, it was no secret that Macready's first season of theatrical management had been a financial failure. He had lost 700 pounds in addition to the 1,800 pounds he could have expected for his own salary. Only the success of two new plays in the spring, *The Lady of Lyons* and Knowles's *Woman's Wit,* had prevented a much greater deficit. These plays had brought good houses and had cost very little. Bulwer-Lytton had returned to Macready the 210 pounds paid to him, and Knowles's fee had been small. These plays had also helped Macready obtain an engagement at the Haymarket for five weeks during his summer recess. Webster was willing to pay Macready 25 pounds a night, four nights a week, as leading actor, if he brought with him the two new plays. The fact was recognized by Macready, who commented in his diary that Knowles's play was a primary object of Webster's interest.[9]

In spite of his financial loss, Macready decided to undertake another year of management.[10] He had been angered and frightened by the success of Charles Kean's London debut at Drury Lane during January.

Reviews had praised Kean, and the Queen had frequently attended his performances. Even Forster, respecting his agreement with Kean, had written a favorable notice, and Macready was furious at this defection:

> I was astonished—dejected—and sickened with disgust at the recreant contradiction of his own strongly expressed opinions in my room on Monday night. . . . And this is my friend! . . . Such men have neither the heart, the courage, nor the honesty to be friends.[11]

The other reviewer he depended upon, William Fox, had been taken off all Drury Lane assignments by the editor of the *Morning Chronicle* in response to Bunn's complaints about prejudiced reviews of his theatre. Although Macready continued to believe that Kean had no merit—"How long is the intelligence of this country to be insulted by his quackeries?" —he was afraid of his competition and preferred the financial risk of management to the uncertainties of uncontrolled competition in a declining market.

On his benefit night at the end of the season he addressed the audience, announcing his intention of continuing the management and discussing his motives for undertaking so burdensome a task. He denied that his motives were mercenary and selfish, asserting that his primary object had been the "wish to elevate my art, and to establish an asylum for it and my brothers and sisters professing it, where they might be secure of equitable treatment, of friendly consideration, and most of all, of that respect which man should show to man." [12]

Phelps, now that his contract had ended, looked for a way to escape from Macready's "asylum," but he found none. The Haymarket offered no hope, both because Macready was going there for the summer and because Webster was still angry about Phelps's departure the previous October. For the winter season Drury Lane would have been an alternative to Covent Garden except that Bunn had decided to devote the theatre entirely to opera. An engagement at one of the minor theatres, like a return to the provinces, would have ended all possibility of becoming a tragedian on the London stage. Therefore, Phelps was forced to sign another contract with Macready for the winter of 1838–1839 on the same terms as before.

After Covent Garden opened for the second season of Macready's management in the fall of 1838, Phelps realized that he was in a worse position than he had been the previous season. Although Macready's announcements listed his company in alphabetical order instead of by rank,[13] it became apparent that John Vandenhoff had been added to the company to play the roles Phelps had expected to act. Anderson, Bennett, Elton, and Warde shared roles of secondary importance, and Phelps was assigned such minor parts as Antonio in *The Tempest,* the First Lord in *As You Like It,* and the High Constable of France in *Henry the Fifth.* Macready's selection of Vandenhoff for the second position in the company must have been motivated by fear of rivalry rather than a desire to strengthen the casts of his productions. His own opinion of Vandenhoff's acting, frequently expressed in his diary, had never been high. He had written of Vandenhoff's Iago: "A poorer, more unmeaning, slouching, ungainly, mindless, unimaginative performance I have never witnessed in any person making pretensions to high rank." [14] Vandenhoff had been prominent on the London stage since his debut in 1834, without winning great popularity or critical esteem. His style was that of an older generation; he seemed stiff and cold to audiences who had seen Edmund Kean and Macready. Like John Philip Kemble, whose style he recalled, he was at his best in such a role as Coriolanus; but when he played this part on the opening night of the new season, critics were cool. The *Morning Herald* (September 25, 1838) remarked that the unusual attention bestowed upon the staging of *Coriolanus* helped make up for the mediocrity of the acting. When Vandenhoff appeared the following week in the leading role of the old comedy *Town and Country* by Thomas Morton, the theatre was half empty.

As the season progressed, empty seats at Covent Garden were noted by reviewers, and the failure of Macready's management was generally expected. A beautifully decorated production of *The Tempest,* garnished with music, and featuring the Shakespearean text liberated from the Dryden-Davenant revision, was attractive to audiences; but because it had been very expensive, a long run was necessary. After fifty-five performances, interspersed with *Hamlet, Werner, Virginius,* and *The Lady of Lyons,* reviewers were complaining of the lack of variety offered at Covent Garden.[15]

In the meantime Drury Lane was attracting good houses with opera, enhanced by an afterpiece featuring live horses, lambs, and lions; and the Haymarket was profiting from the success of another new comedy by Sheridan Knowles. Macready's attempts to produce attractive afterpieces, both operas and farces, had not been successful. Since he chose the works himself and directed many of the rehearsals, and since he had no ear for music and very little sense of humor, it is not surprising that most of them failed. His worst setback was the failure of the Christmas pantomime, on which he had spent 1,500 pounds. After this catastrophe, the proprietors informed Macready that they planned to advertise the theatre to be let, since the failure of his management was expected any day.

Macready, however, had unusual determination, and he also had friends who were both wealthy and influential. By January 16, a special subscription for his management had brought in 1,000 pounds, which Forster presented to him. On January 23, he received word that the Queen would command a performance at Covent Garden—a boon which he had obtained through the efforts of his cousin, Marianne Skerrett, who held a position in the Queen's household. During February the Queen paid three visits to the theatre, atoning in some measure for her earlier attention to Drury Lane, where the lions had particularly attracted her interest. On February 9, Macready learned that the Anti-Corn Law League, of which his friend Fox of the *Chronicle* was a prominent member, would rent Covent Garden for their annual meeting (even though they could have rented Drury Lane for 50 pounds less). In addition to these specific remedies for his financial embarrassment, he had the manuscript of a new play from the pen of his friend Bulwer-Lytton and the promise of Stanfield's help in painting the scenery for *Henry the Fifth*.

The new play, a historical drama called *Richelieu,* was an unqualified success and ran for thirty-seven nights. *Henry the Fifth,* in which the Chorus's speeches were illustrated by a diorama painted by Stanfield, was moderately successful in spite of critical condemnation of its emphasis on spectacle at the cost of acting. With these two productions, Macready retrieved some of his losses and was able to continue the season until July 16, 1839, when the Queen's presence again assured an overflowing house.

In spite of his many troubles during the season, Macready would have undertaken a third year of management except for a bitter quarrel with the proprietors of the theatre about the terms of his lesseeship. His subleasing of Covent Garden to the Anti-Corn Law League had been objected to as highly improper and outside his rights as manager. Macready refused to admit any wrong on his part or to discuss restitution of the rental fee. He angrily declared his retirement from the management, while denouncing the proprietors (knaves, blackguards), the actors (traitors, slaves), and the newspaper reviewers (ignorant coxcombs, vile and low-minded creatures) to his friends and in the pages of his diary. Although his last performance was greeted by a full house of cheering and applauding supporters, he had to leave the theatre without his wardrobe, because the proprietors would not allow him to remove his trunks until their claims were paid.

Phelps could look back on the season with no more satisfaction than Macready. Another year had been wasted without significant advancement in his profession. His Cassius (with Macready as Brutus, Vandenhoff as Mark Antony, and Bennett as Caesar) had been especially noticed by audience and reviewers, but the play had been performed only two nights. He had also gained recognition for his acting in the small part of Father Joseph in *Richelieu* and had the satisfaction of finding himself mentioned immediately after Macready in the reviews, even though Helen Faucit, Anderson, and Elton played roles of greater prominence; but this kind of recognition was a long way from the reputation he had once hoped to make in London.

Financial problems were also pressing upon Phelps. In the previous year, he had given a financial bond for a friend (perhaps a close relative) who almost at once fell seriously into debt. In order to pay the obligation, he had been forced to borrow a large sum of money at 45 percent interest. Since then he had found his salary inadequate to keep up the interest payments and maintain his growing family, which now included in addition to his own three children, a nephew who had come to live with him after the death of Phelps's older brother. During May, 1839, his affairs were in so desperate a state that he offered to leave the theatre to avoid the unpleasantness of possible arrest. Macready, who had more than once retrieved both Warde and Anderson from debtors' prison by advancing money on their salaries, willingly lent Phelps 50 pounds, to be repaid from his salary. The end of Macready's management took away his only sure hope of employment in London.

Macready was also concerned about finding a place to act in London during the next winter season. With Covent Garden and Drury Lane both closed to him, because of his violent quarrels with the proprietors of one and the lessee of the other, he was forced to try some means of extending dramatic privileges to another theatre, although he was still unwilling to support a bill for the repeal of the monopoly. He applied to the Lord Chamberlain for a special license that would grant him the right to form a company and present legitimate drama at whatever theatre he could lease. Bulwer-Lytton exerted his influence to secure this personal license for Macready, but without success. Macready was therefore limited to the Haymarket, where Webster offered him an engagement beginning in August, with the excellent salary of 100 pounds a week. He accepted the offer and recommended to Webster that he engage Willmott (his prompter at Covent Garden and an actor of minor parts), James Anderson, and Mary Huddart (now Mrs. Warner, since her marriage in December) as supporting actors. He was not happy about the change in his status, from manager to hired actor and from the great winter theatre to the smaller Haymarket with its summer patent; and when he learned that Webster had engaged Charles Kean as his star during June and July, he was angry at Webster and despairing about the future of drama in London:

The man is a fool, there is no hope from him. *The art is all at sea again.*[16]

Webster was now the only successful producer of legitimate drama in London. He had been successful where other managers had failed, because he had chosen the one patent theatre of a proper size for presenting plays and because he had consistently put his managerial interests ahead of his acting career. At the Haymarket he did not have to spend huge sums for spectacular settings of his plays in order to attract full houses. One comedian like William Farren or John Buckstone, in this theatre where his slightest gestures could be seen and his words clearly heard, could fill the house night after night. Webster had obtained a good company for comedy, and he had been willing to pay a popular playwright like Knowles sufficiently well to assure a supply of new comedies. As an actor, he was willing to accept the verdict of the box office, placing other comedians ahead of himself in rank of popularity. Careful, though not lavish, staging, good acting, and variety of dramatic fare had made the Haymarket attractive to audiences.

Webster also had the advantage of his theatre's reputation for summer entertainment. He had adopted the policy of engaging the most admired actors from other theatres for his summer season, when they normally would not be engaged. This novel practice of featuring one famous actor after another was referred to by reviewers as Webster's star system. Although they did not entirely approve, they had to admit its attractiveness. Some of his stars came from the minor houses as well as from the patent theatres. Thus he drew upon a wider audience than a strictly legitimate theatre could attract, competing with the Olympic and the Adelphi—the two minor theatres patronized by fashionable society. When the winter season began and his stars went back to their regular companies, Webster fell back on his own company with their talent for comedy. With the collapse of Macready's management and the conversion of Drury Lane to an opera house, Webster looked forward in the autumn of 1839 to a long season running through most of the winter and featuring tragedy as well as comedy. His "summer patent" was now extremely valuable, and he intended to stretch it to the limit of the law.

It is typical of Webster's managerial acumen that he engaged Phelps to come to the Haymarket as chief supporting actor during Macready's stay. He knew how much enthusiasm Phelps's debut had aroused, and he was not deterred by Macready's strong suggestion that Anderson should be engaged as second lead. He deliberately used the attraction of a possible rival to Macready by advertising Phelps prominently on his bills early in August. It was probably a shock to Macready to see an advertisement headed in this manner:

First appearance this season of the eminent tragedian
Mr. MACREADY
First appearance of
Mr. PHELPS
and
Miss HELEN FAUCIT

Phelps had realized as soon as he was engaged by Webster that Macready might take offense. On June 20 he tactfully told Macready of the engagement and evidently assured him of the modesty of his own ambition. Macready wrote in his diary, "Mr. Phelps called, and spoke to me about his engagement at Haymarket; seemed to entertain very sensible views." Phelps's disarming tactics were sufficiently effective to gain Macready's agreement to Webster's proposal that the two actors alternate in the leading roles of *Othello*.

Their first appearance was August 19, with Macready as Othello, Phelps as Iago, Helen Faucit as Desdemona, and Mrs. Warner as Emilia. This strong cast attracted a full house, including a number of critics. During the course of the play it became evident that the audience was responding more warmly to Phelps's Iago than to Macready's Othello, and the next morning most of the reviews reflected the preference of the audience. The *Morning Chronicle,* however, gaves its usual high praise to Macready's performance. In attempting to account for the coldness of the audience Fox chose a most unfortunate explanation:

> In the two scenes with Iago we think he a little injured the effect of his performance by playing too backward on the stage: the working of his countenance could not well be discerned.

In these words Fox, who had a complete admiration for his friend and nearly as complete ignorance of stage practices, innocently described Macready in the act of upstaging his rival.

On August 26 the performance was repeated with the same kind of reaction. Macready could never act his best without the stimulus of applause, and in the comparatively small theatre he was doubly embarrassed by lack of response to his points. After a performance of Claude Melnotte on August 21 he had referred to the Haymarket in his diary as a "dog-hole of a theatre" and remarked, "The audience is so close upon me, and yet I cannot feel their sympathy." On the twenty-ninth he said, "Acted Othello with as much energy as I could—and in some instances well; but the audience did not seem to sympathize with me; at least I did not feel their sympathy."

In the alternate performances, when the two roles were reversed, Phelps scored an unmistakable triumph as Othello. The naturalness of his acting, unbroken by the artistic effects of Macready's style, and his greater tenderness in the scenes with Desdemona carried the audience along on a tide of sympathy which broke into thunderous applause at the end of the play. Macready was also an excellent Iago. The subtle touches, intelligent reading, and artistic control of his acting made it a great performance, which critics highly praised. The *Weekly Dispatch* (September 1, 1839), which had particularly disapproved of Macready's Othello, pronounced him the best Iago on the stage. At the same time the reviewer made this comment on Phelps's Othello:

> He was of all things that which we have never witnessed since the death of Kean—natural. There were no stage tricks in him, and though he wanted dignity and even energy, he was always true to nature. Mr. Phelps is as much superior to Macready as Othello, as Macready is superior to Cooper as Iago.

Another reviewer, an admirer of Macready, also preferred Phelps's Othello:

> We have hitherto on the whole given the preference to Macready's Othello to that of the elder Kean, but we are now convinced that the Othello of Mr. Phelps is the Othello of Shakespeare.[17]

These reviews disturbed Macready, and on September 2 when Phelps acted Othello for the second time, Macready became so angry at the response of the audience that he lost his temper on the stage, revealing his discomfiture clearly enough that the incident was remembered by critics years later.[18] Macready realized that he had behaved badly and wrote his regret in his diary:

> Acted Iago very unsatisfactorily, and *quite lost my temper—an inexcusable fault*. The audience applauded Othello, Mr. Phelps, who got through the part very respectably, but seemed not to understand me. They called for me after Mr. Phelps, but I was undressed and did not go.

It is characteristic of Macready that he refused a curtain call when it came only after Phelps's tumultuous reception. He was extremely sensitive in the matter of applause, and on one occasion he had refused to appear before the curtain because he heard one or two voices raised for Vandenhoff. It is also characteristic that he could regret losing his temper and at the same time resolve to put Phelps safely out of the way for the rest of the season, without ever admitting, even to himself, that Phelps was any more than a "very respectable" actor.

He spent the next day at home, hurriedly looking over plays to find himself a new role. The following day he told Webster that he would not act in *Othello* again, proposing *The Merchant of Venice* instead. Although he of course found Webster reluctant to withdraw a play which had been attracting full houses—"Mr. Webster is playing his game of tradesman with me"—he was determined to impose his will. He set to work at once to get possession of a new play of sufficient merit to be of use in bargaining with Webster. First he saw Robert Browning, who had been working on a play for him, but he was disappointed in the manuscript of *King Victor*. He asked Forster to look into Sheridan Knowles's latest play, since he was not himself on good terms with Knowles; but Forster reported that it was "good, but not overwhelming." He turned to his friend Bulwer-Lytton, who began at once to write a new play. Before the end of the month he had presented *The Sea-Captain* to Macready.

In the meantime, Macready rehearsed Shylock, which he acted for the first time on September 30. In his own words, it was "an utter failure." Fox's attempt to praise it provoked direct contradiction from the *Spectator* and other reviewers who resented the *Chronicle's* evident partisanship. The *Weekly Dispatch* pronounced it the worst piece of acting ever seen. Although the production of *The Merchant of Venice* lowered Macready's reputation and was considered by many to have been an unfortunate mistake, it achieved the end Macready had desired: Phelps had been effectively removed from prominence, and in the role of Antonio he could not be dangerous. This new instance of Macready's suppression so angered Phelps that he showed his resentment on the stage. According to the *Spectator* (October 12, 1839), he "walked through the part of Antonio undertaker-fashion." In *The Sea-Captain,* which did not achieve the success of Bulwer-Lytton's earlier plays, Phelps had a very minor role. During the rest of the Haymarket season, which ran until January, he was given no opportunity to distinguish himself above other actors in the company.

During the autumn, the two winter theatres had opened. Mme. Vestris, universally admired for her management of the Olympic during the previous seven years, had taken the lesseeship of Covent Garden. It was a gigantic task, since she undertook the project entirely on her own resources, without the influential friends who had backed Macready's effort. As a heroine of burlettas, admired for her charm, beauty, and singing, she could not claim to be the supporter of legitimate drama. The *Weekly Dispatch* complained that her company lacked tragedians, noting the absence of Macready, Phelps, and Elton from her playbills. Nevertheless, her first production was *Love's Labour's Lost,* a play which had not been seen since the Restoration, followed by Sheridan's *The School for Scandal* and Fletcher's *Rule a Wife and Have a Wife.* She had gathered a talented group of comic actors, including Charles Mathews (her husband), George Bartley, Robert Keeley, and William Farren, and two tragedians, John Cooper and James Anderson (to whom she paid double the salary he had received from Macready). Good comic acting, aided by attractive staging, drew moderately good houses. The attendance was greatest on "Olympic nights," when burlettas of the type she had made famous in the minor theatre were produced at Covent Garden.

Bunn, overtaken by his debts, had left Drury Lane, which was now in the hands of W. J. Hammond, former manager of the Strand Theater, where he had specialized in burlesques of American life and manners.

He engaged Warde, Elton, and Mrs. Warner from Macready's old company and two new actors, Fanny Cooper and Henry Marston. They played *Richard the Third* and *Romeo and Juliet* to sparse audiences. Macready and Phelps joined the company in January when the Haymarket closed for its legally required winter recess, and they played for seven weeks alternating *Macbeth* and a new drama called *Mary Stuart,* which had the characteristics and few of the virtues of other tragedies written expressly for Macready, and drew smaller houses than the well-worn *Macbeth.*

Phelps, along with Mrs. Warner, who recently had been reduced to secondary roles by Macready's preference for Helen Faucit, planned to stay at Drury Lane after Easter, when Macready's return to the Haymarket would leave them in possession of leading roles; but Hammond disappeared suddenly at the end of February, leaving debts of 8,000 pounds. With the closing of Drury Lane they were forced to accept Webster's offer of contracts for the 1840 "summer" season. During March and April Mrs. Warner was leading lady at the Haymarket because of Helen Faucit's illness, while Phelps played the Ghost to Macready's Hamlet and Father Joseph to his Richelieu. The arrival of Charles Kean in June sent Macready to the provinces.

Chares Kean came to the Haymarket in the summer of 1840 as a star, and Phelps once again was assigned to support him. During the years since they had acted together in Sheffield under Butler's management, they had followed different courses in their quest for a prominent position on the London stage. Kean had always played leading roles. His famous name had stimulated interest wherever he acted, and he had been willing to take short engagements at many different provincial theatres. He had also made an American tour—an almost certain method of earning money for an English actor of repute who had the stamina needed to face the rigors of traveling long distances under difficult conditions. His first appearance in London, in January, 1838, had been carefully limited to twenty nights at 50 pounds a night (double what Macready had been getting). This engagement and a second one at the Haymarket in 1839, again limited to a few weeks, had been successful. He had not made the test of long-continued popularity, and he had not yet established himself as a Shakespearean actor. So far his fame, aside from his Hamlet, which had been considered refreshingly new, rested upon his performances of contemporary plays that bordered on melodrama. In the summer of 1840 he was announced at the Haymarket as Macbeth, Richard the Third,

Shylock, and Hamlet—thus making a serious bid for laurels as a tragedian.

Phelps, who had played three of the same roles with distinction at the Haymarket three years earlier, now found himself as the Ghost in *Hamlet,* Henry the Sixth in *Richard the Third,* and the eternal Macduff. This assignment was more galling than his previous subordination to Macready because Kean had neither the acknowledged position nor the ability to interpret Shakespeare that Macready possessed. He was less interested in the interpretation of character and the precise meaning of lines than in clever stage effects. Audiences found his performances lively and interesting, but most critics found him unconvincing. Reviewers who did not like Macready's style, like Bayle Bernard of the *Weekly Dispatch,* were more favorable to Kean, but even the *Weekly Dispatch* (July 12, 1840) complained that he often had the wrong emphasis upon lines and frequently ruined a Shakespearean passage for the sake of a purely theatrical effect. Bernard said that whereas Macready's Macbeth was cold and calculated, Kean's was hurried and sloppy. Other reviewers found Kean simply grotesque in his Shakespearean characters. The *Morning Herald* (August 4, 1840) spoke briefly of "Mr. Charles Kean's vigorous and most elaborate misrepresentation of Macbeth" and went on without further comment to review the afterpiece of the evening's bill. Two days later, after seeing Kean's Shylock, the same reviewer declared:

> We have now seen Mr. Charles Kean in all his Shakespearean parts, and our strengthened conviction is, that he is merely a noisy, yet most tricky commonplace.

In general, Kean's six-week engagement at the Haymarket lessened the enthusiasm he had created in earlier appearances and brought unfavorable opinions from most critics.

In the lacuna between Kean's departure and Macready's return Phelps shared the Haymarket stage with James Wallack, a well-known actor of romantic heroes, who had just returned to London after six years in New York. They played together in Holcroft's *The Road to Ruin,* and Phelps made a hit as Old Dornton—a role created by the celebrated comedian Joseph Munden, who was much admired by Charles Lamb. The *Weekly Dispatch* (September 20, 1840) paid Phelps a high compliment: "We cannot conceive that . . . Munden, with his drollery, could have filled the part of Mr. Dornton better than Mr. Phelps." Reviewers said that the play drew the largest audiences of the summer.

When Macready returned in September, armed with a new play,

Master Clarke, written by his friend T. J. Serle, he resumed control of casting at the Haymarket and assigned Phelps such a minor role that he openly sulked through it. The *Morning Herald* (September 28, 1840) reprimanded him for revenging bad parts on the unfortunate audience. In the next production, Byron's *Werner,* Phelps threw himself into the role of Gabor and won favorable reviews, but this success annoyed Macready, who retaliated by denying him the part of Smooth which Bulwer-Lytton had intended for him in writing a new comedy for Macready called *Money.*[19] The rest of the Haymarket season, which lasted until March 13, 1841, was devoted to the new play, and during these three months Phelps was completely idle, although he drew his salary.

He was constantly looking for any other possible engagement, but the London theatre of 1840, reflecting the economic depression in all England, offered a dreary picture. Only the theatres which attracted the upper classes had sufficient audiences, and most of these were devoted to non-dramatic entertainment. Mme. Vestris was gallantly carrying on her management of Covent Garden, running into debt but supported by the devotion of her company; but she had no place for another tragedian. Drury Lane had become the home of promenade concerts. Among the minor theatres, both the English Opera House and the St. James's (Prince's) were fashionable opera houses. A new theatre, richly decorated and equipped with a special royal box, had been built in Oxford Street and opened in October as the Princess's Theatre; but it was also devoted to promenade concerts. The Adelphi was presenting tableaux. The Olympic, which was the only prominent theatre to attempt melodrama and farce in the season of 1840–1841, had been forced to close for lack of audiences. Even the Strand had been converted to ballet. Aside from the Haymarket, the only theatre in London successfully presenting plays was Sadler's Wells, which had risen to prominence during this depressed season. Although the populous district which supported this theatre was suffering severe economic distress, Sadler's Wells was attracting good houses with its domestic melodramas, sea stories, and adaptations of novels. Henry Marston, who had made his debut under Hammond's ill-fated management, was leading a competent company in acting those forms of minor drama which were regarded as no infringement upon the patent rights of the legitimate theatres.

During November of 1840, there was a serious attempt to reopen Drury Lane for dramatic performances. A group of playwrights, including John Heraud, R. H. Horne, and George Stephens, proposed a joint management, financed by a number of shareholders who might be persuaded to invest in such a venture, and dedicated to the production of poetic drama—particularly the plays that had been refused by managers of the patent theatres. Some of the members of this group, which called itself the Council of Dramatic Authors or the Syncretics, had sufficient wealth to back such an enterprise, and they had enough influence to obtain assurance of the Queen's patronage. Phelps was offered the position of leading actor in the company, if he would contribute 500 pounds as a shareholder. He accepted eagerly, hoping to escape from Macready's domination of the Haymarket. The Syncretics had reached the point of discussing terms with the proprietors of Drury Lane, when suddenly the managing committee of the theatre withdrew from negotiations, stating that the theatre was no longer for lease. The project was therefore abandoned.

It was rumored that Macready was responsible for the sudden change of policy on the part of the proprietors and that he was motivated in his intervention by fear of losing his control of the stage.[20] It is true that Macready addressed a petition to the Lord Chamberlain in December with reference to Drury Lane. He was very angry at the answer he received on December 23, which referred him to the proprietors, and he decided at once to call upon his influential friend, Lord Lansdowne. On January 3, according to his diary, he confided to Forster his "notion of engrossing a large share of Drury Lane Theatre," and on February 2 he began negotiations with the proprietors about the terms of his lease. Whether or not he deliberately intervened to prevent the lease of the theatre by the Syncretics, his expression of interest in the theatre did remove it from their reach.

Macready had more immediate and personal reasons for his sudden interest in resuming the management of a patent theatre. On December 19, he had spoken so intemperately to Webster on the stage of the Haymarket in the presence of other actors that Webster had demanded an apology. The quarrel, according to Macready, had developed out of the attempt by other actors to diminish the effectiveness of his acting in *Money*:

> Acted Evelyn pretty fairly, not pleased with some unfair advantages taken by Helen Faucit. . . . Mr. Webster was laughing during the concluding speech, which checked me twice and very nearly made me lose the word.

I spoke (which there was no need to do) to him about it when the curtain fell, and he flatly denied it. I (*indiscreetly*) said it was of little consequence to me what he asserted or what he denied. I was very hasty, *but
nothing can justify anger!*

In spite of this effort at minimizing the incident, Macready probably
realized that he had jeopardized any future engagement at the Haymarket
after his contract for 1841, which was already signed, had expired.

Whatever his motive, Macready had decided to lease Drury Lane and
had nearly completed arrangements by the end of February. Seldom in the
history of the English stage has a management received so long an advance notice as Macready's projected lesseeship of Drury Lane. More than
a year elapsed between his note to the Lord Chamberlain in 1840 and his
opening night on December 27, 1841. It is not surprising that the group
of playwrights who had wanted to lease the theatre, when they saw it
empty for most of the year, felt that Macready had deliberately prevented
their projected experiment as managers.

After the collapse of the Syncretics' proposal, Phelps had no alternative
to the Haymarket and decided to accept Webster's offer of a three-year
contract, hoping that the end of Macready's (now limited) stay would
give him his long-awaited opportunity. During May and June he played
very minor parts while first Macready and Helen Faucit and later Charles
Kean and Ellen Tree were the stars at the Haymarket. On July 10 the
Theatrical Journal announced that "Mr. Macready will not be able to
open Drury Lane until the 26th of December, as his engagements at the
Haymarket preclude him from leaving that theatre." This was bad news
for the proprietors of Drury Lane, who were receiving no rent while
Macready held the theatre unused, and also for Webster, who would have
to pay Macready 100 pounds a week although he had failed to draw good
houses after the novelty of *Money* had worn off. For Phelps it meant another postponement of his hopes—after so many disappointments—and
the prospect threw him into despair. When Webster assigned him the role
of Friar Laurence in the old stage version of *Romeo and Juliet* with
Charles Kean playing Romeo, Phelps refused to act and angrily resigned
from the theatre.

Utterly damning reviews of Kean's Romeo were small comfort to
Phelps, who faced a return to the provinces without having established
his reputation in London. During the four years since his debut, in spite
of the restrictions of the theatrical monopoly and the decline of interest

in drama, opportunities had appeared, and he had used them well; but each had been removed by Macready's careful control.

An unexpected offer from the Syncretics, a group who also felt themselves to be victims of Macready's domination, gave Phelps employment for the rest of the summer of 1841. They offered him the position of stage manager and leading actor for the production of a new play called *Martinuzzi,* written by George Stephens, one of their members. Stephens, a man of considerable wealth, leased the English Opera House (Lyceum Theatre) for one month beginning August 26 and paid the actors' salaries. In order to circumvent the monopoly law the play was arranged in three acts instead of five, equipped with songs and musical interludes, and advertised as a concert. Phelps engaged Mrs. Warner and Elton as chief supporting actors, assumed the direction of rehearsals, and gave his advice on staging.

Unfortunately, *Martinuzzi* was a very bad play. Stephens's verse was so turgid and obscure that even the skill of practiced Shakespearean actors could not make it intelligible. Absence of dramatic interest and clumsiness in technical matters produced absurdities of situation more ludicrous than the absurdity of language, which provoked titters of laughter from the audience. Stephens could afford to keep the play on the stage for a month, although he offended the professional theatre by persisting in the face of damning reviews. He supplied a claque and "forced the pit" (filled the pit by the gift of free tickets so that paying patrons would have to buy box seats)—practices used by regular theatrical managers under stressful situations.

Although reviewers condemned the play, they gave Phelps credit for a convincing piece of acting under difficult conditions, and the audience, most of whom had never seen him in a prominent role, discovered him to be an impressive actor. For Phelps the experience of directing a play was perhaps the greatest benefit of his engagement.

Before *Martinuzzi* had come to the end of its month-long run, Macready's agent, Thomas Serle, called upon Phelps at his home for the purpose of persuading him to join Macready's company at Drury Lane for the winter season of 1841–1842. Phelps, along with the rest of the theatrical world, knew that Macready had leased Drury Lane, and since no company had yet been announced, he was not entirely surprised by Serle's visit. He had evidently discussed with his wife and nephew the possibility of signing another contract with Macready and found them both opposed.[21] He had some hope of an offer from Mme. Vestris, who was beginning her third year as manager of Covent Garden, and his wife urged him to wait for that possibility rather than have any further dealings with Macready. If he failed to get an offer from Covent Garden, he could make an American tour. Serle was persuasive, and his proposal included Macready's assurances that Phelps would be given nothing less than the most prominent supporting roles, along with some leading roles, in Macready's new management. The interview was long, but in the end Phelps found the offer sufficiently attractive to win his acceptance. He preferred to risk Macready's treatment rather than face the possibility of unemployment or separation from his family in the bad times of 1841. Considering the hazards of sea travel he was probably wise, since three of his colleagues lost their lives at sea (Elton, Power, and Brooke). Both his wife and his nephew tried to dissuade him from the contract with Macready, whom they thoroughly distrusted; but he declared himself satisfied with its terms.

During the interval between the closing of *Martinuzzi* on September 26 and the beginning of Macready's management on December 27, Phelps spent several weeks at provincial theatres. Then, early in December, he returned to London for a series of performances at the Surrey—a transpontine theatre more famous for its hippodramatic pieces than for poetic drama. This unexpected offer of a starring engagement in London came from the enterprising management of Davidge and Jones, who dared open violation of the monopoly law, trusting that the Surrey's distance from the theatrical center of London would give excuse for lack of strict enforcement. Sadler's Wells, under Marston's leadership, had several times in the past year taken the same risk without suffering any penalty. The managers of the Surrey had gathered an adequate company and were presenting Shakespeare to full houses when Phelps arrived to fill his engagement.

Although performances at the Surrey were not usually reviewed by London's leading theatrical critics, the announcement of Phelps's appearance brought at least one reviewer to the theatre on his opening night, and the following article appeared in the *Sun* of December 7, 1841:

> Mr. Phelps commenced an engagement here for a limited number of nights last evening, and chose the character of Lucius Junius Brutus, in Howard Payne's tragedy of *Brutus,* for his *début* before a Surrey audience. This character was written expressly for the late Edmund Kean, then in the

zenith of his fame, and in the full enjoyment of all his energies, and Kean at once made it his own. Since his death the tragedy has seldom been produced, the stage possessing no actor qualified to represent the arduous character of Brutus. This reason, however, no longer exists. Mr. Phelps is an excellent representative of Brutus. Since the days of Kean there has been no Brutus at all approaching Mr. Phelps. His oration over the dead body of Lucretia was beautifully given, his warm and natural style of eloquence contrasting most favourably with the monotonous syllabic declamation to which of late we have been too much accustomed. The whole of the two last acts was magnificent; from the first expression of horrible suspicion that his son may be a criminal, in the fourth act, to the fearful condemnation of that guilty son, at the conclusion of the fifth, when the stern duty of the patriot has been fulfilled to the letter, the Roman becomes humane, and the Consul softens into the man and the father—all was given with a truthfulness to nature which stamps Mr. Phelps as an actor of high genius. We hope frequently to see him in impassioned characters such as this, which give full scope for the exhibition of the play of the feelings. He was called for at the fall of the curtain, and loudly applauded.

Such unqualified praise, in an age when reviewers generally preferred the display of discriminating judgment to enthusiasm, suggests that Phelps might have ascended quickly to fame if he had been given many such opportunities to show his ability. But such a review, particularly the implied comparison with Macready, whose "monotonous syllabic declamation" had often been criticized, was more likely to diminish his opportunities than to increase his reputation. The hope expressed by the reviewer that Phelps would frequently be seen in such characters was not to be realized while Macready controlled the assignment of roles.

While Phelps was at the Surrey, where he also acted Virginius (in the play by Sheridan Knowles), King Lear, and Cassius (in *Julius Caesar*), he was studying the role of Shylock for the opening of Drury Lane. Macready had asked him to play the role in the event that he himself remained at the Haymarket, where his contract did not expire until January 15. Past experience should have warned Phelps of the unlikelihood of his obtaining such a boon from Macready. Perhaps Macready had honestly intended to allow Phelps greater prominence under his new management, feeling that the past three years had sufficiently lessened the danger of Phelps's sudden rise to fame. If this was the case, the announcement of Phelps's starring engagement at the Surrey may have changed his mind.

Whatever his intention, Macready did not allow Phelps to play Shylock. Instead, he abruptly left the Haymarket on December 7. His departure was called a "secession" by the *Spectator,* and he parted from Webster in open hostility.

The casting of *The Merchant of Venice* caused several problems. Although Phelps accepted Antonio without complaint and Bennett agreed to play the minor part of the Duke, G. V. Brooke refused to accept either Salanio or Salerio and withdrew from the company before the opening night. Brooke had been famous as a "child Roscius" some years before and had been scheduled to make his first appearance in London as a mature actor during this season at Drury Lane, but Macready's first assignment convinced him that he would be given no opportunity to show his ability to London audiences. He went back to the provinces and did not return to London until Macready's domination had ended, and then he immediately rose to the highest peak of popularity. The final announcement of the cast for *The Merchant of Venice* brought a protest from the *Sunday Times* (December 12, 1841), which cited Bennett's role as "a continuation of the *levelling* system, so pertinaciously insisted upon by Mr. Macready."

Macready's first season as manager of Drury Lane was even less successful than those at Covent Garden. There was no new play by Bulwer-Lytton but instead a dull tragedy called *Gisippus* by Gerald Griffin, which Macready had revised with a free hand, dividing one character between two actors and giving fullest prominence to his own part. The most successful production of the season was a lavishly staged opera, Handel's *Acis and Galatea.*

Phelps was given minor roles in most plays and excluded entirely from the cast of *Gisippus,* which Macready kept running for twenty performances to very thin houses; but he had the leading role in a "petite comedy" which served as the afterpiece for the Handel opera. It was a three-act play called *Prisoner of War,* by Douglas Jerrold, which did not rank as legitimate drama and occupied very little of Macready's attention. Jerrold, however, was no mere theatrical hack of the sort who provided dramatic fare for the minor theatres by translating French plays into English. The dramatic critic of *Punch* and an amateur actor of some reputation, he had written three successful melodramas which were among the first to bring the continental genre into typically English settings. His originality and his mastery of dramatic techniques, aided by the talented acting of a good cast, made *Prisoner of War* unexpectedly attractive. Jerrold's play, with Phelps and the two Keeleys, on the same bill with Handel's opera, drew the best houses of the season and ran longer than any of the five-act plays produced.

During the run of *Prisoner of War,* Douglas Jerrold and Phelps met again and reminisced about their early days in London twenty years before when they had worked side by side in a newspaper office. Jerrold recalled his prediction that Phelps would never earn more than 25 shillings a week as an actor and good naturedly admitted his misjudgment.[22] Phelps was now earning 20 pounds a week.

In this season Phelps finally rid himself of the debt he had contracted for a friend's security when he first came to London. The exorbitant rate of 45 percent interest had kept him near bankruptcy for five years. Now he asked Macready for a loan of 300 pounds, with his life insurance as security, to be paid back out of his weekly salary over the period of their two-year contract.[23] Macready agreed to the proposal and did so in such a gracious manner that Phelps never forgot his kindness. The means of liquidating his old debt with its crippling rate of interest gave him a financial security he had never known, and his gratitude to Macready partly canceled the professional grievances he had previously felt.

The unsuccessful season at Drury Lane forced Macready to close the theatre early, after barely six months of his management, leaving the Haymarket again in sole possession of the legitimate drama in London. Macready, to whom the Haymarket was now barred because of his quarrel with Webster, departed for Dublin and Birmingham, taking Helen Faucit as his leading lady. Webster, who had a forgiving nature and was more interested in the financial success of his management than past disagreements, engaged Phelps for the summer as chief supporting actor to Charles Kean and Ellen Tree (now Mrs. Kean). He commissioned Sheridan Knowles to write a play for this cast, and the result, *The Rose of Arragon,* was a success. The *Sunday Times* (June 5, 1842) unhesitatingly pronounced Knowles the best contemporary writer of poetic drama and praised him for providing a play so admirably suited to the cast. Phelps in the role of a crafty and despicable villain, Almagro, rather surprisingly dominated the play. According to this reviewer, he was "the perfection of a cool, designing villain," and his performance "as magnificent a piece of acting as we have ever beheld." Even the *Weekly Dispatch,* always partial to Kean, found no character better acted than Almagro. In the third act,

where the interest of the play centers in the villain, Phelps captivated the
audience by the compelling realism of this unsympathetic antagonist and
by the ease of his acting, which contrasted noticeably with Kean's artificial
style. *Punch* (July 16, 1842) humorously remarked upon Kean's discomfiture:

> The comparative effect of the acting of the two gentlemen is now well
> known. Mr. Phelps . . . did, on Monday last, in full Haymarket green-
> room, present to Mr. Charles Kean a very handsome silver—*extinguisher!*

Soon afterward, when *The Rose of Arragon* had run for nearly two
months, the Keans left for a tour of the Continent, amid rumors that
Phelps's success had shortened their stay at the Haymarket.[24] Webster
then advertised Phelps in a series of leading roles. He played Sir Giles
Overreach in Massinger's *A New Way To Pay Old Debts,* where he again
showed his skill in making an exaggerated villain credible on the stage.
He also played Duke Aranza in *The Honeymoon,* a comedy modeled
upon the Elizabethan type, written by John Tobin in 1805. In both plays
Phelps had the excellent support of Webster's perennially good company
of comedians, including William Farren, Mrs. Nisbett, and Mrs. Glover.

When Macready reopened Drury Lane in October, 1842, Phelps returned to his former position with a wider reputation than he had ever
had. Audiences and critics looked forward to his reappearance on the
stage of the great national theatre, and they were disappointed when he
was assigned only insignificant parts. During this season reviews frequently objected to Macready's preference of Anderson, Elton, and a new
actor, John Ryder, to Phelps for important roles. In the first major production of the season, *As You Like It,* Phelps was given the part of Old
Adam—"a very unprofitable part for him," remarked one critic, after
praising his performance. In the important production of Congreve's *Love
for Love* (adapted to suit nineteenth-century taste), critics noticed his
excellent performance of the very minor part of Scandal, remarking that
the role was "wholly unworthy of the actor." A typical comment is one
that appeared in the *Dramatic and Musical Review* (April 29, 1843) after
he had played a small part in Knowles's new play *The Secretary*:

> Phelps, in Lord Byerdale, had little more to do than those who are usually
> called upon to represent obdurate and wicked stage noblemen, who are
> ever scowling on humble lovers; in other hands, the character would have

been intensely disagreeable, but Phelps's excellent acting was apparent more than ever in this part.

The most important production of the season was *King John,* put on the stage with lavish scenic decoration in which careful attention had been paid to historical detail. Indeed, the emphasis upon the scenery provoked unfavorable comment from many reviewers, who complained that acting had been submerged in spectacle. Others objected to the acting itself— that it was noisy and that most of the actors imitated Macready's manner. Helen Faucit, who lacked the power needed for such a role as Queen Constance, was never more grievously miscast. Critics spoke of her acting as the "sheer impotence of rant," and "the bodily suffering of some very noisy woman," asserting that she reduced the dignity of the Queen to the level of a scold. One reviewer said that "boisterousness is the hallmark of the acting of *all* save Phelps as Hubert." [25] In contrast to the rest of the actors, Phelps seemed natural, unstrained, and sincere. Although he played a small part, he left an indelible impression on the audience. Even the lordly *Times,* whose reviews this season had the tone of polite congratulations to Macready without much serious dramatic criticism, noticed Phelps's performance:

> Phelps was an admirable Hubert; an actor with more manly pathos than any on the stage, he managed his pathos with great skill. [October 25, 1842.]

The *Morning Post* (October 25, 1842) contained this paragraph:

> As Hubert is the finest character in the poet's conception, so was it acted with the most consistent power. . . . [Phelps] is one of the few living men who touch our hearts, and this, not by loud words and hurried delivery and strong tones (although his strength is plentiful), but by the genial undercurrent of living feeling which is ever leaping and throbbing under the surface of his acting. He calls forth a tear by the only magic that can do so—the strong persuasion that his grief or passion is actually grappling with the very roots of his own heart.

King John also brought Phelps to the notice of the Queen, who was so much affected by his Hubert that she commanded him, dressed in the costume of the role, to sit for a portrait to the painter Sir William Ross.

During October and November, Phelps was assigned two prominent roles: Old Dornton in *The Road to Ruin* and Iago. *The Road to Ruin* was performed on an "off night" when Macready did not act, Tuesday, October 18. No provision had been made for adequate staging, and the scenery was put together out of old remnants. But the excellent acting of Phelps, Anderson, and Mrs. Stirling in the leading roles lifted the comedy into prominence. The *Morning Post* had an enthusiastic review the next day, commenting that "as the audience laughed heartily at the capital acting, and endured the dingy scenery, the *Road to Ruin* will of course be a repeated comedy." A second performance was given the following Tuesday, but then the play was abruptly withdrawn and the theatre closed on the three subsequent Tuesday nights. A similar treatment was given to his Iago. When *Othello* was first performed on October 20 with Macready as the Moor, Phelps was warmly applauded for his Iago. Forster, in his review of the play, tried to minimize Phelps's success, but his remarks provoked a letter to the *Theatrical Journal* of October 29, protesting the *Examiner*'s misrepresentation and describing the audience's enthusiastic reception of Phelps's Iago. After the third performance of *Othello* on successive Thursday evenings, this play was also withdrawn, and on the following Thursday Drury Lane was closed for the evening.

Although Phelps, being thoroughly accustomed to Macready's practices, bore his disappointment with reasonable equanimity, two new members of the company had already begun to object to the manager's despotism. Mme. Vestris and Charles Mathews, who had been persuaded to come to Drury Lane after the collapse of their management of Covent Garden, had been too long in the professional theatre to accept his unusual practices. So long as they acted only in afterpieces, there was little cause for quarrel. Their great success during the early weeks of the season in Planché's *Follies of a Night* had the dual advantage of attracting audiences to the theatre without suggesting any rivalry with Macready. But Macready insisted upon Mathews's playing Roderigo in *Othello* (a role which, as might have been predicted, he played badly) and a servant in *The Rivals*. Mathews protested, but capitulated. Then, early in October, Macready assigned Mme. Vestris the small part of Venus in an elaborate production of the Dryden-Purcell opera *King Arthur*. This assignment, as Macready well knew, was peculiarly insulting to the famous Vestris. She had originally conceived the idea of producing *King Arthur* as an operatic extravaganza under her management at Covent Garden, but before she had begun work on it Macready had announced its forthcoming production at Drury Lane, eighteen months ahead of its actual appearance.[26] Having forestalled her production, in which she would have had the leading role, he now asked her to play a minor part, preferring for the leading role his young protégée Priscilla Horton, for whom he was planning a course of singing lessons. It is difficult to see what motive Macready could have had beyond a desire to humiliate Mme. Vestris. The attraction of the bewitching Vestris in the leading role would have insured the success of *King Arthur,* and surely the public expected to see her in it. For these reasons, it was no ordinary grievance that brought Mathews into Macready's office on October 8, although Macready pretended that it was a trivial matter:

> Mr. C. Mathews held a very long and *very silly* conversation with me, which I tried to receive as patiently as possible. I see he is not to be managed to any advantage.

Macready did not seem to realize that the Mathewses, unlike other actors in the company, were not limited by the theatrical monopoly. Their protest of October 8 was a warning of the storm that broke on November 5, when they led the entire company in opposition to the manager.

On that Saturday, the weekly payday, the actors discovered that a percentage of their salaries had been deducted because the theatre had been closed on the previous Tuesday night (when Macready had preferred not to risk another performance of *The Road to Ruin*). Such a salary deduction was wholly without precedent in legitimate theatres. Since the actors had been engaged at a fixed weekly rate for the entire season and were not allowed to act at any other theatre while under engagement to him, Macready's new practice was tantamount to an unexpected cut in salary. The anger of all the actors was aroused, and when they discovered that the deduction had been extended to the lowest ranks—even to the cleaners and sweepers, whose regular salary in some cases was only 15 shillings a week—they were disgusted by the pettiness of the device. They knew that Macready had arranged to have his own salary included among the working expenses of the theatre, separate from the normal pay roll, and they may have guessed that his reason for closing the theatre on that night had been personal jealousy instead of economy.

Mme. Vestris and Charles Mathews, who had themselves managed a patent theatre for three years, felt that Macready had committed an outrage which should not be ignored and went to his office at once. After a stormy three-hour session, during which Macready made no concessions, they resigned from the company, making clear their intention of publishing their grievance (which appeared shortly afterward in the *Morning Post*). Macready, having called in his three officials, Anderson, Willmott, and Serle, declared that there was nothing in the actors' contracts forbidding such deduction. "I felt my own strength and was very cool," he wrote in his diary that night, but on the following Wednesday morning (after another Tuesday night closing) when he arrived at the theatre, the whole company was in open rebellion. His response was a stern reprimand and a threat to close the theatre until they were ready to continue rehearsals for *King Arthur*:

> Spoke *very strongly* to the whole community, actors and band, to the effect that they were wanting in proper feeling and duty, and that I was indifferent to the carrying on the theatre, but if the piece were not ready for Saturday, I would close the theatre till it should be.[27]

This threat, supported by the closing of the theatre on Thursday, Saturday, and the following Tuesday, forced the company into submission. No one followed the example set by Mme. Vestris and Charles Mathews. Macready explained the unusual closings to his public by the statement that additional time was needed to prepare the great production of *King Arthur*.

On November 16 the spectacular version of Dryden's tragedy accompanied by Purcell's music finally appeared on the stage of Drury Lane. It was well received by the first night audience, but the combination of tragedy with elaborate scenery and music brought neither critical esteem nor popular audiences. The work ran as a second feature, with *King John* and other new major productions, for twenty-seven performances, but it was not sufficiently attractive to repay its tremendous cost.

Macready needed a good new play, like Knowles's *Virginius* or Bulwer-Lytton's *Richelieu,* to make the season a success. In December he put on *The Patrician's Daughter* by Westland Marston, although he was uneasy about attempting a blank verse tragedy in a contemporary setting and troubled by the fact that Helen Faucit had the title role. Apparently his fears were confirmed by the performance. Anderson reports that "Helen Faucit, Mrs. Warner, and Phelps were excellent," omitting mention of Macready.[28] The *Spectator* (December 17, 1842) was more explicit:

> Mr. Phelps's personation of the Earl is admirable for quietude and unaffected propriety: Mr. Macready's style of acting is unsuited to the man

of fashion; and the rest of the male performers do not appear like persons accustomed to move in upper society.

The play provoked some interest but lasted only eleven performances.

Macready continued to search among the plays in his possession for something suitable. A tragedy called *Athelwold* by William Smith seemed to be a possibility, but after rereading it Macready decided that there was not sufficient emphasis on the leading role. He feared that the secondary part of Dunstan might become too prominent on the stage. He then turned to the manuscript of *A Blot in the 'Scutcheon,* which Browning had given him more than a year before. This play did not satisfy him, and he continued to look for something else. "Searched, hunted, ruminated; could find nothing," he wrote in his diary on January 26. In the absence of any alternative he finally took Browning's manuscript to Drury Lane in a despairing and resentful mood. Instead of asking Browning to read the play to his actors (as he often did when the author was a friend) or having it read by the stage manager (the usual custom), he gave the task to his prompter Willmott and left the room. Willmott, a close associate of Macready for many years, must have sensed his dissatisfaction with the play, and therefore displayed his talent as a low comedian in the reading, particularly in the women's roles, producing much laughter in the green room. The next day, Macready told Browning that the actors had laughed at his play and advised him to revise the second act.[29]

Although Macready's attitude was not encouraging, Browning agreed to work on alterations. When he arrived at Drury Lane on January 31 with the revised manuscript, to keep an appointment with Macready, he was rudely received by the doorkeeper and kept waiting. He found Macready brusque and condescending and apparently reluctant to produce the play. Macready's attitude may have been nothing more than an overflowing of general resentment, but it was perhaps a deliberate effort to compel a sensitive author to accept drastic revision of his work. If so, Macready found Browning far less docile than he had expected. "I fear he is a very conceited man," he wrote that evening in his diary. This statement, coupled with his further remark that he had afterward read Browning's altered version "with great difficulty, being *very unwell,*" indicates that he was burning with indignation and anger against Browning. The epithets "conceited," "self-sufficient," and "impertinent" in the diaries are almost always connected with a serious quarrel, and the expression "unwell," with underlining, generally is a sign of uncontrollable anger.

The following morning he stayed at home and tried to work on revision of the play, but by the time Serle stopped in with business from the theatre he had decided to divorce himself from further concern with *A Blot in the 'Scutcheon.* "I told him of my inability to meet my work— that I *could not* play this part of Browning's unless the whole work of the theatre stopped, that I thought it best to reduce it to its proper form— three acts, and let Phelps do it on all accounts." The additional statement that "he concurred with me" is the usual remark after airing his grievances to Serle, his most comforting adviser. He then turned immediately to work on *Much Ado about Nothing* and a spectacular musical version of *Comus,* both of which he decided to produce on the same bill, as soon as possible.

Phelps was ready for a rehearsal of Browning's play three days later on February 4. Perhaps Macready, in directing the rehearsal, began to doubt his wisdom in throwing away the role of Lord Tresham. Some event, omitted from the published portion of his diary, severely disturbed Macready that day. The entry for February 5 shows a sorely troubled mind:

> Very little sleep last night, and this morning found me dejected, desponding—almost despairing. I have wished to be right—I cannot say that I have always tried to be right, or that I have tried enough—I have not. Perhaps that is the cause of my present unhappiness. I wish life could be past with me, so that I could leave my blessed children with hope and my dearest wife in worldly comfort. God forgive—forgive and aid me.

If these remarks indicate that Macready regretted giving the role of Tresham to Phelps, then the news he received the next morning, that Phelps was too ill to attend rehearsal, must have seemed the answer to his prayer. He at once decided to understudy the part. As rehearsals continued during the week and Phelps remained ill, Macready alternated between hope and despair about the success of the play, but his final decision was to act Tresham if Phelps could not. On February 10, the day before *A Blot in the 'Scutcheon* was scheduled to open, Macready stayed home to study the part.

> Began consideration and study of the part of Tresham, which was to occupy my single thoughts till accomplished. About a quarter past one a note came from Willmott, informing me that Mr. Phelps would do the part, if he "died for it," so that my time had been lost.

He then went to Drury Lane for the penultimate rehearsal.

> Offered to give to Browning and Mr. Phelps the benefit of my considera-
> tion and study in the cuts, etc. I had made one I thought particularly
> valuable, not letting Tresham die, but consigning him to a convent. Brown-
> ing, however, in the worst taste, manner, and spirit, declined any further
> alterations, expressing himself perfectly satisfied with the manner in which
> Mr. Phelps executed Lord Tresham. I had no more to say. I could only
> think Mr. Browning a very disagreeable and offensively mannered person.
> *Voilà tout!*

Macready's suggested revision of the ending, although it was not used,
has been preserved in the original manuscript of the play, which is in the
library of Yale University.[30] Browning's reaction to this last-minute suggestion is preserved in the same place, below what Macready had written:

> The above, in Macready's handwriting, was the substitution for [what]
> he found written: this to avoid giving the piece the dignity of a Tragedy,
> and Mr. Phelps the distinction of playing in one!

The last rehearsal, on February 11, was conducted with apparent
civility between author and manager. Browning had mastered his anger
sufficiently to make an attempt at reconciliation. He may have been well
enough pleased with the acting to forgive Macready's high-handed treatment of himself and shabby staging of his play in old scenery and costumes. Macready wrote that evening that he had made "many valuable
improvements" during the rehearsal.

The performance went well. The audience responded with tumultuous
applause, demanding Phelps's appearance before the curtain and calling
loudly for the author. Browning did not rise to the call, even when
Anderson, who as stage manager had come before the curtain to receive
the audience's verdict on the play, begged the author to come forward if
he was present. Anderson responded to the applause with the customary
announcement that the play would be performed three nights a week.
Macready, watching from a box, was angry that he had not been included
in this demonstration of approval nor consulted about "giving out" the
play for future performance. The entry in his diary fails even to mention
the fact that the play succeeded—usually his most important concern on
an opening night:

Saw the play of *Blot on the 'Scutcheon,* which was badly acted in Phelps's and Mrs. Stirling's parts—pretty well in Anderson's, very well in Helen Faucit's. I was *angry* after the play about the call being directed without me.

Reviews of *A Blot in the 'Scutcheon* were highly favorable, and for the first time in Macready's management even unfriendly critics were enthusiastic. The *Morning Post* (February 13, 1843) for example, had a long review of the play, describing it as "an unequivocal success" and a work of "genuine genius." The reviewer noted that the scenery was old and some of it unmistakably the same as that used in *The Patrician's Daughter,* but he congratulated Macready on "the change of policy" that brought this play to the stage and praised the acting in general, giving this description of Phelps as Tresham:

> Phelps took the part which Macready would otherwise have acted, and if we missed a little of that refinement which carries the latter actor so triumphantly through his blotchy mannerisms, it is due to Mr. Phelps to say that in other respects he gave a singular passion and power to the proud brother, which we believe could have been shown by no other actor than himself. The whirlwind of rage and hate with which he compels Mertoun to draw were terribly true. The whole soul—its love, its masculine sense, and its reason—seemed lost in the madness of the moment; and each savage phrase was thrown out with a lightning-like rapidity and violence from the cloud and storm of his passion, that brought the reality and fear of that dark and momentary insanity singularly home to the listeners. . . . The actor was forgotten in the terrible truth of his fiery utterance. . . . Equally fine was the manner in which the man-slayer suffered the madness of his guilt to subside when the lover of his sister lay dying at his feet. And as an isolated beauty, still earlier in the drama, we may mark the tone in which loathing, and affection, and disbelief were struggling as he bade Mildred "not to lean upon him," after he has heard from his retainer Gerard the tale which involves her dishonour. At the conclusion Mr. Phelps was vociferously called for.

The *Era* (February 12, 1843) also pronounced the play "entirely successful" and had high praise for Phelps:

> The manner in which the play was acted reflects the highest credit on the Drury Lane company, and the absence of Mr. Macready from the cast was as little regretted as it possibly could be. Phelps, who performed the brother, was fearfully effective in his impersonation of the angry and

agonized patrician, who shrinks from the fear of the blot upon his 'scutcheon. In the great scene in which he detects the lurking lover, and, dragging him out into the light, taunts him till he draws his sword,—although he will not name himself, or uncover his face,—the actor was powerful, and almost terrific. The passion of his rage reminded us vividly of Edmund Kean, and such praise is no common compliment.

The *Dramatic and Musical Review* (Feb. 18, 1843) was critical of the play itself and gave Phelps a large share of the credit for its success on the stage:

> Mr. Phelps had a long and difficult part, on which the whole weight of the piece rested, and he bore his burthen admirably. His appeal to his sister to disprove the charge, and the feeling and energy with which he denounces her treachery (as he supposes) to his friend Mertoun, were masterly and natural. Whenever Mr. Phelps has had an opportunity of displaying his ability, he has invariably made a highly favourable impression upon the audience. He was loudly called for at the conclusion.

Laudatory reviews brought many playgoers to Drury Lane for subsequent performances. On February 25, the *Theatrical Journal* noted that "the new tragedy of the Blot on the 'Scutcheon has been three times represented to full and admiring audiences since our last publication." To the ordinary observer Browning's play seemed destined for a long run and Macready's management for better fortune. At the end of the week, however, the play was withdrawn and never performed again under Macready's management.

Phelps apparently accepted Macready's characteristic action without bitterness. Browning, however, was totally shocked by the withdrawal of his successful play, especially after it had survived its hasty and shabby staging. He could hardly believe that a friend, with whom he had shared not only a warm social relationship but serious professional concerns, would treat him in such a manner. He never willingly met Macready again, and when they passed in the street, Browning turned away to avoid speaking. Macready seems to have been rather surprised at Browning's attitude:

> *March 18th.*—Went out; met Browning, who was startled into accosting me, but seeming to remember that he did not intend to do so, started off in great haste. What but contempt, which one ought not to feel, can we with galled spirit feel for these wretched insects about one? Oh God! how is it all to end?

Although there can be little question that Macready suppressed Browning's play chiefly to remove Phelps from prominence, it appears that Macready was able to deceive himself about his own action. Only four days after the last performance of *A Blot in the 'Scutcheon,* he wrote the following paragraph in his diary:

March 1st.—Dow called; gave me some curious information respecting Mr. C. Kean's refusal to allow Mr. Phelps to act with him in Knowles's play *The Rose of Aragon,* which shows him to be what I have long considered—a most despicable person—a mere pitiful quack.

Dow undoubtedly had firsthand knowledge about the sudden termination of *The Rose of Arragon* when the Keans abruptly left for the Continent in the summer of 1842, because he had often been backstage at the Haymarket and had given a supper party to celebrate Knowles's achievement after the play's successful opening. But it is surprising that Dow chose this occasion to discuss Kean's behavior toward Phelps, and even more surprising that Macready was able to condemn Kean with such indignation for retreating from competition with him.

The rest of the season did not go well. On April 8 Macready had to sell another 1,200 pounds of securities in order to meet the deficit at Drury Lane. Later in the month he regained some of his money by subletting the theatre to the Anti-Corn Law League, but the proprietors of Drury Lane reprimanded him for this bold use of his lesseeship.

In spite of all his difficulties and his serious financial losses, Macready was eager to continue as lessee of the patent theatre for another season, and he tried every means available to induce the proprietors to give him another lease on his terms. Undaunted by their repeated declarations that they would not allow him the privilege of subletting the theatre or consider any further reduction in rent, Macready called upon high-placed friends who might influence the managing committee. At the same time, ignoring the committee's discouraging responses, he began to engage a company for the winter of 1843–1844, asking each actor to accept a reduction of his salary by one third. He recorded in his diary that Anderson, Phelps, Keeley, Hudson, Mrs. Nisbett, and Mrs. Stirling had agreed to his proposition. Mrs. Warner, who had seen most of her well-known roles—even Lady Macbeth—given to Helen Faucit, refused. So great was his confidence that he spoke to representatives from the Anti-Corn Law

League about their subletting the theatre during the next season and was delighted to hear that they wanted it for fourteen nights.

On the first two days of June when the managing committee was meeting at Westminster, Macready drove down and paced the Hall many hours, waiting to hear news of their decision. After a lengthy debate the proprietors resolved that any lessee must take responsibility for the minimum rent and could not be allowed to sublet the theatre at his own discretion. As soon as Macready was informed of the committee's decision he decided upon June 12 for his closing night and immediately wrote to his cousin, Marianne Skerrett, asking her to apply to the Queen for a command on that night.

During his last week as manager of a patent theatre Macready took one important action which affected the future of the English stage: he saw Drinkwater Bethune, parliamentary draftsman to the government, about drawing up a petition for the repeal of the theatrical monopoly. It is hard to escape the conclusion that this sudden reversal of his stand, coming within a week of his failure to obtain the lesseeship of Drury Lane, was motivated by spite. Macready was well aware of the importance to the proprietors of their exclusive patents. The terms of the petition for repeal (which Macready succeeded in having read to the House by the Home Secretary himself) were entirely personal. In it he attacked the patent holders as if they were his avowed enemies:

> They are armed by law with the power to prevent your Petitioner from exercising his art and calling in any other theatre, and to declare that, unless he live on such terms as they may prescribe to him, he shall not . . . live at all.[31]

The petition, and more especially the attitude expressed in it, angered the proprietors of the patent theatres. According to Macready's diary,[32] Lord Glengall, speaking in the House of Lords, said that Macready's petition was "more marked by self-sufficiency, self-conceit, and vanity than any petition ever presented to that House."

Nevertheless, Macready's influence, which had been an important factor in preserving the monopoly against the petitions of authors, actors, and managers of minor theatres, now quickly destroyed it. Only nine weeks after his private conference with Bethune, the Theatres Regulation Bill was passed by both Houses of Parliament. On August 22, 1843, the two-hundred-year-old prohibition was removed, and the freedom to produce plays was granted to all licensed theatres in London.

Macready asked Phelps to accompany him to America, but Phelps refused. The London stage, so long restricted by legal and personal monopoly, now offered freedom of opportunity to actors. Unfortunately for actors like Phelps, such opportunity depended upon finding a manager willing to break tradition by converting one of the fashionable and comfortable minor theatres into a home for serious drama; and no such manager appeared. Their stages were occupied by farce, burlesque, nautical melodrama, romances pirated from the plots of popular novels, extravaganzas, and domestic pieces. The English Opera House alternated between concerts and melodramas. At the Olympic Mme. Celeste and John Webster were presenting French translations; at the St. James's, a theatre patronized by the highest level of society, the plays were entirely in French. The new Princess's Theatre might have provided excellent housing for dramatic productions, since it was well situated, comfortable, and of a good size for presenting plays; but its new manager, J. M. Maddox, chose the safer venture of opera. Bunn had again taken Drury Lane, announcing his intention of producing only opera, ballet, and spectacle. Even Webster had temporarily abandoned five-act plays and was presenting at the Haymarket the lighter kind of short pieces associated with the minor theatres.

During the summer of 1843 the actors from Macready's disbanded company desperately searched for employment. E. W. Elton, James Anderson, James Hudson, and Helen Faucit had gone to provincial theatres soon after the closing of Drury Lane. Elton, on his way home from Edinburgh, was shipwrecked and lost his life at sea, leaving his large family nearly destitute. This tragedy emphasized the miserable condition of the legitimate theatre, since his former colleagues, most of them unemployed, had some difficulty finding opportunities to give benefit performances for his widow's relief. In this distressing situation, Thomas Greenwood, lessee of Sadler's Wells, where Elton had occasionally appeared, offered his theatre for a benefit performance. On August 5 *Othello* was performed there with Phelps and Mrs. Warner in the leading roles and Henry Marston of the local company as Iago. The West End actors were surprised at the size of the audience, which brought in 70 pounds for Elton's family, because they had not expected many local patrons of Sadler's Wells to attend a Shakespearean play.

Although after August 22 legitimacy was legally dead, and although the evidence of recent years had indicated that drama could not be produced profitably in the huge national theatres, the tradition of a hundred and fifty years was so compelling that actors turned to the old patent theatres as if by instinct. Toward the end of August, Henry Wallack (brother of the actor James Wallack, who was now back in America) suggested to the members of Macready's old company that they band together under his management to produce plays at Covent Garden. Phelps, Anderson, Bennett, Mrs. Warner, and Mrs. Nisbett agreed. John Vandenhoff and his daughter joined them. Their hope of success lay in their intention to reduce the prices of admission and to abandon "Macreadyism" by sharing leading roles and providing strong casts for such plays as *Julius Caesar* which require a number of talented actors. But the project was hastily organized and lacked sufficient financial resources to survive the failure of their first new play—a dreary, conventional drama called *Woman* by Dion Boucicault, whose *London Assurance* had introduced a fresh spirit to the theatre in 1841.

There was no alternative now left to the actors in London, and most resigned themselves to a winter in provincial theatres. According to the *Theatrical Journal* (October 28, 1843), Anderson in a desperate attempt to stay in London applied to Alfred Bunn for an engagement, offering his services to Drury Lane as leading tragedian for the sum of 30 pounds a week. Bunn, remaining firm in his policy of producing opera, sent him a short answer:

Dear A.,
—You can't sing.
Yours, etc.
A. Bunn

Nearly all of London's prominent actors had had experience in theatres in parts of England, Scotland, and Ireland and were aware of the difficulties they might encounter during a winter in the provinces. They were hardly prepared, however, for the peculiar conditions of 1843–1844. Provincial theatres already had too many displaced London actors, and this surfeit of stars came at a time when drama was no more popular in other cities than in London. Only short engagements at low salaries could be found. Phelps, Mrs. Warner, Anderson, and the two Keeleys obtained a joint engagement for the second half of November at the Bath Theatre, and they spent the intervening six weeks in whatever positions they could find.

Phelps went to Liverpool for the first half of November to fill an engagement with Malone Raymond, manager of the Liver Theatre. Advertised as a London celebrity, he played Hamlet, Richard III, Macbeth, and Shylock on successive nights. This schedule was a strain on both his physical and financial resources, since he had to study roles he had not acted for a number of years and had also to provide his own costumes. The expenditure of effort and money proved worthwhile as increasing audiences showed approval of the new tragedian. During the second week Raymond offered him an extension of his engagement, to begin after he returned from Bath.

At Bath the first performance was *Othello,* with Anderson, Phelps, and Mrs. Warner in the leading roles. Phelps's daily letters to his wife comment upon the small audience and other aspects of this engagement:

> Tuesday
>
> We opened last night to a bad house—Othello. Made a great hit and hope and think it will yet turn out well. Bath is a beautiful place and the theatre the best I ever acted in.

> Thursday
>
> Send me the grey wig I wore for the "Patrician's Daughter." . . . Shylock tonight. I think we shall do well here yet.

> Friday
>
> We play here next week of course for our own benefits. I shall have about £10 to receive for this week.

> Sunday
>
> We are getting on a little better but still bad. The papers speak in the highest terms of me.[33]

That the last statement was not an exaggeration is shown by a review from the Bath *Herald*:

> We cannot, we think, even though we be charged with indulging in fulsome adulation, too highly extol the matchless performance of Mr. Phelps as the double-faced Iago. We have seen many attempt this character, but never did we see it so inimitably sustained as on this occasion. It was not merely that the text was delivered with correctness and fluency, or that his look and attitude were in perfect keeping with the part—there was something even more, which we find it difficult to describe, but which many who were present could not, we think, but have been forcibly struck with. We mean the inimitable manner in which he identified himself with

the character, so that from the very first moment he appeared on the stage, until his exit in the last scene, the illusion was so admirably kept up, that the spectator only saw before him the hypocritical, cold-blooded, and remorseless villain; indeed, so strongly impressed was this idea upon the mind, that when Othello stabs him, a feeling of delight (if we may so express ourselves) thrilled the bosoms of many present. We have never heard more enthusiastic applause greet any actor.[34]

This warmly appreciative audience had been cool toward Macready during his last appearance there in 1836, and it was not an unsophisticated audience, since many prominent London actors had played in Bath. The *Herald*'s enthusiasm for Phelps and particularly for his identification with the character is similar to the reaction of Exeter critics during Phelps's first appearance in Exeter. The unusual praise and the similarity of the criticism are good evidence that Phelps would have achieved a high place on the London stage during the intervening seven years if he had not been so completely suppressed by Macready's domination of the legitimate theatres.

Phelps returned to Liverpool before the end of December and acted there during most of January and February. Raymond had reduced the prices of admission so that audiences were large in spite of competition from the Theatre Royal in Liverpool, which featured first Vandenhoff and then Charles Kean under Benjamin Webster's management. At the Liver Phelps held the position of stage manager as well as leading actor of the company, assuming a large share of responsibility in Raymond's management. He worked hard, playing a different role every evening and directing the daily rehearsals of the company. His strenuous efforts were rewarded by an increase in the number of appreciative playgoers among the audience. On the first night of the annual holiday pantomime when spectators usually cared very little about the tragedy which preceded the featured entertainment, Phelps wrote to his wife, "It was crammed but I never played to a quicker audience." Two other letters mention full houses:

We were very full again last night to Macbeth. Scores went from the doors. Richard tonight.

I have had a very long rehearsal of Virginius. The house was full last night to Hamlet. It is a bad job that the prices are lowered as the house will not hold £60 now.

Low prices were a recognition of bad times in the "hungry forties" in England. Besides low wages actors in the provinces had to contend with dishonest managers. Anderson says that the manager of the Bath theatre absconded with their salaries, and Phelps wrote from Glasgow that the manager had given him only 38 pounds after his benefit when the house had seemed a full 50 pounds. His income, even under Raymond's generous management, was so meager that he had to send home immediately whatever he earned, reserving the smallest possible amount for his own expenses. His letter of December 30, 1843, reveals his own financial circumstances and the poverty of those he saw around him in Liverpool:

> I meant to have sent you half a sovreign with this—but this morning when I came down to breakfast I found a poor woman waiting for me who turned out to be a person whom I lodged with a week at Ulverston and who sent me a wig (which I wore last night) to Dumfries. She was then very comfortably off, but a widow—has been reduced to go to service and is come to Liverpool in distressed circumstances and some complaint in her leg to go into the infirmary. She told so pitiful a tale that I could not help giving all I had £1—and must now wait till tomorrow to get more.

Except for a few weeks in Preston, Phelps stayed with Raymond until the middle of February. He continued the long rehearsals and worked on stage grouping, drilling the supers. Such practices, which Phelps had observed under Macready's management, were rare in the provincial theatre; but Phelps clearly enjoyed trying to make the performances as polished as he could. He even paid 50 pounds for the rights to a new play by Henry Spicer.

But he was homesick as well as overworked. "I wish to heaven I could get any thing to do in London," he wrote his wife. At the end of February he went home for two weeks, but he found no possibility of acting in London. In March he played in Belfast to small houses and then went on to Glasgow, where the theatre was so badly constructed that a third of the audience could not see the stage. He reported to his wife, "if it is any consolation," that Vandenhoff and his daughter were not drawing half as many people as he had been and that Charles Kean was playing to very bad houses. Helen Faucit had "middling" audiences at Dundee, but Phelps, following her during Passion Week, found the boxes empty because the upper classes belonged to the English church. He could not go on to Edinburgh because Charles Kean was playing there, and he had no other prospects, so in the middle of April he went home.

He had written his wife to send him a playbill of the opening night at the English Opera House because he was "curious to know what they are about," but he found that the new lessees, his friends the Keeleys, were specializing in burlesque. Spicer had suggested producing his play at Sadler's Wells, but Phelps found this an unlikely proposal.

He had been home for almost a month—a desperate month during which he hardly dared think of the future—when Thomas Greenwood, the lessee of Sadler's Wells, called upon him with the proposal that he become co-lessee and manager of his suburban theatre. Greenwood had already made the same proposal to John Vandenhoff and Walter Lacy, but they had refused to consider it seriously. The theatre's location outside the West End—the traditional center of the theatrical world, which contained twenty of London's theatres—and the long-standing reputation of Sadler's Wells as a place of low amusements and rough audiences removed it from consideration as a home for poetic drama. It was a theatre for clowns, acrobats, and sensational melodrama, not for Shakespeare. If poetic drama could not find a profitable home in the West End, where education and wealth might be expected to provide a sufficient audience, how could anyone hope to establish it in a community of shopkeepers and laborers?

Greenwood, however, had excellent arguments based on intimate knowledge of the theatre; and Phelps was induced by the desperation of his own situation to listen. Greenwood's grandfather had been Kemble's scene painter at the patent theatres. Since 1792, when the elder Greenwood retired, the family had been associated with Sadler's Wells. His grandson was a well-known and respected member of the local community, the proprietor of an apothecary shop in Islington, who wrote pantomimes and minor pieces for the theatre. For the past three years he had been co-lessee of Sadler's Wells with R. Honner, and then sole lessee, with Henry Marston as his stage manager. During that time the theatre had become known as a good minor house with competent acting and conscientious staging. The last season had not been financially successful, and his recent attempts to interest other managers in sharing the lesseeship had failed, but Greenwood felt certain that he and Phelps together could convert Sadler's Wells to a "legitimate" theatre.

Phelps was not wholly convinced, but he liked Greenwood, and he had confidence in his own abilities to manage a theatre; so he agreed to a trial period and persuaded Mrs. Warner to share the venture with him as leading actress and partner. On May 25, two days before the usual Whit Monday opening, the *Theatrical Journal,* with a hint of incredulity in the tone of the article, announced that Mr. Phelps and Mrs. Warner had taken Sadler's Wells for a limited period:

> Macbeth will be the first performance, the *legitimate* will be the order of the day. . . . We trust the Islingtonians will support so bold and arduous an undertaking.

III

Manager of Sadler's Wells

THE theatre of which Phelps now found himself manager had the longest history of any theatre in London, possibly in England. It had begun as a Musick-House, built in the 1680's by a man named Sadler to provide entertainment for the crowds of people attracted to his garden by the discovery there of a buried medieval well to which miraculous healing powers were attributed. The entertainment of musicians, dancers, and fighting cocks soon eclipsed the attraction of the well, and the place became popular for rowdy amusements. In 1744 it was indicted by a grand jury as a place injurious to morals. A new owner, Rosomon, changed the entertainment to pantomime, harlequinade, and burletta, and he enjoyed a long and successful management. In 1765 he replaced the old wooden building with an attractive stone theatre, capable of seating 2,500 persons —as large an audience as the two patent theatres of his day—and fitted with pit, boxes, and galleries. Wine was served during the performances, and there were special ledges for bottles built in the backs of the seats. Entertainment varied from pantomime to troops of performing dogs, tightrope walkers, racing ponies, and annual visits of Grimaldi, the famous clown. Among the most popular items in the eighteenth century was a dramatization of Hogarth's *The Harlot's Progress,* set to music by John Frederick Lampe, which achieved a popularity rivaling that achieved by *The Beggar's Opera* in higher ranks of society.

During the early years of the nineteenth century Sadler's Wells acquired a new attraction with the installation of a huge water tank under the stage for the production of aquatic spectacles. This tank (90 feet long, 25 feet wide, and 5 feet deep) and a second tank above the stage to give waterfall effects—both supplied with water from the New River alongside the theatre—provided such remarkable realism in the performance of sea stories that Sadler's Wells became for thirty years the home of the "nautical drama." *The Sea Devil, Ocean of Life, Cataract of the Ganges,* and *Paul the Pilot* were major attractions. By 1840, when this novelty had begun to fade, less exotic forms of melodrama began to appear as the standard fare. These included domestic pieces with such titles as *The Outcast Woman, Woman's Love,* and *Intemperance;* adaptations of the novels of Scott and Dickens, pirated by unknown dramatists; plays with local subjects such as *Old Blue Lion of Gray's Inn* and *The Watchmaker of Clerkenwell;* and many farces. Occasionally a five-act play was produced, risking the penalty for infringement of the rights of the patent theatres: *Rienzi* in 1839, *Pizarro, The Merchant of Venice,* and *Macbeth* in 1840, a week's round of Shakespeare in the summer of 1841, and *She Stoops to Conquer* and *Faust* in 1842.

An extreme catholicity of taste characterized the Sadler's Wells audience during the years immediately preceding Phelps's management. Other minor theatres each had a particular specialty, but the patrons of Sadler's Wells in the course of one year, 1840, not only supported the regular company, acting melodramas with unusual competence, but also welcomed with overflowing houses the appearances of such outside performers as Grimaldi, the Chareni family on the tightrope, a group of distinguished actors in *Macbeth,* Carter's menagerie of tamed animals, various vocal artists, and Ducrow's horse company (for which the water tank was converted into an arena). During the course of a single evening, this audience seemed equally delighted by a performance of the tragedy *Faust* and an afterpiece in which a live monkey was the chief attraction. Their preference for pantomime had brought to the theatre some of the best writers, performers, and set designers in that field, so that the Christmas pantomime at Sadler's Wells was famous throughout London and usually ran for several months.

The nature of this audience is difficult to assess. It was frequently described by reviewers as "noisy" or "uproarious." The *Theatrical Journal* records several occasions when the impatience of the audience forced actors to get through a play as fast as possible, without regard for the meaning of the lines, in order to clear the stage for a more popular entertainment scheduled to follow. During the pantomime season of 1841, when spectators were attracted from all of London, the *Theatrical Journal* remarked that "the crowds of respectable persons who take their families to witness the performance of the pantomime is surprising." This comment would seem to indicate that respectable persons did not usually attend Sadler's Wells, and indeed this inference is supported by the particular, although rare, emphasis upon the respectability and quiet behavior of the audience.[1] There is a hint that the character of the audience varied according to the type of entertainment offered. On June 10, 1843, the *Theatrical Journal* noted that "this theatre opened on Monday for the season, the audience being one of the most respectable we have witnessed for years." Attributing this unusual circumstance to "the great respect Mr. Greenwood commands in the community," the reviewer added, "We hope to see a continuation of such audiences." Phelps, assuming the management a year later, would have echoed this sentiment.

The theatre itself possessed many advantages. Most important, the rent was considerably lower than theatres of the West End. For example, the lease cost one third that of the English Opera House, in which Phelps had been interested.[2] Although it was so far from the West End as to be completely out of the usual circuit of regular playgoers, it could be reached by an eightpenny fare from Regent Street. Habit as much as distance had consigned Sadler's Wells to its local, suburban audience. The old-fashioned exterior of the building was not without charm, and its site, on the banks of Sir Hugh Myddleton's New River, was unusually attractive. Its appearance is described by James Cook (in *The Actor's Notebook*, a two-penny weekly which lasted for only six months) as he found it in 1841:

> There is a great pleasantness in the aspect of Sadler's Wells Theatre, at the present fine season, which cannot, we think, fail to be attractive to the passers-by. There are the trees, the cool river, and the well-cropped grass at the margin. The neighbourhood itself is vastly picturesque, what may be called the barrier walls between the bustle and noise, and country quietude, being only a little way off.

The theatre's interior, which had been improved the year before by the installation of backs on all the seats in the pit, was comfortable, well ventilated, and conveniently arranged for seeing and hearing. Although reviewers, comparing its size with the vastness of the nineteenth-century Covent Garden and Drury Lane, sometimes referred to Sadler's Wells as a little theatre, the house could seat 2,600 without crowding—only a thousand less than the patent theatres. This unusual capacity was achieved through the extraordinary length of the pit, which was much greater than that of any other theatre in London. Designed to accommodate a lower class audience, it had fewer boxes than theatres of the West End, reserving most of its space for pit benches and gallery, at a shilling or sixpence a seat. The following comparison of measurements of the important London theatres published in the *Theatrical Journal* of July 17, 1841, clearly distinguishes Sadler's Wells from other theatres:

	Width of Proscenium	Width of Stage	Depth of Stage	Stage to Center Box
Drury Lane	40¾	78	60	50
Covent Garden	38¾	81½	67½	54
Haymarket	23	57	42	38
Adelphi	24	37	56	—
Astley's	40	78	67	50
English Opera	34	67	50½	43
Olympic	22	50	41½	26
Oxford St.	27	58	62	—
Queen's	18	35	32	27
Sadler's Wells	27	50	50	115
Strand	24	58	21	20
Surrey	30	70	63½	49
Victoria	31½	68	60	36

Its large pit was the dominant characteristic of Sadler's Wells, and the thousand occupants of its benches determined the character of the audience. Spectators in this part of the house had the advantages of fairly comfortable seats (since the backs had been added) and a full view of the stage, at the cost of 1 shilling for admittance and some physical discomfort in the rush for a seat. This distinctive feature—a large, reasonably comfortable, and inexpensive pit—combined with the location of the theatre in a densely populated neighborhood to insure a popular audience, characterized by the tastes and attitudes of the relatively uneducated lower-middle class typical of suburban London in 1840.

This circumstance had been an advantage to previous managers, most of whom were successful in suiting their entertainment to the taste of the neighborhood. To Phelps and Mrs. Warner, the size of the pit must have seemed an embarrassment, both because it limited the space that could be sold at higher prices and because it invited domination of the theatre by a class of society generally thought incapable of understanding serious drama. In the patent theatres during the first half of the nineteenth century, the pit (traditionally, as in the twentieth century, the preferred section of a theatre) had lost importance. Ever since the enlargement of Covent Garden and Drury Lane, Shakespearean actors had looked increasingly to patrons of the boxes for their chief support. Patrons of the pit usually preferred spectacle, dancing, and music to traditional Shakespearean acting. Many arrived at half-price time, when the tragedy was almost over, and demanded spectacular afterpieces. Because of their recent experience in the legitimate theatres, the new managers of Sadler's Wells probably did not look upon its out-sized pit as an advantage.

Despite their misgivings, the three lessees of Sadler's Wells put every effort into their project. Greenwood assumed the position of acting manager, taking responsibility for all aspects of theatrical management except for the production of five-act plays. Mrs. Warner's husband, a tavern keeper, became treasurer. Phelps was the stage manager, or in twentieth century terms, director. He immediately set about his first task, that of finding actors. He was able to engage a number of actors from Macready's former company, who might not have considered Sadler's Wells had there been any West End theatre open to them. He engaged George Bennett as Second Tragedian, J. W. Ray as First Old Man, T. H. Lacy as Heavy Father, and James Hudson, Collins, Hield, J. Binge, and C. White as Utility Men. Also from Macready's old company came his Leading Comic Actress, Fanny Cooper (Mrs. T. H. Lacy). Henry Scharf, son of the German lithographer George Scharf and formerly a scene painter for Macready, became Low Comedian of the new company. He kept some of the actors who had been at Sadler's Wells during previous seasons: Henry Marston for Second Lead and Mrs. Marston as First Old Woman; John Webster for Walking Gentleman and principal actor in afterpieces; Charles Fenton as Second Low Comedian; F. Fenton and Finlay, the scene painters; and "Pepper" Williams, a minor actor who was to serve as prompter. Other members of the company, including singers and dancers for afterpieces, were recruited from the minor theatres of London: Anthony Younge from the Strand, Forman from the Adelphi, T. H. Higge from the Princess's, Morton from the Surrey, Morelli from the Victoria, and Miss Lebatt from the Olympic.

With this company Phelps rehearsed *Macbeth* while Greenwood directed preparations for the operetta and farce which were to fill out the first night's program. Together they planned settings and costuming for the tragedy, and Phelps, watching Greenwood manipulate the resources of his theatre, realized that he had acquired a talented partner in his undertaking. In little more than a week the combined efforts of these two men, with the help of Fenton's talents, produced a setting for *Macbeth* which elicited a gasp of admiration from the first-night audience.

Before the opening night, Phelps prepared a statement about the new management, which was printed on handbills and distributed in the neighborhood surrounding the theatre. Its purpose was not merely to advertise their new project; frequent use of the word "respectable" indicates that it was also designed to warn some of the usual patrons of Sadler's Wells of a decided change in the type of entertainment to be offered.

> Mrs. Warner and Mr. Phelps, of the Theatres Royal, Drury Lane, Covent Garden, and Haymarket, present their respectful compliments, and request attention to the following outlines of a plan which they trust will not be without interest for the respectable inhabitants of this neighbourhood.
>
> Mrs. Warner and Mr. Phelps embarked their exertions in the management and performances of Sadler's Wells Theatre, in the hope of constantly rendering it what a Theatre ought to be; a place for justly representing the works of our great dramatic poets. This undertaking is commenced at a time when the stages which have been exclusively called "Patent," are closed, or devoted to very different objects from that of presenting the real drama of England, and when the law has placed all theatres upon an equal footing of security and respectability, leaving no difference, except in the objects and conduct of the managements.
>
> These circumstances justify the notion that each separate division of an immense metropolis, with its 2,000,000 of inhabitants, may have its own well-conducted theatre within a reasonable distance of the homes of its patrons.
>
> For the North of London, they offer an entertainment selected from the first stock drama in the world, reinforced by such novelties as can be produced by diligence and liberality, intending that the quality of their novelties shall constantly improve as time will be gained to procure and prepare them; and a Company of acknowledged talent, playing such characters as they must be called upon to sustain at Drury Lane and Covent Garden, were these houses now devoted to the drama. These attractions are placed in a theatre where all can see and hear, and at a price fairly within the habitual means of all.

They commence under the disadvantage of very short preparation, and they are aware that some errors and deficiencies are quite inseparable from such a circumstance. They trust that their names are a sufficient guarantee for the honest endeavour to deserve public patronage, and they promise that the trust of the Public and its encouragement shall be met by continued zeal and liberality, increasing constantly with the means of shewing it. They will endeavour to confirm what may be found satisfactory, remove what may be at first deficient, and above all exalt the entertainments, and with them the tastes of their audiences.

They feel assured that such an endeavour is not unworthy of the kind encouragement of the more highly educated and influential classes. There may be differences of opinion as to the existence of Theatres altogether; there can be none as to the truth that if theatres are to exist, they should aim at the highest possible refinement, and produce the most intellectual class of enjoyment which their audiences can receive.

They intend to continue their attempt as long as they can feel reasonable hope of making Sadler's Wells Theatre the resort of the respectable inhabitants of the neighbourhood, for the highest purpose of theatrical entertainment.

Any Patron with whom this Circular is left, will on sending an address card to the Box Office, have an admission for One forwarded, as it is the wish of the management, and their motive for this departure from their otherwise strict system of giving no Orders, to afford to those who may take an interest in their plan, an opportunity of judging for themselves, and to speak of the undertaking as they may think it deserves.[3]

When the theatre opened on May 27, 1844, Phelps, his company, and a large portion of the audience were venturing into uncharted territory. Even Macready, playing Hamlet in Mobile and St. Louis during the spring of 1844, was traveling a more familiar road to theatrical success than the one Phelps was pursuing three miles from Charing Cross. When Macready walked off a steamboat into a prairie town, his arrival had been expected, his reputation was known, and his audience had seen other performances of Shakespeare. A week's round of tragedy was less surprising to the steamship owners, fur dealers, and slave traders of Mississippi than to most inhabitants of Islington; and to Shakespearean actors the populous suburban area of northern London was a more remote wilderness than the young cities of America.

Except for the handbill distributed to local residents, the opening of Sadler's Wells was virtually unheralded. No advertisement appeared in the *Times*. Phelps, with his characteristic distaste for "puffing," had not made the rounds of the important newspapers with offers of free seats in exchange for favorable reviews—a practice used by Macready and most other theatrical managers of the time. Perhaps even such attention to the press would not have induced many reviewers to make the trip to Sadler's Wells, although it was Phelps's first appearance on a London stage in the role of Macbeth. The theatrical profession generally held little hope for the experiment of converting Sadler's Wells into a "legitimate" theatre. The *Athenaeum* (May 25, 1844) commented that nothing but the desperate nature of contemporary theatrical conditions could have driven these distinguished actors to such a locality, expressing without conviction the hope that their performances would improve the taste of the neighborhood. *Punch* (July 13, 1844) congratulated the actors for "the zeal which has impelled them thus to consecrate a temple to the Drama in the remote waste of Islington."

Such predictions had left the management unprepared for the size of the audience that poured into the theatre on the evening of May 27. Approximately twelve hundred persons thronged the gallery, and a thousand more crowded the benches in the pit. Even the boxes, at 2 shillings a seat, were filled to their capacity of six hundred. Greenwood hastily dispatched stage hands to the overflowing lobbies to erect platforms so that those who were standing might have some view of the stage.

When the curtain rose, a current of excitement seemed to run through the house. There was a suppressed exclamation of surprsie and admiration, evidently inspired by the stage setting. And then the audience became perfectly still. Instead of the usual rustling and settling down of an experienced group of playgoers, there was the silence of an expectant throng waiting to catch every word spoken on the stage. The actors, sensing an unusual sympathy across the footlights, put their best efforts into the performance, even though they were occasionally disconcerted by the reaction of the audience. Well-known speeches and famous points produced astonishingly unpredictable results. The expected round of applause was sometimes replaced by utter silence or by an awestruck shudder. The most surprising reaction of all came at the end of Act One with these lines:

MACBETH: If we should fail?
LADY MACBETH: We fail?—
          But screw your courage to the sticking place
          And we'll not fail.

Here the audience broke into spontaneous cheers. The actors were startled until they realized that an immediate and personal interpretation was being given to the words. The audience was interrupting the play to assure Phelps and Mrs. Warner that their new management of Sadler's Wells would not fail.[4]

To Phelps, who was as much interested in reaction to his first performance of Macbeth as in the audience's response to the new management, this performance must have been nerve-wracking. His choice of Macready's most famous Shakespearean role indicates that he looked upon his gamble at Sadler's Wells primarily as an opportunity to win a reputation after many years of frustration.

Had his Macbeth appeared on the stage of Drury Lane, critics and audience would have instantly recognized a difference between his interpretation and Macready's. From the moment he strode on the stage, a soldier utterly confident in his own strength, his vigor and commanding presence contrasted with the more gentlemanly bearing and introspective nature of Macready's well-known interpretation. The important differences in the conception of the role were not noticed by the audience at Sadler's Wells, who had never seen Macready. Instead, thy succumbed with uncritical willingness to the illusion of reality which Phelps gave to the character on the stage. In the intensity of his suffering this Macbeth seemed actually to be racked with emotion. He walked and gestured with a convincing naturalness which masked the actor's art. He spoke Shakespeare's poetry, not to be sure, in the manner of every-day speech, but with fluency and appropriate shading that were never distorted for immediate theatrical effect. A sophisticated audience would have recognized a new identification of actor and character and a departure from the traditional attitude which presented the character as a work of art created jointly by playwright and actor, consciously held up to view for the approval of the audience.

This quality of Phelps's acting, although noticed and described by the enthusiastic critics in Exeter, and more recently in Bath, had scarcely been glimpsed by London audiences during the seven years of his restriction to minor roles. Now it was admired by an audience whose response would matter less to the theatrical world than that of a provincial audience. Although his success with the Islingtonians was indeed complete—breathless silence testified to their rapt absorption in the play—it could not be regarded as an important triumph. The few critics who came to this opening night were distracted by their unfamiliar surroundings, the unusual character of the audience, the absence of their colleagues, and the total impropriety of presenting Shakespeare in such a place. Under these circumstances they could not give complete attention to Phelps's interpretation and compare it with other Macbeths they had seen. They saw that the spectators were moved not by admiration of the actor's art but by an impression of immediate reality which held them silent until he left the stage. The intensity of their sympathy and the unrestrained cheering that followed each scene appeared to be evidence of their naiveté. Therefore, the reaction of the audience was to a certain extent discounted by the critics, who felt the need to preserve some detachment from the uninhibited enthusiasm around them. Their attitude is reflected in the *Athenaeum*'s review (June 1, 1844), which begins with an explanation of "the unwonted circumstance of our noticing either the 'doings or pretences' of this almost forgotten theatre" and records these impressions of Phelps's Macbeth:

> Mr. Phelps we have never seen before in Macbeth, and it was certainly the ablest performance in which he has yet exhibited. Since Edmund Kean's we have seen nothing better for vigor and vivid effect. It is essentially distinct from, and stands in contrast with Mr. Macready's, which, however fine and classical in its conception, is but too obviously open to the Scotch sneer of presenting "a very respectable gentleman in considerable difficulties," so studied is it in all its parts, and subdued into commonplace by too much artifice; fretfulness, moreover, substituting high passion in the fifth act. The straightforward and right earnest energy of Mr. Phelps's acting, on the contrary, made all present contemplate the business as one of seriousness and reality; while the occasional pathos of his declamation thrilled the heart within many a rude bosom with unwonted emotion. The spectators were visibly agitated, and incapable of resisting the impulse.

Phelps's performance was not the only notable one in this production of *Macbeth*. Mrs. Warner's Lady Macbeth, although not new to the London critics, seemed more than usually impressive. A handsome and imposing woman, she was naturally well qualified to play a dominating and regal character. Her acting was of the polished, elegant, and dignified style associated with the Kembles. She had both the physical stamina and the imagination necessary for the taxing role of Lady Macbeth. Although in comparison with Phelps her acting removed a character farther from the audience and inspired as much awe as sympathy, she was capable of expressing emotion with unusual force. She was less concerned to give an impression of sincerity than to present the full passion and poetic beauty of a role. This appearance as Lady Macbeth was important to Mrs. Warner's career because in recent years she had been restricted by Macready's preference for Helen Faucit. Not only had he confined her to a narrow range of tragedy, reserving for Miss Faucit the lighter roles and younger heroines, but he had even refused to allow her Lady Macbeth in his last season at Drury Lane, until Helen Faucit's obvious failure in the role forced him to recast it. At Sadler's Wells Mrs. Warner was reasserting her preeminence in this important part. The *Theatrical Journal* (June 1, 1844) recognized her claim:

> Her performance is marked with a boldness of character no other actress can approach; and her figure, face, and action, combine what we consider Lady Macbeth ought to possess. She was most deservedly applauded, and she perhaps, never took greater pains to please her auditory.

The rest of the cast, particularly Henry Marston as Macduff and (T.) H. Lacy as Banquo, showed themselves competent and experienced Shakespearean actors. Although preparations had been hurried, the tragedy was carefully performed and well staged. It was followed by Greenwood's new farce, *A Row in the Buildings,* with John Webster as the principal actor, and a new operetta, *The Hunter's Bride,* featuring Miss Lebatt.

The audience left the theatre with no doubts about the changed condition of Sadler's Wells. The excellence of the company and the concerted effort revealed by the completeness of the first night's performance had assured them that the new managers were serious in their purpose. On the other side of the curtain, the actors finished their night's work with a new opinion about the possible success of their enterprise. They had been surprised by the large number of spectators, their attentive silence, and their unmistakable encouragement of the undertaking. What had happened on the opening night at Sadler's Wells was surprising and of great importance for the future of the English stage, but newspaper critics, most of whom had not witnessed the performance, were still unaware of the new development—the first indication that repeal of the theatrical monopoly had opened an unexpected way to successful management. On May 29, the *Times* for the first time contained an advertisement for Sadler's Wells and a brief notice of *Macbeth* with the comment that "To play one of Shakespeare's tragedies at this place is a bold undertaking." The *Morning Post* of May 28 discussed the entertainments at the Lyceum, the Princess's, the Surrey, Astley's, St. James's, Covent Garden, and Drury Lane, but made no mention of Sadler's Wells. The *Observer* of June 1 mentioned the fact of the opening of the new management, but indicated that the reviewer had not attended the performance.

Only one of the prominent London critics revealed any degree of confidence in Phelps's venture, and this, surprisingly, was Bayle Bernard of the *Weekly Dispatch*. Bernard, the outspoken critic whom Macready had sued for libel, might have been expected to oppose the continued existence of classic drama. An author of successful minor drama, including farces and petite comedies, an uncompromising critic of Macready's managements, and an admirer of Charles Kean, he might well have condemned the attempt at Sadler's Wells as a mere extension of an obsolete form of drama to untried audiences. Instead, he predicted success for the new management if comedy, tragedy, and racy farce were presented and well performed, asserting that these types of entertainment—the traditional fare of the patent theatres—would be more appealing to any audience than "outrageous, noisy, and unnatural melodrama and 'domestic,' and sickly absurdities." This opinion throws new light upon the condition of the Victorian theatre: evidently, a critic could condemn Macready and still uphold traditional drama, and a writer of minor pieces could insist upon a distinction between good and bad melodrama.

Phelps allowed *Macbeth* to run for six nights in a row while he prepared the second production, *Othello,* which also ran for a week. The theatre continued to be full every night, although few critics were attracted to the performances. The reviewer for *Lloyd's Weekly London Newspaper* made the lonely pilgrimage from the West End to see *Othello* and was favorably impressed with the production as a whole and particularly with the improvement in Phelps's interpretation of the Moor since he had last seen it in Exeter in 1837. There can be no clearer indication of the effect of Macready's suppression of Phelps than this review, which reveals that the excitement caused by Phelps's acting in Exeter was felt again by a London critic after seven years.

During June and July many new plays were added to the repertory. An initial venture into eighteenth-century comedy with George Colman's *The Jealous Wife* proved so successful that *The Rivals, The School for Scandal,* and *The Provoked Husband* (Vanbrurgh-Cibber) were soon added. *The Jealous Wife* brought the critic of the *Morning Post* to the theatre for the first time. He was surprised to find Mrs. Warner an excellent Mrs. Oakley, since this role had been Helen Faucit's under Macready's management. He pronounced it the best Mrs. Oakley he had ever seen. In general, he seemed rather bewildred by the transformation of the old theatre into a home for polite comedy. He wrote on June 19, "It may be safely asserted that such a dramatic entertainment as Sadler's Wells now offers was never before enjoyed at similar prices." Phelps's ability to act in plays of this genre also evoked some surprise. The *Weekly Dispatch,* which had disapproved of his Falkland in Macready's production of *The Rivals,* highly praised his Major Oakley. Of his Lord Townley in *The Provoked Husband* the reviewer declared, "It is infinitely superior to Macready's—there is more of the gentleman in the character—less irritability, with greater dignity." This was a high compliment to an actor who previously had been "typed" by Macready's casting as the rough, blunt soldier.

The Merchant of Venice, Byron's *Werner,* Kotzebue's *The Stranger,* and Knowles's *Virginius* alternated with comedy in the growing repertory. Shylock added to Phelps's reputation. The *Weekly Dispatch* (June 30 and July 14, 1844) called it by far his best part and praised the "bold, vigorous, and natural" interpretation. After seeing his Virginius, the same critic said that he played "with energy and bursts of impetuous passion and genuine feeling that we hardly thought him capable of giving."

The few critics who came to the theatre during June and July said that the manner in which these plays were acted and staged raised Sadler's Wells to the level of the best London theatres. Settings were appropriate and intelligently planned. Reviews indicate that the acting had begun to show the results of Phelps's long and painstaking rehearsals and attention to minor roles. The company's daily workout had little resemblance to Macready's terrifying rehearsals, with their outbursts of anger and physical violence, but Phelps's gentleness and patience cloaked an equal determination to achieve perfection. In July the company was strengthened by the arrival of George Bennett, who had not been able to appear earlier.

On July 29 *Hamlet* was performed for the first time, and an overflowing audience was attracted by the announcement of this most popular of all tragedies. Several London reviewers made their first visit to Sadler's Wells for the sake of measuring Phelps's ability in this important role and comparing him with other tragedians. Phelps, aware of the importance of his first appearance as Hamlet, had deferred performance of the tragedy until he had had time to make it a finished production. The result surprised even those critics who had visited Sadler's Wells in recent months. The *Theatrical Journal* said that the splendor of the scenery was beyond description, and the *Athenaeum* called the gravedigger scene "almost magical in its effect." Other reviewers, who had not visited the theatre under its new management, were astonished that so insignificant a theatre could afford such beautiful scenery and costumes.

Phelps's Hamlet and, indeed, the acting of all the cast, were found to be on a level with that of the former national theatres. Phelps was closely compared with other actors, while Mrs. Warner and George Bennett as the Queen and King were said to be superior to other actors who had recently appeared in these roles. Reviewers approved of the performance and the audience watched with a rapt attention that hardly distinguished play-acting from reality.

With the production of *King John* at the end of September, Sadler's Wells began to be regarded as the real dramatic center of London. The costuming and scenery, carefully designed for historical accuracy, were sufficiently splendid to lift the theatre out of the "minor" category. An eye for stage design and an ingenuity in solving problems posed by the text, aided by Greenwood's knowledge of the commercial aspects, enabled Phelps to devise a setting which critics compared with Macready's memorable production at Drury Lane. In the matter of casting he was not hampered by Macready's prejudices and fears. Mrs. Warner (who should have played the part at Drury Lane) was called "magnificent" in the role of Constance. Bennett was the Hubert and Marston a gallant Faulconbridge. Of Phelps's first appearance in London as King John, one reviewer wrote

> He has more real genius in him than any actor of our time, and it is now making itself manifest. He was kept down by the overbearing power of Macready; but not disadvantageously, for all the while he was gathering strength and acquiring a mastery of his high art, the fruits of which are now ripening. A small theatre is the true test of an actor's genius. Tricks won't do there, all must be genuine; and therefore it is that really great actors are always greatest and the most enjoyable where they are the centre upon which eye and ear are absorbed. . . . Phelps's personation of the monarch is extremely fine, but he must beware lest he unconsciously act Macready's instead of his own conception of the character.[5]

Extremely favorable reviews of *King John* and the absence of other dramatic productions in the autumn of 1844 brought playgoers from central London in increasing numbers. By the second week of performances there was an unusual demand for seats in the boxes, which at 2 shillings were considered too expensive by most local patrons of the theatre. The narrow stairway to the boxes, which had not been designed for accommodating large numbers, became so crowded that one evening, according to the *Theatrical Journal* (November 2, 1844), "Mr. Greenwood was obliged to assist upon the stairs leading to the boxes, to take admission money from ladies who were suffering the pressure of the crowd to such an extent, that several were carried away fainting." Such a scene, in marked contrast to the sparse audiences at Drury Lane, presaged a new era in theatrical history.

Phelps accomplished an unbelievable amount of work during this first season of his management. Besides playing the leading role six nights a week in a variety of plays and directing daily rehearsals, he designed the settings for many of the productions and experimented with new arrangements of the action and new devices of staging. The *Theatrical Journal* expressed the fear that the new manager was working beyond his strength, but apparently Phelps had unusual stamina. Besides his work at the theatre he was reading plays at home in an attempt to expand the traditional repertory both with neglected works of known playwrights and new plays worthy of performance. He prepared an acting text of Massinger's *The City Madam,* which had been performed only a few times in two centuries, and made it one of the most successful plays of the season. His greatest triumph was a production of *Richard the Third* from Shakespeare's text, without any of Colley Cibber's alterations and additions which had dominated the play since 1700. His one new play of the season, *The Priest's Daughter* by Thomas J. Serle, was written in stilted poetic language and depended upon good acting to keep it alive for eight performances.

The two plays most frequently acted during the first season were Macready's former vehicles, *The Bridal* (an adaptation of *The Maid's Tragedy* by Beaumont and Fletcher) and Bulwer-Lytton's *The Lady of Lyons.* Phelps fitted easily into parts written for Macready and was successful in them without insisting upon total domination of the stage. In fact, Sadler's Wells was beginning to be noticed for the high quality of the whole performance, especially the competent acting of minor roles. *John Bull* (November 16, 1844) remarked upon this feature of *The Lady of Lyons*:

> The effect of this play (and the remark may be extended to all the plays represented at this theatre) is much increased by the *general* quality of the performance. The company does not (like many others) consist of a star or two and a heap of rubbish; but its members are adequate to the parts allotted to them, and perform them with intelligence and verisimilitude.

The same reviewer apologized for the negligence of critics toward the new experiment at Sadler's Wells:

> We feel conscious that the excellent company now established at this theatre have not received from us, nor indeed from the press generally, the degree of attention to which they are justly entitled.

Critics' reluctance to recognize Sadler's Wells as an important playhouse is exemplified by the attitude of the *Observer*. This reviewer had noted the opening production of *Macbeth* in his column, without going to see it, although no other theatre attracted him that night. During the summer he had regularly reviewed plays at the Haymarket and operas at Her Majesty's, remarking occasionally upon the fact of dramatic performances "in the unlikely vicinity of Sadler's Wells." On August 18 after *Hamlet* had been played there, he recognized the fact that the national drama had taken shelter in the outskirts of the city but stated that "we shall patiently wait for its return . . . to some situation nearer its old neighbourhoods." To his complaints about the location of Sadler's Wells he added his assertion that Phelps and Mrs. Warner were second-rate actors and that their management lacked the means to put on performances of the highest quality. During the winter season he reviewed unsatisfactory performances at Drury Lane and the Princess's while pleading for a good company appearing in legitimate drama at a centrally located theatre. When at last he went to Sadler's Wells in December to see *The Lady of Lyons,* his surprise is amusingly evident in the changed tone of his remarks. He found that the play was produced "in a manner for which we could hardly have given them credit" and that it was "capitally acted." He declared that Mrs. Warner had more versatility of talent than generally supposed, and he wrote that "Phelps was always a favourite with us, and more so when we saw a disposition in some quarters to repress him, and to keep him out of even second-rate characters." [6]

The repertory of the season included the traditional Christmas panto-mime, which was produced on Boxing Day and ran for many weeks, sharing the stage nightly with a comedy or tragedy. Because of Green-wood's competence in this genre, Phelps had none of Macready's troubles with the annual pantomime—neither the time-consuming preparations nor the financial failures. And he did not follow Macready in featuring a spectacular Easter piece.

In this season's pantomime Greenwood inserted a note of self congratu-lation to the managers by having his narrator describe Sadler's Wells as a refuge for Shakespeare "turned out of doors by dancing Belles." This was a reference to the use of Covent Garden and Drury Lane for opera and ballet—a change from hallowed custom that was to trouble the conscience of Londoners for many years, even though the legal basis for the monopoly had been abolished.

The theatre was closed for Holy Week in the middle of March, but it reopened for three weeks before ending its long season. Several nights in April were devoted to the customary benefit performances for the manager and leading actors of the company. On these occasions novelties were performed for the sake of attracting the largest possible audience on a single night, especially those patrons who had attended regularly and therefore had seen the usual repertory. For his own benefit Phelps played two roles: Rover in O'Keeffe's comedy *Wild Oats* and the lead in the afterpiece. For Greenwood's benefit he put on the rarely acted *Soldier's Daughter* by Andrew Cherry. The last performance of the season, on April 10, for Mrs. Warner's benefit included both *The School for Scandal* and *Henry the Eighth,* the latter featuring her Queen Kather-ine and Phelps's performance of Wolsey.

Phelps could take his month's vacation with the assurance that he had at last found a permanent position. After the uncertainties of the previous twenty-five years he was assured of a steady income large enough to sup-port his family. He knew that he had not achieved a reputation rivaling Macready's and probably assumed that he could never achieve it if he remained at Sadler's Wells. While critics congratulated Sadler's Wells on taking over the leadership in drama once held by the two national theatres, they often in the same breath expressed the hope that Phelps would soon transfer his management to a theatre in the West End. This is a typical comment upon Phelps's success:

We trust, however, that it being now proved not only that there is genius
to embody the British drama, but an audience to appreciate it, they . . .
will remove to some theatre more central, but not much larger, where they
may hope, not in vain, nightly to gather round them the intellect of this
metropolis.[7]

There was a tacit assumption in the highest circles of London society
that a nationally important theatre could not exist outside the limited
area which they had been accustomed to regard as the theatrical center
of England. *Punch* (October 19, 1844) recognized the irrationality of
this prejudice and ridiculed it in a satiric description of Queen Victoria
attending Sadler's Wells with King Louis Philippe and presenting
Phelps with a cross of the Legion of Honor. *Punch* was aiming his
satire at Macready as well as the Queen. Macready was soon to appear before the King of France at a special performance in Paris, and he actually did receive from Louis Philippe a golden poinard set with sapphires
(which he later discovered to be only silver gilt and paste). The contrast with Phelps was clear, and the point of the satire was the nobility's
attitude toward Sadler's Wells. Obviously such a visit was, to the con-
ventionally minded, unthinkable, even though Sadler's Wells was at this
time not only an excellent theatre, but the only theatre in London presenting serious drama.

Phelps did not consider the possibility suggested by reviewers of moving his management to central London, even when he had the opportunity of leasing the Lyceum—a theatre he liked for its size and interior
arrangements. In Islington he had found an actor's most important re-
quirement—an audience. After years of watching Macready struggle
with half empty houses he was fully aware of the lack of interest in
drama which currently prevailed in the upper classes. No one had
suffered more than Phelps from the change in taste that had emptied
theatres and filled opera houses. At Sadler's Wells he had found an audience that must have surpassed his highest hopes. Indeed, such an
audience is rarely found anywhere. It was so numerous that on many
occasions hundreds of would-be spectators could not be admitted, and
its attentiveness was remarkable even when the house was uncomfortably crowded. One writer says that the audience listened with "such
perfect stillness as quickened the sense to hear the faintest whisper from
the stage." [8] And this was an age when the behavior of audiences was
customarily far less polite than the well-mannered patrons of our con-

temporary theatre. The audience perhaps lacked the discrimination of the experienced playgoer, but it was free of his prejudices. An initial deference to Phelps's judgment indicated a willingness to learn. Newcomers to the theatre were as much surprised by the behavior of the audience as by the excellence of the performance. The theatrical critic of *Punch* (September 14, 1844) after his first few visits to Sadler's Wells advised his readers to make a pilgrimage there just to see an audience "so possessed and delighted."

There was something else, too—a special rapport, or perhaps merely mutual respect, between actors and audience. Both took the theatre seriously. There was no fickleness on the part of the audience nor cheap pretense on the stage. Phelps, as an honest workman, was rewarded with honest appreciation and loyalty. A visitor to the theatre in 1846 commented: "There always appears, both in actors and the audience, a sort of heartiness and good-will between them which is quite delightful." [9] Attendance was so regular that members of the audience learned to know each other by sight. Phelps apparently felt at home with this audience, with whom he shared attitudes and assumptions characteristic of Victorian middle-class society. It was evident that he worked hard and with the pride of a good craftsman in making as finished a piece of work as he possibly could. Nor did he adopt the attitude, characteristic of many celebrated actors, that his profession set him apart from ordinary men. He soon moved his family to a house in Islington[10] and became an established member of the community. Off the stage, because of his retiring manner and modest style of living, he might have been taken for a member of the audience. He was a little shocked when one of his daughters was refused admission to a private school nearby because of her father's profession, but he recognized this prejudice as the exception rather than the rule. Most Islingtonians were proud of the distinction Phelps had brought to the north of London. One local resident, the editor of the *Theatrical Journal,* succinctly expressed the contemporary view of the importance of Phelps's management:

> This theatre may be said to be fully established now in public favour for the acting of the legitimate drama, a circumstance which will never be forgotten in the annals of the stage.[11]

Reviewers were surprised that the kind of audience which patronized Sadler's Wells could understand and enjoy serious drama. They spoke with wonder of the workingmen, shop girls, tradesmen, clerks, and "innumerable kinds of wage earners" who thronged the theatre and seemed better able to appreciate Shakespeare than the wealthy and fashionable audiences of the West End. They cited the behavior of the humble people at Sadler's Wells as an example to the more privileged classes.

This audience, largely drawn from the district surrounding the theatre, undoubtedly contained some of the same people who had attended Sadler's Wells in the days of sensational melodrama. *Punch* (September 27, 1845) humorously asserted that Phelps had civilized the natives of Islington:

> The night charges of the various police-stations of the neighbourhood have sensibly diminished, and men—before considered irredeemable bacchanals —are now nightly known to bring their wives and little ones to listen to the solemn and sportive truths of Shakespeare.

Some years later, Charles Dickens published in his popular magazine *Household Words* (IV (1851), 25–27) a circumstantial account of the "taming" of the audience in Phelps's first weeks as manager. Many subsequent writers have repeated this story,[12] which has a certain dramatic appeal characteristic of its author. But the story of uproar in the gallery and of Phelps's throwing a cloak over his costume and running to the gallery to silence the noise is contrary to all contemporary descriptions of Phelps's first audiences. From the very first night, when the house sat in admiring silence at *Macbeth,* Phelps's audience was noticeably different from the one which had patronized Sadler's Wells a few weeks earlier. It was still a local audience, but it had lost at least the more vulgar element of former audiences, and probably now included many new patrons who had not previously been attracted to Sadler's Wells. One has only to read the weekly issues of the *Theatrical Journal* for the spring of 1844 to be assured of this change. Because the editor, William Beestow, was a resident of Islington, this journal always followed the affairs of Sadler's Wells closely.[13] In reviewing a performance of *Othello* in the second week of Phelps's management, he speaks particularly of the audience in the sixpenny gallery when he says that "the play was listened to with the greatest attention." On June 29, just a month after Phelps's opening, he asserts that the composition of the audience at Sadler's Wells "is now entirely changed; and here may be seen an assemblage equal in respectability to any house in the metropolis."

Moreover, Dickens's story is specifically denied by Phelps's nephew in his biography (pages 16-17), and assertions about the audience made by Dickens in a speech at the Theatrical Fund dinner of 1857 were greeted with cries of "No, no!" from at least one guest at the table.[14] To Dickens and others who came to Sadler's Wells from other parts of London only after Phelps's management was well established, the character of the audience was puzzling. Unaware of the social distinctions in such a suburb as Islington, they assumed that these lower middle class people were the same as those formerly known for their rowdiness. It is not surprising that they attributed this seemingly miraculous transformation to the civilizing influence of Shakespeare and to Phelps's strenuous efforts. But the *Theatrical Journal* (August 23, 1845) more accurately records the transformation of the audience with such statements as "The house has been well attended every night by the more respectable portion of the immediate neighbourhood."

The nature of this audience had already determined two continuing policies of Phelps's management: low prices of admission and the repertory system. He had not raised the prices when he took over the theatre, although the additional expense of expanding the company and providing new scenery, as well as the long-established precedent of high prices at the patent theatres, might well have persuaded him that an increase in prices was justified. He kept the same prices even after the crowded houses of the first season indicated the appeal of his productions. The purses of his spectators were the limiting factor. It mattered little that they could now see the best dramatic productions in London for the same price they had formerly paid to see *Intemperance* and *Paul the Pilot*. The boxes were 2 shillings, the pit 1 shilling, and the gallery sixpence. At Covent Garden, Drury Lane, and the Haymarket, the pit cost 3 shillings, and the boxes varied from 5 to 7.

The repertory system was equally important for the audience at Sadler's Wells, with its regular weekly patrons. Frequent change of program encouraged this regular attendance. The assurance of full houses, in turn, offset the expense of maintaining a large repertory by lessening the risk of failure even with an unpopular production. It also encouraged a variety in selection and some experimentation. The following list, arranged in order of popularity, includes all the five-act plays produced during the first season:

		Number of Nights
Shakespeare		
	Hamlet	28
	Richard the Third	24
	King John	21
	Macbeth	14
	Othello	10
	Merchant of Venice	6
	Henry the Eighth (three-act version)	1
Old plays		
	The Bridal (Beaumont & Fletcher)	30
	City Madam (Massinger)	13
	The Rivals (Sheridan)	9
	The Provoked Husband (Vanbrugh)	8
	School for Scandal (Sheridan)	7
	Road to Ruin (Holcroft)	4
	A New Way to Pay Old Debts (Massinger)	3
	Wild Oats (O'Keeffe)	3
	The Jealous Wife (Colman)	2
	The Wonder (Mrs. Centlivre)	2
Romantic and Victorian		
	Lady of Lyons (Bulwer-Lytton)	32
	Werner (Byron)	8
	The Priest's Daughter (Serle)	8
	The Stranger (Kotzebue)	6
	The Wife (Knowles)	5
	Virginius (Knowles)	4
	The Iron Chest (Colman the younger)	3
	Soldier's Daughter (Cherry)	3
	Hunchback (Knowles)	2

The second season of Phelps's management, which began after a month's recess on May 12, 1845, followed much the same course as the first. Three new plays were introduced to the stage this season, and all of them succeeded in drawing audiences for nine to eleven performances without exciting any lasting interest. Bulwer-Lytton's *Richelieu* with thirty-seven performances and his comedy *Money* with sixteen led in popularity the twenty-four non-Shakespearean plays performed this season. Three more Shakespearean plays were added to the repertory, including *King Lear* from the original text with the Fool fully restored for the first time since Nahum Tate's revision, and an exceedingly attractive production of the seldom-acted *The Winter's Tale,* which ran for forty-five nights. The most unusual play of the season was Massinger's *The Fatal Dowry,* produced "with an effect scarcely to be credited by those who have not witnessed the performance," according to the *Theatrical Journal* (September 6, 1845).

Reviews commented upon the completeness of performances at Sadler's Wells, the relation of parts to the whole, and the care with which even the smallest parts were acted. Phelps had fostered the development of his lesser actors by careful rehearsal and training, but this alone could not have produced the results which reviewers found remarkable. Minor actors seemed to take a pride in their work that indicated more than painstaking tutelage. They showed a willingness to work together for a general effect, frequently forgoing opportunities for winning a round of applause at the expense of distorting the meaning of the lines or the balance of a scene, and thus achieving an impression of *ensemble* that had not been known in the days of jealous competition on the stage of the patent theatres. Macready had drilled, harangued, and demonstrated during his long rehearsals at Drury Lane, but the results were often disappointing. His own performance was intended to dominate a play, leaving small scope for creative performances in the minor roles. When he played Prospero he appropriated some of Ariel's lines into his own part, and when he played a small part like Jaques he took some of the speeches assigned to the First Lord. Those actors who did not compete with him tended to imitate his mannerisms too closely. The "Macready pause" could be detected in the acting of other players, and reviewers complained that they were seeing several copies of the same pattern.

The company at Sadler's Wells worked with a concerted effort and devotion that must have been inspired by Phelps's own attitude. Since he did not like the interrupting rounds of applause which had been traditionally cultivated by actors, he did not use petty devices to dominate the stage nor worry that other players would "mar his effects." He had demonstrated his attitude toward the star system of acting Shakespeare by his production of *Richard the Third,* in which he not only gave up the padded role of Cibber's version but also cut his own role as freely as others in shortening Shakespeare's play. That he produced a *Richard* in which Queen Margaret was the most impressive character must have inspired his company to look beyond individual points in their performances.

The second season fulfilled expectations raised by the first and firmly established the success of the experiment at Sadler's Wells. The audience, which might have decreased in numbers after the novelty of having a legitimate theatre in the neighborhood wore off, had instead increased. There was also a growing number of new patrons attracted from other parts of London. The *Athenaeum* remarked upon the frequent appearance of "men of literary eminence" in the audience, and the *Theatrical Journal* noted that a group of medical students from Bartholomew's Hospital had begun to attend the theatre regularly. Sadler's Wells had survived the competition of Macready's reappearance in London, and Phelps had established himself as an actor of Macready's rank, yet not of the "Macready school." Although reviewers sometimes warned Phelps not to adhere too closely to Macready's interpretation of a role (as in King John), their comments show that he did not imitate Macready's style. The *Theatrical Journal* (May 31, 1845) said, "We were afraid that from having played with Macready he would have fallen into the error so common among the actors of the present day, of imitating the manner of the great tragedian, but we rejoice to say that our fears were groundless." The *Dramatic and Musical Review* (September 12, 1846) in speaking of Phelps's magnificent voice and clearness of speech, praised him for not copying Macready's "studied and methodical" manner.

Macready's three limited engagements at the Princess's during the winter of 1845–1846 had drawn good houses, and the return of serious drama to the Haymarket with Helen Faucit, James Anderson, and the new American actress Charlotte Cushman had created interest among playgoers, but Sadler's Wells remained the only house consistently presenting poetic drama.

Between the second and third seasons Phelps took a recess of two and a half months which he used to remodel and redecorate the theatre, making it more suitable to its new use and more convenient for its larger audience. A portico was built in front to shelter those who waited nightly for the doors to open, and a separate entrance to the boxes was arranged so that patrons of the more expensive seats could avoid the crowds waiting outside. Practice of the early Victorian theatre allowed those who wished seats in the boxes to enter as they arrived and pay a boxkeeper for individual seats, whereas other spectators were not allowed to enter the theatre until a scheduled hour when the opening of the doors was the signal for a grand rush for seats. In 1846 Phelps enlarged the area devoted to box seats and divided it into a dress circle and a second circle to increase the theatre's limited number of higher priced seats. Prices remained the same except for the new first circle, for which the admission was 3 shillings. Playbills announced for the first time that children under three years would not be admitted and that all children entering the pit must pay the full price of admission—1 shilling. The interior was redecorated in a less florid style to provide a simpler background and thus to concentrate attention on the stage.

The most important change at Sadler's Wells, however, was an unhappy one. Mrs. Warner had left the company, and Phelps was to find her irreplaceable. Her reasons for going were apparently personal and domestic. She and Phelps continued to be good friends and to support each other professionally when the occasion arose. Her niece, Miss Huddart, stayed on in the company. Mr. Warner, who had been made the treasurer of the theatre when the new management began, was perhaps the real cause of her withdrawal. He was notoriously unable to manage his own finances, and Greenwood had quarreled with him, probably on sound managerial principles. Whatever the cause, Mrs. Warner's departure was a serious loss. She had contributed to the early success of Phelps's venture by lending the prestige of her reputation and by giving excellent performances of Lady Macbeth, Emilia, Queen Margaret, Hermione, and Queen Gertrude—roles in which she surpassed all other actresses of her time. But she was to be missed even more for the devotion and good-natured cooperation she had shown in her work at Sadler's Wells. The consistently high quality of her acting and her willingness to act roles not particularly suited to her were of crucial importance to a repertory theatre.

Phelps began the third season without having found an actress capable of playing tragic heroines, and therefore chose his repertory carefully to suit the abilities of the remaining company, particularly his two most competent actresses, Fanny Cooper, who lacked the strength for Shakespearean tragedy but was extremely good in comedy, and Mrs. Marston, who had played leading roles in provincial theatres before her marriage and had recently made a hit as Paulina in *The Winter's Tale.*

The choice of *Henry the Fourth, Part One* for the first play of the third season, which began on July 25, 1846, displayed an ability to make the best use of his resources which was one of Phelps's best qualifications for managing a theatre. By choosing a play which had no part suitable for Mrs. Warner he compensated for her absence by exercising a new freedom in the selection of plays, at the same time making her loss as inconspicuous as possible. The audience was less concerned with the absence of her name from the bill than with the prospect of a new play featuring not only two additions to the company but also their favorite, Phelps, in the comic role of Falstaff. The venture proved entirely successful not only for the theatre but for Phelps's future career as a comic actor.

The second play, *Julius Caesar,* was likewise chosen for its many important male roles and the absence of a leading feminine role. Portia was played by Mrs. Brougham, who had been Macready's leading actress at the Princess's in the past season. Two important new actors from the provinces appeared in this play: a young man named Hoskins (who had appeared at Covent Garden in 1843 under the short-lived management of his father-in-law, Henry Wallack) and William Creswick, who had a sufficiently high provincial reputation that he would not under normal conditions have consented to play secondary roles. He made an excellent Cassius, although his acting was noticeably less polished than that of other members of the company. The *Athenaeum* (August 8, 1846) remarked, "What provincial vehemence still clings to him will wear off by collision with the Brutus of Mr. Phelps."

The season went well during the opening weeks, with Mrs. Marston making an excellent Mrs. Quickly, Fanny Cooper playing leads in the non-Shakespearean plays, Creswick winning a London reputation for his Hotspur and Cassius, and Hoskins developing a comic talent.

By the end of August Phelps had found a new leading actress in Miss Laura Addison. She came from Edinburgh with the kind of reputation that excites professional interest in a debut. Macready had recommended her to Phelps, and it was rumored that Webster was watching to see what impression she made at Sadler's Wells. Since she was very young and in Phelps's judgment insufficiently trained for Shakespeare's tragic heroines, he introduced her to London in a contemporary tragedy, *The Patrician's Daughter,* which had not been acted since Macready's attempt at Drury Lane. A full house watched the dual test of play and actress on August 26, 1846, and afterwards declared its unqualified approval of both. Miss Addison showed intelligence and a natural gift for acting that enabled her to grasp the essential nature of the character and to present it with an impression of complete sincerity. She became a favorite with the audience, and reviews predicted a brilliant future for the nineteen-year-old debutante. The *Athenaeum* (August 29, 1846) uttered a small word of caution:

> She has but little to unlearn—a slight occasional excess of action, which experience will soon correct; and what she needs to acquire will not be long in coming, now that she has taken her position in the excellent school of acting, which this theatre, under the management of Mr. Phelps, has become.

Phelps capitalized on the popularity of his new actors by casting Creswick and Miss Addison as Romeo and Juliet in an important production of Shakespeare's play from the original text. It was a bold venture because Charlotte Cushman had made her famous appearance as Romeo at the Haymarket only a year earlier, but it succeeded with critics and audience, establishing beyond doubt the principles of Phelps's management. There was no star in the performance (although Phelps played Charles Kemble's role of Mercutio), and no attempt at modern novelty, but rather an emphasis upon the fullest possible expression of Shakespeare's work, complete in all its parts. Laura Addison gave the audience the pleasure of seeing Juliet played by a girl not yet out of her teens who also had unusual spirit.

Phelps's relation with his actors is illustrated by the casting of *Measure for Measure* in November, 1846. He would have liked to play the part of Angelo; but Creswick refused to play the Duke, and Phelps was afraid that Bennett, whose style had a Kemble stiffness, might incline toward pomposity in such a role. So Phelps played the Duke, assigning Bennett to Angelo. Some of the minor parts were noticeably well played, particularly Lucio, which Hoskins lifted into prominence with delightful humor. Laura Addison's growing popularity reached a new height with her Isabella. It was the most demanding role she had played and a test of her ability to become something more than a girlish heroine. Reviewers felt that she passed the test, acting with the force and emotional intensity demanded of a tragedienne, and they began to compare her with Charlotte Cushman, Helen Faucit, and Mrs. Warner.

As Portia she was not so enthusiastically praised by the critics, perhaps because the role depends more upon artistic finish, but her success with audiences continued. Reviewers commented upon the strong cast which the company supplied for *The Merchant of Venice*. Phelps was the Shylock; Bennett, Antonio; Marston, Bassanio; Hoskins, Gratiano; and Scharf, Launcelot Gobbo. The competent Fanny Cooper, who had not been given many important roles since the arrival of Laura Addison, was an excellent Nerissa.

The audience poured in to see Laura Addison as Mrs. Haller in *The Stranger*. "Dull and extravagant as the play is," said the *Theatrical Journal* of October 31, "nevertheless, when such splendid acting supports it, one cannot be surprised at its great popularity." During November and December she played Helen Faucit's roles in *The Lady of Lyons* and *Money*.

Phelps gave Creswick prominent roles in plays especially chosen to suit him. He appeared as the young heroes of *Venice Preserved, Damon and Pythias,* and *Ion*. Creswick, however, had come to London with greater hopes than his engagement at Sadler's Wells was able to realize. Confident that he could build his reputation more quickly at a West End theatre, he took his benefit night in December and withdrew from the company. By April he was playing leading roles at the Princess's opposite Fanny Kemble, whose return to the stage had caused considerable excitement, and during the summer he acted with Helen Faucit at the Haymarket. He seemed to have found the position Phelps had once sought, but he soon discovered, as did other actors trying to reach the highest rank during these difficult years, that such engagements were of limited duration. After a round of Shakespeare the theatres returned to their usual fare.

In January, 1847, Phelps put on the third unfamiliar Elizabethan play restored to the stage under his management. It was *A King and No King* by Beaumont and Fletcher, and the *Athenaeum* (January 16, 1847) described this production as "perhaps, the most important step yet taken in the serious task of restoring the poetic drama to the stage."

In February appeared the first really successful new play of his management, *Feudal Times* by the Reverend James White. It ran for twenty-five nights this season and was brought back some years later.

Instead of an Easter spectacle Phelps produced *The Tempest* with a magnificence not seen in Shakespearean drama since Macready's management. There were scenic devices like burning rocks, a flying devil, and red fire surrounding Prospero in the scene where he is an invisible witness to the magic banquet, but there was no attempt to make the play primarily a spectacle—nothing like the "flying" Ariel of Macready's production.

The acting claimed the main attention with Phelps as an impressive Prospero, reading the poetry with great skill, and Miss Addison an enchanting Miranda. Julia St. George was a graceful Ariel. If there was one particular attraction, it was Bennett's Caliban, which had been admired in Macready's production. In assuming the brutishness of Caliban, Bennett shed his normal stage manner of somewhat ponderous dignity and became something subhuman—blank in expression with a look of limited intelligence. He caught Caliban's childish vindictiveness and his fawning adulation of Trinculo with such realism that the audience was both repelled and fascinated. To the poetry he gave the imaginative and sensitive reading characteristic of his style, so that his Caliban truly crawled like a beast and talked like a poet.

The total effect of this *Tempest* was of a poetic fantasy. Easter holiday audiences who came expecting to see a glittering spectacle were hushed into silence as the center of interest shifted from setting to the words spoken on the stage. Reviewers said that during the performance the every-day world did not intrude upon the magical one and that Prospero's Epilogue was needed to help break the spell cast upon the audience.

During May a number of unusual plays were presented without careful staging or exhaustive rehearsal. The *Athenaeum* complained of capriciousness in the selection of pieces, but this variety of fare helped spark interest in audiences during the end-of-the-season lull. Thomas Morton's *Town and Country* featured Phelps as Reuben Glenroy and Anthony Younge as Cosey. The *Theatrical Times* (May 15, 1847) found it a "clever and bustling" play. A romantic tragedy, *Bertram* by Charles Maturin, was presented for the sake of giving Laura Addison a chance to play the character of Imogene and Phelps a role in which Kean had been successful. Good acting failed, however, to revive interest in this forgotten play, which the *Athenaeum* (May 29, 1847) said had a meretricious style and an odious subject.

The theatre closed on June 3, ending a season that would have been

notable in any period of theatrical history. Two hundred, fifty-two performances of thiry-one plays had been given, in addition to a variety
of afterpieces and the annual pantomime. Nine of the plays had been
major productions, of unusual interest either for the play itself or for
the acting. Of the afterpieces *Lloyd's Weekly* (June 6, 1847) said that "the
best farces of the most able writers of the day" had been produced, com-
plimenting the management on its preference for English authors over
pirated French pieces. The company had included thirty-six regular
members, three of whom had become important additions to the London stage through their debuts this season. Both acting and staging had
maintained a uniformly high quality, not to be found in any contemporary theatre. An experienced and appreciative audience had filled the
large house, often to overflowing, nearly every night of the season.
Without the patronage of the Queen or of the upper class of London
society, Sadler's Wells had become an unofficial national theatre and a
center for all playgoers seriously interested in drama.

Only two theatres, the Princess's and the Haymarket, offered any
challenge to the pre-eminence of Sadler's Wells. The Princess's, however, only sporadically presented plays. In the autumn of 1846 Macready
had appeared instead at the Surrey, where the magnificent offer of 1,000
pounds for five weeks had overcome his abhorrence of unfashionable
theatres. In the spring of 1847 Fanny Kemble (Mrs. Butler) had returned
from America to appear at the Princess's, but critics found her guilty of
sentimental rant. Later Mrs. Warner and Macready acted *Hamlet* there,
with an incompetent cast and careless staging. At the Haymarket, where
Helen Faucit, William Farren, Mrs. Nisbett, and the Keeleys frequently
appeared, plays were well cast and competently staged; but the dramatic
fare was of uneven quality. Webster had turned to the forms of minor
drama, and many of his productions competed with those of the Adelphi
and the Lyceum rather than with Sadler's Wells. The Keeleys had been
producing successful burlesques at the Lyceum (English Opera House).

Many other forms of entertainment were thriving in London theatres
in 1847 and 1848. Madame Celeste was an admired heroine of melodramas at the Adelphi. Jenny Lind had made her first appearance in
England at Her Majesty's, the most fashionable opera house, during the
spring of 1847 and was rapidly becoming the greatest attraction in London.
Drury Lane had its promenade concerts, with intervals of special features
like the horse troupe which appeared in March, 1848. The Queen's and

the City of London competed with each other in the field of sensational melodrama, both during the same week presenting versions of *The Drama of the Bottle,* based on Cruikshank's drawings.

Sadler's Wells opened for its fourth season on August 22, 1847, with a play that underlined its uniqueness among theatres of its time. Shakespeare's rarely acted *Cymbeline,* a play with almost equal emphasis on a number of roles and no star part, was offered to London theatregoers during a period noted for an interest in famous stars, an admiration for spectacle, and a preference of music to drama. But its reception could have been predicted by anyone acquainted with the audience which now regularly patronized Sadler's Wells. Reviewers had ceased to be surprised when a play generally considered unactable drew a full house of intensely interested spectators. Among those who crowded in to see *Cymbeline* were John Forster and Charles Dickens, who were both prompted to write Phelps after the performance. Forster congratulated him upon his audience as well as his performance and noted the peculiar characteristic of the regular patrons that they insisted upon quiet during the course of a play, quickly teaching newcomers that no noise would be allowed. "They seem to have formed themselves into a police for security of their own enjoyment," he wrote, "and nothing can be more marked than their intelligent appreciation." [15] Dickens's letter mentioned earlier visits and invited friendship.

> Broadstairs, Kent,
> August 29th, 1847

My Dear Sir,

I cannot resist the impulse I feel to thank you for the very great pleasure I derived from the representation of Cymbeline at your theatre on Thursday night. The excellent sense, taste, and feeling manifested throughout; the great beauty of all the stage arrangements; and the respectful consideration (so to speak) shown by every one concerned, for the creation of the poet, gave me extraordinary gratification. Nor could I readily express to you, if I were to try, how strong a sense I have of the great service such a theatre renders to all who visit it, and to the general cause of Literature and Art.

Even at the risk of seeming to intrude this sense upon you, I really cannot help assuring you of my warm interest and admiration. And perhaps you will receive my note with the greater favour, when I confess to having resisted a similar impulse after several former visits to Sadler's Wells, in my unwillingness to trouble you.

Let me hope that I may have the pleasure of associating my public knowledge of you with a more private and personal one than hitherto when I return to town in October; and believe me, my dear Sir,

Faithfully yours,
Charles Dickens

Samuel Phelps, Esquire

The competence of the cast, down to the least important members, and their obvious concern that there should not be a carelessly uttered line in the performance were largely responsible for the success of *Cymbeline*. As Leonatus Posthumus Phelps caught the quick changes of mood and emphasized his transitions from relative calm to violent outbursts of jealousy. Laura Addison gave an intelligent interpretation of Imogen, although there was a lack of smoothness and control in her acting that became more evident as she strove for greater force. Reviewers said that she tended to substitute a strained voice and excited manner for convincing emotion. Marston played Iachimo with more dignity and self-possession than was customary, and thus more plausibly masked his villainy from the other characters, while also giving more importance to some of the finest poetry in the play. Bennett as Belarius, Hoskins and Johnson (a new member of the company) as the disguised brothers, and Scharf as Cloten were all noticed in reviews. A minor actor named Harrington was described as making "quite a feature" of the servant Pisanio.

Cymbeline was performed nineteen times during the early weeks of the fourth season, and its success was recognized as a notable event in contemporary theatrical history. The *Athenaeum* (August 28, 1847), commenting upon this production, praised Phelps's example in taking advantage of the repeal of the theatrical monopoly and expressed the hope that it had brought a new era to the English stage:

> The more poetical of Shakespeare's dramas have here been the most popular. . . . The example thus successfully set is about to be followed elsewhere:—and there is good reason to believe that the liberty now conceded to the stage has given a new start to the Drama.

The remark about a new attempt to transform a minor theatre into a home for drama refers to an announcement that Mrs. Warner had leased the Marylebone Theatre for seven years with the intention of producing the old legitimate repertory.

One result of the general recognition of the success of Sadler's Wells was the respect with which Phelps was now regarded by London's intellectuals. Dickens's letter was the first step in an attempt to draw Phelps into the coterie which included, besides Forster and himself, Macready, Bulwer-Lytton, Talfourd, and other playwrights, critics, and prominent men interested in the contemporary theatre. Macready was the only professional actor among them, and although he was annoyed and embarrassed by the enthusiasm for his profession which led them into amateur theatricals, he enjoyed the group both socially and for its support of his career. Phelps, whose financial position and style of living would not normally have qualified him for so high a level of society, was more strictly limited to a professional relationship to such men. Their wish to bring him into their social circle seems somewhat surprising.

Their attitude can perhaps be explained by the peculiar circumstances of dramatic writing in the early Victorian period. Many writers were seriously interested in the theatre and eager to acquire professional knowledge of the stage. Bulwer-Lytton, Talfourd, the Reverend James White, Browning, and a number of others had converted themselves into playwrights by means of Macready's encouragement, professional advice, and subsequent performance of their plays. Embarrassed by their lack of technical knowledge, they had sought the help of a literate and intelligent professional actor; touchy about the possible rejection of their efforts, they had welcomed friendship with a sympathetic theatrical manager, who would be willing to look at their plays with professional interest and yet spare them the humiliation of formal rejection. And in fact, Macready had been the only theatrical manager likely to be interested in new five-act plays of the more serious and poetic type. Since Phelps now stood in the position Macready had formerly held—the recognized champion of tragedy and comedy in an age of melodrama and burlesque—this group turned to him.

Their interest was not entirely selfish. They had found in Phelps's performances an intelligent knowledge of Shakespeare and an absence of professional trickery that indicated the possibility of a real communication of ideas, such as they enjoyed with Macready. Moreover, his presence in their social circle would have represented the broadening of cultural life to include the middle class, which Dickens and other Victorian writers had recognized. At Sadler's Wells Phelps had destroyed the boundary line which had traditionally separated lower-class suburban audiences from classic English drama in much the same way as Dickens's novels had removed barriers to the widespread enjoyment of literature. And also, Dickens and his friends were aware that they could be useful to Phelps by increasing the interest of the aristocracy in Sadler's Wells. A strong suggestion from Dickens might result in special notice from the Queen, if not a royal visit to Sadler's Wells.

Phelps, however, did not enjoy the kind of social life that Dickens, Macready, and Forster lived. He was studious and even scholarly in his interests and not inclined to conviviality. After a performance, he had supper and went immediately to bed; he would have disliked the kind of congratulatory congregation in his dressing room which Macready encouraged. In contrast to Macready, he disliked all forms of social recognition generally accorded an actor off the stage, and he had a special distaste for anything that might be construed as currying favor with the press or men of influence in other spheres.

His exacting schedule at Sadler's Wells left him very little time for recreation, and he preferred to spend that time with his family. His vacations were devoted to fishing and hunting, sports in which he took great pleasure and had developed unusual skill. His nephew says in his biography that Phelps knew nearly every trout stream in England and seldom missed the first day of the partridge and pheasant season. It is typical of Phelps that he spent his vacations for a number of years at a small town in Kent, taking an interest in local affairs and becoming known to many farmers, without ever revealing his name or profession. Years later when he was acting at Drury Lane, a Kentish farmer rose from his seat in the pit in the midst of the play, giving a loud exclamation of disbelief when he recognized in the Doge of Venice a familiar fisherman of Farningham.

Phelps of course answered Dickens's letter, but when it was followed by invitations to dine at his house, Phelps gave a firm refusal to them all. Dickens at last and reluctantly gave up the attempt to draw Phelps into his circle. They came to be well acquainted, but their appointments and correspondence always concerned professional matters. Occasionally, Dickens's natural sociability would lead him to try again: "Can you come and join our family dinner (we shall be perfectly alone) on Sunday at five?" But in the letter he was careful to provide an alternate appointment in his office, if Phelps preferred.

John Forster was the unofficial ambassador from the playwrights of this group to Phelps. He represented Bulwer-Lytton, Leigh Hunt, the Reverend James White, and other writers in their professional dealings with Sadler's Wells. Sometimes he brought a manuscript for Phelps to read and later conveyed the verdict back to the author. In 1850, he served as an emissary for Macready in asking Phelps's services for Macready's farewell performance. As a reviewer, he was a regular patron of Sadler's Wells, and he often brought distinguished visitors with him. One of Macready's sons saw his first Shakespearen play at Sadler's Wells with Forster. Like Dickens, Forster would have added a personal and social acquaintance to this professional one, but his invitations were politely declined, even when he offered Phelps a choice of any day of the week to suit his convenience.[16]

In September, 1847, Phelps produced *Macbeth* from the original text, one of the most important productions of his career and one that had a lasting effect on the theatre in ridding Shakespeare of "improvements" from the eighteenth century. The staging and the acting both helped to bring out a new interpretation of *Macbeth* seen for the first time without singing and dancing witches. The only disappointment in the performance was Laura Addison's Lady Macbeth. Lacking sufficient power, she had begun to substitute mere vehemence for tragic expression.

In choosing a Rosalind for *As You Like It,* produced the following month, Phelps evidently decided to rely upon the trained ability of Fanny Cooper rather than the somewhat variable talent of his youthful leading actress. Miss Cooper's competence and versatility had been sorely missed during the previous spring when she had joined Macready at the Princess's. Although her Rosalind necessarily lacked the impressiveness that a more forceful actress could have given to the role, it was described as a charming and unique performance, "a highly finished miniature."

The critical praise accorded these two plays previously associated with Macready's name and the success of a second play by his friend James White perhaps awakened Macready's resentment. In February, 1848 he wrote Phelps the following letter:[17]

My dear Sir,
    Understanding that the play of the Bridal is announced at Sadler's Wells Theatre I must beg to inform you that as I intend to act it *myself* during my present engagement, I do not consider it right to extend the permission for its performance at present. Under other circumstances I should not object to the arrangements.

Yours very faithfully,
W. C. Macready

Although Macready had suggested the outline for the revision of *The Maid's Tragedy* and had starred in its initial production, it is hard to know by what means he intended to keep it off the stage at Sadler's Wells. That he had no authority to do so is obvious from a second letter, written to Phelps a few days later on February 23:

> My dear Sir,
>   By this day's paper I perceive to my surprise the play of the Bridal announced at the Marylebone Theatre. "What is done cannot be undone"—in *that* respect; and therefore I would not wish, that the prohibition should wear so *invidious* an appearance as to have any *particular* direction. You will therefore receive this note, if you please, as the requisite permission to perform the play of the Bridal at Sadler's Wells during the remainder of the current season at your own wish.
>
> Yours very faithfully,
> W. C. Macready

Phelps did put on the play (as he had in previous seasons), along with *Werner, The Lady of Lyons,* and *Money,* which had been introduced to the stage by Macready.

The contrast between Phelps's management at Sadler's Wells and the attitude of other London actors is illustrated by a single performance which took place at Covent Garden in December, 1847. The most prominent Shakespearean actors were gathered on one stage to give a benefit performance for the purchase of Shakespeare's house as a national monument. Nine individual scenes from Shakespearean plays were presented, each featuring a single important actor, who had been allowed to choose the scene he preferred and to select supporting actors agreeable to him. This plan, although a disappointment to serious playgoers, made possible a joint performance by stars of such magnitude as Macready, Buckstone, Webster, Helen Faucit, Mme. Vestris, and Mrs. Warner, who would never have agreed to act in a single play together. Macready played the death of Henry the Fourth; Helen Faucit appeared as Juliet with Mrs. Glover as the Nurse; and Mrs. Warner did the statue scene from *The Winter's Tale.* Phelps, who had also been asked to contribute his services to the benefit, put on the second scene of *The Tempest* as it had been performed at Sadler's Wells, taking with him Marston, Bennett, Miss Addison and other members of the company.

A huge audience was attracted by the announcement of such a dis-

1. Samuel Phelps as Cardinal Wolsey. Portrait by Johnston Forbes-Robertson, 1878. Reproduced by permission of the Garrick Club.

2. Sadler's Wells Theatre, drawn and engraved by Daniel Hovell, 1826. Courtesy Harvard Theatre Collection.

3. Interior of Sadler's Wells Theatre showing water tank. Drawn and engraved by Pugin and Rowlandson for R. Ackerman's *Microcosm of London,* 1809. Courtesy Harvard Theatre Collection.

4. Mrs. Warner as Hermione. Steel engraving by Paine of Islington, 1845–1846. Courtesy Harvard Theatre Collection.

5. New entrance at Sadler's Wells, 1846. From a newspaper clipping. Courtesy Harvard Theatre Collection.

6. The company of Sadler's Wells in the green room, dressed for *The Merchant of Venice*. From *Illustrated London News,* January 9, 1847. Courtesy Harvard Theatre Collection.

tinguished cast and by the promise of royal patronage. Although the Queen did not, in fact, appear, the house was uncomfortably crowded. Phelps opened the performance by reading a prologue, written by Charles Knight for the occasion, but the audience refused to quiet down, because they were protesting the overcrowding. After the second interruption, he left the stage without finishing the prologue. Accsutomed to the courteous attention of the audience at Sadler's Wells, he was unwilling to endure the kind of humiliation frequently experienced by actors at the great London theatres. When the difficulties about seating had been settled, the rest of the program went well; and the benefit was considered a success, both artistically and financially. Most reviewers refrained from making comparisons, giving general praise to all the actors. The *Morning Chronicle,* however, showed a characteristic partisanship by extolling the virtues of Macready's acting, while severely criticizing the two actresses with whom Macready had quarreled. "Mr. Macready showed himself the great artist he always appears," wrote the reviewer, but Fanny Kemble as Katherine "was cold, torpid, and monotonous," and Helen Faucit's Juliet was the "most indubitable rant."

The Queen's failure to appear increased the growing resentment against her neglect of English drama. Typical of the feeling among actors is an article entitled "Royal Neglect of English Art," which appeared in the *National Dramatic Biographer.*[18] In it the editor severely criticized the Queen for patronizing Italian opera and the French theatre "night after night," while ignoring all forms of English drama. "No one can tell the time when she has been within the walls of an English theatre," he asserted. During the autumn of 1847, general resentment of the aristocracy had been growing as a large number of business failures threw England into a new monetary crisis. Agitations in Paris for parliamentary and electoral reforms were echoed in England during the winter with riots in London, Manchester, Glasgow, and Edinburgh. The depression of 1848 came upon a theatre already suffering from a fashion set by the nobility. The Haymarket was in serious financial difficulties, while the St. James's (French) Theatre and Her Majesty's Opera enjoyed full houses at extremely high prices. According to the *National Dramatic Biographer,* double boxes on the grand tier at Her Majesty's cost 8,000 pounds per season. Such criticism must have come to the Queen's attention, since she inaugurated a series of private dramatic performances at Windsor Castle. In choosing a director for the royal entertainments she showed a preference which had already been recognized by naming Charles Kean.

Sadler's Wells suffered less than other theatres from the financial depression. On November 27, 1847, the *Theatrical Times* remarked that this theatre had good houses whereas other theatres were having extremely bad attendance. It was also noted by many reviewers that Sadler's Wells now had by far the best company in London. Even when Phelps did not appear in the cast, the acting was sufficiently attractive to bring full houses. In October a large number of spectators came to see Bennett, Laura Addison, and the Marstons in *The Jealous Wife*. Early in December the theatre was crowded for a performance of *The Poor Gentleman,* with Bennett, Hoskins, Mellon, Johnson, the Marstons, and Fanny Cooper in the important roles.

In January, 1848, Phelps continued the emphasis upon comedy with a production of *Twelfth Night.* The *Athenaeum* (January 29, 1848) praised the "great taste and splendour" of the staging, asserting that "this play, with all its beauty and romance, has rarely been better represented." Laura Addison's Viola had buoyancy, mirth, and pertness. Fanny Cooper was Olivia, and the "downright, hearty" Mrs. Marston was Maria. Bennett's Sir Toby, like his Caliban, showed his ability to lay aside the somber manner of his tragic style and project the idiosyncrasies of a comic character with genuine humor. Anthony Younge and Henry Scharf were irresistibly funny as Aguecheek and the Clown, although they played their roles without the buffoonery which comedians had long been accustomed to insert in low comic characters. And in this production Phelps introduced to the stage his Malvolio, an interpretation remembered by a generation of playgoers as one of his best.

Next Phelps played Falstaff in a well-acted and beautifully staged production of *The Merry Wives of Windsor.* On his benefit night he followed this performance with Mrs. Centlivre's *The Wonder,* in which he acted Don Felix.

Alternation of comedy and tragedy underlined the versatility of the company. Fanny Cooper was praised as highly for her Cordelia as for her Mrs. Page, and Scharf accomplished the rare feat of giving distinction to Olivia's Clown and Lear's Fool on alternate nights.

In spite of this variety attendance had fallen off this season at Sadler's Wells, and generally London theatres had a disastrous year. Macready and Charlotte Cushman, appearing together at the Princess's, had cost

Maddox more than they brought in, although he had cut other expenses by hiring the cheapest supporting actors and by using old opera sets for scenery. Mrs. Warner had found her management of the Marylebone Theatre an expensive failure. A last attempt to increase houses by engaging Macready to act with her for six nights (at 300 pounds) was not sufficiently successful to offset the heavy losses she had suffered. Benjamin Webster announced that he had lost 8,000 pounds during his eighteen-month season, which had featured Charles and Ellen Kean and the tragedian Vandenhoff in addition to his regular company.

The London season of 1847–1848 had produced one huge success with the debut of Gustavus V. Brooke at the Olympic Theatre. Having returned to the provinces in 1841 rather than submit to Macready's domination, he now came to London and achieved a wider and more sudden popularity than any actor since Edmund Kean. His fiery delivery of impassioned speeches, particularly in *Othello,* his thorough training, and his personal charm won enthusiastic response. Reviewers found him guilty of playing to the gallery by using startling interpretations of particular passages to win applause and by dazzling his spectators with mere physical force, but audiences were not deterred by unfavorable reviews. For a few months Brooke was the rage of London.

Macready was preparing for another trip to America, where he intended eventually to live in his retirement, and had arranged for a royal command performance at Drury Lane for his own benefit before leaving England. The novel arrangement, unprecedented on the stage, which would net Macready more than a 1,000 pounds in a time of theatrical depression angered London actors and managers, who had recently quarreled publicly with Macready over his support of a French troupe at Drury Lane.[19] This feud, added to old resentment, made it hard for Macready to find actors who would donate their services for his benefit performance. Even Charlotte Cushman, who as an American was not involved in the affair of the French actors, refused Macready's request (perhaps remembering how insultingly he had refused to act for her benefit in Boston). Eventually Macready turned to Phelps:

> 5, Clarence Terrace, Regent's Park
> June 26th, 1848

My Dear Sir,
    You will perceive in this day's announcements, that Her Majesty commands (and I ought to say in the kindest and most considerate manner) a

performance at Drury Lane Theatre for my benefit, the last but one I shall ever take in London, on Monday, July 10th.

On this occasion may I calculate upon the contribution of your valuable aid?—and, if so, will you oblige me by performing King Henry in the three first acts of King Henry VIII., and Major Oakley in The Jealous Wife?

I need scarcely add that I shall consider myself greatly obliged by your acquiescence in my request; but I may beg to intimate my conviction that the committee will be happy to meet your views in any arrangement you may desire.

I remain, my dear Sir,

Very faithfully yours,
W. C. Macready

Phelps's response was a marked contrast to others Macready received:

8, Canonbury Square, Islington,
June 26th, 1848

My Dear Sir,

I have but this moment (four o'clock) received your note, the contents of which have afforded me great pleasure. I will study King Henry: Major Oakley, I believe, I *have* acted, and am most happy in being able to place my poor services at your disposal.

I am, my dear Sir,

Yours faithfully and obliged,
Samuel Phelps[20]

The promptness of Phelps's answer and its warm tone show that he had great respect for Macready and that he no longer resented the treatment he had received at Macready's hands. His own lack of jealousy, his characteristic generosity, and perhaps some feeling of satisfaction at the prospect of assuming the position Macready had so often denied him led him to offer his aid when asked.

It is difficult to know whether he was aware of the current intensification of feeling against Macready. He had not been drawn into the affair of the French actors, probably because his theatre was too far from the center of the theatrical world to make common cause with West End theatres. Although he was on good terms with most London actors and prompt to help in such affairs as the benefit for the purchase of Shakespeare's house, he probably was unaware of professional gossip and day-to-day events in the theatres of central London. He was not a member of the Garrick Club, where such matters were discussed. His ready compliance with

Macready's request would seem to indicate total ignorance of the tense situation in his profession. Macready showed his gratitude by lending him his own costume for King Henry—an unusual mark of favor, which Macready thought sufficiently important to record in his diary.

Although there is no indication that other actors resented Phelps's willingness to act, the bitterness toward Macready increased in the weeks before his benefit. Posters appeared along Bow Street saying, "Who acts for Mr. Macready?" (The title of Mister was known to be especially annoying to Macready, who had hoped for knighthood and bitterly resented the common prefix.) Very few did act for Macready. Mrs. Warner, Mrs. Nisbett, Mrs. Stirling, and Priscilla Horton did. John Ryder, who was again to go with Macready to America, also did. But, in general, the unofficial boycott was remarkable for the evidence of harmony and concerted action in a profession noted for individualism and lack of agreement. Dickens served as stage manager; Forster as general manager; and vacancies in the cast were filled by several actors from Sadler's Wells.

Before the night of the benefit, even Phelps must have become aware of the opposition to Macready. Newspapers criticized the novel arrangements for an actor's benefit and protested the Queen's patronage of such an actor after her long estrangement from the English theatre and patronage of everything foreign, "which has caused the withdrawal of aristocratic influence and support of the English theatre." [21] Hostility to Macready was so openly expressed that before the performance he took the precaution of stationing in the pit seven or eight policemen in plain clothes. This precaution was well advised, since neither the presence of the Queen, nor Macready's direct address to the audience in the middle of the second scene was sufficient to repress the noisy disapprobation expressed by members of the pit and gallery. This behavior, which may be described as violent in comparison with the usual habits of English actors and others connected with the acting profession, should be remembered in any discussion of the fatal Astor Place riot, which ten months later was to terminate Macready's American tour. Although the violence that caused the death of thirty-one New Yorkers is totally reprehensible, resentment of Macready should not be considered a purely trans-Atlantic phenomenon.

Although most of the first act of the tragedy was not heard, Macready went bravely on with the performance. He pretended that overcrowding was the cause of the disturbance, but reviewers said later that the noise increased markedly whenever Macready was on the stage. By contrast, Phelps's appearance was greeted with enthusiastic applause, and he was called before the curtain at the end of the evening's performance. The *Dramatic and Musical Review* (August, 1848) used the occasion to remark upon Macready's former fear and suppression of Phelps:

> We well recollect the openly-expressed chagrin which he felt when, after a performance of "Othello," at the Haymarket, Mr. Phelps, the representative of the Moor, was called before the audience at the end of the tragedy, and Mr. Macready, the Iago of the evening, was suffered to depart to his dressing-room, muttering groans "not loud, but deep," upon the taste of an audience who understood so badly "the text of Shakspere." Witness, also, the manner in which, throughout his connexion with Mr. Macready, that intelligent actor was kept in the background, because he was likely to become a dangerous rival.

Phelps went back to Islington probably less affected by the controversy that surrounded Macready's benefit than many others not directly involved. He was glad to show his honest respect for Macready, while at the same time asserting confidence in his ability to act beside so distinguished an actor without any diminution of his own reputation.

During the summer of 1848 when most London managers were trying to keep expenses to a minimum, Phelps and Greenwood spent a large sum on major alterations of their theatre. Crowding of the entrances, only partially alleviated by the alterations of 1846, had continued to be a problem. They solved it by enlarging the entrance to the boxes and constructing a separate stairway for the dress circle. There were also a new carriage drive and a covered lobby for patrons of the pit. For the first time the backs of the pit benches were upholstered. The principal alterations, however, were behind the curtain. The stage itself was enlarged, and additions were made to the backstage facilities, which had been cramped. A new set of larger and well-lighted dressing rooms was added, and a new green room.

Although Phelps had scheduled a longer recess for the sake of the remodeling, a wet summer slowed the work so much that the theatre was not ready for its opening date at the end of August. He used the time to study plays, but it is evident from letters written to his daughters at school in Kent that the inactivity irked him and that he was worried about the loss of money which would result from several weeks' delay in opening. At the end of August he had a brief engagement at the Brighton theatre, which helped to relieve his depression and gave him a chance to find new actors for his own company. During the second week of September he took his company to the Surrey for a series of performances. A letter of September 16 indicates that they attracted good houses across the Thames:

I have been acting all the week at the *Surrey*—nothing but the eternal *"Lady of Lyons"*—we have had capital houses. We shall soon open the Royal property—you will not know it again, it is so wonderfully improved.[22]

The repertory of 1848–1849 was chosen to show off the new stage facilities of the remodeled theatre and to introduce some important new actors to the London stage. Isabella Glyn, a protégé of Charles Kemble, who had failed through nervousness in her debut as Lady Macbeth at the Olympic in the previous season, successfully launched her career as Volumnia in *Coriolanus.* She then appeared as Hermione in *The Winter's Tale,* Queen Katherine in *Henry the Eighth,* Constance in *King John,* and Margaret in *Richard the Third.* She had the tragic force which Laura Addison (who had gone to the Haymarket) never achieved, and she used the classic style of the Kembles with poses reminiscent of Mrs. Siddons. The critics praised her highly on her debut and for years afterward, but the audience at Sadler's Wells never liked her as well as Laura Addison.

Fletcher's *Rule a Wife and Have a Wife,* which appeared in October, added to the growing list of neglected Elizabethan plays revived at Sadler's Wells. Mme. Vestris had tried it at Covent Garden in a different spirit without much success, but in the Elizabethan style of Phelps's production the comedy became popular and was revived in several seasons.

G. K. Dickinson made his debut in November to a full house as Jaffier in Otway's *Venice Preserved,* and the audience gave him hearty approval. Debuts at Sadler's Wells were usually successful. Whether this should be attributed to Phelps's talent for recognizing promise in a young actor, to the advantage gained by appearing with an excellent company, or to the encouragement of a responsive audience, young actors had better fortune at Sadler's Wells than at other theatres. It is remarkable that most of them would have preferred to make their debuts at the Haymarket or the Princess's, where even the greatest success could win a Shakespearean actor only a limited engagement. Dickinson, like Isabella Glyn, had tried other theatres first; but other managers had been discouraging whereas Phelps and Greenwood gave him a full season's contract not dependent upon the success of his initial appearance.

The *Athenaeum* (November 18, 1848) opined that he was graceful and elegant but too vehement in elocution and gesture. His love scenes were "too amatory for London boards." A more important objection was the limited range of his voice. But such defects could be improved with training, and training was part of the daily work at Sadler's Wells. Critics noted that Miss Glyn was receiving excellent training. Again, the *Athenaeum* (October 21, 1848) spoke of Sadler's Wells as a school:

> The nightly improvement of the young actress in Volumnia has placed her merits beyond question—and owes something, no doubt, to the excellent school of acting in which it has been Miss Glyn's good fortune now to matriculate. One result of its especial training is, that Miss Glyn's elocution is now so distinct that every syllable has due pronunciation.

The finding and training of new actors was a major part of Phelps's occupation as manager, since he found it difficult to hold actors in his suburban theatre once they had achieved sufficient popularity to attract offers from West End theatres. Mrs. Warner had left financial security and a leading position to try for more prominence with fashionable audiences. Creswick had not been satisfied to stay at Sadler's Wells. Miss Cooper had left to join Macready at the Princess's, although it was a limited engagement. Laura Addison had gone to the Haymarket. That these actors would have fared better by remaining at Sadler's Wells seems clear from their subsequent careers. They found that their engagements in the West End were temporary and interspersed with long periods of unemployment. Mrs. Warner finally tried her own hand at managing a suburban theatre, but her failure clouded the rest of her life. Creswick eventually became manager of the Surrey, and for a dozen years produced the old "legitimate" drama, but he never became an actor of first importance, nor did his management achieve the distinction of Phelps's. Laura Addison eventually went to America, and there she found herself competing with Mrs. Warner at rival theatres in New York.

In spite of these examples many actors moved from Sadler's Wells to theatres of greater social prestige. Their attitude is reflected in an anecdote told of Mrs. Brougham, a charming and competent actress, who twice joined the company of Sadler's Wells after the termination of her engagements at the Princess's. According to Godfrey Turner, "she once told Phelps, who apologized for offering her a very small part, that it did not much signify, as it was only a matter between herself and the parish of Clerkenwell." [23] The residents of northern London could offer Mrs. Brougham an appreciative audience and a comfortable income, but they could not give her a great name among the wealthy and fashionable.

The attitude of the aristocracy toward Sadler's Wells was never more obviously displayed than in November, 1848, when a series of dramatic performances to be given at Windsor Castle was announced. With Macready in America, Phelps was easily the foremost actor in London, and his company had long been recognized as superior to that of any other theatre for poetic drama. Nevertheless, the Queen's advisers ignored Sadler's Wells in choosing the players that were to be honored by royal patronage. Charles Kean and other actors who had recently appeared at the Haymarket acted Shakespeare before the royal family. Thus, Mrs. Warner and William Creswick shared with Vandenhoff and the Keans a distinction they would have been denied had they remained at Sadler's Wells. Such patronage was not merely a matter of honor and prestige. After the series was completed Webster announced on the Haymarket bills that *Hamlet* would be performed with the same cast that had played before Her Majesty. The mere announcement filled his theatre for the first time in many months. According to the *Observer,* this was "a proof of the potency of fashion," since the same cast had played *Hamlet* to half-empty houses at the Haymarket in the recent past. Increase in the size of Webster's audience offered little competition to Sadler's Wells, nor did Phelps need the stimulus of royal patronage to provide sufficient audiences for his theatre; but he did suffer from aristocratic prejudice in the matter of attracting and keeping actors who were ambitious to gain a widespread reputation. In some measure Queen Victoria damaged Sadler's Wells, not by her neglect, but by setting a fashion so potent that it robbed Phelps of his actors.

That Sadler's Wells was one of very few successful theatrical managements in London is clear from comments in the newspapers. The *Theatrical Journal* of October 26, 1848, in its prognostication of the London season, said that "the great business of the season will, no doubt, be transacted by Messrs. Maddox, Greenwood, Mathews, and Celeste." Maddox was again producing opera at the Princess's; Charles Mathews and Mme. Vestris were putting on translations of French pieces with taste and style at the Lyceum; Mme. Celeste was the heroine of sentimental domestic drama and plays of Douglas Jerrold and Mark Lemon at the Adelphi. Greenwood's name in this short list indicates that Sadler's Wells ranked in financial success with the houses patronized by West End audiences. It also reveals the lonely prominence of Sadler's Wells as the one theatre successfully producing tragedy and comedy.

Phelps was ill during the early part of the season, after the exhausting week of preparing his first productions in the limited time allowed between the completion of the remodeling and the opening night. For the first time in his management he began regularly to produce plays that did not require his presence in the cast, scheduling them for Friday and Saturday nights. Although these "off night" features received no special attention in staging, they were often interesting for the acting and for the rarity of the plays. In this season he put on George Lovell's *Love's Sacrifice,* a work that many critics felt had been unjustly neglected, and three comedies from the turn of the century: Thomas Morton's *A Cure for the Heartache* and *Speed the Plough* and George Colman's *The Poor Gentleman.* In these plays and in a featured production of *Much Ado about Nothing,* Dickinson, Marston, Hoskins, Bennett, Younge, Scharf, Miss Huddart and Miss Cooper shared the stage, while Phelps and Miss Glyn rested.

Phelps also revived Browning's *A Blot in the 'Scutcheon,* which received critical acclaim without attracting large audiences. One result of its performance was an increase in the number of playwrights who pressed Phelps to read their unacted works. Forster was busily relaying manuscripts and pressing him for early decisions. In one case he asked for the unusual favor of allowing an author to read aloud his own play. The writer was G. H. Lewes, novelist, critic, and translator of French plays for the London stage. Because Forster felt bound by friendship to urge Lewes's' unusual request, Phelps agreed to the arrangement. Unfortunately, he found the play hopeless and could find no way to hide his reaction from the author. The interview proved embarrassing and in fact caused a wound to Lewes's pride. Twenty-five years later he published a book called *On Actors and the Art of Acting* from which he pointedly omitted discussion of Phelps.

Forster was at the same time rather reluctantly pressing Leigh Hunt's suit to Phelps. Victorian writers were distressed by Hunt's poverty and had in the past applied to theatrical managers on behalf of his *Legend of Florence.* Macready had refused to attempt it in spite of Forster's petitions. Mme. Vestris had put it on at Covent Garden although it was not suited to her style of management or the talents of her company and did not succeed. Phelps finally purchased the rights to it and in 1850 made it a featured production, but it lasted only six performances.

He must have felt the injustice of the situation in which he found himself. He was on the one hand nominated by playwrights to the position of preserver and upholder of the national drama, implying the responsibility of producing works unlikely to be financially rewarding, and on the other hand completely ignored by the Queen, whose recognition would have helped support the kind of national theatre he was expected to maintain. Perhaps a trace of resentment may be detected in his decision to perform *The Stranger,* one of the plays Webster was advertising with the caption "as performed at Windsor Castle." Since Phelps had performed the play during every season of his management, his right to put it on during the winter of 1849 could hardly be questioned, but the *Theatrical Journal* (January 25, 1849) assumed that Phelps was in this case deliberately provoking comparison with Webster's company:

> The last performance before the Royal Family was the "Stranger" and Mr. Phelps has taken the lead and had it performed before Mr. Webster could avail himself of bringing it out at the Haymarket. This is showing great tact and judgment; we consider as a whole the characters have been more efficiently cast and acted than they could have been at the Haymarket. Let our readers compare the names in the two bills. Even those who had the honour of appearing before Her Majesty will not vie with the company now performing at the only legitimate theatre in the metropolis.

Toward the end of the season Phelps produced *The Honest Man's Fortune* by Beaumont and Fletcher with moderate success. Then he tried a new play *Calaynos* by George T. Boker, an American, who had published his work before it was ever acted. This choice provoked some controversy on both sides of the Atlantic. The *Theatrical Journal* (May 17, 1849) was reluctant to believe that an American could have written so good a play, remarking that "it abounds with language of the most refined character." An anonymous contributor to the *Stage-Manager* (May 26, 1849) objected on principle to the performance of an American author's work:

> I feel that the acceptance of this play from a foreign hand, although probably Mr. Phelps got it for *nothing,* which very likely induced him to bring it out, is an insult to the English public, who have well supported his house; it is a worse insult to the English Author, and surely if he reads them, or gets them read, among the three or four hundred MS. plays pre-

sented per season to Mr. Phelps he could find *one* better than the Yankee melodrama of *Calaynos*.

The heat of these objections would seem to indicate on the part of the writer a personal interest in plays that had been rejected by Phelps, although the quality of the prose leads one to hope that its author was not, as the editor claimed, "a gentleman of some standing in literature."

The low opinion of American culture expressed by the *Theatrical Journal* was not unusual in mid-nineteenth-century England. Dickens's *American Notes* and *Martin Chuzzlewit* had made their full impact in the past five years. In theatrical circles there was particular feeling against Americans because of the quarrel between Macready and Edwin Forrest. Englishmen had been shocked by Forrest's public hissing of Macready in Edinburgh, followed by his unrepentant letter in the *Times,* since they did not know how great a provocation the American had been given.[24] The open and ill-mannered rivalry between the most prominent tragedians of England and the United States had increased English feeling against foreign competition in the declining English theatre. The feeling in the United States, where English actors demanded high salaries, had recently become far more bitter toward such foreign invasion. By a remarkable coincidence *Calaynos* opened at Sadler's Wells on the same night rioters attacked the Astor Place Theatre, New York, in a violent eruption of hatred for Macready and English snobbery. Although news of the Astor Place riot had not yet reached England when the anti-American contributor to the *Stage-Manager* was composing his letter, he was echoing the sentiments of the enemy in his indictment of plays "from a foreign hand."

In Philadelphia, Boker and his friends were unhappy about Phelps's use of an American play without the author's consent. Since American authors had not yet obtained the protection of a copyright law preventing the use of published plays, they felt themselves at a disadvantage beside their English competitors. Phelps was following accepted practice in appropriating Boker's published play for his stage; and although he was not legally required to pay the author, he did, according to the *Stage-Manager* (May 26, 1849), send him the customary fee for each night the play was performed. Phelps may also have assumed, because of the large number of unacted plays on the market, that a successful production was worth something in itself to the author's future career. As it happened, the production of *Calaynos* at Sadler's Wells was probably a factor influencing the manager of Drury Lane to produce Boker's new and unpublished play, *The Betrothal,* in 1853.

Since Isabella Glyn had abruptly left the company at Easter, Fanny Cooper played the leading role in *Calaynos,* but she fell ill in the middle of May. For this reason the play was withdrawn after nine performances, but it was performed in the following season.

At the end of May in the last week of the season—a period when novelty in the selection of plays was sought for the sake of benefit nights —Phelps made a rare excursion into the field of melodrama by presenting "Monk" Lewis's *Castle Spectre.* Reviewers were generally critical when a theatre known as "legitimate" produced melodrama. Webster's recent failings in this regard, and especially his presentation of many translations from French originals, had been cited as reason for the unsuitability of the Queen's choice of his company for performances at Windsor Castle. Until now Phelps had strictly avoided any plays that would not have been considered worthy of the patent theatres. If he was at all concerned that he might be censured by the critics for performing *Castle Spectre,* he may have felt that he would be excused for resorting to popular drama on a benefit night at the end of a long season. He might also have pleaded that the inclusion of Tobin's comedy *The Honeymoon* (in the shortened acting version) as an afterpiece went far to legitimatize the evening's entertainment.

It was not, however, the critics who objected to Phelps's choice of Lewis's gothic melodrama; it was the audience. They found the play dull, and they expressed their opinion in unmistakable, though good-natured, disapproval. The *Theatrical Journal* (May 31, 1849) reported that the actors "failed to create the least interest throughout the evening, although they laboured hard to obtain the meed of applause that generally falls to their share in the ordinary course of their performance."

The taste of the audience which now regularly patronized Sadler's Wells was well formed and discriminating. Although at the beginning of his management Phelps may have led the audience and helped to shape their preferences, they had long since created their own standards of judgment. Their preference for poetic plays, for original texts over acting versions, and for a more natural style of acting over the formal and classical style had been clearly displayed in their applause and patronage. They were less influenced by the opinion of reviewers than most audiences. Since Phelps could not afford, Macready-fashion, to ignore the preferences of his audience, he generally respected their judgment. After one performance of *Castle Spectre,* there were no more attempts to substitute melodrama for tragedy and comedy.

The choice of afterpieces had always posed a problem for Greenwood and Phelps. It was gradually made clear that the audience did not like the kind of broad farce which was popular at many of London's minor theatres. They demanded pieces of more than ephemeral interest, and they expected them to be well acted or, in the case of musical pieces, well sung. That the management did not always satisfy their taste is indicated by occasional criticisms in the *Theatrical Journal* mentioning objections to a particular piece or complaining of lack of variety in the offerings. There was the additional problem of satisfying the patrons who came chiefly to see the afterpieces and were admitted for half price at nine o'clock, when the major play of the evening was more than half over. Greenwood presented as many as sixty-five different afterpieces in one season, in addition to the annual pantomime, which usually ran for a month after Christmas. Although performances ended promptly at eleven-thirty, an earlier hour than customary at some of the fashionable London theatres, there was no attempt at Sadler's Wells to abandon the old custom of half-price admission or to shorten the bill by omitting afterpieces. In fact there were often two short pieces after the major play of the evening.

Types of afterpiece included farce, interlude, *petite* comedy, *petite* drama, burletta, operetta, musical drama, and shortened versions of five-act comedies. Among the authors represented were Inchbald and Sheridan, in addition to the well-known contemporary writers: Buckstone, Planché, Dibdin, Poole, Jerrold, Dance, Bernard, and Greenwood. Actors for afterpieces were used in minor parts of comedy and tragedy, and a few like Hoskins and Fanny Cooper were able to play important roles in both forms of entertainment. Singers, dancers, and musicians were hired specially for afterpieces, and these performers were expensive, as Macready had discovered, because of the preference of fashionable society for musical entertainment. Phelps, unlike Macready, never attempted to compete with West End theatres in the realm of music, and generally the musical performances at Sadler's Wells were undistinguished. The farces and short comedies were of uneven quality, although they were chosen with a preference for original English pieces over translations from the French.

The fifth season of Phelps's management had run for 198 nights, presenting seven Shakespearean plays and twenty other tragedies and comedies. Houses had continued to be good in spite of hard times and a raging epidemic of cholera. During the winter there had been daily reports in the newspapers of the number of cases of cholera, which often exceeded a thousand in London. In one "infant refuge" (for workhouse babies) a hundred and forty-six children had died. Widespread agitation for social and political reforms continued. That a theatre devoted to drama succeeded in attracting the residents of northern London during a period of such hardship is a remarkable fact. One moralizing reviewer commented that "there are shop-girls whose genuine enjoyment of the fine dramas produced here would put to shame the corrupted taste of some even of the very highest ladies in the land." [25]

The opening of the new season in August, 1849, revealed more changes in the company. Fanny Cooper had again left Sadler's Wells, this time to become Creswick's leading actress at the Surrey. Phelps replaced her with a lively and polished actress from Dublin, Helen Fitzpatrick, who made a hit in her debut as Letitia Hardy in *The Belle's Stratagem.* Her talent for polite comedy gave Phelps a chance to put on a number of other plays not commonly seen on the Victorian stage: Colley Cibber's *She Would and She Would Not,* Mrs. Centlivre's *The Busy-Body,* and Goldsmith's *She Stoops to Conquer.* Henry Scharf had gone to the Olympic, where Brooke was scheduled to appear after Christmas, and he was replaced at Sadler's Wells by Henry Nye.

When Miss Glyn returned from France in the middle of September, she appeared as Portia in *The Merchant of Venice* and Isabella in *Measure for Measure,* lifting both these heroines to an emotional level usually reserved for tragedy. Then she became Cleopatra in the first successful production of Shakespeare's play in two centuries. Without laying aside the dignity which characterized her style of acting, she caught the sexual attractiveness, caprice, and vanity of Cleopatra and gave a striking performance which led some reviewers to pronounce her the first actress of her day.

Phelps gave *Antony and Cleopatra* a lavish setting, more magnificent than any previous production, but his expense was repaid by a run of twenty-two performances. During the rest of the season other members of the company had an opportunity to appear in roles especially suited to their talents: Phelps in Sir Giles Overreach, Dickinson in Claude Melnotte of *The Lady of Lyons,* and Helen Fitzpatrick in Juliana of *The Honeymoon.*

Again the following season the major production displayed Miss Glyn's abilities. She played the title role in Webster's *The Duchess of Malfi,* which had not been seen on the stage since 1707. In spite of critics' objections to the "revolting nature" and "criminal tendency" of the tragedy, it was highly successful with the audience. Phelps laid aside his usual repertory system and performed the play every night during most of January, 1851.

In 1850–1851, for the first time since undertaking the management of Sadler's Wells, Phelps faced competition from several London theatres. Although neither Creswick's management of the Surrey nor Mrs. Nisbett's new attempt to run the Marylebone was likely to become an important rival, G. V. Brooke at the Olympic, James Anderson at Drury Lane, Macready in his farewell season at the Haymarket, and Charles Kean as the new manager of the Princess's were, collectively, a threat to the status of Sadler's Wells. They drew some of that group of playgoers who had been coming to Islington from other parts of London, and they enjoyed a prestige which attracted Phelps's best actors. Mrs. Marston followed Scharf to the Olympic. Dickinson and Nye had left the company during the summer, along with several actors of less importance. Despite the fact that these actors were generally disappointed in their hopes—Mrs. Marston soon left the Olympic, and both Dickinson and Scharf went to America in 1850—the pull of the West End continued. Before this season opened Phelps had regretfully accepted Henry Marston's decision to leave Sadler's Wells to find a more prominent position in the theatrical world. The Marstons could hardly be replaced, not only because of their talents in certain roles but also because of their invaluable experience in the variety of parts required of actors in a repertory theatre. It was said that neither had ever played a role badly. When they found no engagement in London, they decided upon a provincial tour, leaving their daughter Jenny to make her stage debut at Sadler's Wells.

Phelps chose plays he thought best suited to his depleted company. No new Shakespearean play was added to the repertory, but twelve of the twenty he had already produced were revived this season, including an impressive *Hamlet.* In October Henry Marston returned, and Phelps gratefully cast him as Benedick in *Much Ado about Nothing.* His reappearance brought cheers from the audience. *The Duchess of Malfi* kept the house full during much of the winter, but it also increased Isabella Glyn's reputation so markedly that Webster offered her an engagement, which she immediately accepted. Dwindling attendance and Miss Glyn's departure induced Phelps to close the theatre abruptly on March 26, ten days before the compulsory recess for Holy Week.

For Macready's last performance, a benefit and royal command at Drury Lane on February 26, 1851, John Forster had written Phelps asking him to volunteer his services. This Phelps promptly did and appeared as Macduff on that gala night when Drury Lane was sold out before the performance, some seats at the incredible price of 3 pounds each. This crowded house—"as brilliant an audience as ever congregated within the walls of a theatre"—took the occasion of Macready's retirement to nominate Phelps as his successor. *Lloyd's Weekly* (March 2, 1851) described their action:

> We must not omit to mention how the house marked and duly acknowledged the worthy spirit which dictated Mr. Phelps to come forward and impersonate Macduff. He was loudly cheered on his first appearance on the scene, so much so as to delay the progress of the tragedy for some minutes. His performance throughout was loudly applauded, and at the termination of the fourth act, the audience was vociferous in demanding his appearance before the curtain. Mr. Macready's retirement leaves Mr. Phelps in possession of the foremost place in tragedy.

Macready was less eager to give Phelps public recognition and rejected the suggestion made by Dickens and Forster that he make Phelps an honorary vice-president of his farewell banquet. He did, however, single out Phelps in his speech at the banquet, not as an actor, but as a manager who had raised a degraded theatre to respectability "by the learned and tasteful spirit of his productions." [26]

Phelps's eighth season opened early, on July 28, 1851, for a special series of farewell performances by Mrs. Warner, who was about to sail for America. After Macready's disastrous experience only two years earlier, an American tour was admittedly a desperate expedient, but Mrs. Warner was in severe financial difficulties brought on by the failure of her management and increased by her husband's irresponsibility. The two-week engagement was highly successful. According to the *Theatrical Journal* (July 30, 1851), the opening night attracted "one of the most crowded, and to all appearances enlightened, audiences that ever graced the Theatre Royal, Sadler's Wells," and Mrs. Warner's performance of the Queen in *Henry the Eighth* was "as fresh and powerful as ever." Good houses continued through performances of *The Winter's Tale* and *The*

Merchant of Venice. For her last night Mrs. Warner chose Lady Macbeth. Had she known that it was to be her last performance on an English
stage, she could not have chosen a role better suited to display the distinctive features of her acting: unusual force, intelligent characterization, and
expert reading of Shakespeare's poetry. Nor could she have found a more
talented company or more appreciative audience than those who wished
her *bon voyage* on August 9, 1851.

Mrs. Warner's performances engendered an excitement among playgoers which continued for several weeks afterward, as two rival actresses
challenged comparison by acting Lady Macbeth: Isabella Glyn at Sadler's
Wells and Helen Faucit at the Olympic. A number of reviews compared
the three actresses. Critics generally agreed that Helen Faucit's grace and
delicacy could not be matched by Mrs. Warner or Miss Glyn, but they
found her deficient in the force required for Lady Macbeth and in the
ability to read Shakespeare's poetry. A critic in the *Stage-Manager* (April
7, 1849) had complained that "she has almost neglected elocution, like
the generality of the modern school, who seem to think it beneath them
to learn how to read." Isabella Glyn was granted superiority in energy,
but many critics disliked her formal style, chanting cadences, and posed
attitudes. Mrs. Warner's acting had some of the same old-fashioned
stiffness, but it was much closer to the taste of her time, though without
the ease of Helen Faucit's acting. She combined unusual power with an
ability to project both the meaning and rhythm of Shakespearean poetry.

In their performances of Lady Macbeth in 1851 both Mrs. Warner and
Miss Glyn had the great advantage of playing in a finished production,
intelligently directed, capably acted in every role, and carefully staged.
Miss Faucit had an inadequate company and makeshift production. The
company at Sadler's Wells had been strengthened this season by the
return of Mrs. Marston and by the engagement of several new actors of
some promise. Frederick Robinson, whom Phelps had found in Edinburgh, made his London debut as Cromwell in *Henry the Eighth,* and
showed himself a good replacement for Dickinson. An experienced comedian, Barrett, had been engaged for leading comic roles; and J. W.
Ray had come to replace Anthony Younge as First Old Man. A young
actress, Fanny Vining, also appeared at Sadler's Wells for the first time.
The yearly appearance of fresh actors, generally unknown to London
audiences, distinguished Phelps's management from others. The star
system had become so firmly entrenched that most managers no longer

tried to maintain a full company of competent actors for minor roles. Playwrights and audiences concentrated their attention upon one or two leading actors and seldom made serious demands upon the supporting cast. A discerning critic writing in the *Theatrical Journal* of July 3, 1851, suggested that the decline of Shakespearean drama could be attributed to the fact that most theatres could no longer supply a sufficient number of actors to fill the cast of a Shakespearean play. In contrast to other theatres Sadler's Wells introduced, trained, and lifted into prominence several new actors each season.

Phelps's avoidance of the star system was put to a severe test in the autumn of 1851 through the opposition of Isabella Glyn, who had returned from the Haymarket. From the beginning she had asked for star billing, which he had refused to grant. He had, however, allowed her to play all the great heroines of the classical repertory and had given her in Cleopatra and the Duchess of Malfi the opportunity to create two important characters for the theatre of her time. As the second play of this season he produced the tragedy *Fazio* so that she might challenge comparison with Charlotte Cushman, who had played its heroine, Bianca, recently in London. Critical approval of her Lady Macbeth and Bianca during the first week of the season led Miss Glyn to refuse to play the Queen in *Hamlet,* which had been announced for the following Monday, August 18, on the grounds that the part was too slight for an actress of her reputation. When Phelps assigned her the role, she is reported to have asked whether John Philip Kemble had ever been asked to play in a pantomime.[27] Phelps, who had suffered much from Miss Glyn's attitude during her three seasons at Sadler's Wells, insisted that she play Queen Gertrude or suffer dismissal for breach of contract. She chose to leave the company.

That she felt herself to be unfairly treated is evident from comments in the *Athenaeum* of August 23.

> In the full tide of theatrical success—and after only one week's exercise of her perfected powers—Miss Glyn's name has been suddenly withdrawn from the bills of Sadler's Wells Theatre. There are rumours abroad to account for the fact which are not very favourable to the management; but it is difficult to believe that they can have been willing parties to their own loss,—for there is no actress on the stage to replace Miss Glyn.

In the following issue there was a letter from Miss Glyn complaining of Phelps's "moral breach of contract" in assigning her a role which she was bound to play only by a formal clause in her contract. She also asserted that she had refused the part on grounds of etiquette, because Phelps required her to "play up to him" as Hamlet. Her charges were answered by a leading article in the *Theatrical Journal* of September 10, in which the editor pointed out that both Mrs. Warner and Laura Addison had played Queen Gertrude at Sadler's Wells. The article contains a statement about the usual interpretation of a contract for "heavy business" in a repertory company:

> A lady who is engaged at a great theatre for leading business, we think, might be allowed, if she particularly objected, to refuse the Queen of Denmark, but in a limited company, where numbers and remuneration have to be fitted according to the prices, the locality can afford to pay . . . the term "heavy" certainly is always expected to include every character in that department, whether ordinary, prominent, or principal.

Phelps was perhaps unwise in dismissing so valuable an actress as Isabella Glyn. Possibly the willingness of most members of his company to accept his practices in casting had accustomed him to an unusual degree of cooperation. Mrs. Warner's recent visit had undoubtedly left its impression of good-natured adaptability to repertory practices. Phelps's own abhorrence of stardom probably made him less sympathetic than some managers to the humors of a prima donna, and he may have been unnecessarily harsh to the ambitious young actress. On the other hand, he could hardly afford to have a leading actress who objected to roles that would normally fall to her lot. His own exacting schedule of work left him little time to meet the emergencies caused by her unexpected objections; and twice before she had left Sadler's Wells abruptly. Nor could he allow the *esprit de corps* which was a major asset of his company to be endangered for the sake of one actress, no matter how great her talents.

Phelps faced a difficult season after her departure. Miss Goddard, who immediately took over the roles of Queen Gertrude and Lady Macbeth, seemed very weak after Isabella Glyn. Fanny Vining, who made her debut as Beatrice in *Much Ado about Nothing,* was young and almost untrained. Phelps gave careful direction to both actresses, coaching them in delivery of the lines and in interpreting roles so they fitted into the total effect of the play. Evidences of his training were noted by reviewers. On November 12, the *Theatrical Journal* cited Miss Vining's satisfactory performances as a good example of his managerial methods:

Her delivery, like Mr. Phelps's, is free from mannerism, each word is understood as she utters it, effect is not strained after. The grand is eschewed for the plain and straightforward, and the poetry is given with a respect for the author and a just appreciation of the theme.

As soon as possible Phelps altered his repertory for the season, choosing plays that contained good roles for the strongest members of his company. A variety of comedies from eighteenth and nineteenth century dramatists featured one member of the company after another. Barrett played Old Dornton, showing the experienced skill of an actor who had been trained in the school of William Dowton and Joseph Munden. J. W. Ray became an excellent Sir Peter Teazle, and then joined Hoskins and Mrs. Marston in *Secrets Worth Knowing,* a comedy by Thomas Morton which had not been seen on the stage for many years. Marston was applauded as St. Pierre in *The Wife,* a role Phelps had played formerly. Another of Knowles's comedies, *The Love Chase,* showed off Helen Fitzpatrick's charm. Frederick Robinson, whose progress in his first season was watched carefully by important reviewers, scored a hit as Claude Melnotte. The *Athenaeum* (November 8, 1851) pronounced him "a great acquisition to the modern stage."

Suitable Shakespearean plays were harder to find. *Henry the Fourth* featured Barrett as a richly humorous Falstaff. *Julius Caesar* with Phelps, Bennett, and Robinson in the leading roles elicited the comment from the *Theatrical Journal* (September 10, 1851) that "we have rarely seen a piece so perfectly cast in all its parts." For a great tragedy that could be played without a strong actress, Phelps looked beyond the usual repertory and decided to concentrate all the resources of his theatre upon a production of *Timon of Athens,* a play generally thought to be lacking in dramatic interest and therefore almost never performed. At Sadler's Wells in a lavish production with excellent acting it proved one of the most successful plays, running thirty-one performances in this season and ten in the revival of 1856–1857.

Sadler's Wells had a second hit this season with a new play called *Ingomar,* by Mrs. Maria Lovell. Although Anderson had produced it at Drury Lane the previous season, Phelps knew that many of his audience could not have seen it. He also felt that it would do no harm to provoke comparison with Drury Lane in the acting and staging of a contemporary play. He was not disappointed. *Ingomar* ran twenty-five nights, and critics made the intended comparison, giving the verdict to Sadler's Wells.

A third major event of this season was Phelps's assumption of the role of Sir Pertinax MacSycophant in *The Man of the World,* which he introduced on the night of Greenwood's annual benefit. From the first night this performance was hailed as a work of genius. Phelps played the role for twenty years, and it was remembered by playgoers well after the turn of the century.

At the end of the season, in May and June, Phelps played Sir Pertinax in Edinburgh, where critics and audience forgave him the "vile libel on the Scottish people" for the sake of its humor and praised his impeccable Scottish dialect. This engagement in Edinburgh and another in Dublin were Phelps's third provincial tour in recent years. In the summer of 1850 he and Laura Addison had appeared in Manchester, where both had given bad performances because of illness. In 1851 he had shared an engagement with Mrs. Warner in Liverpool. During most of his eighteen years as manager, however, Phelps did not seek provincial engagements, preferring to rest in the summer after his long winter season, which ran from August to April.

In the autumn of 1852 as Phelps began his ninth season of management, he was again plagued with the problem of choosing plays that did not require a strong leading actress. Helen Fitzpatrick had joined Isabella Glyn at Drury Lane in a company that was otherwise undistinguished. To replace her Phelps had brought back Fanny Cooper, always a favorite with the Sadler's Wells audience. Mrs. Ternan, his new tragedienne, was a capable actress without great power. The repertory of this season, and indeed for the rest of Phelps's tenure at Sadler's Wells, reflects his difficulty in finding good actresses.

His first production added a new Shakespearean play—his twenty-third—to the list performed at Sadler's Wells. He put on the almost unknown comedy *All's Well That Ends Well,* playing the part of Parolles. It ran for eleven performances, but critics did not like it. One commented that Sadler's Wells had become "a sort of museum for the exhibition of dramatic curiosities," and dubbed the play an Elizabethan crudity.[28]

Phelps had some success with *A Woman Never Vext* and more with *The City Madam,* but he finally turned to *Henry the Fifth* for his major effort. The staging, with medieval pageantry and settings based upon historical research, was a main feature. In choosing a highly patriotic play and in portraying King Henry, Phelps caught the spirit of the fifties, when England's confidence in her strength and superior wisdom among the nations of the world ran high. Audiences filled the theatre, and reviewers spoke of Phelps's Henry as "amongst the very best things which the modern European stage has produced." [29] The play ran four nights a week in November and six nights a week in January.

Even Queen Victoria did not remain indifferent to the strong appeal of the Sadler's Wells *Henry the Fifth* and for the first time commanded Phelps to play in a performance at Windsor Castle. During the past three years when she had been patronizing the theatre through her master of revels, Charles Kean, critics had complained of her neglect of Phelps and Sadler's Wells. On one occasion a royal performance of *Henry the Fourth* had been canceled because Bartley could not appear as Falstaff, and the *Theatrical Journal* (January 31, 1850) had commented that since Phelps had been acting Falstaff for three weeks to crowded houses, he could easily have substituted. Sadler's Wells had been the only theatre in England to give a benefit performance for the Great Exhibition of 1851, donating all the proceeds of the evening to a committee headed by His Royal Highness the Duke of Cambridge. But it was not until January 7, 1853, that Phelps was asked to act at Windsor Castle. That evening he played King Henry in *King Henry the Fourth, Part Two*. On November 10, 1853, the whole Sadler's Wells production of *Henry the Fifth* was transported to Windsor to initiate the dramatic performances of the new season.

One result of Phelps's acting at Windsor was his decision to produce the second part of *Henry the Fourth* at Sadler's Wells, where he played not only the King but Justice Shallow in the same performance. On the first night the theatre was crowded from floor to ceiling to see Phelps in this *tour de force,* and the audience gave unqualified approval to the dual performance as something more than a display of virtuosity in the art of impersonation. The *Morning Advertiser* (March 18, 1853) said that "it shows that plasticity of imagination which can conceive and represent mankind in all its varied and varying phases, and raises the office of the actor into the highest department of literature and the arts."

The Queen's belated recognition of Phelps, however, could not reverse the fashionable trend, which she had helped to establish, away from traditional English drama to the kind of gentlemanly melodrama Charles Kean was presenting at the Princess's Theatre in Oxford Street. It is reported that she was so moved by the suspense of a scene in *Pauline* that she convulsively clutched the draperies of her box until the denouement.[30]

For the elevation of melodrama to a respected place on the English stage, Charles Kean must be given full credit. By gathering a good company, by seeking out skillful contemporary writers and translators, by producing plays with careful direction, elaborate settings, and refined taste, and by making the most of his own talent for the conventions of melodramatic acting, Kean showed playgoers the potentialities of a genre which had previously been consigned, in England, to the lower classes. Enthusiastic response from fashionable audiences triumphed over the complaints of critics who objected to his importation of French plays. A writer in the *Theatrical Journal* (September 21, 1853), decrying the production of *The Corsican Brothers,* attributed its success to the victory of fashion over the real preferences of the playgoing public:

> Why, then may we ask, is this extraordinary and unnatural thing tolerated in preference to the genuine old English drama? Is it because audiences, in our day, have vitiated tastes? I answer no! emphatically no! Phelps's success is proof to the contrary. It is because the public can get nothing better— because the principle actors of the day, the most fashionable, and at the same time the best, are guilty of introducing that description of French trash with which the stage is inundated—and last, not least, our gracious sovereign patronizes it. Were Phelps in royal favour as Kean is, we should soon find such horrid *omelettes* entirely driven from the stage.

When Kean extended French methods of acting and staging to Shakespearean productions, reviewers were further outraged. During the summer recess of 1853 while Kean was in Paris, one jeering critic remarked that possibly he had gone there to get a hippopotamus to use as the serpent of the Nile. When his new season opened with an elaborately staged *Macbeth, Lloyd's Weekly* (October 9, 1853) commented that "in Garrick's day we had a Macbeth without the costume, and now we have the costume without the Macbeth."

Phelps also opened his season of 1853–1854 with a production of *Macbeth,* but he could not compete with the interest generated by Kean's elaborate production. Although he had engaged three new actors (Lunt from Liverpool, Josephs from Edinburgh, and Rousby from Norwich), he could not compensate for the draining off of his actors to West End theatres. Mellon and Graham had gone to the Princess's, Robinson and Williams to the Lyceum, George Bennett and Miss Vining to Drury

Lane. The *Theatrical Journal* described the remnant as "the ghost of a company" compared with former seasons.

Phelps immediately turned to comedy, taking for himself the role of Sir Peter Teazle in *The School for Scandal,* which had been Bennett's, and making it so much his own that he played it until the end of his career. He then put on four almost forgotten comedies: Cibber's *Love Makes a Man,* Bickerstaffe's *The Hypocrite,* Fielding's *The Miser,* and O'Keeffe's *Wild Oats.* For the major production of the season he chose another rarely acted comedy, Shakespeare's *A Midsummer Night's Dream,* which had been seen on the nineteenth-century stage only in versions that emphasized music, ballet, and spectacle. Phelps's production combined his talent for stage design, now fully developed by years of practice, his ability to direct his company with their fullest cooperation, and his own gift for comic characterization (in the role of Bottom). He never had a greater success. He won approval from spectators, critics, and even from his rival manager, Charles Kean, who imitated the production in his own fashion three years later. *Punch* (October 15, 1853) called upon the Queen to journey to Sadler's Wells, "for hitherto our Elizabeth has not visited our Burbidge." Other reviewers urged all London playgoers to see *A Midsummer Night's Dream* at Sadler's Wells.

Apparently Islingtonians needed no urging to attend a major production at Sadler's Wells. During the first week the house was so full of regular patrons that those less experienced in the methods of gaining entrance found no way to get in. *Lloyd's Weekly* apologized on October 16 for the lack of a review and gave the reason that no boxes had been available, the pit had been packed, and the steep staircase to the gallery had been full of those descending after unsuccessful attempts to find space. Comments upon the reaction of the audience to *A Midsummer Night's Dream* are interesting not only for information about the performance but also for a glimpse into the character of this unusual congregation of playgoers. Their silence impressed the reviewer of *Lloyd's Weekly* when he finally got into the theatre:

> It is our firm belief, from the hushed stillness that reigns at times through the house, that one-half the spectators are dreaming without knowing it, and that they only wake up when the curtain drops, and are surprised to find they have a play-bill in their hand. The belief is strengthened by the fact of the unusual sparingness of the applause. All motion, all action, seems to be involuntarily suspended. Occasionally a loud laugh bursts out, but it

is quickly succeeded by a deep stillness, as of midnight sleep. This feeling is something more than the mere reverence of attention. You would suppose from the silence that closes you in like a dark room, that you were all alone, with your senses far away, wandering you knew not where, but watching intently some strange illusion of a man with an ass's head being kissed by a Fairy Queen.

The *Examiner* (October 15, 1853) noted that the behavior of the audience revealed not only a discriminating appreciation but also knowledge of the text of the play:[31]

> The *Midsummer Night's Dream* abounds in the most delicate passages of Shakespeare's verse. The Sadler's Wells pit has a keen enjoyment for them; the pit and gallery were crowded to the farthest wall on Saturday night with a most earnest audience, among whom many a subdued hush arose, not during, but just before, the delivery of the most charming passages.

That the audience was composed of regular patrons, fiercely loyal to Phelps's management and jealous of his reputation in London, is clear from an incident recorded by the same reviewer:

> When Bottom volunteered to roar high or roar low, a voice from the gallery desired to know whether he could "roar like Brooke." Even the gallery at this theatre, however, resents an interruption, and the unexpected sally was not well received.

G. V. Brooke was at this time starring at Drury Lane, where his vehement acting was delighting boisterous audiences described as "a gross discredit to the public taste."

The warm partisanship of the local audience at Sadler's Wells led some stray visitors to mistake its nature. A writer in the *Theatrical Journal* (February 28, 1850) complained that they were indiscriminate:

> Once bring a man to the footlights, and set the gallery going, and stop them who can—the second man then the third, and on they go calling for everybody, almost down to the supernumeraries, dead stock and live stock, talent and mediocrity.

This correspondent had perhaps strayed into the theatre on the opening night of a season or on a Saturday night when the audience was in a holiday mood. It is not unlikely that on some occasions, like the opening night of a season when the theatre had been redecorated over the summer, that they applauded the dead stock as well as the live stock.

The *esprit de corps* of the audience and its unusual character emphasized the widening gulf between Sadler's Wells and the theatres of central London. Its taste for the now old-fashioned "legitimate" drama and
its status as lower class combined to make Sadler's Wells a backwater,
cut off from the main current of the English theatrical world. *Punch,*
in its review of *A Midsummer Night's Dream,* called Phelps a national
schoolmaster, meaning to emphasize the excellence of his interpretations
of England's greatest poet (and also to contrast his repertory with the
predominantly French fare at fashionable theatres), but many writers
regarded Phelps primarily as an educator of the underprivileged, as if
his greatest achievement was an increase in the cultural level of his audience. A patronizing attitude toward the audience is evident even in
laudatory descriptions of its behavior, as in this one by Henry Morley
in 1857:

> The aspect and behaviour of the pit and gallery at Sadler's Wells during
> the performance of one of Shakespeare's plays cannot fail to impress most
> strongly every visitor who is unaccustomed to the place. There sit our
> working classes in a happy crowd, as orderly and reverent as if they were
> at church, and yet as unrestrained in their enjoyment as if listening to
> stories told them by their own firesides.[32]

That the spectators displayed an aesthetic appreciation far superior to
most audiences is confirmed by many commentators. Sir Henry Irving
long afterward described the intermissions at Sadler's Wells as "one
humming aesthetic debating party," where members of the audience discussed the merits of play and cast.[33] The *Athenaeum* (March 3, 1855) in
reviewing a performance of *Macbeth* remarked upon the numerous spectators "who, with book in hand, followed every verse of the poem as
pronounced by the actor, sometimes criticizing the form of expression,
and always attentive to the lights and shades of emphasis." The *Morning
Advertiser* (November 17, 1856) remarked that the audience watched
"every action of their favourite actors with eagerness, and with an appreciation that bespeaks a cultivated connoiseurship." In drama they preferred the poetic to the frivolous and sensational; in acting they preferred
the intellectual and natural to the melodramatic and artificial. Morley
once noted that "they do not applaud rant at Sadler's Wells." [34]

Their preference for serious drama was clearly shown in the spring
of 1855, when Charles Mathews brought the Lyceum company to act at
Sadler's Wells during the recess. His plays were light comedies trans-

lated from French originals, and his acting was the "free-and-easy" style (in the *Athenaeum*'s phrase). The engagement was a total failure because attendance fell sharply after the first few performances. The explanation offered by the *Athenaeum* (April 28, 1855) for the audience's lack of interest is extremely interesting:

> With an audience composed of persons engaged in the real struggle of life, and sternly occupied in daily efforts "to keep the wolf from the door," the serious drama is preferable to the comic, and the poetic element the very thing that has the needful influence and the fitting interest.

To contemporary American ears, long accustomed to the argument that frivolities of stage and screen must be provided for businessmen because the hard work of their daily lives leaves them too exhausted for intellectual entertainment, this Victorian explanation sounds strange indeed. In 1855, the inhabitants of Islington, who worked long hours six days a week and were further burdened with the financial and human expense of the Crimean War, are said to have no taste for light comedy and farce because they felt an understandable need for serious drama and poetry.

It should be noted that the Victorian words and tone used to describe the social class of the Sadler's Wells audience are apt to mislead twentieth-century readers. "Workingmen" does not mean day laborers, although such a distinction meant less in 1850 than it does now, especially to some of the literary men who visited Sadler's Wells. A commentator of more plebeian background writing in the *Theatrical Journal* of December 3, 1851 described the audience somewhat differently: "Theatres, . . . like railroad carriages, have three divisions, and the aristocracy at the Opera, the middle class at Sadler's Wells, and the mechanics at the saloons, are those on whom they must rely for support." *Punch* (November 20, 1847), facetiously complaining that "the theatres have all become so proper!" said, "You have the Pumps of Islington going to a playhouse which they would formerly have been shocked to be seen in." It is evident from such remarks that the audience of Sadler's Wells was drawn from a higher social level than the term "working classes" seems to imply. Reviewers sometimes commented that it was a more "respectable" class than audiences of the Standard and the Surrey.

Greenwood, who had lived all his life in Islington, knew the tastes and habits of this audience. It was he who persuaded Phelps not to play on Friday and Saturday nights, because he knew from experience that most middle-class Islingtonians would not go to the theatre on those two nights.[35] According to John Coleman, Greenwood filled the house by giving out free tickets, but the actual receipts for Friday and Saturday were always very low, between 12 and 20 pounds.

On other nights of the week, although the gallery was almost entirely composed of local inhabitants, the pit and the boxes contained regular patrons from other parts of London. In the words of Phelps's nephew, the aristocracy of every grade except that of birth was represented. For a brief moment in 1854 it appeared that even the aristocracy of birth might patronize Sadler's Wells. Dickens had undertaken a suit to Colonel Phipps, the new Master of Revels, asking for a royal visit to Sadler's Wells and had almost persuaded Phelps that the request would be granted, although the manager jokingly objected that he had no royal box and that a wall would have to be pulled down to provide a suitable entrance. On February 25, 1854, Dickens wrote the following note to Phelps:

My Dear Sir,
    You will not have to pull down that wall. I am sorry to inform you that the difficulties in the way of the Queen's coming to Sadler's Wells are unsurmountable. But a very just reference is made to you and the theatre in Colonel Phipps's letter.
    Will you come here to-morrow an hour before dinner—that is to say, at five—and let us again review the circumstances?
                                        Faithfully yours always,
                                        Charles Dickens.[36]

And so the Sadler's Wells audience continued to be "totally removed from all fashionable influence."

Although this unfashionableness did immense harm to the reputation of Sadler's Wells both during the time of Phelps's management and ever since, it had little influence upon dramatic critics. Most reviewers protested the effect of aristocratic fashion upon the theatre of the fifties. Their most vehement attacks centered upon the Princess's, which they felt held its high place more because of royal favor than the quality of its productions. The *Examiner* (October 14, 1854) complained that "an excellent play by Mr. Douglas Jerrold, *A Heart of Gold,* has been inadequately, we might almost say contemptuously presented" by Charles Kean's company. The *Athenaeum* (February 25, 1854) castigated Kean for using

Cibber's version of *Richard the Third,* asserting that Sadler's Wells had proved Shakespeare's play to be more effective on the stage. *Lloyd's Weekly* (November 12, 1854) headed a review with the title "Old Clothes at the Princess's" and said that the French piece then being presented had been worn to tatters at the Standard and was now just a thread upon which Kean had hung a series of striking tableaux.

In contrast, their praise of productions at Sadler's Wells frequently occupied several columns and contained thoughtful dramatic criticism inspired by a new understanding of the play through the interpretation given by the performance being reviewed. Six or seven of London's dramatic critics might be described as champions of Sadler's Wells, so frequently and consistently did they praise its performances. The *Theatrical Journal* (April 5, 1854) once protested the "great laudations of the press" and even suggested that one, unnamed, journal must have a financial interest in the theatre.

During the mid-fifties Phelps's management reached the peak of its reputation. A tone of self congratulation was evident in the Christmas pantomime of 1854, which satirized the kinds of amusement offered at other theatres and described Sadler's Wells as the upholder of poetic drama. Phelps and Greenwood had good cause to be proud of the record of their first ten years, in which more than a hundred major plays had been produced. But in this very record can be seen the reason for the beginning of a decline in subsequent years. The repertory of the classic English drama had been nearly exhausted, and there was no new drama of the same genre. More frequent repetition of plays produced in earlier seasons was inevitable, and the few unfamiliar plays that could be added to the repertory were almost certain to be less interesting than earlier productions.

Charles Kean had a distinct advantage in the novelty of melodrama and its supply of new plays—new, at least, to English audiences. One reviewer suggested to Phelps that since the supply of five-act plays was limited, he should enliven his repertory at the end of the season by using some of the plentiful French importations. That such a course would not have interested the audience is indicated by the empty houses which greeted the Lyceum, Adelphi, and Olympic companies when they leased Sadler's Wells in quick succession during the summer of 1855. In fact, Phelps's management continued to be financially profitable throughout its eighteen years, while Webster lost money at the Haymarket, the

Mathewses had to give up their management of the Lyceum, and the Keans retired with heavy losses from the Princess's after nine years.

In the spring of 1853 Mrs. Warner returned from America, incurably ill and in financial distress from her husband's misadventures. After seeing her, Phelps wrote the following letter to Macready, who was now living in retirement at Sherborne and mourning his wife's death:

8, Canonbury Square, Islington
July 21st, 1853

My Dear Sir,

I have within these few days been inexpressibly shocked by hearing from her husband the sad recital of Mrs. Warner's sufferings in America, and her present melancholy condition. During the period of, and since, my business connection with her, I have held in the highest respect and esteem her fine womanly character; indeed, before her departure for the United States I had regarded her with almost the affection of a brother. Not until yesterday could I nerve myself to see her;—the interview I shall never forget; she looks death in the face with the meekness of a Christian and the courage of a hero—as beautiful in face as ever; talked of her approaching end without a tremor; told me what a load of parental care you had generously eased her of (God bless you for it!); then hoped that our future meetings would be regarded as preparatory of her return to America, and kept me listening more than an hour while she related anecdotes of her late experiences there.

Although she said but little on the subject, I am certain that a necessity exists for increasing her pecuniary means. A benefit night at Drury Lane instantly suggested itself to me, and I lose no time in asking your opinion on the subject, and begging also the assistance of your advice. How should it be announced to the public, &c.?

I am sure, my dear Sir, you will pardon my troubling you. Knowing somewhat of your regard for Mrs. Warner, I have not hesitated to do so. I conceive that whatever is done should take place immediately, as the London season is drawing to a close.

I hope you will not deem it an impertinence if I say how deeply I have sympathized with you under your bereavement, and that I am,

My dear Sir,
Ever gratefully and faithfully yours,
Samuel Phelps[37]

W. C. Macready, Esq.

Macready answered with approval, but warned against the difficulties of getting prominent actors to combine in a single performance. Nevertheless, Phelps worked for many months, taking time from his own affairs, attempting to arrange a great benefit night at Drury Lane. When he had to abandon the plan, he formed a committee of prominent actors to solicit contributions to a fund for Mrs. Warner, but no large sum was collected. On December 28, 1853, the *Theatrical Journal* reported that proceedings against Mrs. Warner in the Insolvent Debtors Court had revealed the fact that Phelps had paid 147 pounds to her creditors to preserve her household furniture for her. Finally, in September, 1854, he invited Charlotte Cushman, who was currently starring at the Haymarket, to join him at Sadler's Wells in a performance for the benefit of Mrs. Warner. The American actress generously agreed to play Queen Katherine to Phelps's Wolsey, and with the loyal support of playgoers the benefit was "successful beyond expectation," according to the *Theatrical Journal*. Within a week, however, Mrs. Warner died, and the money intended for her own needs and for her children's future security was claimed by her husband's creditors.

That Phelps was worried and frustrated by the whole affair is evident from Macready's letters to him during these months.[38] The friendship that grew between them must have been some compensation for his other grief; and he must have enjoyed playing with Charlotte Cushman, since he had been several years without an actress of the first rank.

The main business of the season, 1854–1855, was a spectacular production of *Pericles,* which occupied much of Phelps's time. The theatre was closed one night to allow time for final mounting on the stage, and the play ran two months without interruption. It was Phelps's attempt to compete with Charles Kean's revivals at the Princess's, where a magnificent version of Byron's *Sardanapalus* was currently playing. Although the attempt was a success with critics and at the box office, Phelps never again put on a similar spectacle. Perhaps his dislike of playing the same role for many consecutive nights was a primary reason, since the elaborate scenery prevented the usual alternation of repertory. During the rest of his management he returned to the old system, with two or three plays a week.

A rash of failures among theatrical managements in 1855 indicates that audiences had fallen off with the advent of war. Charles Mathews, confessing financial ruin, give up the Lyceum. Laura Seymour and the author Charles Reade, with a strong company including Isabella Glyn, George Vandenhoff, and Barry Sullivan failed at the St. James's. Charles

7. Macready as Macbeth. Portrait by Henry Inman. The Metropolitan Museum of Art, Rogers Fund, 1906.

8. Phelps as Macbeth. From a daguerreotype by Paine of Islington. Courtesy Harvard Theatre Collection.

THEATRE ROYAL.

Sadler's Wells

Lessees, — Messrs. GREENWOOD and PHELPS.

UNDER THE MANAGEMENT OF

Mr. PHELPS.

Monday, Oct. 22, Tuesday 23, Wednesday 24, & Thursday 25

Will be presented (**First Time at this Theatre**) the Tragedy of

ANTONY AND CLEOPATRA

FROM THE TEXT OF SHAKSPERE,

WITH NEW SCENERY, DRESSES AND DECORATIONS.

The Scenery - by - Mr. F. FENTON.

Marc Antony,			Mr. PHELPS
Octavius Cæsar,	Triumvirs of Rome,		Mr. G. K. DICKINSON
M. Æmilius Lepidus,			Mr. HOSKINS
Sextus Pompeius,	— Mr. HENRY MARSTON		
Domitius Enobarbus,			Mr. G. BENNETT
Ventidius,			Mr SCOLEY
Eros,			Mr GRAHAM
Scarus,	Friends to Antony,		Mr FROST
Dercetas,			Mr SMYTHSON
Demetrius,			Mr THOMAS
Philo,			Mr MARCHANT
Mæcenas,			Mr HAMILTON
Agrippa,			Mr H. MELLON
Dolabella,			Mr RIVERS
Proculeius,	Friends to Cæsar,		Mr WILKINS
Thyreus,			Mr H. LEE
Gallus,			Mr DOLMAN
Menas,			Mr KNIGHT
Menecrates,	Friends to Pompey,		Mr W. PITT
Varrius,			Mr FRANKS
Canidius,	(Lieutenant General to Antony)		Mr HARRIS
Euphronius, (an Ambassador from Antony to Cæsar) Mr KENDALL			
Mardian,			Mr BELFORD
Alexis,	Attendants on Cleopatra,		Mrs GRAHAM
Diomedes,			Mr C. FENTON
A Soothsayer, — Mr WILLIAMS	A Clown, — Mr HENRY NYE		
Officers, Sentinels, Messengers, Eunuchs, Guards, Dancers, &c.			
Cleopatra,	(Queen of Egypt)		Miss GLYN
Octavia,	(Sister to Cæsar, and Wife to Antony) Miss ALDRIDGE		
Charmian,			Miss T. BASSANO
Iras,	Attendants on Cleopatra,		Mrs G. SMITH.

Scene : — Dispersed in several parts of the Roman Empire.

To conclude with (for the Third Time) a Farce, by W. MONCRIEFF, entitled The

MISTRESS of the MILL.

Marquis of Pretengil,			Mr H. MELLON
Corney Poppy,			Mr HENRY NYE
Clem,			Mr FRANKS
Matchioness of Pretengil,			Mrs G. SMITH
Flora Granger,			Miss JULIA ST. GEORGE

On FRIDAY and SATURDAY, will be performed for the First Time at this Theatre,

Mrs. CESTLIVRE's Comedy of

THE BUSY BODY

To be followed by a New Farce, entitled

THE FIRST OF MAY

WITH OTHER ENTERTAINMENTS.

Stage Manager, Mr PHELPS,   Acting Manager, Mr T. L. GREENWOOD,
Scene Painter, Mr F. FENTON   The Properties, by Mr HARVEY
Machinist, Mr CAWDERY   The Costumes, by Mr COOMBES and Miss BAILEY
Musical Director,   Mr W. H. MONTGOMERY

BOXES : — First Circle, 3s.   Second ditto, 2s.   PIT, 1s.   GALLERY, 6d.

Half-Price to Boxes only, at Nine o'Clock.

PRIVATE BOXES, £1.1s. & £1.11s.6d. to be obtained on application to Mr AUSTIN, Junr. at the Box-Office; at Mr SAMS' Library,
St James's Street; Mr MITCHELL, Royal Library, Old Bond Street; Mr ANDREWS, New Bond Street; Mr EBERS, Bow
Street; Mr ALLCROFT, Bond Street; and at the Carlton Library 12, Regent Street.
The BOX-OFFICE open from 11 till 3, under the direction of Mr. AUSTIN, Junr.   Bill Inspector, Mr. PHILLIPS.
Children under 3 Years of Age, cannot be admitted, and all Children entering the PIT must pay the Full Price of Admission.
Doors open at Half-past 6, the Entertainments to commence precisely at 7.   S.G. Fairbrother, Printer, 31, Bow Street, Covent Garden

9. Playbill for the first night of *Antony and Cleopatra*, 1849. Courtesy Harvard
Theatre Collection.

10. Daguerreotype portrait of Phelps by Paine. From Tallis's *Drawing-Room Table Book*, 1851. Courtesy Harvard Theatre Collection.

Kean kept an elaborate production of *Henry the Eighth* on his stage for the unprecedented run of a hundred consecutive nights to dwindling houses and complained of heavy losses. A gloomy description of theatrical conditions which appeared in the *Athenaeum* (April 7, 1855) asserted that only in suburban theatres was there any sign of dramatic interest. This assessment was borne out during the summer of 1855 when Isabella Glyn and Henry Marston played at the Standard in *Antony and Cleopatra* and drew capacity crowds from the Shoreditch area. Across the river Creswick and Phelps, alternating in the principal roles of *Othello* and *Julius Caesar,* filled the Surrey.

During the next four seasons dramatic interest centered on Sadler's Wells and the Princess's, the only theatres in London which consistently performed plays and maintained high standards of production. Although both acted Shakespeare, the methods of the two theatres were so different that critics and playgoers generally showed a decided preference for one over the other. Macready, for instance, making his first entrance into a playhouse since his retirement, visited Sadler's Wells in the autumn of 1855 and wrote Phelps a letter of warm congratulation which contained such bitter remarks about Charles Kean's management that Phelps destroyed it.[39]

Another distinguished visitor came to Sadler's Wells in this season, the German novelist Theodor Fontane. He had come to London with a deep interest in the English theatre, particularly in performances of Shakespeare. After attending the Haymarket and the Lyceum he dismissed them as foreign theatres devoted to French plays, Spanish dancers, Italian opera, and Continental magicians. He went to the Princess's to see Kean's *Henry the Eighth,* and there he found a new Shakespeare— a Shakespeare used as a picture gallery and an excuse for ballet and music, with settings created by the joint effort of numismatists, archaeologists, and theatrical machinists. He wrote a review of *Henry the Eighth* for a Berlin newspaper, *Deutsches Kunstblatt.* Then he went to Sadler's Wells, where he became a regular visitor for two seasons as he studied Phelps's methods. From 1855 to 1857 he reviewed six of Phelps's productions for *Deutsches Kunstblatt* and in 1860 he published his reviews along with a general discussion of the English theatre in a long essay entitled *Die Londoner Theater.*[40] His comments are valuable not only for the detailed descriptions of performances at Sadler's Wells but also for the insights of a foreigner's view of the English stage.

Fontane was surprised by Charles Kean's emphasis on spectacle, but after further acquaintance with the London theatre he decided that Kean had adopted a good method for overcoming the apathy of the educated classes toward English drama. He felt that Kean had kept the fashionable theatre from being overwhelmed by French melodrama, or as he called it *Pointiertheithen* (point making).[41] It seemed good to keep Shakespeare, however changed, on the stage, and he found that the Princess's was a step on the way to Sadler's Wells, the true Shakespearean theatre.[42] On the small Islington stage he found much to interest him and much that seemed to him superior to the great court theatre of Berlin, where actors were supported by the state and therefore free of the tyranny of financial success. The position of Sadler's Wells as a *Volksbühne* (people's theatre) was a revelation to Fontane, who knew Shakespeare only as a playwright for educated audiences. The evident enthusiasm and comprehension of Islingtonians convinced him that German productions of Shakespeare were too refined and gentlemanly.

The three things that impressed Fontane most about Sadler's Wells were the remarkable use of settings, the direction of plays by a single intelligence, and the appeal of Shakespeare to many levels of society. He liked the immediacy, the sense of being within the scene, that he found at Sadler's Wells in contrast to the German court theatres, which tended to remove the scene from the audience. After seeing Phelps's productions he concluded that the court theatres had too much space and too much money. He also realized that a director could exercise much more power than was generally believed. The unity, coherence, and balance of performances at Sadler's Wells were unknown in the Berlin theatre.[43] Although he thought that freedom from financial necessity gave German actors the opportunity to develop superior talent, he saw that it also allowed them to emphasize individual interpretations at the expense of the total effect. He rated Phelps as an actor somewhat below Emil Devrient and other great German actors, but he had never found in Berlin the character development, consistency, and inner unity of Phelps's Macbeth, Hamlet, and Falstaff.[44]

This season Phelps introduced two new actresses. Fontane remarks that Margaret Eburne made a rather robust Ophelia but approved her naturalness as Miranda. He really admired Emma Atkinson, a promising tragedienne, whom Phelps was training for the most demanding Shakespearean roles. By the end of the season she was playing Portia, Hermione, and Constance, and in 1856 she undertook Lady Macbeth.

Having found a competent actress, Phelps plunged into an unusually varied repertory. In 1856–1857 he produced fourteen Shakespearean plays, two of them for the first time. In contrast to the long runs at the Princess's, no play was given more than four consecutive performances even though one (*Timon*) was elaborately staged and another (*The Merry Wives*) proved highly attractive to audiences. Interspersed between Shakespearean performances were seventeen other plays of the old legitimate repertory. Phelps himself assumed the widest range of characters, from the irrepressible Falstaff to the misanthropic Timon, from the intellectual Hamlet to the grossly sensual and stupid Christopher Sly, and from the open-hearted Othello to the haughty Coriolanus. In producing *The Taming of the Shrew* Phelps used all five acts and noted on the playbills that it was the twenty-ninth Shakespearean play to appear at Sadler's Wells. In the same season Charles Kean was playing Richard II in a version of the play so drastically cut, in order to give time for lavish spectacle, that much of the meaning was obscure.

Kean drew fashionable audiences, including aristocracy and royalty, but Phelps won the approval of most critics, who preferred his traditional methods to the spectacular productions and new style of acting used by Kean. The *Weekly Dispatch* (September 7, 1856) was sarcastic about the realism of Kean's *Pizarro* and remarked the next week about Phelps's *Macbeth* that "the scenery and the imitations of atmospheric phenomena were excellent, but did not by an undue prominence obscure the beauties of the text." The *Morning Advertiser* (October 13, 1856) condemned Kean's emphasis upon spectacle and specifically contrasted it with the productions at Sadler's Wells:

> The difference between the exhibitions in Oxford Street and Sadler's Wells is exactly this; because at the head of one is a showman, who as lavishly illustrates Pizarro as Macbeth, whilst at the other is an artist, who, though he archaeologically illustrates his author, never forgets that better are bare boards and immovable scenery, with the fervour and genius that can delineate human character and passion, than an overwhelming show that dwarfs the meagre actor to an *homunculus*. Elevating still-life over historic and histrionic ability, and giving to stocks and stones the position of genius and poetry, is a misuse of dramatic art.

The *Examiner* (October 18, 1856) praised the emphasis on poetry rather than scenery at Sadler's Wells and declared that "Shakespeare is not fairly heard when he is made to speak from behind masses of theatrical upholstery."

At the end of this season Phelps was persuaded to make one of his rare public appearances outside the theatre in order to act as chairman of the annual Theatrical Fund Dinner, a philanthropic occasion used to raise money for retired and needy actors. If one can judge from the abstract of the proceedings he was a gracious and well-spoken chairman.[45] His plea for support of the pension fund is interesting for its insistence upon the worthiness of the actor's profession. Unlike Macready, Phelps believed that the theatre was a high calling, "as delightful, as humanizing—ay, and as noble an art, when rightly directed, as can employ the faculties, mental and physical, of man." He defended acting from the charge that its impermanence makes it less important than other arts by arguing that it reaches many men at once and relates them to each other in a common, vivid perception.

> What other artist can, as it were, by a single stroke of his wand electrify the heart and brain of assembled thousands—strike a chord that is felt by all at once in a multitude, compelling them involuntarily to acknowledge their common nature, and wonder at the power that thus exposes them to each other in all the fullness of their humanity?

He asked for the support of the public at large for the Theatrical Fund on the grounds that "civilization, in exercising her influences upon great masses of the people, can receive no higher aid than that rendered her by dramatic exhibition."

Later in the evening Charles Dickens proposed a toast to Phelps, giving a laudatory review of his contributions to the English theatre, noting especially his devotion to Shakespeare, his liberal payments to authors of contemporary plays, and his "sensible subservience of the scene-painter and the mechanist to the real meaning of the play."

It is clear from the tone of Dickens's speech and from the account of the cheers which followed it that the theatrical profession had chosen this occasion to express its admiration for Phelps. He received few honors in his life, partly because he did not seek them, but he must have enjoyed this demonstration of warm regard from his fellow actors. He responded to the toast in a friendly, humorous, and modest tone, admitting to his nervousness and remarking that it was the second time in his life he had ever entered a public room. In the course of his short speech he recounted an anecdote about sending his youngest daughter to a private school in Islington from which she was abruptly dismissed one day, after six months of excellent work and exemplary behavior:

> Good God! I thought, what is amiss? What horrid crime can that little wretch have perpetrated? (Laughter.) Her mother started off in alarm, and had an interview with the school mistress, who thus explained herself: "I have under my roof three young ladies, sisters—daughters, Mrs. Phelps, of a gentleman who is an immediate neighbour of yours. He has been to me, and threatened to remove his three daughters from under my roof if I persist in receiving little Miss Phelps as a pupil, for he will not allow his children to be educated under the same roof with an actor's." (Laughter.) Gentlemen, the moral of this story is, that either in honouring my name as you have just done, you have evidently committed a great error, or the gentleman in question acted the part of a great fool. (Cheers and laughter.)

The long-standing prejudice of Puritan morality against play-acting was still felt in 1850. Phelps and the hard working members of the theatrical profession could laugh at such prejudice from their position of respectability, but only a few decades earlier when the lobbies of the great theatres were used by prostitutes for solicitation and the audiences of the minor theatres were rowdy, the anecdote would not have seemed ridiculous. Phelps himself, by his management of Sadler's Wells, had taken a great step in establishing the worth and serious purpose of theatres.

By 1857 there were unmistakable signs of a new kind of theatre emerging in London. The Haymarket had a success with Tom Taylor's three-act play *An Unequal Match,* following the trend set by his *Masks and Faces* toward a new drama. At the Olympic Frederick Robson was transforming burlesque into something new, attracting full houses and a royal command.

Phelps, seeming to fly in the face of contemporary taste, chose *Love's Labour's Lost* for the important production of his season. A comedy of leisure and wit, with only the slightest plot, and lacking any major role, Shakespeare's comedy would seem to offer little to Victorian audiences, who had a strongly developed taste for exciting incident, spectacular show, farcical comedy, and favorite stars. Not even the charming Vestris had been able to interest London playgoers in *Love's Labour's Lost* when she used it for her opening at Covent Garden in 1839. Nevertheless, at

Sadler's Wells it proved the most successful Shakespearean play of the season, and reviewers found it thoroughly enchanting.

The acquisition of a new actress, Mrs. Charles Young, from Australia, and the return of Helen Fitzpatrick had strengthened the company in comedy. Comments upon the excellence of Marston's Biron (Berowne) bewailed the fact that the new generation of actors had not been trained to play Shakespeare's gentlemen with such grace and understanding. Phelps as Don Adriano, Robinson as the King, Ball and Megreason as the Clowns, and even Williams's young daughter as Moth were important to the success of the play. "Rarely have so many parts been so well played," John Oxenford commented at the end of his long review in the *Times* (October 1, 1857). But perhaps the most important factor in the success of *Love's Labour's Lost* was, as the *Athenaeum* recognized, the discriminating audience that nightly filled the pit of Sadler's Wells. It is a rare group of playgoers who can relish three hours of sophisticated wit, no matter how skillfully delivered by accomplished Shakespearan actors.

In January, 1858, Phelps and his company received a distinction that surprised the fashionable as well as the theatrical world of London. It was announced that they would perform *Macbeth* at Her Majesty's Theatre as the opening play of the festival in celebration of the marriage of the Princess Royal to the Crown Prince of Prussia. No one familiar with the Queen's taste mistook the occasion as a belated recognition of Sadler's Wells, and in fact this mark of royal favor fell upon Phelps only because Charles Kean had refused to act for the festival. He had been affronted at his displacement by Phipps as the Queen's master of revels. An editorial in the *Times* (January 20, 1858) reveals the attitude of the aristocracy toward the relative position of Phelps and Kean:

> By histrionic genius, matured of late years to its highest degree of perfection, and by a splendid style of stage management, that has made the production of each succeeding season eclipse its predecessor, Mr. Charles Kean has made the Princess's Theatre the acknowledged home of the Shakespearian drama. . . . No one could indeed, ignore the unquestionable merits of Mr. Phelps in raising the character of Sadler's-wells, and implanting a veneration for Shakespeare in a public previously accustomed to lower forms of the drama. But, setting all other considerations aside, it is still impossible to regard the Pentonville district as the focus of the metropolitan drama.

Perhaps the tone of the editorial, reinforced by the quaint misspelling of the theatre's name, provoked the following reply in the *Islington Gazette* on January 30:

> The *Times* says that a Shakespearean play without Mr. Kean is like a "Lord Mayor's Show without the Lord Mayor." The resemblance between the Lord Mayor's Show and a Shakespearean tragedy (by Kean) is complete enough: but who goes to see the Lord Mayor? . . . Mr. Kean and his imitators are investing with a meretricious splendour the remains of a drama whose vitality they have helped to destroy. . . . We have only space now to express our astonishment that amongst all the reasons alleged, and the surmises as to the reasons, for the omission of Mr. Kean's name on the occasion, the very simple one that he cannot act Macbeth, and could not easily transport to Her Majesty's the stage properties which at the Princess's he shows in lieu of it, does not seem to have occurred to any one.[46]

The performance itself was of less interest than the controversy it had aroused. The old stage version of *Macbeth,* with a full complement of singing witches, was chosen. The distinguished audience who gathered at the theatre had not come to watch the play. The *Times* remarked that the slight to Kean did not matter because after the royal party arrived, deep in the second act, no one looked at the stage. Perhaps Helen Faucit, who played Lady Macbeth, was offended by the inattention of the audience, since she evidently carried away unpleasant memories of the occasion. In her book *On Some of Shakespeare's Female Characters,* published after Phelp's death, she attacked him as an unfair actor who upstaged her in this performance.

In this season and the next Phelps continued to put on at Sadler's Wells a variety of comedies, featuring the same actors as those in *Love's Labour's Lost.* He included several that were rarely performed: *The Clandestine Marriage* (Colman and Garrick), *The Provoked Husband* (Vanbrugh and Cibber), *The Wheel of Fortune* (Cumberland), and *The Hypocrite* (Bickerstaffe). Reviewers praised the acting and commented upon the uniqueness of a theatre which depended upon acting for its major interest. The *Weekly Dispatch* (October 31, 1858) spoke of the singularly good voices in the company:

> Every man down to a messenger has a sonorous tone. The verse is not only delivered sensibly [with a sense of its meaning], but with such appropriate music.

In training his company to read Shakespeare, Phelps was considerably helped by the encouragement of an intelligent audience. The *Times* (October 23, 1858) commented upon this fact:

> It is already generally known that the audience of Sadler's Wells Theatre is one of the most appreciative on record, and recognizes points which would elsewhere pass totally unobserved.

Sadler's Wells continued to be regarded as a school for actors, even though the gulf between the West End and Islington had widened. The *Weekly Dispatch* (November 21, 1858) in praising Mrs. Young's performance of Charlotte in *The Hypocrite,* makes this clear:

> Anything more playful or more pointed, more buoyant or more sweetly wilful, we have not had the pleasure of beholding for some years. It was a very faithful and finished effort, and served to deepen the conviction which we share with so many others, of the injustice which keeps this lady from a home at the West End. We are aware of the fellow injustice—the robbery thereby of this theatre of her services; but really this is a penalty Mr. Phelps must be content to pay. His theatre is almost the only school of acting in the metropolis, and for some years past we have been accustomed to see the birds trained in his nest take wing westward as soon as he had taught them self-sustainment.

The reviewer's cavalier attitude indicates Phelps's problem in holding good actresses in his unfashionable theatre. At the end of the season Mrs. Young did fly west, where she began a distinguished career.

After the theatre closed on March 15, 1859, Phelps did a surprising thing. He took the regular members of his company and the scenery for seven Shakespearean productions, along with the pantomine of the season, on a tour of the principal cities of Germany. Touring companies were practically unknown in England at the time. Even in America companies had not yet begun to travel. It is hard to understand how a man who was timid about financial risk should have decided upon such a tour, particularly in Germany where the lack of a central government made it impossible to conduct the arrangements through a single agent. The German theatres of the times were court theatres, maintained by the rulers of each section. They were far above Sadler's Wells in financial resources, in size, and in social position. One can only guess at the impulse which led him to assume the expense of transporting his unfashionable little suburban theatre to the great stages that were the pride of German's upper classes. There is no sign either in Fontane's writing or in Phelps's biography that the opinions of the distinguished German critic had reached Phelps's ears. In fact Fontane reports that the appearance of the Sadler's Wells company in Berlin during April, 1859, caused him some anxiety.[47] He writes that he felt like a brother who has extoled the beauties of his absent sister and is suddenly confronted with her appearance among his friends. He feared that the productions which he had found exciting in London and which he had praised highly in reviews in the *Deutsches Kunstblatt* would not inspire equal enthusiasm in the coolly critical audience of Berlin's court theatre.

Indeed, Phelps's opening performance as Othello received only mild approval in Berlin. This partial failure was almost certainly the result of Phelps's usual first-night nervousness. That he still suffered from this old malady, even at Sadler's Wells before a familiar audience, is indicated by a comment in the *Athenaeum* on September 24 of this same year:

> We must recollect that it was the first night of the play; and Mr. Phelps has been frequently inferior on first nights in characters in which subsequently he has won a distinguished reputation.

In Berlin Phelps undoubtedly faced his first night with more than usual dread and therefore played Othello with a constricted voice and stiffness of manner. His second performance, as King Lear, at once counteracted the poor initial impression. A German review (translated into English) which appeared in the *Theatrical Journal* (April 20, 1859) makes this clear:

> If Mr. Phelps, the English Tragedian, by the choice of his first appearance in *Othello* has to a certain degree weakened the great fame which preceded him, he has splendidly restored it in *King Lear*. We do not remember ever since the days of Ludwig Devrient to have received such a powerful impression by the performance of a great tragedy, as the one received at that representation of our guest. We will not deny that we waited with a certain degree of anxiety for the raising of the curtain, lest we should meet again that monotonous, ever-repeating sound of a seemingly artistic declamation with which we were plagued in *Othello,* even to nervous excitement. But we found ourselves agreeably deceived. . . . The first scene . . . gave at once, as our guest performed it, the most perfect insight to that powerful character.

Fontane says that subsequent productions (*Hamlet; Macbeth; Henry the Fourth, Part One; The Merchant of Venice;* and *The Merry Wives*)

were hits which kept the interest of the public rising constantly to the
end of the engagement.

German audiences were accustomed to look for individual scenes and
actors as deserving particular praise, but they found in the Sadler's Wells
company that the *ensemble,* the cooperative effort, was more important
than the individual parts. Miss Atkinson was praised for her Portia,
Robinson for his Bassanio, Miss Eburne for her Cordelia, Belford and
Ray for their comic roles; but the over-all unity of the performances made
the usual kind of criticism irrelevant. The artistry of one actor never
intruded upon the total effect.

One other aspect of the performances which struck German critics
was the staging. Certain scenes were pronounced to be masterpieces of
theatrical production which deserved careful study. More important than
any particular scenes, however, was Phelps's use of staging to interpret
the play. They were surprised at his use of scenery and lighting to set a
mood and give unity to the whole. Fontane quotes a leading critic as
saying that the Sadler's Wells performances "have given us for the first
time a clear understanding of Shakespeare's effectiveness in the theatre
and of the magic of his poetry designed also for the eye." [48]

The Sadler's Wells company was well received in Berlin. Critical interest centered in the Shakespearean plays, but apparently the pantomime
was also successful. A report in the *Theatrical Journal* (May 11, 1859)
said that this thoroughly English form of entertainment with its combination of spectacle, burlesque, ballet, and music charmed a German
audience which included the Prince and Princess of Prussia. Reviews say
nothing about the size of the audiences, perhaps because German actors
were not dependent for their livelihood on nightly receipts. For Phelps
this was the most important consideration, since he had to measure success in financial terms; and he was disappointed in the size of the
houses. From Hamburg he wrote his youngest daughter that besides
honor they had met with nothing but troubles and vexations:

> Our expenses are so enormous, having already paid since we left home
> upwards of £200 for travelling alone, that at Leipsig I made up my mind
> to "cut it" and come home and had got thus far, when the manager here
> wished us to play for three nights,—tomorrow, Saturday and Monday.
> Whether we shall go further or stay here longer depends upon circum-
> stances. . . . The success of the acting has been all we could wish—but

none but the higher classes come to see us and they are not numerous enough to pay.[49]

Their reception in Hamburg was similar to that in Berlin: critical approval and small audiences. By May 15, Phelps was back in London. The *Theatrical Journal* (May 18, 1859) reported that he had broken an engagement to play in Vienna and attributed his "precipitate retreat" from Germany to the fact that Miss Atkinson had proved to be "the most popular *artiste* in the company." One can only guess at the reason for this unkind accusation, but there is no doubt about Phelps's motives in cutting short his tour. His first consideration, clearly, was financial; but he was also worried about his health. On April 18, he had written from Berlin to his doctor in London that he had suffered "the rupture of a small vessel" during an attack of seasickness on the Channel and said that he would try to be in London on April 25.[50] He actually returned two weeks after this appointment, postponing his departure in spite of his worries. He had so little jealousy of other actors in the company that he regularly used the plural in speaking of the performances in his letters home, as if they all shared equally the praise of German critics.

When Phelps opened his sixteenth season at Sadler's Wells in September, 1859, he could congratulate himself that his management had survived Charles Kean's management of the Princess's, even though his rival had enjoyed a royal patronage seldom granted to English managers. Kean's financial failure must have seemed to him a clear justification of his own principles of management, but he also knew that Sadler's Wells could not achieve the first level of importance without the support of the aristocracy. A scrap of a letter to Macready which is preserved among the Phelps papers in the Harvard Theatre Collection reveals his feelings:

> I have just entered upon the sixteenth year of my theatrical management and begin to despair of attracting more notice than I have done—little enough you will say. I begin to feel the cause is in myself—public opinion is said to be generally right and I suppose I have not got in me the elements to persevere to the end. I am quite sure I have done some *good* and think I have disciplined myself to bear a good deal without grumbling.

In November the Queen invited Phelps and his company to perform *Romeo and Juliet* at Windsor Castle, but such patronage was no substitute for the general interest which a royal visit to Sadler's Wells would have aroused,

On October 19, 1859, Phelps introduced a new play to the stage—the thirteenth produced during his management and by far the most successful. The author, Tom Taylor, was known as a writer of the new drama emerging on some West End stages, but for Sadler's Wells he had written at least the semblance of the old five-act poetic play. *The Fool's Revenge,* described as a romantic drama, did not qualify as true tragedy with the critics, but it was well patronized by the audience. The usual fare at Sadler's Wells was beginning to seem old fashioned to some playgoers. The *Theatrical Journal* (March 21, 1860) complained of Phelps's devotion to traditional drama:

> The loftiest, the severest tragedy is represented in all its dreary integrity by solemn veterans: Shakespeare especially—Shakespeare undefiled—textual.

On April 9, 1860, after his own season, Phelps went to the Princess's Theatre for a six-week engagement under Augustus Harris, who had leased the theatre after Charles Kean left. This was the first time that Phelps, now fifty-six years old, had appeared as a star before West End audiences, and he came to the fashionable theatre in Oxford Street almost unknown to the spectators. The announcement of his engagement did not excite much interest among the regular patrons of the Princess's, and he might have played his Sir Pertinax to an empty house on the opening night but for the coincidence that it was a holiday, Easter Monday, which gave Islingtonians an opportunity to make the trip to Oxford Street. The pit was full of admirers, who greeted him with hearty hand clapping that must have surprised those used to the muffled applause of scented gloves. The *Theatrical Journal* described it as "a welcome never before heard in these walls."

He followed Sir Pertinax with Bertuccio (in *The Fool's Revenge*), Richelieu, Falstaff, and Hamlet, a series of roles chosen to display the wide range of his acting. Reviews spoke of his unique position among contemporary actors: the *Morning Advertiser* (April 10, 1860) described him as "the only remaining Shakespearian actor we have in the more ambitious characters." The *Weekly Dispatch* (April 22, 1860), in describing his Sir Pertinax, said:

> Such a conception, and so embodied, is certainly a revival of the truest comedy which we remember to have seen, and a pledge that acting in its best sense is not extinct among us.

But the high praise of critics who already knew Phelps did not at first have any effect upon West End playgoers. James Anderson, his old colleague, went to see him on April 28 and gave a dreary report of the evening.[51] He found *The Fool's Revenge* a "weak piece, written in ambitious blank verse, unsatisfactory in treatment, and disagreeable in plot," and said that Phelps worked hard to win a few hands of applause from a very poor house.

Gradually the fashionable audience of the Princess's became interested in this "new" actor from an old school, who played tragedy and comedy with equal ease. Coroneted carriages began to appear in Oxford Street, and on May 15 the Queen came to watch Phelps as Bertuccio. The *Examiner* (June 23, 1860) commented on the change:

> We have been very glad to observe the thoroughness of the success of Mr. Phelps in Oxford Street—a success all the more genuine for having been gradual. At first there were thin houses, but . . . for some weeks past Mr. Phelps has been performing to full boxes and stalls, and to a crowded pit.

This review had the inevitable comparisons with Charles Kean, who had produced *The Merry Wives of Windsor* at the Princess's nine years before. Phelps's Falstaff was in every way a contrast to Bartley's. Morley suggests that Phelps's untraditional interpretation was preferred by the upper-class audience:

> He takes care to represent [Falstaff] as more than a mere oily sensualist; he is a gentleman by social rank, and a wit whom, as he takes pride in the sharpness of his intellect, it is all the more pleasant for the merry wives of Windsor to outwit.

He also contrasts Phelps's Hamlet with that of Charles Kean:

> Most carefully elaborated, it is yet entirely free from that manifest struggle for expression which made the Hamlet of Mr. Charles Kean toilsome to follow. It must surprise some of the old frequenters of the house to observe how easily and how like a true poem the play now runs. Mr. Phelps never sacrifices anything to love of points.

Phelps's first engagement as leading actor at a fashionable London theatre proved a decided success. He brought critical acclaim and good houses to the Princess's, and the manager engaged him for the following summer.

He returned to Sadler's Wells in 1860 as sole lessee, his partner Greenwood having retired. His commitment to the suburban theatre was shown by the cleaning and redecorating accomplished during the summer recess. He had also engaged several promising actors, including Hermann Vezin, an American who had been a minor actor under Kean, and Mrs. Charles Young, whom Phelps had persuaded to return. (Not long afterward she became Mrs. Vezin, the name by which she is now remembered.)

Two events of the season deserve special mention. One was the performance of *Richelieu* at Windsor Castle by royal command. The other was the debut of Phelps's son Edmund on November 21. He was then twenty-two years old and the only one of six children who chose the theatre as a career, although Robert, the oldest, had written afterpieces for Sadler's Wells before he was admitted to the bar. Edmund made his first appearance as Ulric to his father's Werner. Critics said that he had good personal qualities for acting—graceful bearing, expressive face, and resonant voice—and that he played his first role successfully. An overflowing house applauded him enthusiastically, but undoubtedly it was an occasion when critical judgment was colored by affection and respect for the manager. Phelps must have found his son's performance promising, since he began a serious course of training with him and in the following season cast him in a number of youthful roles.

Otherwise there was no novelty in the season of 1860–1861. The appeal of the performances lay in the uniformly good quality of the acting and staging and a varied repertory. Morley, reviewing *Coriolanus* early in the season, commented that Phelps had followed the course necessary for reviving interest in serious drama:

> He acts national plays in a house small enough to allow all to see, though few may appreciate, the subtlest and most delicate shades of expression proper to the art of the actor; he has a company of performers trained and accustomed to support each other steadily, and peculiarly able to present each play as an effective whole. When the curtain falls upon a play at Sadler's Wells, the audience has not only seen a sight and heard much sound, but it has felt . . . an entire poem.[52]

Using these methods Phelps in one season produced *As You Like It; Coriolanus; Henry the Fourth, Part One; The Winter's Tale; Cymbeline; Othello; The Tempest; Hamlet; Macbeth; The Merchant of Venice; King Lear; King John; Julius Caesar;* and *Romeo and Juliet.* He also produced sixteen other tragedies and comedies. As a whole the season may be regarded as the last flowering of a long theatrical tradition characterized by its emphasis upon the skill of actors in a variety of plays from the classic repertory.

In the summer of 1861 Phelps went back to the Princess's, where he acted in alternation with Fechter as Hamlet. Fechter's new Hamlet, breaking with all tradition in manner and dress, walking with an air of nonchalance and speaking in a colloquial tone, had caused a furor in London during the winter. There could hardly be a greater contrast between two contemporary actors. One, a foreigner who spoke English with an accent, excited audiences by his novelty and charmed them with the elegance of his manner. The other, old fashioned and lacking the refinement that appealed to the highest social class, offered them a traditional interpretation and a melodious reading of blank verse. Because both appeared as mature actors with fully developed styles before a public unaccustomed to their acting, the contrast was sudden and pointed.

Phelps's vigor was as surprising to many West End playgoers as Fechter's nonchalance. The *Morning Advertiser* (May 24, 1861) commented that the awful force of Lear's curse as Phelps delivered it was rather too strong for "the refined ears of our conventional times." (One wonders what Macready's would have seemed to this audience.) It is surprising that Phelps's Lear did compete with Fechter for the attention of playgoers, but apparently it did.[53] He drew full houses, and the usual frequenters of the Princess's, according to reviewers, were visibly shaken by the emotional force of his acting. Insistent rounds of applause called him before the curtain at the end of each act.

Critical comment about the two actors is especially interesting because of the juxtaposition of the two styles of acting—one looking back to Betterton and the other looking ahead to Sir Laurence Olivier. According to the taste of the individual critic, the strength of one style seemed the weakness of the other. Fechter's smoothness and graceful elegance made Phelps seem stiff; his use of gesture and pose to give intense emphasis or sudden new meaning made Phelps's acting seem subdued; his variety of pace and intonation made Phelps's speech seem monotonous. For other critics the situation was reversed: the majesty of Phelps's Lear, the consummate art of his declamation, and the profound thought revealed by his interpretation made Fechter's Hamlet seem melodramatic and trivial.

When he returned to Sadler's Wells for the season of 1861-1862, Phelps's management declined into mediocrity. He had again lost his best actors to West End theatres. Mrs. Young was now at the Haymarket, playing Portia to the Shylock of a new American actor named Edwin Booth. Hermann Vezin, who had been Fechter's Laertes, was starring in modern plays at the Lyceum. Mrs. Marston was at the Olympic. Her husband and a number of lesser actors had also left Sadler's Wells, so that Phelps was forced to organize a new company—a task that even his energy and resourcefulness might have failed to accomplish except that a number of American actors had been driven to London by the Civil War in the United States. Four of them appeared at Sadler's Wells. The best of them, Mrs. D. P. Bowers, was well received, and her success had the usual result: she moved to the Lyceum in October.

Except for Emma Atkinson, Barrett, Ball, and a few minor actors, Phelps faced a company in need of thorough schooling before it could give a skilled and cohesive performance. One reviewer complained that "the manager himself is the whole dramatic corps." Its inadequacy for Shakespeare forced Phelps to give up the complete texts he had been accustomed to use and to substitute the old acting versions, which had smaller casts and concentrated interest in the leading role. Playbills show no Lady Macduff in the cast of *Macbeth*. *Henry the Fourth, Part Two*, was severely cut. *Richard the Third* was performed from Cibber's version. The only Shakespearean revival which could be compared with those of former years was *A Midsummer Night's Dream* produced with new settings. The cast, aside from Phelps, was undistinguished but gave a competent rendering that showed careful direction.

Phelps's management had depended on actors. His difficulty in finding and keeping actors showed the impossibility of maintaining for much longer a theatre so cut off from the mainstream of English drama. The contrast between Sadler's Wells and the main current of theatrical development is pointed up by two articles in the *Times* on November 11 and 12, 1862. The first records the fact that Falconer's *Peep O'Day* had just completed a year's run at the Lyceum, commenting that "the uninterrupted succession of 300 and odd performances is, we believe, without precedent." The second article reviews a new three-act play by Watts Phillips with this apology:

> Five act plays are now such rare phenomena that when an original piece in three acts, with the pretension of being more than a long melodrama, makes its appearance on the theatrical boards, we feel compelled to attach to it the degree of importance which once belonged alone to works constructed according to the old form of legitimacy.

The long run and the three-act prose play had established themselves on the stage. The repertory system and the five-act poetic play had all but disappeared.

In spite of the obvious decline of Sadler's Wells an appreciative audience continued to fill the theatre. They remained critical and attentive although their interest was now almost entirely devoted to Phelps's acting. Their attitude toward the new members of the company can be inferred from the *Athenaeum's* remark that Mrs. Bowers "is happily now placed in a school where the audience will soon correct her errors, and teach her reverence for the great poets whom she will have to interpret."

Even as late as 1862 Sadler's Wells preserved something of the traditional English drama that could inspire high praise from a newcomer to the theatre. A French visitor to London, Hector Malot, found the fashionable theatres full of imitations or translations of French plays.[54] Shakespeare was performed only when one of these pieces failed and nothing was ready to replace it. His plays were given perfunctory performances with dingy settings. Malot was surprised to discover that Shakespeare was still alive at an unimportant suburban theatre:

> De vrai, il y avait un petit théâtre où il régnait encore, *Sadler's Wells,* et où on le jouait respectueusement, avec tous les bons principes et le tradition, devant un public qu'il passionne et enthousiasme.

At Sadler's Wells Malot also found a superior actor after having been discouraged by the poor quality of the acting in West End theatres:

> Cependant, dans cette pauvreté, quelques noms sortent de la foule: M. Phelps, l'interprète de Shakspeare, comédien véritablement anglais et qui, à mon sense, laisse loin derrière lui les deux rivaus que le monde élégant lui oppose: M. Kean, qui n' a de son père que le nom, et M. Fechter, qui nous avons vu autrefois à Paris.

Critical approval, financial success, and a devoted audience could not preserve a theatre so isolated from the center of English culture. In the end Phelps was defeated by the prevailing taste of *"le monde élégant."* The fact that such an actor as Hermann Vezin left Sadler's Wells, where he played Romeo, Orlando, and Prince Hal to overflowing and enthusiastic audiences, to join the Lyceum company where he appeared six nights a week for more than a year in the cast of *Peep O'Day* is an indication of the power of fashion.

Phelps's management ended almost without announcement on March

14, 1862. His decision to give up Sadler's Wells was sudden and came from a personal tragedy, the discovery that Mrs. Phelps was dying of cancer. After thirty-four years of a marriage which had been distinguished by unusual devotion on both sides, he found himself unable to face his strenuous job as actor-manager without his wife's support. What strength he had was needed to conceal his despair from her and continue his career in some easier way.

To his colleagues and to his family Phelps explained his sudden decision to give up the management by pleading the strain of the last two years. Since Greenwood's retirement, he had been forced to assume responsibility for many practical aspects of the management which formerly he had safely entrusted to his partner. Although Malone Raymond, his old friend from Liverpool, was officially the acting manager, he proved no substitute for Greenwood. Phelps's explanation was readily accepted, and since the theatre had already been let for the summer, he had time to find another lessee before autumn. Within a few months he had transferred his lease to Miss Lucette, who proposed to convert Sadler's Wells into a house for opera, burletta, and light dramatic fare.

There was no public announcement of Phelps's retirement from Sadler's Wells. During the summer of 1862 he acted at the Standard and in Liverpool. In October he returned to Sadler's Wells to act a series of six plays during three weeks, partly to help the new management establish itself. Without any statement that these were farewell performances, Phelps played *Richelieu, Hamlet, Othello, The Merchant of Venice, The Fool's Revenge,* and *Julius Caesar* supported by a few actors from his old company, his son Edmund, and William Creswick. Only on the last night was there a notice printed on the playbill that it would be his final appearance at Sadler's Wells—a display of modesty which some reviewers considered excessive. "Here is Mr. Phelps," wrote *Punch* (November 29, 1862), "retiring from Sadler's Wells in such a modest quiet way that people knew nothing about it until the thing was done. . . . Mr. Phelps slips out of sight with neither flummery nor fuss, and so modestly takes leave of us that we have scarce the opportunity to say how much we liked him."

After Phelps's departure Sadler's Wells began a steady decline. Burletta and melodrama were performed without much success until 1871, when the theatre became a skating rink and then an arena for prize fights. In 1878 Mrs. Bateman of the Lyceum took the lease and completely remodeled the decayed building for the purpose of presenting plays. For a short period Sadler's Wells regained something of its former status, and according to Hermann Vezin the audience attracted by her management still showed the effects of Phelps's long sojourn:

> It was the best an actor could play to. They expressed their disapprobation of what they did not like, but not offensively, while on the other hand, the most delicate effect an actor might produce, were it only by a change of facial expression, a subtle vocal inflection, was sure of meeting immediate recognition.[55]

In 1893 the theatre became a music hall and later a cinema until it again fell into disrepair and was closed. In 1927 the old theatre was completely demolished and another Sadler's Wells rebuilt on the same site under Lilian Baylis's leadership. Since then, except for the war years, when the theatre served as a shelter, the story of Sadler's Wells has been connected with the Old Vic, a history too well known to be recounted here.

Some memory of Phelps's management lingered on in the acting profession for many years. In 1883 Michael Williams wrote:

> To have played with Phelps, at Sadler's Wells, is yet the proudest boast of those who survive from his old company; and many of our best actors and actresses have owed their fame to the training which they received, in early life, at "The Theatre."[56]

Phelps and Shakespeare: Actor

As an actor and producer of Shakespearean plays, Phelps's reputation is far below his accomplishment. In producing under his management at Sadler's Wells thirty-one plays—more than 1,600 nights of Shakespearean drama—without any patronage except that of the audience, he succeeded where Macready and Charles Kean failed in attracting audiences, in winning widespread critical approval, and in the financial success of his venture. The chief reason for neglect of his work, although it seems almost incredible in the more egalitarian climate of the twentieth century, lies in the potency of aristocratic and fashionable taste, asserted in the Victorian period and unconsciously accepted by subsequent generations. In considering Phelps as an actor and a manager, one has to lay aside prejudices and take a fresh look at the contemporary evidence.

In the field of Shakespearean acting Phelps is now generally considered as a follower of Macready. Yet he was thirty-three years old, an actor with fifteen years' experience, and a promising contender for the highest rank before he first saw Macready on the stage. On this evidence the charge that he was a follower of Macready could be dismissed except for the fact that it was sometimes made by critics of his own time. A number of such comments lead to the conclusion that there was some similarity in their acting.

Macready, like the other great actors in the history of the English stage, was successful not only because of his individual genius, but also because he could interpret tragic heroes in terms understood by his own generation. As Edmund Kean had expressed on the stage some of the passionate force of the Romantic spirit, so Macready embodied the emotions which most concerned his contemporaries in the early Victorian period. His diary reveals many personal attributes and concerns that are characteristic of the temper of the age. His outward reserve and seeming coldness, broken occasionally by the eruption of violent emotion, his constant introspection and self-justification, his unflagging pursuit of the highest standards of excellence in his work, his faith in God, and his idealization of family life belong to the spirit of the transitional period between the Romantics and the Victorians. This complex of emotions and ideas inevitably colored his interpretation of characters on the stage, not so noticeably that it obscured his intelligent grasp of the author's meaning, but sufficiently to mark certain roles in which he touched the basic concerns of the day with the cogency of truth. His Macbeth was far more introspective than earlier Macbeths. He gave Shakespeare's King John a sensitive portrayal which possibly has never been surpassed for its subtle insight into that complex character. His Lear, with its vigorous authority, troubled sense of sin, and emphasis upon the moral lessons learned through experience, had special meaning for that generation.

Phelps, born a decade after Macready, shared with him many of the assumptions and ideals that were peculiarly characteristic of the mid-nineteenth century. And furthermore, although he was not troubled by the pride, ambition, violent temper, and habitual introspection which plagued Macready, in other respects their temperaments were remarkably similar. Phelps had the same seriousness of purpose, moral convictions, devotion to hard work, and intellectual approach to his art. On the stage Phelps eventually found himself most at home in the characters which Macready did best: Macbeth, King John, Lear, Virginius, and Richelieu. These were not perhaps Phelps's greatest portrayals, but he could play them with intuitive sympathy.

More important than these resemblances in attitude and ideals was the similarity of their approach to the art of acting. They both, separately and without direct influence upon each other, had introduced a new way of looking at dramatic characterization which modified the traditions they had inherited in the theatre to make them relevant to the thought of a new age. At the end of the eighteenth century, actors had been concerned primarily with the external aspects of characterization. Kemble and Mrs. Siddons excelled in portraying a character with such perfection of external detail and such consistency of speech, movement, and pose that it gave the impression of truthfulness and grandeur found in a classic statue. Edmund Kean by contrast had frequently broken through the external characterization to give glimpses into the soul of the character he was acting, so that instead of seeing the hero from the outside, the audience suddenly looked into his internal being and felt an echo of his emotion. Macready and Phelps, more thoroughly influenced by the age of Romanticism, with its emphasis upon the psychological and emotional aspects of human life, sought to present on the stage the internal characterization of a man—not with the intuitive insight of Kean's flashes, but with the consistency and perfection of detail which the Kembles had achieved in external characterization.

The attempt to present a thoroughly consistent psychological portrait of a character was a new approach to dramatic art, even though it developed out of the methods used by the Kembles and Kean and resulted from a different emphasis rather than a total break with tradition. Macready and Phelps in studying a role found it more important to ask "How did this man feel?" or "What was he thinking?" than the older questions: "How did this man act?" and "How did he appear to others?" In their acting they used spiritual and psychological suggestion to show the character from the inside—the emotions and thoughts underlying, and sometimes at variance with, his words and overt actions.

So important a change of approach to dramatic art, presented almost simultaneously by two gifted actors, inevitably led critics to see a common basis of their acting, especially since other prominent actors of their time did not share it. (Vandenhoff followed the Kembles' approach; Brooke followed Kean's; and Charles Kean, although he ushered in a new realistic style of acting, was always concerned with external characterization.) But in fact Macready and Phelps differed radically in their styles of acting.

Macready was far more consciously artistic, with carefully planned effects achieved by the use of pause, variations of tempo and pitch, and particular emphasis on pieces of stage business. Although his style was less elevated than that of the Kembles, it was no less affected. His mannerisms were so easily imitated that many of the actors who worked with him adopted, almost unconsciously, the "Macready pause" and other characteristics of his style. He used the same effects in every performance, so that if you saw his Hamlet a hundred times you would see him pull out his white handkerchief at the same line of the text. His left leg always exited half a moment after his body when he went off to murder Duncan. And he expected the audience to recognize and applaud his artistry frequently during a performance.

This style was the antithesis of Phelps's identification with the char-

acter, his avoidance of points, and the concealment of art in his performances. He was like Kean in abandoning himself to the character and in the
variation between one performance and another of the same role. Going
beyond Macready's aim of making the audience see the character from
the inside, Phelps often made them feel the same emotions as the character. This "pathos," as the critics termed it, was an important feature of
Phelps's acting.

Usually critics found the differences between Macready and Phelps
more striking than their resemblances. In some roles, however, their similar approach to dramatic art—the emphasis upon internal characterization
and the use of subtle details to portray it—was especially evident. In these
characters, particularly King John, Richelieu, and Werner, critics complained that Phelps imitated Macready. Toward the end of his career,
many years after Macready's retirement, some critics who had never seen
Macready act assumed that Phelps resembled him, partly because his
acting differed so radically from the new school.

TRAGIC ROLES

In Hamlet Phelps displayed the characteristics of his own acting which
differed from the actors before him in its sense of identification with the
character and from actors after him in his superb elocution. A contemporary critic contrasted him with other actors of his time in these words:

> He presents Hamlet, in its artistic *ensemble,* better than any actor I ever
> saw. Charles Kean is simply absurd in the part—violates every rule of
> decency, and is intensely ridiculous. Macready was great in it; but particular
> passages stood out too much: you thought too frequently of Shakespeare's
> beautiful language, and too rarely of the character he had conceived.[1]

The interpretation which Phelps presented was a courtly, intellectual,
and spiritual Hamlet, who was shaken to the depths of his being by the
knowledge imparted by the Ghost. It was not the passionate sufferer Edmund Kean had portrayed, with all the poignancy of his grief and despondency, but rather a philosophic mind whose assumptions about the
universe had been destroyed. Hamlet's royal grace and dignity and his
tendency toward speculative thought were emphasized by Phelps, perhaps
at the cost of the emotional side of the character. Many critics thought he
lacked passion in the scenes with the Queen and with Ophelia. They

agreed that he was excellent in the scenes with the players, the courtiers, and the gravedigger.

One advantage of his interpretation was that it provided solutions to some of the traditional "problems" in *Hamlet*. His tremendous outburst of emotion at the Ghost's disclosure of the murder, for example, provided a credible basis for his irrational manner in the following scene with Horatio and Marcellus, so that Hamlet's distraction could not be mistaken for actual madness. Phelps showed Hamlet at once possessed by a sorrow so deep that he could find no adequate response and therefore turned to humor, first indicated by his frivolous responses to the Ghost's command, "Swear." His parting with Ophelia was seen in reference to his probing concern with the meaning of life, not primarily as emotional reaction.

The *Athenaeum* (September 19, 1857) spoke of the "serenity, also, that was almost religious in the air of the character and befitted the great theme of immortality with which Hamlet's mind is constantly burdened." Not all critics liked Phelps's interpretation. Westland Marston found it "quaintly droll" and Towse said that it was heavy. *Tallis's Dramatic Magazine* (November, 1850) described it as "elaborately impressive, meditative, and courtly, and decidedly one of the best embodiments of the character, though not one of the most impassioned, that has ever appeared on the stage." *Lloyd's Weekly* (December 7, 1851) said that the emotional impact of the performance came from the over-all impression that everything was consonant with the character, so that the forces of actor and poet concurred at every point.

Phelps's Hamlet reminded the German novelist, Fontane, of Emil Devrient's acting of the role, except that Devrient was a younger prince and interpreted his distraction as real madness.[2] Fontane says that Phelps made Hamlet consciously superior in intellect and knowledge as well as in royal position—a man who used his doubly superior position to mistreat the whole world. He spoke the soliloquies simply, almost too simply, without loudness or passion, not making his art compete with that of the poet. Like English reviewers, Fontane found the Mousetrap scene one of the best in Phelps's performance. The outburst of full voice and energy carried such conviction that Fontane forgot he was in a theatre and looked upon the scene as upon a real event.

Fontane notes several interesting bits of stage business in the performance. He mentions that during Hamlet's farewell scene with Ophelia he left the stage after each "farewell" and returned abruptly to continue the speech. This was a traditional piece of business which Fontane, looking with fresh eyes, found effective.[3] He also found very striking the arrangement of the scene in Gertrude's bedroom. Here Phelps followed Macready's practice of hanging the walls with life-sized portraits of the Danish kings. The room was lit with dim, flickering light. Suddenly the Ghost with a loud noise stepped out of one of the frames. Even in the dim light the King could be recognized, dressed in a rich black robe edged with gold and purple and wearing a crown above his deathly pale face. Hamlet, hands stretched forward, body bent back, spoke softly and imploringly as the Ghost strode past him. Then in his growing anger prompted by the Ghost's words Hamlet caught his mother's arm and twisted it. Her cry of pain seemed real to Fontane—not moderated as it would have been in a German theatre; and he found it very moving.

In the duel with Laertes Phelps introduced a new method of accomplishing the exchange of rapiers. After he was wounded, he had a convulsive reaction which jerked his rapier and caused both blades to fall on the floor. As he stood briefly dazed by the wound and unable to pick up his own rapier, Laertes retrieved them both, watching Hamlet closely. Hamlet suddenly recovered from the physical weakness and snatched one of the foils from Laertes' slack hand, continuing the match without being aware of the exchange. Fontane found this device a happy solution to the problem of the text, because it preserved Hamlet's innocence and still avoided the improbability usually felt when Laertes allows Hamlet to pick up the wrong rapier.

The *Athenaeum* (August 3, 1844) described Phelps's first Hamlet at Sadler's Wells as "an exceedingly natural impersonation, without exaggeration of manner or anxiety to make points." The use of the word "natural" must be understood in nineteenth-century terms, since it quite clearly does not mean imitation of the manner of everyday life and conversational speech to which we have become accustomed on the twentieth-century stage. His acting seemed natural because he preserved the dramatic integrity of the character, omitting famous points and submerging his own personality in that of his creation. Evidence of the reality of his Hamlet occurred on one of the first nights he played it at Sadler's Wells. There had been some noise in the pit at the beginning of the play because of overcrowding, but silence reigned after the problem had been settled and the audience had been caught by the intense emotions of Hamlet. When they heard him say that the groundlings were capable of nothing but noise, they took the speech as a personal affront.[4] This reaction may be attributed partly to the naivete of the new audience at Sadler's Wells, who did not know *Hamlet* until they saw it that night; but almost a decade later an experienced playgoer came to Sadler's Wells and had the same impression of immediacy in Phelps's acting:

> I have seen your Hamlet this evening for the first time; and for the first time have I seen the mind of that noble and exquisite creation embodied and rendered palpable to the eye and heart of the spectator. I have seen several stage Hamlets, but never Shakespeare's till now. So fresh, so new, so clear is your portraiture that I could not avoid troubling you with the expression of my pleasure and my obligation. I am ignorant of Mr. Charles Kemble's Hamlet; but nobody since his time has made us feel, as you do, Hamlet's grief, his filial love—in all its depth and fulness—and the exquisite refinement and spirituality of his character. These are so finely expressed that the agony of his situation and the utter repugnance of its requirements to his nature are intensely felt throughout the play. Moreover, the real worshippers of Shakespeare owe you a world of thanks for giving them a performance free from stage quackeries and conventional tricks. It is inexpressibly refreshing to see the forms and dictates of simple nature so faithfully adhered to. Nothing can surpass the beauty and affecting power of the chamber scene with the Queen—so new in style, yet so simple and truthful, but so tremendous in effect. Never have I witnessed that scene before without a wretched violation of all truth, propriety, and force, in order that the Queen shall throw herself in to the arms of Hamlet (who is obviously preparing himself for the event) for the purpose of making a stage tableau. I must tell you also that I felt convinced this evening that had the stage exhibited in former times any such plain and obvious interpretation of the story and character of Hamlet as yours, the many disquisitions and squabbles about Hamlet's consistency and madness would never have arisen.[5]

Phelps's Hamlet was "natural," then, in the sense that it avoided conventional tricks like the stage tableau in the bedroom scene.

Another characteristic of Phelps's Hamlet which requires some explanation is skilled elocution. At the beginning of Phelps's management elocution, or declamation, was still considered the basis of the art of acting. Careful development of vocal tone, range, and volume and constant practice in enunciation, emphasis, and phrasing were of major importance in an actor's training. Modern distaste for the heightened style (which is known to most of us now only in the melodramatic genre of "ham" acting) has cut us off from any interest in poetic expression on the stage. Our acute sensitivity to realistic intonation has made us insensitive to the rhythms of poetry, purity of tone, and subtlety of phrasing.

In Phelps's Hamlet, as in all his acting, elocution was of primary importance. His best physical asset was a deep, resonant, and powerful voice, which had been deliberately trained through years of practice. He had sung opera in his provincial days, and there was a musical quality in his declamation which was especially noticed in comparison with the unmelodious character of Macready's speech. On public occasions, such as the benefit for the purchase of Shakespeare's house, Phelps was frequently asked to declaim the ode written for the occasion, since even among actors he was noted for the beauty of his voice. In rehearsing a part he worked to perfect details of emphasis and phrasing so that he read the lines with a subtlety and precision that made nuances of meaning clear to pit and gallery. *Lloyd's Weekly* (August 4, 1844) in summarizing his first performance of Hamlet at Sadler's Wells, singled out this aspect as the most important: "The success of Mr. Phelps was complete; his voice is excellent, and he commands it to any utterance; his judgment is sound, and his taste correct."

Because Macready had already made Macbeth one of his specialties before Phelps arrived in London, the latter did not include the role in the series he played for his debut at the Haymarket. His own interpretation, developed during his provincial years, was not seen in London until he played it for the opening of his management of Sadler's Wells in 1844. From then on he played it more frequently than any other part except Hamlet almost to the end of his life.

Phelps was the first actor since the Restoration to act in a totally Shakespearean *Macbeth,* stripped of D'Avenant's improvements and complete with the scenes formerly left out of the stage version. The evil force of the three Weird Sisters, felt more strongly and pervadingly, the break in tension caused by the Porter's entrance, and the removal of Macbeth's death agonies from the stage—all affected Phelps's interpretation of the hero. He was less hag-ridden than most of his predecessors and more fiery, showing Macbeth possessed by a more fundamental force of evil than singing witches. He was resolute, bold, confident, quick in decision, and imperious, even in dealing with the Weird Sisters. The energy, breadth, and strength of his Macbeth distinguished it from that of Macready and, in later years, from that of Edwin Booth.

Some critics, like Westland Marston, who preferred Macready's interpretation, found Phelps too rugged, and they missed the haunted air of Macready's Macbeth. Others, like J. R. Towse, felt that he had the correct interpretation:

> As Macbeth he was less imaginative, poetic, and pathetic than Booth (I am thinking of the latter's collapse after the apparition of Banquo), but more robust and terrible, and, to my mind, closer to the spirit of Shakespeare.[6]

Although Phelps's Macbeth had moments of remorseful and sullen despondency, he never showed complete collapse, but was only temporarily unnerved and shaken. He gave few physical symptoms of mental agony, depending instead upon the descriptive emphasis of the words to convey the depth of his suffering. For example, in the dagger soliloquy (like Macready) he gave no sudden start but merely stared fixedly at a point in space while his quietly intense speech conveyed the sense of the reality of the dagger created by his tortured imagination. He expressed horror rather than terror at this apparition. Some reviewers, used to the elaborate physical posturing and abrupt variations of tempo in Macready's reading, felt that Phelps had "failed" in this scene. Others found his quiet intensity more impressive.

All the critics, whether they found Phelps's acting in this role truly great or merely accomplished and skillful, remarked upon the consistency of the whole. Having projected his conception of the character in the first scene, he did not let it lapse through overemphasis on famous points or through failure of physical stamina. His interpretation required much energy, and he admitted that he could not play Macbeth more than two nights consecutively, but he was usually able to maintain the force of tragic expression, without falling into mere excitability, until the final curtain. There is little doubt that it lacked the accumulation of detail and intellectual subtleties of Macready's Macbeth, but it was praised for the harmony of the whole portrait and an intelligent sensitivity to the poetry:

> Mr. Phelps's performance was conceived in the highest poetry—with no "false starts," no spouting, no pointed ranting, no misdirected energy that fires the unreflecting many into sudden admiration. . . . Certainly we have never seen the character so completely portrayed; the key-note being struck gently at the first, the harmony was preserved throughout. Some particular scenes other actors might give more grace or force to, but as an entire conception of the valiant chieftain . . . we have never seen it rivalled.[7]

And in the words of a later critic, "No subsequent impersonation of the part has been equal to it in justness of proportion, vigor, or picturesqueness." [8]

Phelps's interpretation of Lear was also influenced by his use of the complete text, with the Fool fully restored to his place in the tragedy. The traditional stage version, even after Macready's partial restoration, ended the first act with Lear's curse of Goneril, transposed from the middle of scene four. This "improvement" on Shakespeare provided the actor with a grand climax and gave the audience an impression of Lear's strength as the curtain fell on act one.

With the curse replaced in its proper position and scene five restored, Lear's period of confidence was considerably shortened, and premonition of his helplessness clearly given. In Phelps's restoration the act closed on a Lear already fearing madness. He avoided strong emphasis upon the curse, preventing the customary round of applause, in order to blend it into the changed tone of the whole scene when related to scene five. Since no curtain fell between the scenes, consistency of characterization was important. A few critics failed to understand Phelps's purpose and criticized him for not making this famous point, but the critic of the *Athenaeum* (November 8, 1845) both understood and approved Phelps's new reading of the curse:

> It is much to the actor's credit that he sacrificed his professional ambition to the proprieties of the scene. Having restored the curse to its original place in the drama, Mr. Phelps was judiciously careful not to give it undue effect by being too vehement. He chastened and toned it down to the proper emphasis required by its rightful position. Was it on that account less effective with the audience? Not a whit.

In contrast to his Macbeth, which was more vigorous and commanding than the usual interpretation, Phelps's Lear was less so. He made Lear an old man, assuming the appearance, gait, and voice of an octogenarian. In the first scene his actions seemed the result of rash anger and a certain rigidity of mind brought on by age rather than evidence of a moral defect. Macready, following the "tragic flaw" theory of drama, made his Lear arrogant and domineering in the first act, and in the rest of the play he emphasized passages of philosophic comment to show that Lear gained wisdom through suffering. Phelps, on the contrary, emphasized the suffering of Lear, probing the depths of his agony in despair and degradation. He depicted the suffering and did not try to explain it.

From the first act, where his interpretation was significantly reinforced by the inclusion of scene five, to the last, his Lear was dominated by a pervading consciousness of his daughters' rejection of him. This one painful idea was seen to be always with him, coloring thought and action, both when he was insane and when he was trying to penetrate the meaning of existence through philosophic reflection. He used Lear's suffering to illuminate the meaning and passion of Shakespeare's language—the opposite to Macready's course of using the language to explain the suffering.

He was more the father than the king, and some critics felt that he lacked sufficient royal dignity and physical vigor. Westland Marston thought that his "indignant and convulsive grief was harrowing," and that "in his irony extremes met, and misery laughed and jested," but he found Phelps's Lear not truly tragic, since it excited compassion rather than awe.[9] Against this assertion by a critic who seldom visited Sadler's Wells should be placed the following quotation from *Bell's Weekly Messenger*:

> The majesty, as well as the paternal tenderness of Lear, is preserved throughout; the grief, despair, and madness are kingly; and the business which the action inspires is heightened by the consciousness of the greatness of the mind that is suffering.[10]

Two further descriptions of Phelps's Lear compare him with other actors. The first from the *Court Journal* appeared on November 8, 1845, when Phelps and Macready were both playing Lear in London:

> There was a fearful beauty in some of his bursts of passionate anger, which we have never seen exceeded. But it was in the last two acts that Phelps proved himself, not merely an excellent and admirable, but a great actor. . . . There was, we are disposed to think—or rather, were compelled to feel—a greater depth, simplicity and unity of purpose, and a more perfect embodiment of that purpose than even in the great performance of Macready himself.

The second is from the American critic Towse, who saw Phelps only at the end of his career:

> His Lear . . . was one of the most satisfying interpretations of that unactable conception that I have seen. It was ruggedly majestic in the opening scenes, tempestuous in passion, and infinitely pitiful in the shifting humors of its degradation and despair. In vocal and elocutionary resource it was

superb. It combined the strength of Forrest with the subtle intelligence of Edwin Booth.[11]

In tragic roles Phelps acted with an abandonment of feeling that sometimes caused him visibly to tremble from head to foot, and so completely was he submerged in the character that he seemed not to be acting. The *Athenaeum* (April 1, 1848) remarked upon "the apparent absence of histrionic art" in his Lear, and the *Daily Telegraph* (November 4, 1861) said that in Othello he "merely yields himself as it were to the torrent of emotion flowing through his heart, and is borne along without any effort on its impetuous current." His Othello was a profoundly moving performance which won the sympathy of the audience by its strong emotional appeal.

As with his Lear, some critics found him overly pathetic as Othello. Certainly he lacked the loftiness of Macready's interpretation, and this was noted in his first years at Sadler's Wells; but reviewers of the sixties did not complain of any lack of tragic elevation. There is a possibility that Macready's more pretentious and consciously artistic style would have seemed pompous to audiences who had seen the familiar style of Charles Kean and Charles Fechter. In comparison with Fechter Phelps was praised for his dignity in the role of Othello:

> His natural dignity, however, gives all the requisite sustenance to the character, and we think he admirably hits the *juste milieu* between stage pomposity and a common-place familiarity. Though he is as easy and natural as may be, he nevertheless understands that there is in the senate, on guard, and in public generally, something more of artificial manners than when unrobed in his harem he takes his ease. In the grand scenes of the last three acts, where the passion predominates, his great artistic power is shown, and his mingled rage and grief are finely expressed. . . . The great and pathetic speech of the farewell to his occupation was given with consummate art and force, and the images rose one after another into a grand climax, till they were all scattered by the last despairing line. This mixture of elocutionary power and deep feeling Mr. Phelps is probably the only man on our stage who can properly render; and it is the perfection of his art.[12]

Punch (November 16, 1861) in attacking the sentimental and artificial pathos of melodramatic acting, contrasted the true pathos of Phelps's Othello:

Not being sentimental, his pathos is most touching in its natural simplicity; instance specially the farewell to his soldier's occupation, and the low voice and quivering lip with which he sobs the answer "not a jot—not a jot," and in the outbreak of his jealousy he gives the fullest utterance to the passion of the text.

Towse also speaks of the superb elocution and the dignity of his Othello, asserting that his address to the senate exceeded Booth's in soldierly simplicity and natural dignity.[13]

Phelps showed Othello in the first two acts to be tranquil, modest, but conscious of his own worth, moving easily with a kind of barbaric pomp on official occasions, and profoundly happy in his love. The only hint of the storm to follow came in the scene after the midnight brawl when he demanded, "Who began it?" and with sudden intense heat said:

> Now, by heaven,
> My blood begins my safer guides to rule;
> And passion, having my best judgment collied,
> Assays to lead the way.

The excitement of the third and fourth acts came like a storm after this calm beginning. Doubt, suspicion, tenderness, jealousy, hatred, fury, and self-mortification were shown with passionate intensity in voice, gesture, and facial expression. In the fifth act he was solemn and depressed as he carried out his determination to kill Desdemona. His subdued manner made the horror of the situation more palpable than the strong emphasis used by other actors. He played in this low key throughout the murder, the revelation of Iago's villainy, and his own despair, relying upon the force of Shakespeare's language to express the depth of his feeling.

Phelps liked to alternate the roles of Othello and Iago whenever he played with another actor capable of doing both. At Sadler's Wells he did not often have the opportunity, since Marston made a good Iago but lacked sufficient strength for Othello. In 1850 when his excellent light comedian, Hoskins, wanted to play Othello for his benefit night, Phelps welcomed the chance to show the audience his Iago. That his interpretation took them by surprise is indicated by a review in the *Theatrical Journal* (December 26, 1850):

It gives us great pleasure to pronounce him superior to any other actor of the present day in this character. He gave a new reading to the part. We never saw so natural a piece of acting since the palmy days of E. Kean.

Only one opinion seemed to prevail throughout the theatre and that was that he never has been seen to so much advantage in any other character.

The "new reading" which Phelps had given Iago was a credibility that made the character seem real. He did not smirk, scowl, nor address the audience behind the back of other characters. He allowed only his sharp intelligence and a certain watchfulness to show underneath his pose of open-hearted honesty. He appeared to be the blunt soldier, the humble servant, or the gay companion. His malignity was revealed only in the effect of his actions.

At the end he was proudly erect and made his exit with a glance of unspeakable scorn—no ordinary villain's look of hate, but a frighteningly powerful defiance of human sympathy. The acting was "natural" in the sense that he made no points in the role and gave no thrilling highlights. For this reason some critics found his Iago unimpressive. Towse called it unimaginative. One advantage of his interpretation was that it made credible Othello's trust in his lieutenant.

Phelps played Iago many times after leaving Sadler's Wells, and even in the later years was still praised for his naturalness in comparison with the usual stage Iago. The Manchester *Sphinx* on November 27, 1869, said:

> Mr. Phelps's by-play and naturalness in this character are remarkable. Most actors deliver Iago's asides in a loud voice, and to the audience. Mr. Phelps repeats them quietly and rapidly to himself.[14]

During his long management of Sadler's Wells, Phelps played Leontes more frequently than any other Shakespearean hero except Hamlet. His acting was an important factor in the success of *The Winter's Tale,* a play formerly regarded by many critics as "closet drama." Leontes had previously been interpreted as a kind of lesser Othello—a man with a high sense of honor and a trusting love of his wife who is betrayed into unjust suspicion. Phelps, on the contrary, adopted the interpretation set forth by Coleridge that he is a man by nature jealous. From his first appearance he showed a temperament easily aroused to suspicion by inadequate cause. There was a violence in his love for Hermione that seemed to snatch eagerly at occasions for tormenting both her and himself. He was moody, prone to abrupt withdrawal into his own thoughts, and continually worried about what others were thinking of him. His injustice to his wife seemed rather the result of his fear of ridicule than the reaction of a man sensitive to the loss of his honor. It was not, in this interpretation, a sympathetic character, and yet it was so convincing on the stage that spectators were held in the grip of the emotions displayed. They felt the climax of the statue scene with a palpable shock.

Critics were quick to recognize the importance of Phelps's new reading of the character. His success was felt to be a demonstration of the correctness of Coleridge's interpretation, and its insight provided the basis for a new understanding of *The Winter's Tale*, both in the psychological characterization of the hero and in the motivation for the play's action. With Leontes as an imitation of Othello, Shakespeare's presentation of the nature of a jealous man had been blurred by misreading, and the events of the action had seemed to lack sufficient motivation.

In the later years of his management when reviewers had become accustomed to the acting of Charles Kean, they were struck by the majesty of Phelps's Leontes and by the depth and variety of his emotions. The *Weekly Dispatch* (October 10, 1858) spoke of his "perfect ebb of the soul" in portraying Leontes' desolate misery after his loss of Hermione. This kind of gradual transition from one state of mind to another, with an underlying struggle of emotions, was a special feature of Phelps's acting—as much a part of his style as Macready's rapid transitions were of his.

The slow transition was a central part of his portrayal of Timon of Athens. In the early scenes he had a dignity that marked the man as an aristocrat, and he showed a liberal comradeship that provided a natural explanation for his reckless generosity. His manner was easy, his gestures large, his voice smooth and full. This interpretation contrasted with that of Edmund Kean, who had adopted an air of cynicism early in the play.

At the discovery of his friends' ingratitude, Phelps's first outbursts had the fierce indignation of a sensitive man terribly shocked. Gradually he made the transition into bitterness, showing the inner struggle of one emotion against another as painful realization forced itself upon Timon's unwilling mind. The change was climaxed by the curse at the end of the third act, which reviewers said he delivered with the force of prophetic inspiration.

As the curtain opened on the fourth act, he was seen sitting on the ground in a pose that conveyed the total change in Timon's nature. Self-containment and isolation were expressed in physical terms. By gesture and bearing and by tone of voice he kept this characterization prominent through the rest of the tragedy, in his anger, in the mocking raillery of his dispute with Apemantus, and in his bitter calm. At the same time he preserved a dignity from his former position which contrasted with the snarling meanness of Apemantus, increasing the sense of tragedy by the juxtaposition of a noble mind suffering from its isolation and the misery-loving misanthrope.

That this interpretation was effective on the stage is indicated by the success of *Timon of Athens* at Sadler's Wells, where its first production ran for a month and a half. Critics found the character unexpectedly interesting, and the *Morning Advertiser* (October 13, 1856) said that Timon could be compared with Hamlet and Lear in humanity and in nobility of character.

Phelps used the gradual transition to interpret Shakespeare's Brutus. At the beginning of *Julius Caesar* he brought out the calmness and firmness of Brutus, contrasting him at every point with the excitable and irritable Cassius. Gradually, and without loss of dignity, he allowed Brutus to show increasing jealousy and ambition until these emotions reached a climax in the second act, giving credible motivation for the murder of Caesar. In the last two acts he assumed a calm heroism, with moments of tenderness that fully engaged the sympathy of the audience.

It is notable that Phelps chose Brutus for his farewell performance at Sadler's Wells, since it is not a showy part capable of inspiring great applause. In fact many actors have avoided the role because it offers little opportunity for dazzling the audience with great moments, and because the fretful and caustic Cassius can easily command more interest. (Macready disliked playing it, especially with Phelps as Cassius.) But Phelps had a gift for showing a noble and heroic mind under an unassuming exterior in a way that appealed to Victorian audiences.

This same talent made his Henry V a favorite. In the regal dignity and courtly manner of the early scenes, the biting sarcasm of his reply to the French king, and the stern justice of his sentence upon the traitors, the role gives any actor some effective scenes, but in the third and fourth acts an actor must be able to be eloquent without spouting. Phelps delivered the heroic speeches with stirring passion but made a swift transition into the simple and colloquial as if his British nature was embarrassed by this display of emotion. The same soldierly avoidance of an open expression of emotion made the wooing of Katherine a delightful scene— "as excellent a piece of high comedy as we have seen," said the *Morning Advertiser* (October 26, 1852). His modest, soldierly, and eloquent King

Henry won superlatives from many critics. The *Daily News* said that he "has a patent for performing the character of a great-souled, aspiring, energetic man, and stands unrivalled as the actor of heroes—the most genuine impersonator of nobility of mind." [15]

In some types of Shakespearean tragic roles Phelps was not effective. He could not play the passionate lover and never willingly acted Romeo. In *Antony and Cleopatra* his best scenes were those in which he turned to the affairs of Rome, especially those depicting his struggle to free himself from Cleopatra's hold. Aboard Pompey's galley he caught Antony's sensual abandonment to drunken revelry, delighting the audience with the humor of the scene and pointing up the essential difference between the character of Antony and that of the prudent Caesar. But he was unconvincing in the Egyptian scenes.

Nor had he any talent for the dashing young hero. He knew that he was an inadequate Hotspur and rarely played the role.[16] In Coriolanus most critics felt that he had neither the lofty disdain of John Kemble nor the psychological subtlety of Macready. He did not fall into Edmund Kean's error of expressing ungovernable anger, but his dignity lacked aristocratic pride. It is some tribute to his acting that he was able to overcome the natural prejudice of the plebeian Sadler's Wells audience and win their sympathy for so alien a hero.

In two Shakespearean plays Phelps took up minor roles which other tragedians had played before him. Charles Kemble's Mercutio was well remembered when Phelps appeared in the role in 1846. The chief difference between the two was that Kemble had tended to dominate the play whereas Phelps kept the character in proportion to the play. Even the famous Queen Mab speech, which traditionally had been delivered as a separate little oration, he spoke as part of the dialogue in Mercutio's characteristic tone and manner. Similarly, when he played Jaques, a role Macready had taken at Drury Lane, Phelps did not make a "point" of the Seven Ages speech. He gave a new interpretation of Jaques, portraying him as a man with only the detachment and not the bitterness of a cynic. Assuming an air of reflective indolence, he showed a pensive rather than a sullen melancholy. The *Dramatic and Musical Review* (December 18, 1847) called it "without doubt, the best upon the stage." The *Times* (October 26, 1857), which had once criticized Macready's Jaques for its "overstraining at light and shade," praised Phelps for avoiding the usual points.

COMIC ROLES

As a young actor in the provinces Phelps had often played comic roles, and even at Exeter when he was establishing his reputation as a tragedian, he once played the lead in the comic afterpiece. On the London stage in the Macready years he had given some indication of his talent for comedy in performances of Old Dornton (*Road to Ruin*) and Captain Channel (*Prisoner of War*), but it was not until his third season at Sadler's Wells that Phelps launched a career in comedy which is unique among English tragedians.

His assumption of Falstaff in *Henry the Fourth, Part One* was a surprise to critics and audience in the autumn of 1846. His tragic style, with its force and emotional depth, had not prepared them for his transformation into the witty, roguish knight. Temperamentally and physically he was indeed not suited to the role; but he succeeded through intelligence, imagination, and professional skill in creating a believable and fascinating, though unusual, Falstaff. The performance at once established him as a comic actor of the first rank.

His interpretation had very little of the self-enjoyment, the sensuality, and the quality actors call "unction," which had been traditionally associated with the character of Falstaff. He emphasized instead the lively intelligence and a certain aristocratic suaveness, creating a Falstaff with a dry, caustic humor, a self-possessed effrontery, and what the critics caught as "Yankee shrewdness." The portrait was sufficiently well done, both in clearly establishing this conception and in bringing out the details that gave it convincing life on the stage, to be a success if only as a *tour de force;* but it seems to have been more than that. The German critic Fontane called it "perhaps his greatest role." [18] For many years there was no other Falstaff on the stage that could rival it, and although most reviewers said that it was not the ideal Falstaff, they enjoyed it.

In his Falstaff of *The Merry Wives of Windsor* Phelps used the same method: skillful accumulation of small details of characterization, a thoroughly finished portrait, and emphasis upon sarcastic wit. But he created a different Falstaff for this comedy. Here, according to Fontane, he was above all a knight, a gentleman who observes standards of decorum even in vulgar situations. He had the unshakeable calm of shameless cynicism, giving the impression that he felt he would be conferring an honor upon a lower-class woman by seducing her. He was just as fat, but he dressed his corpulence with care, wore his white curly hair and beard neatly clipped, and presented an elegance of appearance and manner that distinguished him from the Falstaff of the historical plays.

Again some thought he lacked exuberance and spontaneity. James Anderson complained of his dryness and remarked that he should always have been fried in lard before a performance.[19] The humor of his interpretation arose from Falstaff's wit, and the comedy of the play as a whole was perhaps increased by emphasis upon his intelligence, which made him more of a match for the merry wives.

In Falstaff Phelps was forced to alter the traditional interpretation because of his own physique and personality, but in Malvolio he broke with tradition for a more important reason. For many generations comic actors had used theatrical devices and conscious humor to provoke laughter from the audience, with little regard for Shakespeare's intention or for the relation of the character to the rest of the scene. J. P. Harley, the Bottom and Trinculo of the older generation, would fix his eye on a man in the pit and direct all his humor at him until the man laughed. It was a trick he had learned from Joseph Munden and an indication of the technique used by a traditional comedian. William Farren also would frequently turn directly to the audience instead of addressing his speeches to the other actors when he had a point to make. Buckstone, Wright, and Compton had developed idiosyncracies of speech, gesture, and dress so that they could make an audience laugh before they had delivered the first line of a role. They did not aim primarily at interpretation of character, but used words and situations as springboards for their own humor. Even in Shakespeare's time comedians took liberties with the text to show off their clowning.

Malvolio was traditionally played with a comic strut and smirk, and his lines were delivered with an emphasis designed to provoke laughter. In 1847 Phelps introduced a new interpretation, consistent in its parts and related to the whole play, which was recognized at once as an inspired piece of acting. Basing his conception upon the characterization given by Olivia early in the play, "O, you are sick of self-love, Malvolio," he made Malvolio the embodiment of colossal conceit.[20] Carrying himself with a frozen calm of self-esteem, he walked with a heaviness that implied a consciousness of his own grandeur, and there was condescension in every gesture. His face was gravely serious through sheer emptiness of expression, and his eyelids were lowered in disdain. So completely was every facial expression, gesture, and bodily movement controlled to impersonate Malvolio that in his first appearance Phelps was not recognized by the audience, who certainly knew him well, until he began to speak.

He seemed to ignore the presence of those he despised. The twittings of the Clown provoked from him only a passing shade of pity. Even the news of Olivia's love for him was received calmly, with the air of approving her good judgment. When he followed her supposed instructions to be opposite with a kinsman and surly with the servants, he did so only by displaying a more assured sense of his own elevation, changing his former condescension to open contempt. The smile which she requested he seemed to bestow as a reward for her wisdom in loving him; and in spite of his effort to cast upon her a beam of gracious warmth, the smile he produced was one of intense satisfaction with himself. He bore his imprisonment with the patience of one who does not doubt the eventual triumph of his own righteousness. When at last the plot against him was revealed, his eyes opened wide during the moment of comprehension, but closed again as the consciousness of his own worth once more took possession. He began to withdraw in state, without a word, when the Fool's taunt about the whirligig of time gave him a second thought about the future. Returning with as much haste as dignity allowed, he uttered his final threat with the contempt of grandeur.

This Malvolio provoked less immediate laughter than overtly comic performances of the role, because Phelps did not interfere with the essential humor of the character by emphasizing a funny line to make a point. Nor did he convert the role into seriousness as Irving and other actors after him have done, by showing Malvolio to be mistreated and by giving his last speech as a serious curse. There was no sentimentality in Phelps's interpretation. It was a complete portrait of fatuous vanity, delightfully funny during the performance but so vividly presented that it left a lasting impression on the spectator of something more than mere amusement. His Malvolio was admired by audiences until the end of his career and pleased a number of critics who did not like his tragic style.

In *A Midsummer Night's Dream* Phelps's portrayal of Bottom was an expression of his interpretation of the whole play—a poetic fantasy with the atmosphere of an actual dream. In the opening scenes he was the conceited and nervous weaver, with red nose, shaggy hair, and a look of sottish stupidity, revealing his restlessness by constant gesticulation and the angularity of his movements, and showing self-importance by an equal emphasis upon all his words. *Punch* (October 15, 1853) said that Phelps caught the asinine qualities of Bottom so well that the ass's head was not needed to mark him as an ass:

> When Bottom, in the first scene, desires to be Wall, and Moonshine, and Lion, his conceit brays aloud, but brays with undeveloped ears. But herein is the genius of our actor. The traditional bully Bottom is a dull, stupid, mouthing ass, with no force save in his dullness. Bottom, as played by Mr. Phelps, is an ass with a vehemence, a will, a vigour in his conceit, but still an ass. An ass that fantastically kicks his heels to the right and left, but still an ass. An ass that has the most prolonged variations of his utterance— nevertheless it is braying, and nothing better.

One reviewer saw him as a "despot of low life who has gained a character for intellect among his companions by force of mere dogmatism."[21] Marston speaks of the calmness of his self-conceit, expressed rather by signs of inward relish of his own ability than by boisterous display; to Morley he seemed "a strange, elaborate, and uncouth dream-figure," as grotesque as a man seen in a nightmare.[22] In the fairy scenes Bottom was subtly changed, as if a mist had also been thrown over his character. Morley carefully describes the difference:

> The violent gesticulations become stillness, and the hands are fixed on the breast. They are busy with unperceived business of managing the movements of the ass's head, but it is not for that reason they are so perfectly still. The change of manner is a part of the conception. The dream-figure is dreaming, there is dream within dream; Bottom is quiet; his humour becomes more unctuous, but Bottom is translated. He accepts all that happens, quietly, as dreamers do; and the ass's head we also accept quietly, for we too are in the middle of our dream, and it does not create surprise. Not a touch of comedy was missed in this capital piece of acting, yet Bottom was completely incorporated with the Midsummer Night's Dream, made an essential part of it, as unsubstantial, as airy and refined as all the rest. Quite masterly was the delivery by Mr. Phelps of the speech of Bottom on awakening. He was still a man subdued, but subdued by the sudden plunge into a state of an unfathomable wonder. His dream clings about him, he cannot sever the real from the unreal, and still we are made to feel that his reality itself is but a fiction. The preoccupation continues to be manifest during his next scene with the players, and his parting, "No more words; away; go away," was in the tone of a man who had lived with spirits and was not yet perfectly returned into the flesh.

Phelps had given special attention to designing the ass's head so that it would carry out his interpretation. The ears and features were controlled by strings, which Phelps worked invisibly with his fingers. The movements of the head were not used to provoke laughter, but only to aid in the actor's expression of the character. In a letter to his wife written in 1867 when he was playing Bottom in Liverpool, he contrasts the ass's head of the local theatre with his own:[23]

> I am very glad I have brought the Donkey's head, for though they have a new one it is not good. It is a most *impudent* looking ass instead of the *stupid* sleek thing it should be for Bottom. It looks impossible that it should *sleep*. I should be dreadfully annoyed if I had to wear it.

Phelps's success in realizing Shakespeare's character on the stage is indicated both by the enthusiasm of a large and diverse group of critics and by the similarity of their reactions. They grasped the essence of his interpretation and approved of it as thoroughly Shakespearean while praising his portrayal as one of the great achievements of the English stage. *Punch*'s review began with the statement that bully Bottom had been "translated" by Phelps, "translated from matter-of-fact into poetic humor; translated from the commonplace tradition of the play-house to a thing subtly grotesque—rarely, and heroically whimsical . . . from dull tradition to purest, airiest Shakespeare."

Phelps used the same fresh approach to several less important comic roles. As Don Adriano, the Spaniard of *Love's Labour's Lost,* whose affected finery of speech and dress contrast ludicrously with the poverty underneath the surface, he avoided the conventions of the stage fop. Although he had the complacency of his Malvolio, an evident lack of intelligence and a ridiculous dependence upon his tiny page kept the character in a lighter vein. He emphasized the euphuistic phraseology and the good humor characteristic of the whole comedy. His Parolles in *All's Well That Ends Well* was a thorough characterization of the coward and braggart without adventitious humor.

In *Henry the Fourth, Part Two,* Phelps displayed the plasticity of his acting by playing both the old King and Justice Shallow. Towse speaks of the complete metamorphosis in bulk, gait, and manner of speech which Phelps achieved from one role to the other. As Shallow his voice was a childish treble—"dislocated and broken, shrill, voluble, hesitant, pompous, or tetchy," and the King's voice was full of "melody, imagination, and pictorial power." [24] In his dying scene when the king is lying in bed, the actor must convey by his voice alone the character of the man and his conflicting emotions. A critic who saw one of Phelps's last performances found this scene impressively moving:

> The broken emphasis with which he articulates the single word "Harry" conveys whole volumes of pathos, and speaks an affectionate reconciliation which a careful culling of all the words of endearment in an entire language could not equal. We are mistaken if any actor of the past half century has approached Mr. Phelps in this most impressive situation.[25]

In playing Shallow Phelps used his talent for revealing the underlying thoughts of a character who is attempting to repress or conceal them. Shallow's fear of death showed through all his pretended indifference and assumed mirth. After hearing that old Double is dead, Shallow turns quickly to happier thoughts, but as Phelps played it the dismal reminder could be seen to persist under the feverish high spirits and his delighted welcome of Falstaff. Marston summarizes his description of Phelps's Shallow in these words:

> Such are my recollections of Phelps's Justice Shallow, and of the moral impression which it left; while the various phases of the man—his dreary libertine vaunts, his clinging to life and yearning for distraction against ugly thoughts, and the overdone merriment which could not cloak his apprehensions—were delivered with that ease and precision of expression— just to the finest *nuance*—which he had so happily cultivated in comedy; the garrulity of age, accompanied by what may be called an air of rustic courtliness, giving fresh individuality to the part.[26]

One source of Phelps's success in getting all the humor out of such a role is indicated by Towse's statement that "he solved puzzles of the dialogue with unfailing ingenuity, giving it cohesion and sequence." Careful study of the text combined with what Towse called "sheer mimetic intuition" to make his Justice Shallow a masterpiece of humor.

The switch from one character to the other appears to have been more than a *tour de force*. In all his acting Phelps used his body as well as voice to express the character he played, so a dual role merely placed in juxtaposition two of his creations; and in this case he was peculiarly well suited to both parts. The *Morning Advertiser* (March 18, 1853) described it as a truly great performance:

The step from the grand and energetic Bolingbroke to the paltry-minded Shallow is a wide one, and the two characters may be said each to lie on the extreme confines of human nature. To mark by caricature the strong contrast between the two is within the capacity of a small artist; but to give in its breadth and depth the deep paternal affection, the right royal dignity, and the setting in death of an energetic mind of the largest scope, and in the same hour to delineate the expiring fatuity of a vain, feeble, and petty intellect and character, is an exercise of the histrionic art that is not often witnessed.

Phelps's methods of using detail of characterization can be seen in Morley's description of his Christopher Sly:

Mr. Phelps, who is the best Hamlet now upon the stage, banishes from his face every spark of intelligence while representing Sly. Partly he effects this by keeping the eyes out of court as witnesses of intelligence. The lids are drooped in the heavy slumberousness of a stupid nature; there is no such thing as a glance of intelligence allowed to escape from under them; the eyes are hidden almost entirely when they are not widely exposed in a stupid stare. The acting of this little sketch is, indeed, throughout most careful and elaborate. There is, as we have said, no flinching from the perfect and emphatical expression of the broader lights and shadows of the character, Christopher is at first sensually drunk; and when, after his awakening in the lord's house, the page is introduced to him as his lady wife, another chord of sensuality is touched, the brute hugs and becomes amorous. Of the imagination that, even when there are offered to the sensual body new delights of the appetite, is yet unable to soar beyond the reach already attained, Mr. Phelps, in the details of his acting, gives a variety of well-conceived suggestions. Thus, to the invitation, "Will't please your mightiness to wash your hands?" Christopher, when he has grasped the fact that a basin is being held before him in which he must wash, enters upon such a wash as sooty hands of tinkers only can require, and having made an end of washing and bespattering, lifts up instinctively the corner of his velvet robe to dry his hands upon.[27]

Occasionally, for a benefit, Phelps followed a performance of a tragic hero with a comic lead in the afterpiece, delighting the audience with his versatility. Charles Rice, who fought his way through a mob of would-be spectators on one of these occasions, records his opinion in his diary for March 20, 1850:

I would not have missed Phelps's Jeremy Diddler for a Pound. To say no man could play it so well, who could equally shine in Macbeth would be weakly praise;—in my opinion no light Comedian of the present day could perform it near so well.—It was one of the greatest performances as to individuality of character I ever witnessed![28]

CRITICAL ESTIMATE

In assessing Phelps's place among Shakespearean actors certain judgments are easily made. In the range and variety of his acting only Garrick approached him. In his search for anonymity in a role—avoidance of points, transformation of physique, voice, and manner, and careful use of details for characterization—he differed from all the famous tragedians who preceded him on the English stage. In the pathos of his acting and the emotional involvement of the audience he exceeded his predecessors. He was like Macready in consistency of characterization, but he did not equal Macready in psychological subtlety. He had some of Edmund Kean's passionate force, but he did not achieve the thrilling climaxes of Kean. He had some of the strength and dignity of the Kemble family, but he lacked their personal grace and poise. During the years of his prime his voice was more resonant, musical, and flexible than any actor within living memory of contemporary reviewers.

In other areas of comparison judgment is more difficult. Would Phelps's style seem hopelessly stilted and artificial today? In what sense was he a traditional actor, as opposed to Charles Kean, Sir Henry Irving, and perhaps Edwin Booth? To attempt an answer to these questions it is necessary to understand the revolution in Shakespearean acting which began at the Princess's under Charles Kean's management.

Kean had always excelled in theatrically effective points—a style frequently condemned as stagey and tricky in his Shakespearean roles but well suited to the melodramatic parts in which he had been most successful. In the 1850's Kean modified his style by adopting a quieter manner, a restrained voice, and the more casual demeanor of the drawing room. He replaced the declamatory style and passionate force of traditional acting (for which his voice and figure were not well suited) with the concentrated intensity of a lowered voice and with realism of detail in portraying the peculiarities of a character. In *The Corsican Brothers* he surprised audiences by showing that contemporary dress and manners need not be impediments to tragic expression. Macready's dislike of modern dress parts undoubtedly arose from a fear that the elevation of his tragic style would seem incongruous with everyday clothes, and this was not an uncommon feeling in the nineteenth-century theatre. Kean solved the problem by developing a tragic style that suited the clothes. That it was not a natural style in the sense we now use the term is abundantly clear. His best roles were those of a grotesque and exaggerated character, and the effectiveness of his acting still depended upon points even though achieved by new methods. Audiences waited with breathless attention for the famous moment in *The Corsican Brothers* when Kean would take the blood-stained handkerchief from his lips, revealing with deliberate nonchalance his mortal wound. In *Pizarro,* which was according to the *Weekly Dispatch* (September 7, 1856) the first time Kean acted without rant, he thrilled the audience by catching an overhanging branch to swing himself over a chasm.

Kean used his new manner in Shakespearean roles as well as melodrama, and critics generally found it superior to his former style although many recognized that something had been lost in substituting a contemporary idiom for traditional declamation. Even such a critic as Westland Marston, who wrote plays for the Princess's and thoroughly approved Kean's new style of acting, carefully distinguished the virtues of the restrained and familiar manner from those of poetic imagination in a great tragedian. Perhaps his best statement of the difference occurs in a description of Ellen Kean's Lady Macbeth:

> It might have been predicted that Mrs. Charles Kean would scarcely make a striking Lady Macbeth. With her fine intensity of feeling, fervour of exposition, and power to translate herself into various types of life, she could hardly be said to combine imagination in its strictly poetic sense. She loved to seize those traits which bring a character within the range of actual life—no doubt an excellent method generally, though its sole use hardly suits those types which, while essentially true, are too remote and awful for familiar treatment. . . . There was a sort of artificial moderation in her rendering of Lady Macbeth's terrible adjurations. It seemed as though she had doubted that an actual woman could have uttered them, and had therefore striven to given them reality by softening their extravagance. From the hints of one or two mighty phrases, on the other hand, an imagination like that of Mrs. Siddons would, one may conceive, seize the *soul* of the woman, take *that* as the reality, and care little whether the probabilities of actual expression were overpassed or otherwise.[29]

Phelps's early experience in stock companies—a training which Kean had missed by beginning his career as a star—had given him a mastery of the body of knowledge about acting which had been handed down through many generations. Like Macready, Edmund Kean, and others before them, he developed his own style within the compass of a well-known tradition. Whatever modifications he made, whether in a basic matter like style or in a small piece of stage business, were made knowingly and not by chance. Moreover, even such changes were governed by the same assumptions about the art of acting and the nature of theatrical performance that had prevailed in Shakespeare's time. To Phelps as to Shakespeare the stage was a place for presenting the creations of poetic imagination, and the actor's art consisted in realizing the poetry as much as character and action. Although these assumptions had long since been challenged on the Continent by the emergence of the Romantic drama and the concept of a more strictly representational theatre, they were unquestioned in England until Charles Kean applied to tragedy and comedy the methods and style associated with melodrama. Phelps and most of the regular members of his company remained untouched by the new trend toward the familiar style. While Kean and his followers were trying to "soften the extravagance" of Shakespeare's language and "seize those traits which bring a character within the range of actual life," Phelps was working hard to teach an untrained generation of actors how to read blank verse and how to "seize the soul" of the character without worrying whether the probabilities of actual expression were exceeded. Although the word "natural" was used to describe both actors, two different meanings were intended: Kean's acting was natural in its assumption of contemporary modes of speech and gesture; Phelps's acting was natural in its "truthfulness to nature," that is in probing the human soul and in avoiding theatrical effects.

Fontane's opinion of the acting at Sadler's Wells is interesting because the style was so foreign to the acting he knew in Germany. He was used to performances more restrained, gentlemanly, and consciously artistic than even Charles Kean's style. At Sadler's Wells he discovered that traditional English actors played with a passionate abandon, that audiences enjoyed battle scenes and terror on the stage, and that such an actor as Phelps could hold the spectator in the grip of the emotions he portrayed. He decided that Germans had been underplaying Shakespeare. He says that Phelps's acting convinced him of the power of pathos, even when it decidedly goes astray, and of the superiority of the natural style over the obviously artistic.[30]

German critics who saw him in 1859 generally support Fontane's view that Phelps's acting was distinguished for the consistency of his delineation of each character and for the absence of artificiality in his style. A reviewer quoted in the *Theatrical Journal* (April 20, 1859) said:

> Phelps solved the most difficult problem of the Tragedian—viz., to speak in the only manner to be approved of—to speak in those tones appropriate to the real sentiments of the passion in all its shades of dignity, deep sorrow, despair mounting to deep destruction. . . . We never met an unnatural display of art, or a far-fetched effect, seeking only for the hurried applause of the mass.

Later, a Hamburg critic writing in *Der Freischütz,* expressed a similar opinion:

> Phelps is a male Ristori, as true to nature and as careful in study, as genial and free in production, and as obedient to rule as the celebrated Italian. His Lear is a living fact; he is an artistic creation in the highest sense of the word. We cannot especially notice any particular scene, for each is a necessary consequence of its predecessor. . . . The expression of his passion followed the course of events step by step, and the climax was rooted in the design of the character.[31]

Another German critic, whom Fontane regarded highly, praised Phelps's Shylock for its total unity and harmony of tone as well as for the strength of his portrayal.[32]

Most English critics at first preferred the traditional style for Shakespeare, asserting that Kean's style was wrong for poetic drama. Phelps was praised for his ability to present a true interpretation of great tragic heroes, for his skill in reading poetry, and for the absence of all trickery in his acting. Nevertheless, the influence of the new style wrought a subtle change of taste which began to make traditional acting seem old-fashioned. Critics might condemn Kean's acrobatics in *Pizarro* as utterly irrelevant to tragic expression, but a week later they would find the *Macbeth* at Sadler's Wells a little less spirited than they had remembered from previous seasons. They might deplore the artificial moderation of Ellen Kean's delivery of Lady Macbeth's speeches, but as their ears became accustomed to the more varied intonation and speed of a conversational style, they began to feel that the traditional poetic style was heavy and slow.

In the autumn of 1856 reviews first began to reflect this change in taste. The *Theatrical Journal* (September 10, 1856) in commenting upon Phelps's Macbeth remarked, "We thought at times there was a monotony in his delivery we had not noticed before." The *Athenaeum* (September 13, 1856) made a similar comment upon the whole company:

> The long experience of this company with the Shakesperian modes of expression and habits of thought gives them a command over the dialogue not generally appreciable elsewhere. The weight of the delivery, however, in these "fast days," may be regarded by some as extreme; but those who still linger with pleasure on the recollection of the elocution that distinguished the stage in past times are glad to meet with the traces of it that are still recognizable on the Islington boards.

In subsequent seasons there was increasing criticism of monotony and over-distinct pronunciation in Phelps's delivery. Although his biographers in *The Life* explain this by saying that in his years at Sadler's Wells he had gradually adopted a more measured elocution so that the audience at the back of the long pit could hear every word, this explanation is not convincing. If Phelps had slowed his pace to achieve clearer enunciation, the complaints about his delivery would have been made equally of his tragic and comic roles, whereas they are restricted to the tragic. Moreover, the time required for a performance would have increased over the years if the actors at Sadler's Wells had slowed their delivery, and there is no indication that performances in 1860 ran longer than performances in 1844. Therefore it seems clear that Phelps's delivery appeared to be slow and measured to critics of the late fifties because they had become accustomed to the new style of rapid and conversational delivery.

Fechter's appearance as Hamlet in 1861 was the greatest single event in this evolution from the traditional to the modern school of acting. By discarding the flaxen wig and black velvet doublet, by introducing new interpretations of the meaning of lines, and by ignoring stage conventions, Fechter freed English actors from bondage to the past and established the principle of innovation in acting Shakespeare. So complete was his triumph that his style was at once accepted and widely imitated, and his methods have continued in force for a century. We, today, are so used to fresh interpretations and absence of convention in Shakespearean acting that it is difficult to imagine the excitement caused by Fechter's Hamlet. His subtlety in using action to bring out the hidden meaning of a line, his finesse in showing sudden changes of mood, the ease of his manner, and his conversational mode of speech gave the stage a new sophistication and an exciting realism which delighted London.

As in the case of Charles Kean, the critics generally objected to fashionable taste; and when Fechter applied his methods to Othello, they protested that *Othello* without grandeur may easily become a domestic melodrama, particularly when the poetry is slurred and when innovations in stage business emphasize the sensational aspects of the play. In the scene before the senate Fechter assumed an air of careless indifference. In the second act he was less a soldier than a newlywed, expressing petulance rather than anger over the riot which erupts in the night. In the last act his severe cutting of the text, his playing of the murder with a violent physical struggle in full view of the audience, and his unexpected stabbing of Iago instead of himself—all served to translate tragedy into the rapid action, superficiality, and glibness of melodrama. The *Daily Telegraph* (November 4, 1861) asserted that his "pathos is certainly not that of a Moor; it is scarcely that of a *man*." The *Morning Advertiser* (November 4, 1861) complained of his commonplace familiarity and his search for bizarre readings. Morley was shocked by one instance of Fechter's use of gesture and intense emphasis upon certain words to give an entirely new reading.[33] He cites an instance in the fifth act. Fechter picked up a looking glass from Desdemona's bed and stared into it while he delivered the speech "It is the cause, it is the cause," implying by the gesture and by his emphasis upon the pronoun that his black skin was the cause of his misfortunes. Such wrenching of the meaning from the author's intention is typical of the new school and utterly foreign to the tradition in which Phelps acted.

The comparison of Phelps's traditional style of acting with Fechter's new style is given another dimension by reviewers' comments upon the acting of G. V. Brooke, who was playing Othello at Drury Lane in October, 1861. Although Brooke had never fulfilled the promise of his triumphant debut in 1848, his fiery delivery and vocal force attracted many playgoers. Like the American actor Edwin Forrest, he excelled in the physical strength of his acting—an important ingredient of the tragic force of a traditional actor; but his failure to achieve real insight into the nature of the tragic hero prevented him, like Forrest, from entering the first rank of tragedians. An American observer once remarked that Brooke played the entire role of Othello in italics.

Most reviewers found him guilty of rant. The *Morning Advertiser* (November 4, 1861) contrasted his "stage pomposity" with Fechter's "common-place familiarity" as the two extremes between which Phelps followed the proper mean. The clear distinction made by nineteenth-century critics between bombast or rant and tragic acting shows that the "ham" actor of the late nineteenth century, although he may have preserved elements of the traditional style, was not a true representative of traditional acting. As early as 1860 the actor George Vandenhoff complained that the advent of lower-class audiences into the patent theatres had led to a perversion of traditional acting:

> Rant has taken the place of passion; extravagance has banished simple nature and truth. That "smoothness and temperance" which Shakespeare inculcated, and which was once considered the *acme* of art . . . is now regarded as "slow"; and as the sign, not of a proper self-control and well-regulated taste, but of a want of energy and power.[34]

In contrast to Brooke, Phelps did not rant.

After Fechter and Charles Kean, audiences generally developed a taste for a less vigorous and elevated style in Shakespearean acting than that traditionally used before 1850. Phelps himself appears to have modified his acting during this decade. The *Athenaeum* (October 6, 1860), for instance, commented that as Prospero he used "a more familiar style of utterance than formerly . . . perhaps in obedience to modern taste." His Hamlet of the following year elicited these remarks from the *Athenaeum* (October 19, 1861):

> Mr. Phelps's style has of late also changed for the better. It is much less declamatory and irregular than it used to be, and he cultivates more the softer tones of his voice. It may be objected that his present subdued style is not so salient as his more demonstrative manner. . . . The quiet elocution is certainly somewhat oppressive from its monotony, but it is perfectly consistent with taste and judgment.

Thus, Phelps's style in his later years was even farther from the conscious artistry which made points of famous speeches and emphasized physical force in declamation—aspects of the traditional style which survived in William Creswick and John Ryder unredeemed by the genius of Macready or Edmund Kean.

For this reason his acting was probably better suited to the task of bringing poetic drama to the audiences of his later years, accustomed as they were to more realistic modes of expression, than actors with whom he was compared in his early career. For many spectators in the late sixties he succeeded in conveying the grandeur and heightened emotion of the traditional style without offending the contemporary taste for a more familiar speech and manner. In his Othello of 1864 at Drury Lane, one of the older dramatic critics found a nearly perfect development of tragic expression:

> He has now utterly cast aside the stage traditions, and all traces of the manners of his predecessors; and he gives a pure, original, and highly-wrought portrait, entirely from his own study. The last lingering bursts of the great Kean, who invented them; the gurgling spasms wherewith Macready expressed his agonies, are no longer to be traced; nor is there scarcely to be found in the portrayal any filling up of the emotion with conventional tones and mere elocutionary skill. He has molded the conception in his intellect until it comes pure and perfect from him; and the portrait, a whole-length one, is complete in all its grandeur.[35]

To be sure, Phelps did not please all the audience at West End theatres in his later years. A new generation of playgoers who looked first of all for refinement and restraint of manner found him coarse and exaggerated in style. Frederic Harrison, who preferred the "naturalness, simplicity, and delicacy" of the European theatre, condemned him (along with Macready and other traditional actors) for his total inability to portray the manners of dukes, counts, and baronets on the stage. Apparently he saw Phelps only once and pronounced him "as bad an actor as stupidity and mannerism can make a man," complaining also of a "constant burring" in his speech.[36] It is true that Phelps used a rolled or trilled "r" in some words as an aid to theatrical expression, just as he used clear vowel sounds and distinct consonants not found in everyday English speech.[37] To those whose taste demanded realism in acting, any attempt to carry on the traditional style would seem mannered and unnatural. Sir Theodore Martin also preferred a more refined and moderated style. When Phelps was playing with Helen Faucit in 1864, he complained that Phelps's Macbeth was unmannerly, loud, and ignoble and that he spoke "as no man ever spoke in real life." [38]

A number of critics who saw Phelps only in his old age found him unsatisfactory in tragedy while they praised his comic roles in the highest terms. But even these admired his performance of Cardinal Wolsey, which he played at the end of his life when he was more than seventy years old. Joseph Knight made this comment on his Wolsey:

> Never fortunate or successful in the presentation of passion or heroic re- solve, Mr. Phelps shows himself an admirable actor the moment the internal workings of a nature compounded of qualities noble and sordid have to be depicted. His presentation of Wolsey is perfect.[39]

By 1875 Phelps was being compared with Henry Irving, then known as the leading Shakespearean actor on the stage. His Shylock had intro- duced a new sociological dimension to the interpretation of *The Merchant of Venice,* with his portrayal of the Jew as a victim of social prejudice. Irving had also followed Kean and Fechter in a more familiar and melo- dramatic style, although he had the psychological subtlety which Mac- ready had introduced to the stage. The contrast between Phelps's Shy- lock and Irving's was marked. Critics used to Irving's interpretation were surprised at the "wonderful force and manliness" of Phelps's Shylock, and with the old actor's "delicate appreciation of the value of words." He used the traditional reading of the character, keeping his Jew a responsi- ble man. His race and creed were made part of the characterization— neither a display of anti-Semitism nor an excuse for Shylock's actions. In the early scenes he emphasized the irony and distrust expressed in his speech with Christians; and although bitter vindictiveness did not appear until after Jessica's flight, in the last two acts he did not attempt to soften its force. Compared with Irving's Shylock, which strained the meaning of the text to make the character wholly sympathetic, Phelps's portrayal seemed more heroic, healthy, and natural.

Similarly, his Wolsey had a manliness that contrasted with the ascetic and intellectual priest of Irving's interpretation. Towse was impressed with the vital, formidable, and dominant personality of Phelps's Wolsey.[40] He was arrogant, curt, and imperious in speech and action, with a biting sarcasm that hit its mark. Although his aspect and carriage sometimes suggested the humble origin which justified Buckingham's epithet of "butcher's cur," he never relaxed his superior attitude toward the nobles, even after the King's crushing rebuke. In contrast to Irving, Phelps did not use sympathy for the underdog in portraying Shylock or Wolsey. The characters remained heroic, without melodramatic coloring or the excuse of psychological and sociological causes.

And yet Phelps's Wolsey seemed to some critics more moving and convincing than that of Irving. Moy Thomas notes that the fall of Wolsey, as Phelps showed it, was seen not from without but from within.[41] There were no points, no outbursts of fury, no displays of picturesque action, no fuming or chafing, and no undue raising of the voice at any point. Wolsey's feelings were conveyed almost entirely through the spoken words, which Phelps's imagination and skill in delivery interpreted with full meaning, nobility, and pathos. "It is herein that this great actor's power is most conspicuous," writes Thomas. "In the sovereign quality of sincerity of utterance Mr. Phelps is not even approached by any living rival." Thomas predicts that when the relief of finding an actor like Irving, who broke up the old tradition, wears off, "it will be seen how greatly deficient he is in the quality of tone and emphasis so managed as to touch the heart and imagination of his hearers." This, according to Thomas, was the most important quality of Phelps's acting. The second was his "command of attitude and gesture, soberly and moderately used." The third quality was consistency of interpretation: "A performance like that of Mr. Phelps in the part of Wolsey is set, like a piece of music, in a certain key, and all its parts stand in some relation to each other."

The same comparison with Irving was made by Manchester critics when Phelps acted Wolsey at the Prince's Theatre in the following season.

> The self-contented repose of the first act, and the politic anxiousness of the second were, as usual, clearly distinguished from the overthrow—never passing into the indignity of a collapse—of the third. It is a peculiarly happy touch that Mr. Phelps's Cardinal holds his head erect when doing obeisance to the King at the very moment when disgrace is upon him; and the emotion of the scene with Cromwell is an emotion only, though a deep and bitter one, not a theatrical metamorphosis of the man.[42]

This reviewer also expresses a fear often found in comments upon Phelps's last performances:

> Let it be hoped that with him the tradition of an utterance which enables every person in the audience to hear and to understand an author's text will not be lost to the English stage. Without this a dramatic performance of Shakespeare himself reduces itself on the stage to a succession of "points," and in the audience to a succession of "sensations."

The *Manchester Guardian* contrasted Phelps's acting in Wolsey to that of other actors in the cast, which showed "the mischievous, we had almost said demoralizing, influence of Irving":

Here there is true acting—the mirror held up to nature,—a living human being, swept by true if stormy impulses, for whom all that is said and done in his presence has a true and close interest, a sensitive instrument that responds to every touch, powerful or delicate, with appropriate note. . . . At its close it rises into absolute grandeur.[43]

That these critics were not merely old-fashioned purists unwilling to accept the style of acting which belonged to a new age is indicated by the fulfillment of their dire prophecies. Realistic and melodramatic acting, aided by spectacle, have failed to interest the majority of the public in Shakespeare, and those scholarly playgoers who wish to see his works acted are repelled by the distortion of poetry and meaning by actors who have not been trained in the difficult art of reading blank verse and have little acquaintance with Elizabethan modes of speech.

Some English critics, most notably William Archer, felt that Edwin Booth in America had escaped the influence of Charles Kean and Fechter, and that he preserved the traditional style.[44] Reaction to his English debut indicates that most critics found little of the traditional in his acting, and even in America an old tragedian, E. L. Davenport, placed Booth in the new age of long runs and "type" casting.[45] Other evidence, however, suggests that he may indeed have shared with Phelps the distinction of being of the "old school" in a new age.

Perhaps in a twentieth-century theatre we would find Phelps too declamatory and unnatural to allow us full enjoyment of his acting, although surely Macready, Edmund Kean, and John Philip Kemble would seem more unnatural. Because their performances are not preserved, we can make such judgments only by relying upon the criticisms of contemporary witnesses who are unprejudiced and capable—not John Forster on Macready, Sir Theodore Martin on Helen Faucit, or John Coleman on anyone—and upon the verdict of audiences expressed in records of attendance. In Phelps's case there is evidence that he was an actor of the first rank. Among reviewers of his time who considered him the best Shakespearean actor on the stage are John Heraud of the *Athenaeum,* Douglas Jerrold of *Punch,* Henry Morley of the *Examiner,* John Oxenford of the *Times,* Bayle Bernard of the *Weekly Dispatch,* and F. G. Tomlins of the *Advertiser.* These men were literary critics or playwrights as well as theatrical reviewers, and none was a close personal friend of Phelps. In attracting audiences to watch his acting—without the adventitious appeal of royal appearances, fashionableness, attractive leading actresses, lavish spectacle, or musical accompaniment—Phelps surpassed all contemporary Shakespearean actors. If we would find him dull or extravagant on our stage we ought perhaps to reconsider our taste in Shakespearean acting.

One critic who saw him only after the new methods had become established made this judgment:

> We may in truth assert that Mr. Phelps was not only the finest tragedian— he was the soundest, the most learned, and the most conscientious actor that the present generation has ever known. . . . In every character . . . which this truly great artist attempted, his reading invariably bore the stamp of most careful study, united to a scrupulous regard for the author's meaning, and a strict adherence to the author's text. To these was added, in rare perfection, that fine and stately method of elocution which, we are told, was the leading characteristic of the old school, and which is now so little cultivated as to be almost extinct.[46]

V

Phelps and Shakespeare: Manager

THE theatrical manager of the nineteenth century had far more general responsibility than any single person in our present day theatre. He was the lessee of house and property, responsible for its financial matters and for its physical upkeep. He was the manager of a company of actors, whom he selected, paid by the season, trained, and assigned to roles. He was a producer of plays, with full responsibility for reading plays, for choosing which should be performed, and for revising the author's text as he deemed advisable. He was the stage designer, determining the number of scenes and planning the settings, costumes, properties, and lighting for each play. He was the director of each production, supervising rehearsals and coordinating all the parts of a stage performance. Frequently he was also the leading actor.

True, many nineteenth-century managers carried out some of these duties in a most perfunctory way. Since acting was the most important aspect of performances in the traditional theatre, settings often received little attention; and since actors were professional specialists who had played the same role many times, they would accept very little direction at rehearsals. The resulting stage performances did not have the cohesiveness and balance we expect in the theatre today.

The first co-ordinated productions, with a single over-all direction of mounting and acting, appeared not in the legitimate theatres but at the Olympic under Mme. Vestris and Charles Mathews. Their management from 1831 to 1839 presented burletta and light comedy in settings that were consistent in style and suited to the plays, although they did not aim at historical authenticity. The managers also rehearsed their actors with care, attempting to erase traditional conventionalities and achieve the more realistic style characteristic of their own acting.

Macready at Covent Garden and Drury Lane took up the trend toward historical accuracy in costuming and setting begun by the Kembles and established it on the London stage. He also followed Mathews and Vestris in their concept of the total stage picture and its appropriateness to the spirit of the play. His rehearsals were more thorough than any previously known to the legitimate stage, but he was hampered by traditional concepts of acting. Although he gave careful direction to supernumeraries and some minor actors, he did not attempt to express his idea of a play through the acting of supporting players, except perhaps for Helen Faucit, his protégé. Most of his actors would not have accepted such direction, not only because of established custom, but also because Macready's insistence upon complete domination of the stage increased rivalry among them.

DIRECTING THE COMPANY

When Phelps became co-lessee of Sadler's Wells in 1844, he may have expected to do no more directing of rehearsals than Macready had, even though he had spent much of the previous winter training a group of provincial actors at the minor theatre in Liverpool where they had formerly not acted Shakespeare. With Mrs. Warner, George Bennett, Henry Marston, Fanny Cooper, and John Webster in the company at Sadler's Wells, he probably felt that the plays would act themselves while he saved his energies for more urgent tasks. But within the first year of his management, Phelps began to train his company, not only drilling them at rehearsals as Macready had, but working to blend individual parts into the whole and coaching actors in interpretation to make a coherent performance expressing the mood, themes, and underlying meaning of the play.

Phelps was the first Shakespearean manager to achieve this kind of control over his company because of two factors that distinguished his management from his predecessors at the legitimate theatres. The first was that many of his actors needed more instruction than those formerly gathered on the great patent stages. Anthony Younge, for example, had acted at minor theatres before Phelps made him First Old Man of the company, and it was natural that he should accept training for such roles as Polonius and Autolycus. Henry Scharf, who played Shakespeare's clowns, had spent one year on provincial stages when Phelps hired him. Laura Addison, like a number of other leading actresses brought to Sadler's Wells, was young and untrained. By the third season of Phelps's management critics spoke of Sadler's Wells as a school of acting.

The second factor that made Sadler's Wells different from previous managements was the character of the manager. Unlike most leading actors Phelps was an extremely modest man, and his dislike of personal prominence showed itself in many ways. He never "puffed" his performances by advertisement. He avoided acquaintance with reviewers and did not cultivate their favor by the usual practice of giving free seats to the press. Once, early in his management, after a performance of Othello, he sternly lectured the audience for having demanded a curtain call.[1] On the stage he showed no jealousy of other actors and allowed secondary roles full prominence—a rare trait in the competitive atmosphere of the early nineteenth-century theatre, which manifested itself in his first season of management. Even in such a play as *The Bridal,* which Knowles had adapted to give overwhelming prominence to Macready's role, critics were surprised at the importance of Marston, Bennett, and Fanny Cooper in the performance at Sadler's Wells when Phelps played Melantius.[2] The most convincing demonstration of his attitude was his restoration of Shakespeare's text of *Richard the Third.* In his first season as leading actor at a London theatre he gave up one of the most celebrated acting parts in the stock repertory for the far less colorful and dominant role of Shakespeare's play. In a letter purporting to be written by an old actor of provincial celebrity, *Punch* (March 15, 1845) parodied professional reaction to the change:

> I beg to protest against the Tragedy of *Richard the Third* as now played at Sadler's Wells Theatre. Mr. Phelps calls it a restoration of Shakespeare's text. He may call it what he likes; but it is a death-blow to my line in the profession. Sir, I have played *Richard* not less than twelve country circuits. My "Off with his head" business invariably secured me nine rounds, and an invitation to dinner from the Mayor. My tent scene was great, and my "Begone, thou troublest me, I'm not i' the vein," was a crusher. All these points are cut out by Mr. Phelps. . . . Why, Sir, Phelps' *Richard* is a tame part. . . . I doubt if there's a good start or a decent scowl from beginning to end of it. Besides, there are at least half-a-dozen parts in his version that kill *Richard's* business. I don't think he has the stage to himself in a single scene.

The reaction in his own company was a willing cooperation with the manager—a new attitude that allowed him to become more like the twentieth-century director than the traditional stage manager. His daily rehearsals were long and arduous. For an opening night of *Coriolanus* he once worked his company from 11:00 in the morning until nearly 1:00 the next morning.[3] Painstaking care in rehearsal continued through his eighteen years of management, long after his company had become accustomed to playing together. The rehearsals for *The Fool's Revenge* in 1859 are described by the author of the play, who worked with many other managers before and after his experience at Sadler's Wells:

I never saw rehearsals more thorough, more careful, or more business-like. Phelps was as able as he was indefatigable in stage management. He did the work of guidance and governance of his actors singly, and of the action as a whole. . . . He had something of the irritability of Macready, and was not slow to give stupid, or, still more, careless people the rough side of his tongue; but his heart was so evidently in his work, he was so thoroughly master of the business he was directing, he so evidently thought of and for all, never sacrificing other actors to himself, that his little ruggednesses and fiercenesses never rankled, and were rarely resented even at the moment. Then his example of strenuous diligence operated on all about him, and made them attentive and strenuous too in their several degrees, so that no time was lost; and though the rehearsals were so strict and elaborate they took up no more time than more slipshod ones would have done. In short, rehearsal, as I saw it in the case of my own play at Sadler's Wells, was what rehearsal should be, continuous, well-considered, patient shaping of the play for public performance, in which not merely the groupings and movements of the personages were attended to, but the delivery of every speech watched, nay, the emphasis and pronunciation of every word noted. . . . When the play was produced on the 18th of October, 1857 [1859], after three weeks of patient and laborious rehearsal, more than equivalent to twice as much time less well employed, the good result was apparent in a smooth, level, and satisfactory performance, with no stage hitch in scenery, speech, or movement, in which nothing had been left to chance.[4]

Many actors have testified to the good relations Phelps maintained with his company even though he insisted on high standards. Lewis Ball, the Low Comedian for several years, once missed his call and kept Phelps waiting on the stage for five minutes, but he found that a frank admission of his fault resulted in nothing more than a reprimand and admonition that it should never happen again. Phelps's combination of strictness and tolerance produced what Richard Lee called "the perfect artistic confederacy of his company":

> Tolerant of everything but inefficiency, not once only, but twenty times in succession, would he put those showing incompetency through their gestures or their words. If the histrionic power were in them, Phelps would draw it out; if it were not, he would drive it in.[5]

The result of such rehearsals was first noticed in the performance of minor roles. In August of his first season the *Sun* (August 22, 1844) remarked of *The Bridal*:

> Take it altogether, we know not when we have seen a tragedy acted so admirably as a whole—there was not a weak point in it.

Some years later Morley cited the performance of minor roles as one of the most important features at Sadler's Wells:

> Every member of the company is taught to regard the poetry he speaks according to its nature rather than its quantity. The personators . . . say what Shakespeare has assigned to them to say with as much care, and as much certainty that it will be listened to with due respect, as if they were themselves Timons, Hamlets, or Macbeths. . . . Nothing is slurred; a servant who has anything to say says it in earnest, making his words heard and their meaning felt.[6]

Another result of Phelps's careful tutelage appeared in the fresh interpretation of characters. Although reviewers did not always recognize Phelps's hand in another actor's performance, their comments frequently reveal evidence of his work. They praised Laura Addison's new and more natural reading of Juliet without the traditional stage conventionalities and "all those exaggerations of manner which are usually premitted to change the sublime into the ridiculous." In 1853 a new member of the company from the provinces was commended for a similar improvement in the role of Joseph Surface in *The School for Scandal*:

> Mr. Lunt's impersonation of the hypocritical Joseph merits general approval; it was quiet, easy, and *natural,* and divested of that absurd stage conventionality in motion and in language which is the curse of the drama.[7]

Similarly, the *Weekly Dispatch* (October 16, 1859) congratulated J. W. Ray for playing Polonius as a man of intelligence and feeling instead of the "drivelling buffoon" of stage tradition.

Phelps's new approach to Shakespeare's comic characters, which appeared in his own acting of Malvolio and Bottom, was evident in the portrayal of Shakespeare's clowns at Sadler's Wells. During his eighteen years of management the whole gallery of those delightful creations was exhibited on his stage, played in the first years by Henry Scharf, later by Henry Nye and then Lewis Ball. Their performances differed from tradition in the same way Phelps's comedy differed from that of Farren and Munden. Instead of using the roles as vehicles for their own comic talent, they avoided extraneous humor and personal idiosyncracies that might blur the individuality of Shakespeare's conception or distort the role out of its proper relation to the rest of the play. Scharf created Feste, Touchstone, and Lear's Fool as vividly distinct characters, and critics often remarked that Shakespeare's humor lost nothing with the absence of buffoonery.

So also, the comic characters like Dogberry, Stephano, and Sir Andrew Aguecheek, traditionally assigned to the First Old Man of the company, were interpreted individually and without clowning by Anthony Younge and later by J. W. Ray. Charles Rice noted in his diary (December 11, 1850) that when Younge appeared on the stage in a character, the audience did not always recognize him:

> A. Younge in Autolycus display'd a versatility and loss of self quite refreshing in a Comic Actor;—Buckstone and Wright and Keely may always be sworn to; but Compton and Younge possess variety, and make a playbill sometimes a necessary for the audience to refer to.

Phelps's direction made Shakespeare's comic characters more natural and credible on the stage, just as Charles Mathews initiated realistic comedy in modern plays by transforming the characters of burlesque into drawing room gentlemen. The parallel trends of the same period resulted in a change of taste among London playgoers which became evident in a very few years. A striking instance occurred under Kean's management of the Princess's when the audience openly showed its disapproval of Wright's clowning, so that Kean was forced to withdraw him from the casts although his contract continued through the season.[8]

Phelps's insistence upon faithfulness to Shakespeare's conception when his actors played the clowns stemmed from his concern for the balance and harmony of the whole performance. A buffoon could destroy the mood of a scene or distort the relation of characters to one another. In his own acting Phelps had always tried to convey the total impression of a character and to avoid anything—points, set speeches, applause—which might blur the image. In his management he began to develop this same concern for the total impression of a performance with the result that productions at Sadler's Wells had an internal unity never before displayed in Shakespearean performances.

Reviewers groped for words to describe it. In *Twelfth Night* there was a harmony and balance that gave the effect, one critic said, of a well-played symphony. The first explicit statement came from the *Theatrical Journal* (August 15, 1850) at the beginning of Phelps's seventh season:

> There is a wide difference between Drury, Haymarket, and Sadler's Wells. At the two former, the actors and actresses are thrown on their own resources! at the latter they are pupils, receiving instructions in every character they are cast for. At the former, you applaud the actor's own conception; at Sadler's Wells you never know how much of the praise belongs to the manager. Mr. Phelps knows full well that he is much above his company; his desire is to form a picture, for all to work in the same direction and towards one model.

In the following year the *Theatrical Journal* (November 12, 1851) used the word "accordance" to describe the same aspect of productions at Sadler's Wells:

> Completeness has ever been the one great characteristic of the present management; from the trunk of the tree to the weakest of the branches accordance has always been visible.

Charles Dickens wrote that at Sadler's Wells "every artist in his degree has been taught to adapt his part, in the complete effect, to all the other parts uniting to make up the whole." [9] According to the *Athenaeum* (October 21, 1854), the influence of the stage manager was manifest throughout a performance at Sadler's Wells:

> Everyone has been evidently disciplined, so as to preserve order and relation. . . . We miss therefore the inspiration of individual actors, but we catch the pervading agency of a presiding intelligence, which insures the requisite unity.

Morley called it poetry:

> A main cause of the success of Mr. Phelps in his Shakespearean revivals is, that he shows in his author above all things the poet. Shakespeare's plays are always poems, as performed at Sadler's Wells. . . . The actors are

content also to be subordinated to the play, learn doubtless at rehearsals how to subdue excesses of expression that by giving undue force to one part would destroy the balance of the whole, and blend their work in such a way as to produce everywhere the right emphasis. If Mr. Phelps takes upon himself the character which needs the most elaborate development, however carefully and perfectly he may produce his own impression of his part, he never by his acting drags it out of its place in the drama. He takes heed that every part, even the meanest, shall have in the acting as much prominence as Shakespeare gave it in his plan, and it is for this reason that with actors, many of whom are anything but "stars," the result most to be desired is really obtained. Shakespeare appears in his integrity, and his plays are found to affect audiences less as dramas in a common sense than as great poems.[10]

Whatever language the critics used to describe Phelps's control over the acting in his productions—whether they described it in musical terms as a well-played symphony, in the terms of plastic arts as a picture or a model, in literary terms as a poem—they found this "pervading agency of a presiding intelligence" a new and excellent method of making Shakespeare come to life on the stage.

STAGING

Phelps followed tradition in making the acting of a play the most important aspect of any production; but he was also concerned with staging, and in this area, too, he introduced a new principle, basically different from any of his predecessors in Shakespearean production. Macready pointed the way with his theory of appropriate settings which illustrated the text in the most complete possible fashion. His *As You Like It* was, according to his prompter, "the most wonderfully perfect representation of court, and pastoral life, ever witnessed on the English stage." [11] His *King John* presented gorgeous medieval pageantry with careful historical accuracy. And there were times when Macready seemed to go beyond illustration of the plays to use settings for creating a mood (the dignity of the Venetian senate in *Othello*, and the somber darkness of his *Macbeth*), and in one case perhaps for symbolic meaning (the solitary tower in Antium in relation to the banished Coriolanus).[12] Macready himself, however, stated his own theory of staging as "truth of illustration" and the transfer of a picture from the poet's mind to the stage.[13] And his practice bore out this theory. In *King Henry the Fifth* he spent a large sum of money and much of his own time in the creation of a diorama to illustrate the speeches of the Chorus.

At the beginning of his management Phelps followed Macready's practices in staging. His settings were appropriate, historically accurate, planned with an eye for the whole stage picture, and newly designed for each important production. Although his stage and his budget did not allow him to decorate so lavishly as Macready, he made up for this by giving careful staging to every play. There is good evidence that his management did more than Macready's own to establish his practices in the English theatre. In the first place, Phelps's management lasted eighteen years as compared with the scant four seasons of Macready's management. Macready's *Henry the Fifth* ran for twenty-two nights; Phelps's three productions of *Henry the Fifth* ran for a total of fifty-six nights. A reviewer in the *Morning Advertiser* (October 25, 1858) credited the first of these with establishing the trend toward archaeology and realism followed by Charles Kean:

> When Phelps first produced this grand dramatic history . . . the custom of illustrating archaeologically, and realizing by the minutest attention to costumes and properties, had not then become the established mode of presenting theatrical productions. It was very greatly owing to the example of the energetic lessees of this remote and small theatre that such became the rule.

Many times during his management reviewers compared Phelps's staging favorably with Macready's. Of the Sadler's Wells *Macbeth* the *Morning Chronicle* (September 28, 1847) said:

> In point of pageantry, some of Mr. Macready's Shakespearian revivals may have been more gorgeous; but we question whether, even in these cases, the resources of Drury-Lane were handled with the tact, taste, and effect which the management of the smaller theatre have shown in bringing their more limited means into operation.

Speaking of the same *Macbeth,* the *Theatrical Journal* (October 2, 1847) declared that no Shakespearean play had ever been so beautifully staged. *Lloyd's Weekly* (November 3, 1850) said of *Cymbeline* that few plays had ever come to the stage in such a handsome setting or with such careful consistency in costuming and decoration. There is abundant testimony from many reviewers that a high standard of scenic design was maintained at Sadler's Wells for all performances, even those stock pieces which never were featured as "productions."

Phelps differed from Macready, and even more from Charles Kean, in that he did not aim at realism in his settings, nor did he allow the scenery to overshadow the actors. In his search for a realistic pastoral scene Macready had introduced live dogs to the sets for *As You Like It*. His *King John* placed such emphasis upon views of Gothic architecture and pictures of life in medieval times that most reviewers treated his production as a spectacle rather than a play, devoting their reviews largely to a description of the scenery. Kean went further on the road which Macready had explored, becoming more elaborate and more carefully historical in his settings. His attention to details, his greater use of machinery, and his more ambitious set constructions reversed the earlier trend toward complete Shakespearean texts. At the Princess's, lines had to be omitted to allow time for scene shifting and pageantry. Macready had omitted the lines of the first scene of *The Tempest* in order to show a realistic shipwreck on the stage. Charles Kean's shipwreck was so much more elaborate that it took a twenty-minute intermission to clear the stage for the next scene (and the first spoken words) of the play.[14] It is reported that Kean once scolded an actor for paying too much attention to the lines he was speaking and too little to the properties he was using. "Make more of the key, sir," he shouted to the offender. "Good God, you give it him as if it was a common room-door-key! Let the audience see it, sir; make 'em feel it, sir; impress upon 'em that it is a key of the period."[15]

Kean's methods were followed by Sir Henry Irving, Beerbohm Tree, and George Alexander, the scene carpenter gradually becoming more important than the scene painter. Beerbohm Tree's production of *A Midsummer Night's Dream* had live rabbits running through the wood near Athens. By 1900 the emphasis upon spectacular and historically correct productions of Shakespeare had combined with the trend to realism in the new drama (begun by Mme. Vestris). The result was a completeness of splendor and realism which has been surpassed only in motion pictures.

Although the trend toward realism may have been furthered by Phelps's staging, he did not aim at realism. The concept of a realistic milieu in which lifelike action might take place would have been nearly as foreign to him as to Garrick. Ideas of appropriateness in scenery and costume had changed since Garrick (who played Macbeth in powdered wig and frock coat), but Phelps would equally have deplored the limitation of the actor's freedom and the spectator's imagination which realistic settings have imposed.

At Sadler's Wells green baize still covered the boards; stage doors stood prominently at either side of the stage in front of the proscenium arch; and there was an apron jutting forward into the auditorium so that much of the action took place in front of the curtain fall line. To change a scene a pair of shutters (flats) could be rolled on the floor grooves from each side of the stage until they met in the center. For the next scene this pair might be removed to disclose a new setting. The canvas backdrop could be arranged to roll from side to side, giving a panoramic effect (used in the diorama), or it could be dropped to reveal a new painted background. The stage also had traps, each equipped with a platform that could rise from below stage level to carry actors up into the center of the scene.

Phelps used this stage with ingenuity and imagination to solve the problems posed by Shakespearean plays in an age that demanded scenery with some semblance of reality. He did not change to the box set, which other managers began to use for the sake of greater realism in settings, but kept the old system of flats and wings moving on fixed grooves and a rolling or tumbling backcloth. He changed scenes in full view of the audience, and the curtain was not usually lowered until the end of each act. Intermissions between acts rarely exceeded five minutes.

His methods of staging, because they ran counter to the trend toward lavish spectacle and literal realism, have been ignored in most theatrical history, but they had more influence on subsequent practice than is generally recognized. In *Richard the Third* of the first season, he divided the stage down the middle to provide for simultaneous action. In the *Macbeth* of 1847 he used gauze and lighting so effectively in the witch scenes that the *Weekly Dispatch* (October 3, 1847) asserted that Sadler's Wells had produced the first real illusion of supernatural witches on the English stage. Of his *Hamlet* in 1851 a critic wrote to Phelps:

There is nothing new in saying that ghosts never knew how to vanish till they learned to do so at Sadler's Wells. You have taught managers the use of darkness.[16]

Contemporary critics approved of Phelps's staging and praised him for adopting the proper course between overdecoration and carelessness in presenting Shakespeare. Tom Taylor, in describing the production of his own play at Sadler's Wells, said:

That was before the days of absolute realism and scrupulous archaeology; but not in the most precise and martinettish West End theatre of the time could more pains have been taken to realize correctness in essentials, and, above all, consistency of dresses and scenery, architecture, properties, and appliances, than in Sadler's Wells. In this respect Phelps seemed to me to hit the true mean between too much and too little as regards show, cost, and keeping in stage externals. All was thought of, and all was done that conduces to effect; nothing neglected that was needed to help the picture or impress the imagination. But there was no pedantry, no idle or ostentatious outlay, no insisting on archaeological minutiae for their own sake.[17]

Henry Morley said that "the scenery is always beautiful, but it is not allowed to draw attention from the poet, with whose whole conception it is made to blend in the most perfect harmony."[18] The *Athenaeum* (September 17, 1859) contrasted Phelps's management with that of Charles Kean:

He . . . called to his aid a moderate proportion of spectacle, which, however, was strictly illustrative of the play, and for the most part what it ought to be, suggestive only, not exhaustive.

Fontane's opinion of Kean's spectacular productions was that in the historical plays (*Henry the Eighth, King John,* and *Richard the Second*) his pageantry and external decoration did not overwhelm Shakespeare's work, but that in *The Winter's Tale* and *The Tempest* the poetry broke under the load of extraneous decoration and mechanical apparatus. He also noted that because Kean's method left nothing to the imagination everything had to be perfectly realized on the stage, even to the last member of the chorus—a demanding goal which Kean often achieved.[19] Of Phelps's productions Fontane said that they were not a display of magnificence but of truth.[20] He praised the historical accuracy of the settings at Sadler's Wells and the realism of certain effects, like the roll of thunder and the clatter of rain, but he was chiefly impressed by the suggestive use of scenery and lighting to create the mood and heighten the effect of the drama.

By the mid-fifties when Fontane visited Sadler's Wells, Phelps had developed and put into practice a new theory of stage decoration, which went beyond illustration of the text to interpretation of the play. Critics first noticed a new relationship between scenery and dramatic art in the *Macbeth* of 1847, especially in his method of presenting the Weird Sisters. The *Athenaeum* (October 2, 1847) said, "On the whole, we know not that we have ever seen *Macbeth* put more effectively on the stage than it is now at this house—ever felt its moral more impressively conveyed in stage representation." Of *The Winter's Tale* reviewers said that the spirit of the play spoke through the scenic decoration. The *Theatrical Journal* (November 23, 1848) commented on the "thorough completeness" of *Much Ado about Nothing,* noting that the staging was remarkable for its success in carrying out the mood of the comedy. Henry Morley saw a dramatic purpose in the scenic decoration even in the case of *Pericles,* the one spectacle Phelps produced:

> Of the scenery indeed it is to be said that so much splendour of decoration is rarely governed by so pure a taste. The play, of which the text is instability of fortune, has its characteristic place of action on the sea. Pericles is perpetually shown (literally as well as metaphorically) tempest-tos't.[21]

The relationship between staging and interpretation was clearest in Phelps's *Midsummer Night's Dream.* "Mr. Phelps has never for a minute lost sight of the main idea which governs the whole play," Morley wrote, "and this is the great secret of his success in the presentation of it." [22]

> He knew that he was to present merely shadows; that spectators, as Puck reminds them in the epilogue, are to think they have slumbered on their seats, and that what appeared before them have been visions. Everything has been subdued . . . to this ruling idea.

Lloyd's Weekly (October 23, 1853) said that the scenic devices transformed flesh and blood actors into the creatures of a dream, so that the spirit and meaning of the play came across the footlights. He noted, in contrast with the usual kind of scenic decoration, that "there is no grand effect produced."

Not all critics understood the basic difference in Phelps's method. In the preceding issue of the same weekly a critic had remarked, "We should not be surprised at Mr. Charles Kean's helping himself to all the principal effects, as he did in *Macbeth.*" Although this prediction was in a sense fulfilled by Kean's producing *A Midsummer Night's Dream* three years later, he used stage effects for such an entirely different purpose that he could never really copy from Sadler's Wells. Phelps shows that he was well aware of the difference in method in a letter to his wife written in April, 1867, when he was in Liverpool appearing as Bottom.

> The Theatre is more like a *palace* than anything else. I never saw any thing approaching it. . . . The stage has every possible requirement. But alas! the "Midsummer Night" is a wretched hash! The scenery like it was at the Princess's. The whole thing as inferior to mine as this Theatre is superior to Sadler's Wells. I have taken care my scenes are done in my own way as nearly as possible. I was in the Theatre yesterday from eleven till four—back again at seven and staid till ½ past eleven.[23]

The "wretched hash" which Phelps was working long hours to revise was not the result of carelessness in acting or slovenly staging; it was rather a misinterpretation of the play, set in an elaborate picture of a tinsel fairyland. His objection to the scenery was that it failed to express the meaning of Shakespeare's play.

Finally, in 1858, the perceptive reviewer for the *Weekly Dispatch,* who had watched Phelps's methods from the beginning of his management, pronounced him "a veritable dramatic reformer" for his introduction and successful practice of a new idea in theatrical management:

> When our stage records are written by some future Victor or Collier, his achievement will stand out as the most interesting event of the last twenty years. . . . [Phelps] resolved to view all the means within his reach as a whole—as material which, if systematized, developed and subjected in proper relation to a central idea, would, however moderate in merit, acquire force from mere harmony, and leave a sense of completeness in all their results which could not fail to content, if it did not always electrify. . . . Without dwelling on the gratification which such a system must have afforded to the genuine play-goer, there is another view of its merits which we may briefly allude to. It has the additional value of being thoroughly practical. It is a system which any manager with common sense and common industry may put into force. Thus its creation is a positive boon to the Drama.[24]

How new and radically different Phelps's system was can be seen through the eyes of the German visitor Fontane, since he came upon it suddenly after it was fully developed. He saw at once that the plays at Sadler's Wells were directed by a single intelligence. He noted the subordination and molding of individual parts to form a unified whole, the consistency of interpretation throughout a play (instead of scene by scene), and the use of scenery to strengthen the interpretation. Such practices were unknown in Germany. Visits to other London theatres soon convinced him that they were equally new to England, and he realized that Phelps's system could revolutionize the theatre.[25]

TEXTS OF THE PLAYS

A corollary to Phelps's principle of completeness in dramatic performance was his practice of using Shakespeare's text in preference to an acting version. He did more than any single manager to restore the original versions of Shakespeare's plays to the theatre.

After the end of the Restoration period with its urge to improve Shakespeare by neoclassical standards, Garrick began the gradual process of ridding the plays of such revisions. But Garrick wrote his own ending to *Romeo and Juliet*, and other actors after him prepared stage versions of the plays, with cutting and transposition of scenes. The ideal of original Shakespearean texts came from outside the theatre, with the new veneration for "the Bard" in the Romantic critics of the early nineteenth century. Macready, influenced by these writers, fought his inclinations as an actor and set himself a goal of restoring pure Shakespeare to the stage. He removed the last of Dryden and D'Avenant from *The Tempest*, and he replaced the Fool in *King Lear*, but his reservations about Shakespeare's judgment and his own practices as a star actor militated against sole dependence upon Shakespeare's text. He restored only part of the Fool's role, declaring in his diary that in his opinion such violent contrasts weary and annoy audiences. In *As You Like It* he discarded the usual acting version for the orignial text, but before the play was performed he had again taken out many of the passages usually omitted, and he had appropriated some of the First Lord's speeches into his own part of Jaques.[26] In *The Tempest* he omitted the first scene for the sake of spectacle and removed some of Ariel's speeches to his part of Prospero. Thus, his practices, both as an "illustrator" in staging and as a dominating actor, resulted in further cutting from some of the acting versions.

Phelps began in his first season a long program of restoring unadulterated Shakespeare to the stage by using a completely Shakespearean text of *Richard the Third*. Macready had once attempted a compromise, keeping some of Colley Cibber's work, but the resulting patchwork did not succeed on the stage.

The long life of Cibber's *Richard the Third* in the theatre can be attributed to the effectiveness of the leading role, to which Cibber had sacrificed the rest of Shakespeare's play. He omitted many characters, most notably Margaret, who in Shakespeare is nearly as important as Richard. He left out most of the scenes in which Richard does not appear, so that the leading actor was hardly ever off the stage. He did, however, add one scene of his own writing without Richard: the murder of the two little princes, which in the original is mercifully only reported. He also added a love story by enlarging the role of Anne and by making Richard more romantic in his suit for her hand. These changes had converted the play into an excellent vehicle for the leading actor, who could use all the tricks of his trade in the portrayal of a monstrous villain. Cibber gave him many telling points and some highly effective individual lines. Even in the twentieth century, performances of Shakespeare's *Richard the Third* have included "Off with his head! So much for Buckingham" and other lines beloved of actors.

When Phelps played this Richard in Exeter, critics noted that his interpretation was closer to Shakespeare's portrayal and that he minimized the theatrical effects of Cibber's adaptation. As soon as he became manager of his own theatre he discarded Cibber.

In restoring an original Shakespearean text to the stage a nineteenth-century manager faced a considerable task. First, he had to cut the play to three hours' performing time (including about fifteen minutes for intermissions between acts). He also had to divide it into scenes to accommodate it to a stage far less flexible than Shakespeare's. And he had to remove or replace expressions which the censor's office would not permit on grounds of indecency or blasphemy. The word "God" could not be spoken on the stage, even in a prayer. The Lord Chamberlain was so sensitive to echoes of blasphemous expressions that in the fifth act of *Lear* "bloody knife" was changed to "bloody weapon," presumably on the grounds that the more exalted noun removed the adjective from suspicion, although the situation makes clear that Shakespeare means real blood. All words referring to the reproductive process were forbidden. "Thy womb" became "thy self." Illicit social practices were unmentionable. "Bawd" became "woman," and "bastard" became "base born."

A copy of Phelps's prompt book for *Richard the Third* in the Folger Shakespeare Library preserves the acting text used at Sadler's Wells.[27] He cut about 1,480 lines from the play's total of 3,600. Although this seems a drastic revision to us who know Shakespeare primarily on the printed page rather than in the theatre, it was not an unusual amount for standard acting versions. What remained was still a longer play than an uncut *Macbeth*. The cutting was carefully done, line by line, and nearly evenly distributed throughout all the acts and all the major characters. Of the thirty-eight named characters twelve minor ones are omitted, some of their lines being transferred to other appropriate characters. Four short scenes are completely omitted, as well as the conversation between the Duchess of York and Clarence's children in the second scene of act two. Lines from act two, scene five, are made into a new scene inserted after the opening scene of act three. The murder of Clarence is performed offstage, keeping his dream speech but omitting his pleading with the murderers. Actual tampering with Shakespeare's lines is limited to the customary bowdlerizing.

The total effect of this cutting was to shorten the play and somewhat condense the action. Phelps made no attempt to present an uncut version of Shakespeare—a twentieth-century ideal which came into vogue only after Shakespeare had ceased to be the mainstay of the commercial theatre. He tried to present as much of the original as could be fitted into nineteenth-century theatre practice.

In his second season Phelps presented *King Lear* from Shakespeare's text without transposition or omission of scenes, removing the last trace of Nahum Tate's tamperings, which had dominated the play since 1681. The reviewer of the *Athenaeum* (November 8, 1845), who had disapproved the dislocations and omissions kept by Macready, said:

> We have lived to see all this, at length, effectually reformed. . . . We announce this restoration with pleasure—for, to speak the truth, it is the only one which has been made in perfect good faith, and with a full reliance on the poet.

An examination of Phelps's prompt book shows that the pattern of cutting is the same as that used in *Richard the Third*, except that much less was cut.[28] Only 750 lines were cut from over 3,000 in the original text. This made an unusually long performance.

In the text of *Lear* there was a greater problem of indecent words than in *Richard*, but since most of the offending passages are in prose, the pruning could be accomplished with great economy. There were only two cuts of any length in the Fool's part: the fifteen-line flippant soliloquy at the end of act three, scene two, and forty lines in III, iv—the mock trial. In the rest of the play the only significant change was in the blinding of Gloucester, which Phelps did not try to play on the stage. Some lines were omitted to soften the brutality of the scene—the beard pulling, for example—and several others to alter the meaning so that the actual blinding could be deferred and be presumed to happen offstage at the end of the scene. This version was the closest to Shakespeare's scene that any manager had attempted for more than a century, and even in this modified form the scene was felt to be too brutal in actual performance. Phelps retained it for several seasons in spite of critical protest, but in the production of 1855 he omitted all of the scene from line 70 to the end.

Faithfulness to Shakespeare's text contributed to the surprising success of *The Winter's Tale* at Sadler's Wells. The *Athenaeum* (December 6, 1845) found it a special merit that "nearly every word of the original text is repeated, and that the second scene of the fifth act, so long wont to be mutilated, is restored." Phelps also restored Leontes' final speech—a typically Shakespearean ending, in which Paulina is given a husband and the characters are hurried off to discuss the startling events just transpired. He omitted several interpolated speeches which had long been part of the acting text. His prompt book in the Folger Shakespeare Library shows that about 700 lines were cut, many of them for the sake of avoiding language that would not have passed the censor. The acting time, including intermissions, was a full three hours.

The Sadler's Wells production of *Romeo and Juliet* in 1846 featured the complete restoration of Shakespeare's text. Since 1680 when Otway's *Caius Marius* appeared, *Romeo and Juliet* had suffered from adapters. Mme. Vestris had replaced Garrick's happy ending with the original, but with many omissions. Phelps presented what critics described as "an entire perfect version of the text, for the first time." His prompt book in the Folger Library shows that only 490 lines were cut—chiefly the Prologues to the first and second acts, and the clowning of Peter with the musicians in IV, v. Reviews report that the restoration of passages usually omitted was fully justified by their effect on the play, since they helped give probability to the motivation of the characters.

Encouraged by the response of his audience to original texts, Phelps in 1847 took a giant step in his production of *Macbeth*. Most of D'Avenant's tampering had been swept away by Garrick's production of 1744, but one important alteration persisted and was still incorporated in the acting text used in the nineteenth century. This was the perversion of the Weird Sisters into a large number of singing and dancing witches, led by a prominent Hecate, whose incantations (taken by D'Avenant from the plays of an earlier generation) were an important feature of the tragedy. Even the admiration for Shakespeare's genius developed by the Romantic movement had failed to dislodge these witches. Their presence was justified by the argument that they increased the importance of the Weird Sisters and by the conviction that the beautiful music (then attributed to Matthew Locke, but now thought to be the work of the youthful Purcell) which accompanied their songs and dances enhanced the effect of the play. Certainly no actor had seriously considered removing them, although they existed at the expense of many Shakespearean lines, which had been cut in order to give time for song and ballet. Lady Macduff and the Porter had been completely omitted; Lady Macbeth did not appear in the discovery scene; and throughout the play a number of individual speeches had been left out of the acting text.

Phelps discarded the acting version and based his production on the original text, nearly all of which was included in the performance. Since *Macbeth* is one of the shorter plays, only 192 lines had to be omitted to reduce it to an acting time of three hours.[29] Lady Macduff was restored and also the Porter, except that the second half of his speech had to be omitted because of its obscenity. The only other significant omissions were the short scene between Lennox and another lord at the end of the third act, and the brief appearance of the English doctor. The lovely music so long associated with the play was presented between the acts.

Phelps's restoration of the original text of *Macbeth* was considered a bold venture. Many critics felt that the acting version was close enough to the original to make restoration unnecessary except for the satisfaction of a few purists, and they thought that much would be lost in theatrical performance if D'Avenant's witch scenes were removed. Even the critics who had championed the cause of original texts were not eager to see some of the omissions in the acting version restored to the stage. The introduction of the Porter to the Victorian theatre was rather a risky undertaking, and the scene between Lady Macduff and her child seemed too painful for representation on the stage. Both of these scenes were in fact criticized by some reviewers after they had seen the performance at

Sadler's Wells. When, in the last scene, Phelps not only included Malcolm's final speech but also followed Shakespeare's direction that Macbeth's head be brought in on a pole, most reviewers objected. One critic suggested that Phelps's veneration for original texts might have led him to have the actor's very head cut off if he had not been playing the part himself. As in the case of the blinding of Gloucester, Phelps eventually yielded to critical opinion, and in later performances omitted the murder of Macduff's son and the business of the head on the pole.

By the time Phelps came to the task of preparing his acting text for *Antony and Cleopatra,* he had had sufficient experience to enable him to take a fresh look at the traditional methods of cutting texts for stage presentation. *Antony and Cleopatra* was almost unknown in the theatre. Dryden's *All for Love* had replaced it early in the eighteenth century, and Garrick's attempt to reintroduce Shakespeare's play had only limited success. In 1813 Kemble had presented a compound of Dryden and Shakespeare, with Charles Young and Mrs. Faucit in the leading roles, but this version was short lived. Bunn's production of 1833, still showing the influence of Dryden on the text, with Macready as Antony, was also a failure. When Phelps decided to produce Shakespeare's original play, he had as free a hand as if he were dealing with a new work. There was no acting text, no tradition of previous interpretations by famous actors, and no precedent in staging.

The universal practice of editors in reducing Shakespearean plays to the customary three-hour performance had been to remove short passages, varying from one to twenty lines, from individual speeches throughout the play, shortening every scene. Some small scenes and a number of minor characters were frequently omitted, but the bulk of the reduction was achieved by a careful and ubiquitous cutting that left no scene intact. Phelps had followed this method in cutting *Richard the Third* and (much less drastically) *Romeo and Juliet* and *King Lear*. In *Antony and Cleopatra* he used a new method. He left most of the scenes untouched, preserving on the stage nearly every line of those scenes which were played. To reduce the length of the play, he omitted ten scenes entirely and removed considerable sections from three others.[30]

All of act one was presented except the Soothsayer's appearance. He kept all of act two except scene five. In act three, scenes one, two, three, four, eight, and nine were omitted. In act four, scenes two, three, and seven were omitted. Scene nine (Enobarbus' death) was transposed to precede scene four. In the last act he cut the section in which Cleopatra's concealment of her wealth is revealed to Caesar by Seleucus, some of the Clown's lines, and some of the Guards' comments upon Cleopatra's death. Throughout the rest of the play few words were removed or changed, and these few were almost exclusively to avoid difficulty with the censor. The word "eunuch" was avoided, for example, and other minor adaptations to the change in manners from Elizabeth's day to Victoria's were made. The economy of Phelps's cutting is shown by the fact that the total of all omissions was less than 650 lines.

The result was a play that retained all the elements of Shakespeare's style, most notably the baroque richness that normally disappeared in acting versions. Some of the scenes would certainly be regretted, particularly III, iii, in which Cleopatra's vanity is pointedly displayed, and IV, ii, in which Antony sinks to a level below the maintenance of self-respect; but most of the omitted scenes are devoted to explanation or comment, not essential to plot or characterization. Some method of reducing the number of changes of scene would have had to be devised, whether or not the length of the performance had been a consideration. Forty-two changes, even in the days of grooved flats and tumbling backcloths, would have bewildered and tired the audience. On the other hand, the texture of *Antony and Cleopatra,* which can be compared to a closely woven and richly decorated tapestry, could hardly have been cut and spliced without blurring its effect. In the acting version which Phelps prepared, the wealth of poetry and fullness of characterization were largely preserved.

Timon of Athens, practically unknown in the theatre, required less cutting. Only 400 lines were removed to reduce the play to three hours.[31] The cutting was again concentrated in certain sections, particularly the last two acts, where Phelps omitted some of Timon's curses and the final appearance of the Poet and Painter. The first three acts were left nearly intact, except for the passage between Apemantus and the Fool. About ten lines were removed for reasons of decorum. There was no transposing of scenes. The acting text was very close to Shakespeare's original.

I have not seen Phelps's prompt book for *Hamlet,* but he apparently used a more complete text than usual. Fontane remarks that at Sadler's Wells *Hamlet* was almost intact, without the usual bits cut from every scene, except that the entire scene of Claudius at prayer was omitted.

In the other Shakespearean tragedies for which his prompt books are preserved at the Folger Library, Phelps used the standard acting texts. His

Julius Caesar was Kemble's version, to which he added only a few lines. His *King John* book is the one used under Macready at Drury Lane. His *Coriolanus* was apparently the same acting version used by Macready at Covent Garden in 1838. Entire scenes are omitted, including the three Volscian scenes from act one, the first three scenes of act four, and the fourth and fifth scenes of act five. All other scenes have lost some lines. The total number of lines omitted approaches 1800, or nearly half the play. There is also an interpolation of thirty-four lines. Critics, who had come to expect original texts at Sadler's Wells, objected to this use of an acting version. The *Athenaeum* (September 30, 1848) complained that the wholesale cutting altered the tone and meaning in many places. The *Theatrical Times* (October 7, 1848) on the other hand, having previously objected to Phelps's "mania" for restoring texts, approved his use of the acting version, declaring that the first act was "judiciously consolidated."

In *Pericles* and in many of the comedies Phelps resurrected from oblivion, his major problem in preparing an acting text was conformance to Victorian standards of decorum. Not only the Lord Chamberlain's office but also many critics objected to "indelicate" situations and "license of language" found in Elizabethan and Jacobean writers. A few had disapproved of *Antony and Cleopatra* on moral grounds, particularly the *Theatrical Journal* (November 1, 1849), whose conservative editor was sensitive in such matters:

> There is, however, little or nothing to elevate and purify in this play. It appeals to the lowest passions, and in spite of its poetry, is sometimes disgusting. This is the reason why it does not long retain possession of the stage in these refined times.

The opening scene of *Pericles* contains the riddle stating the relationship between the Princess and her father and later Pericles' explicit remarks about its nature. Phelps retained the scene but suppressed the riddle and any clear reference to its meaning. The *Athenaeum* (October 21, 1854), always a champion of original texts, objected to this cutting:

> Mr. Phelps, in altering this play for representation, has simply, at the risk of unintelligibility, omitted all the passages that express the crime which he deems unfitting to be named, and barely retained the pantomimic outline of the events that send Pericles forth upon his voyage.

But it is impossible to imagine that incest could be freely discussed on the Victorian stage.

The two scenes in the brothel at Mytilene were condensed into one, with the omission of many lines and the substitution of less specific words for some of Shakespeare's.[32] In the line "And prostitute me to the basest groom," the word "sacrifice" was substituted for "prostitute." Most reviewers praised Phelps for his tact in the alterations, and Morley said that "the plot of the drama was not compromised by a false delicacy." [33]

In *Pericles* Phelps also omitted the chorus character Gower because he did not have an actor he felt capable of making such a difficult role effective on the stage. "Certainly," Morley commented, "unless he could have been himself the Gower as well as the Pericles of the piece, the frequent introduction of a story-telling gentleman in a long coat and long curls would have been an extremely hazardous experiment, even before such an earnest audience as that at Sadler's Wells."

The plot of *All's Well That End Well* presented a problem similar to that of *Pericles*. One reviewer asserted that the plot was "indelicate, even beyond the limits usually conceded to Elizabethan dramatists" and remarked that Sadler's Wells "is a sort of museum for the exhibition of dramatic curiosities, and we have no more right to be astounded at finding some Elizabethan crudity within its precincts than at finding a Buddhist idol in a missionary collection." [34] These protests were made in spite of the fact that Phelps had altered the plot so that the production of the ring was the only condition named in Bertram's letter. The omission of the more important motive of the action, although necessary on the nineteenth-century stage, must have greatly weakened the plot.

In *The Comedy of Errors* Phelps used the original text as the basis for his acting text, but he inserted some of the interpolated passages which he found in old acting versions and followed custom in the omission of many lines. Markings in his prompt book indicate that in some seasons he replaced most of the interpolations with the original passages and restored many of the lines formerly omitted.[35] In the longer version only about 230 lines were cut. The use of a more complete text may have been suggested by the response of the audience to a play which had not been popular in the theatre for a generation. Like several other productions under Phelps's management, *The Comedy of Errors* appealed more to the audience than to critics. Reviewers called it primitive, crude, and extravagant. The *Weekly Dispatch* (November 18, 1855) said that an abridged version would have been better; but the *Athenaeum* (November 17, 1855) reported that the audience enjoyed the full play and laughed heartily.

Critics also found *The Taming of the Shrew* a dull play. It was usually seen as an afterpiece made up of the Katherine and Petruchio scenes, although Benjamin Webster had once played the entire comedy including the Induction. Phelps restored the whole play, cutting very few lines except in the last scene, which was much abbreviated.[36] The *Morning Advertiser* (November 17, 1856) did not entirely approve:

> The entire five acts were rigidly played, and it must be confessed that to hackneyed play-goers of the modern school, the earlier scenes occasionally dragged; but the audience, we firmly believe, would not have lost a word.

The *Athenaeum* (November 22, 1856), with its customary approval of complete texts, said that the comic scenes were enhanced by their setting within the whole play and declared that the humor was greater.

In *The Two Gentlemen of Verona* and *Love's Labour's Lost,* both rare on the stage, Phelps used Shakespeare's text.[37] From *The Two Gentlemen* he omitted only 135 lines; from *Love's Labour's Lost,* 580 lines. His method of cutting by chunks rather than snippets left the delicate play of wit in the euphuistic comedy undisturbed.

Although *Measure for Measure* was a little outside the limits of the standard Shakespearean repertory, it was not unknown on the stage, so that Phelps was able to use an acting version already shortened and pruned, to which he added ten short passages, nearly all in verse, from the original text.[38] The bowdlerization was approved even by the *Athenaeum* (November 7, 1846):

> The comic portion of the plot told well, and excited extraordinary merriment. But the dialogue was well weeded:—not an offensive phrase was left, and the fun was not the less for being deprived of its indelicacy.

Phelps's most important textual restoration in the field of comedy was *A Midsummer Night's Dream.* The few performances of this play during the nineteenth century had tended toward the operatic, with emphasis on interpolated songs and dances set to Mendelssohn's music. A production at Covent Garden in 1840 featured beautiful staging and the singing and dancing of Mme. Vestris. Shakespeare's play, unadorned, had seldom tempted actors, and it was generally considered too poetic and imaginative a work for actual representation. Hazlitt's disappointment with a performance in 1816 led him to the conclusion that it was as idle to attempt to embody the fancy of it as to personate Wall or Moonshine.[39]

Phelps, however, set out to embody the fancy of it, and his first principle was reliance on Shakespeare's text. Without the songs and dances he had time for all but 300 lines of the original, and he reconverted the play of Pyramus and Thisbe from opera to spoken dialogue.[40] The result was one of the greatest triumphs of his management, and no critic complained that the text was too long.

Removal of songs from *The Merry Wives of Windsor* also allowed time for a more complete version than the one usually seen in the theatre. For the text of *Twelfth Night* Phelps used Oxberry's Edition, the standard acting version prepared from performances at the patent theatres a generation earlier; but his prompt book contains a number of lines from Shakespeare's original added to the printed text.[41] He also removed the lines interpolated in the last scene, and restored the proper order of scenes which had been transposed.

For *The Tempest* Phelps used a copy of Shakespeare's text rather than a published acting version.[42] In 1847 he followed Macready in substituting a simulated shipwreck for the spoken words of the first scene, but in subsequent productions he restored the scene. In *As You Like It* he used the original text, from which he omitted only 230 lines.[42]

The comic scenes of the Henry plays presented a greater problem of eliminating indecencies, but in *Henry the Fourth, Part One,* Phelps restored nearly all the original text, including Glendower's role, usually omitted from the play.[43] *Henry the Fourth, Part Two,* was not often performed on the nineteenth-century stage, partly because of the Doll Tearsheet scenes. Phelps used the old acting text from Covent Garden edited by Mrs. Inchbald, to which he added a few Shakespearean lines.[44] Critics said that the "dangerous" scenes were so funny on the stage that the voice of propriety was lost in gales of laughter.

In *Henry the Fifth* Phelps used a fairly complete version including the speeches of the Chorus, which succeeded in holding the attention of the audience without the illustration of a diorama.[45] According to the *Morning Advertiser* (October 26, 1852), Marston rescued this difficult role from tedium and made his appearances come as a welcome relief from the noise and conflict of the play.

Henry the Eighth was usually played not only in an acting version, which omitted the fifth act and severely abbreviated the rest, but also in a three-act truncation ending with the fall of Wolsey. In his first seasons Phelps followed this custom, but in 1849 he used the whole acting text, restoring Queen Katherine's important last scene and making her a figure of equal prominence with Wolsey.

To summarize Phelps's treatment of Shakespearean texts: he restored to the stage in the original text three plays which had been seen since the Restoration period only in adaptations (*Richard the Third, Antony and Cleopatra, Timon of Athens*); from three others he removed the last remnants of such adaptations (*King Lear, Romeo and Juliet, Macbeth*); in seven plays he discarded acting texts for the original; and he brought to the stage in the Shakespearean text four other plays seldom acted since the closing of the theatres in 1642. In fourteen other plays he used the customary acting texts, but in at least four of these he reintroduced lines or characters from Shakespeare's text. Although Charles Kean and his followers took a different road in Shakespearean production, with increasingly shortened texts, Phelps's success at Sadler's Wells is a strong argument for the actability of the original Shakespearean plays.

SOME IMPORTANT PRODUCTIONS

Perhaps the best way to understand Phelps's methods of producing Shakespeare is to look at some of his productions in detail. In about a dozen cases there are contemporary accounts sufficiently specific in description and diverse in source to make such examination possible. These plays are treated below in order of their appearance at Sadler's Wells.

Phelps's first thoroughly finished production was his *Hamlet* of August, 1844. It had taken him three months to marshal the resources of his new management into a truly integrated performance with carefully designed staging; and he concentrated his efforts on the tragedy perennially most interesting to audiences, critics, and actors. The scenery was declared to be splendid beyond belief for such a theatre, but the effectiveness of the staging was not achieved primarily through lavish decoration. The new setting for *Hamlet* displayed Phelps's talent for stage arrangements, as well as Greenwood's resourcefulness and the ability of two fine scene painters, Frederick Fenton and A. Finlay.

Phelps modified traditional practice in several instances. The most important innovation occurred in the Ghost scenes, where for the first time a natural covering was provided for the Ghost's entrances and exits. The usual method, since stage traps had fallen into disuse, was that the Ghost merely walked on and off, taking care to be as silent as possible.

But even the use of felt slippers to deaden the sound of mail on bare boards could hardly mask the solid substance of the actor, especially since he customarily stood "within truncheon's reach of the footlights." [46] There had been no covering of darkness, since the device of lowering the lights had only rarely been used in theatres before 1844.[47] Although gas lighting had replaced oil and candles at most theatres in London during the previous twenty years, making manipulation of the lights far easier, managers had not yet discovered the dramatic use of a darkened stage. In the *Hamlet* of 1844, Phelps for the first time presented an insubstantial Ghost, who seemed to appear and vanish by supernatural means. The scenes are described in some detail by the *Theatrical Journal* (October 12, 1844):

> Every one recollects the manner in which the Ghost used to stalk on and off in the first scene; at this little theatre the scene exhibits an extensive view of a castle by moonlight, with beacon pillars; the distant portions are lit up by the moon's rays, while the fore part lays in deep shadow, and so casts a gloom over the stage, greatly in unison with the coming action, and tends to give an unearthly appearance to the Ghost, which other theatres have failed in. We only see the reflection of, but not the moon—an evidence of great taste. In the distance a beacon fire is blazing, nearer to the audience is another beacon not lit up. . . . The Ghost enters, moves slowly across the stage in an angular direction towards the beacon pillar, behind which it glides, when a burst of light shows it melting away in the far distance. . . . The second appearance of the Ghost gives us a still more extensive range of the castle by moonlight, if anything better painted than the first; on one side rises a range of arches, which, concealing the moon, casts a shadow over one side of the stage. The Ghost comes up some stairs—as if it has led Hamlet to a higher range of the battlements—crosses the stage, and stands within the gloom of the arches; when it disappears, it gradually glides under the arches till the eye loses it in their "dim obscurity."

The effectiveness and simplicity of these scenes are typical of Phelps's techniques in staging. His methods, clearly seen for the first time in this *Hamlet* and developed in later productions, derived from an actor's concern to solve problems posed by the play—not as in much Victorian staging, from a pleasure in decoration as an end in itself.

Although the staging of *Hamlet* received unusual attention in reviews, both audience and critics were primarily interested in the acting. A strong cast was provided by the Sadler's Wells company of the first season, with

Mrs. Warner as a striking Queen Gertrude, George Bennett as a King who seemed an adversary worthy of Hamlet, and Henry Marston as an exceptionally good Ghost. Marston was a talented and well-trained actor who had failed to achieve prominence largely because of a faulty voice, which was husky and uneven. As the Ghost, his voice was an asset, and therefore did not obscure his ability to develop an imaginative interpretation. Instead of speaking in a monotone, as actors usually did in this role, he gave expression to the words and a human personality to the Ghost under his solemn and supernatural exterior, evoking the dignity of a great man and the tenderness of his former love for the Queen. It was a superior piece of acting, which gradually became recognized as the best portrayal of the Ghost to be seen on any stage.

A later production of *Hamlet* is described in one of the most interesting of Fontane's reviews, although he saw the play in a season when it was not a featured revival nor provided with a strong cast.[48] Margaret Eburne's Ophelia was rather insensitive; the King (in Bennett's absence) seemed insignificant; and the Horatio was stiff. Nevertheless, Fontane found the performance one of the most impressive he had ever seen, attributing the success of the production to Phelps's direction.

He rated the Ghost scenes among the highest achievements in the contemporary theatre and carefully described their effectiveness. He says that the play opened on a stage nearly dark and that as the scene progressed the audience caught the feeling of the supernatural so that there was no sound in the theatre as the Ghost appeared. Fontane found the illusion so compelling that his blood ran hot and cold. The Horatio, whose carriage was ungraceful on a lighted stage, spoke through the darkness in a lovely full bass voice, which ran through the scene like a bell. Fontane says that the voice was unforgetable and made a triumph of the role.

In the second Ghost scene, he says that the excellent staging and perfect *ensemble* of the acting created an illusion which held the spectator spellbound. As Hamlet followed the Ghost, the scene changed "as if by magic" so that the edge of the rampart containing the entrance to a cave suddenly appeared, and the Ghost stood in shimmering armor "like a strip of light" in its dark entrance, while Hamlet climbed up as if from steps below the stage. During the Ghost's speech the stage lightened to gray except at the mouth of the cave, where it was still dark. At his farewell he disappeared "like a falling star" inaudible and motionless into darkness. With the last glint of his armor, the sun's rays broke over the cliff, revealing the sea and figure of Hamlet, equally silent and still. Fontane reports that the scene as a whole shook him as much as anything he had ever seen in a theatre.

When Phelps challenged tradition with his production of Shakespeare's *Richard the Third,* he faced serious problems of staging which Cibber had avoided. The "old Actor" of *Punch* (March 15, 1845) alluded to this difference: "And as for the getting up, it's twenty times as expensive as the original piece—I mean Colley Cibber's."

Act five posed the greatest problems, since the preparations for the battle of Bosworth Field are depicted through alternating appearances of both leaders accompanied by their retinues, culminating in the night scene and the appearance of the ghosts simultaneously to Richard and Richmond asleep in their tents. Cibber, faced with the less flexible Restoration stage, had simply omitted Richmond from the ghost scenes. Phelps restricted himself to Shakespeare's text and general design but still tried to present the play with the scenic beauty and semblance of realism demanded by a nineteenth-century audience.

He designed a divided set in which the action proceeded on both sides of the stage simultaneously, as if separated by some distance. The illusion was created by depicting a large open field which appeared to be divided by a small brook running from a grove of trees at center back to the center front. Richard entered from stage right and ordered his men to pitch his tent, which they did onstage. Later Richmond's tent was pitched across the brook, and the attention of the audience was directed to his side of the stage as that conversation became audible, while the other faded to silence without any break in the action of the scene.

When the two leaders had retired into their tents to sleep, the stage was darkened by dimming the lights and by pulling up a gauze designed with successive layers of thickness, which extended across the stage behind the tents. A platform carrying the ghosts rose to stage level behind the several layers of gauze. When the gauze was let down gradually, its successively thinner texture slowly revealed the ghosts, as if they had materialized out of the air.[49]

These devices had primarily a functional purpose. The double set avoided the numerous exits and entrances, which are distracting on a picture stage, and regained the concentration of action intended by Shakespeare. It also produced a scene that was quite lovely in its effect. The movements of officers and messengers in the two camps, with their variety of costumes and banners, gave it a sparkling brilliance on the stage. The *News of the World* (February 23, 1845) described it as "a picture of remarkable perfection." The same review relates the impression of the ghosts' appearance from the spectator's point of view:

> Night having closed in with a kind of dioramic effect, two cressets are planted at the entrance of Richard's tent, which throw a faint light over the forepart of the scene; whilst in the background the ghosts of Clarence, Lady Anne, the Princes, and Buckingham are advanced between the two tents by some ingenious process, but so far only as to be dimly visible to the audience; this partial obscurity, and the deep stillness that is preserved on the stage, just allow the imagination to play without over-exciting it.

The "partial obscurity" was the final layer of gauze, thin enough to be invisible in the dim light, which still remained between the actors and the audience.

Shakespeare's play was a very different work from Cibber's. The character of Margaret, totally missing in Cibber, resumed her important position. Clarence, Stanley, and Hastings reappeared. The part of Richard, already much shorter than in Cibber, had been cut in proportion to other roles, but nevertheless, Shakespeare's Richard emerged, giving to the stage a new character—a Richard of wit, sarcasm, and humor, who operates by the superiority of his intelligence and who allows himself the leisure to examine his own nature, "to sport with the moods of his own mind," in the words of the *Athenaeum* (March 1, 1845). Phelps played it with "a sort of jovial *abandon*," which was shockingly different from the blustering brutality of the traditional stage Richard. So were his unhurried ease and quietness of manner as he accomplished his ends and looked upon the havoc he had created. It was a personality controlled by high intelligence, monstrous only in its force and in its detachment from human emotion. It was not an interpretation calculated to win rounds of applause. Some critics who praised it admitted that the role lacked the color of Cibber's; and a reviewer in the *Theatrical Journal* (March 1, 1845) was as disappointed as *Punch*'s "old Actor." He complained that many telling points were left out and that those which were substituted (his

word) failed to give equal effect. He was able to praise Mrs. Warner's
Margaret but dismissed Phelps's Richard by declaring the character so
altered that it had become a minor role.

The character of Margaret, new to the stage, dominated the whole
play. Mrs. Warner had the majesty and force needed for such a role. Her
bitter curses, delivered with unforgettable emphasis, seemed to hover over
the action of the play as her prophecies were gradually realized. She gave
the impression of having more than human significance—"a mystery and
a symbol, embodying the spirit of the fearful strife." [50]

Other actors received special mention for their performances in
Richard the Third. In fact, the success of Shakespeare's play depends
upon the ability of secondary actors, since minor characters bear a great
part of the dialogue. The company of Sadler's Wells, with a skill learned
in nine months of Phelps's careful tutelage, was fully competent to bring
these small parts to life. Reviewers were surprised to find how much importance such a minor character as Tyrrell assumed on the stage.

Although critical opinion was not entirely unanimous on the merits of
Shakespeare's *Richard the Third* as compared with Cibber's, the audience
gave it unequivocal approval. The *Theatrical Journal* said that the play
had created a sensation. The theatre was so crowded for the first week
that every available space was taken, even on temporary benches set up
in the passageway behind the boxes. The play ran on through March and
April to a total of twenty-four performances. Although Cibber's version
reappeared in other theatres and Phelps himself used it at the end of his
management, when he could find no actress capable of playing Margaret,
the success of his two productions of Shakespeare's play proved its effectiveness on the stage.

The *King Lear* of 1845 attracted attention not only because it was the
first performance of the whole Shakespearean text, but also because Macready had returned to London and was acting Lear at a small theatre
where he could be clearly seen and heard for the first time. Although
critics carefully compared the two tragedians in their interpretation of the
leading role, the major difference in the two performances was in the
total effect of acting and staging. At the Princess', Maddox provided such
a poor company and shabby settings that the audience frankly came to see
only Macready, whereas at Sadler's Wells Phelps had produced a truly
coordinated and balanced performance. One critic said:

There is a studious avoidance of anything like a sacrifice of propriety to engage attention for the leading part. King Lear is not the one engrossing object, surrounded by cyphers, but the center of a group of varied characters, each possessing marked distinctive features.[51]

The *Athenaeum* (November 8, 1845) has a tantalizing description of the scenery:

The tragedy is placed upon the stage, too, in that ideal and simple style of scenic appointment which befits an altogether fabulous period. It has accordingly all the air and severity of a classical drama. Only in one respect has too much been done. The storm . . . is too naturally rendered—it is not imitation, but realization.

Other reviewers are less explicit about the setting, saying only that it was "well conceived" and "in admirable keeping," so that one can only guess how Phelps achieved the simplicity and severity mentioned by the *Athenaeum*. The *Theatrical Journal* (November 15, 1845) was not sensitive to the contrast between the more stylized sets and the naturalism of the storm scene, which the reviewer declared was worth traveling a hundred miles to see:

We have witnessed many attempts of this description, but nothing like this, it is certainly the most effective of anything we have ever seen of the kind.

In producing *Romeo and Juliet* from the original text, Phelps took a fresh look at the problems of staging. Because of the persistence of the altered versions, this play was not equipped with so complete a tradition of stage arrangements and stage business as some other Shakespearean plays, and evidently he felt that customary practice left much to be desired. His careful study produced a number of changes which were commended for their simplicity and smoothness.

The most striking example was in the last scene, which Phelps presented for the first time according to the implied directions in Shakespeare's text. Romeo carried the body of Paris upstage into the vault and stayed there after his discovery of Juliet, not returning to the footlights for his final speech and action. When Juliet woke, she too played her final part in the vault, and the center of the stage remained empty. There was a moment of silence before the stage was suddenly filled by the hurried entrances of the watchmen and servants and all who arrive to comment upon the scene framed by the opening to the vault. The effectiveness of this arrangement, its symbolic value, and its faithfulness to the text might have recommended it to managers before Phelps, except that this arrangement denies the two leading actors the opportunity to make their last speeches close to the footlights. The *Athenaeum* (September 19, 1846) commented that Phelps proved that Shakespeare was wiser than the players had been.

The acting of the whole cast was characterized by the traditionalism and concerted effort that distinguished Sadler's Wells from other theatres. A youthful Juliet, who could deliver Shakespeare's verse with sensitivity to meaning and a sense of its rhythm while impressing the audience with the sincerity of her passion, and a Romeo who did not overemphasize his role were equally unusual on the Victorian stage. Mrs. Marston's performance of the Nurse "requires no praise," declared the *Theatrical Journal* (September 14, 1859). "She is now the only one of a school almost extinct." Even in the production of 1859, Phelps played Mercutio with buoyancy and spirit. Reviewers said that he appeared young, gay, and careless, although he was fifty-five years old.

In *Romeo and Juliet,* as in *King Lear,* critics commented that the restored text made a long play, but that the greater prominence given minor roles increased its interest on the stage.

It was a surprise to critics and playgoers to discover how profoundly all of *Macbeth* was affected by the removal of D'Avenant's additions. They said that it was a revelation of Shakespeare's consummate art that the importance of the Weird Sisters was made clear with so few words and with such a sparing use of the supernatural. The transformation of the witches from a crowd of singing and dancing beings that filled the stage with their magic rites to three dim apparitions who breathed evil with their quiet words changed them from corporal to spiritual entities and from physical prominence in several scenes to a pervading influence over the whole tragedy. A new interpretation of the meaning of *Macbeth* emerged: the hero was seen to be not merely hag-ridden but engaged in a soul-scarring struggle with the power of evil.[52]

The new interpretation of the Weird Sisters was brought out by Phelps's staging of the play. House lights dimmed, the curtain rose on a murky scene of heath and mist, against which the three shadowy figures, illuminated only by a flickering light, could be dimly seen. Fontane says that in the first scene the witches were only appearances—dark figures against a dark background, two gray locks moving in the wind.[53] The darkness of the stage and the ominous presence of these mysterious figures combined with the brief eleven lines of dialogue to set the dark, foreboding mood of the play. At the end of the scene they seemed to withdraw into the air. Their disappearance was accomplished by means of a gauze curtain made of gradually thickened folds, which was pulled up by invisible threads from the stage floor to the borders.[54] The first stretch of the curtain was so sheer that it was not perceptible to the audience, who were not aware of the device used to make the Weird Sisters vanish. Their last words, "hover through the fog and filthy air," echoed in the spectator's ear, reinforcing the impression that the witches, though now invisible, had not left the stage. Their presence was felt throughout the course of the tragedy.

In their second appearance the Weird Sisters were more clearly visible. They stood on a hill under two old spruce trees, the only vegetation in the stark landscape of the Scottish highlands. The trees served the practical purpose of masking the edges of the gauze curtain, which was again drawn up to make them disappear after their colloquy with Macbeth. The impression of vanishing was echoed in Macbeth's "What seem'd corporal melted / As breath into the wind." Behind the opaque lower section of the gauze the three actors silently left the stage; and while Macbeth and Banquo discussed their experience, the gauze was lowered slowly and imperceptibly. The effect was of a haze sinking to the ground, and there appeared to be a gradual brightening of the atmosphere recently clouded by the presence of evil. Increasing light on the stage revealed a distant view of the victorious army, recalling the audience to present reality and Macbeth's outward circumstances.

The effect of these first scenes upon an audience accustomed to the sound and movement of D'Avenant's witches must have been shocking, but critics were less impressed with the novelty of the staging than with its rightness. The opening scene was, in Fontane's words, "an overture of terror." Phelps's staging expressed the mood and the theme of the play.

The opening scene of act two carried on the theme of terror. The curtain rose on a darkened stage, which the flickering torch carried by Fleance revealed to be a great hall in the castle. To keep the tense atmosphere of the murder scene, which might have become remote from the audience in the dim reaches of the large hall, Phelps made use of an unusual feature of Sadler's Wells—the stage doors on the right and left in front of the proscenium arch. Few London theatres still possessed these relics of the early English stage, and generally they had long since fallen out of use as the demand for increased realism had forced actors to retreat behind the line marked by the fall of the curtain. Phelps used one stage door as the entrance to Macbeth's bedroom and the other as Duncan's, so that the scene was played on the apron of the stage. While Macbeth soliloquized on the imaginary dagger, a ray of light from his half-opened bedroom door illuminated the playing area. At the end of the scene he walked to the other door, opened it, and with a peal of thunder in the distance entered Duncan's room. There was a moment of stillness on the empty stage, and then Lady Macbeth entered through the half-opened door, crossed the stage, and looked into Duncan's bedroom. The horror of her words, "He is about it," was increased by the nearness of the door to the audience and by the gloomy patch of light that fell across the stage as she opened it. Fontane felt that everything worked together to produce the height of terror. He comments, "Art and stage can do nothing more."

The discovery of Duncan's murder was made a scene of sudden terror through a vivid imitation of the awakening of a great castle upon Macduff's alarm. Tramping was first heard offstage, as if from distant galleries. Then the soldiers, clansmen, retainers, and servants began to enter, holding weapons of various types, as if hastily snatched. The darkness was broken by the casual illumination of torches carried by some of those who were running to answer the alarm.

Innovations in staging were noticed by experienced critics, who knew every detail of the traditional "business" and could compare Phelp's practice with that of Macready, Kean, and the Kembles. Phelps followed an old tradition (temporarily abandoned by Kemble) in using the physical presence of Banquo's ghost, to which Bennett's imposing form gave substantial reality. His entrances and exits were accomplished by various means, one using the trap and one masked by a clever arrangement of serving men.[55] Phelps devised a new arrangement of the tables in the banquet scene, and this provoked comment from reviewers, who granted the improvement in the general effect but were quick to point out his serious mistake in placing himself downstage of Banquo's ghost, so that the expression on his face—an important element of the scene—was lost to a large part of the audience. Recognizing the justness of the criticism, Phelps revised his arrangement of the banquet in the production of 1848.

The battle scenes of the fifth act also departed from stage tradition. Instead of using the convention of trumpet flourishes to indicate general action offstage while individual pairs of combatants entered and departed, Phelps simulated the battle on the stage behind a massive gothic balustrade, which masked the soldiers' movements. The device gave some impression of the confusion of battle and allowed individuals from both armies to appear and speak audibly by approaching the balustrade, as if struggling through the fighting crowd to the higher ground near the castle. Macbeth, Macduff, and Siward appeared alternately without lapse of time or loss of interest in the scene. This arrangement would not have been possible with the usual acting version of Macbeth, since it provided no suitable place for viewing the details of Macbeth's fight with Macduff and his death agonies—a highlight of Macready's performance. Critics complimented Phelps on his self-sacrifice in giving up this famous "point."

Still another innovation was the change in costuming from the customary Scottish tartans to more primitive-looking mantles of a heavy, dark material that fell from the shoulders in folds. The new dress was not only historically more accurate, but also served to emphasize the somber tone of the whole setting of the tragedy.

Reviewers praised the staging in the highest terms. Some lamented the absence of the music which had accompanied the witches' scenes, but most agreed with the *Athenaeum* (October 2, 1847) that "the manner of presentment of these mysterious beings on this occasion gave to them far more of spiritual impressiveness than ever they derived from music and from number." The Weird Sisters were well played by Younge, Scharf (who also played the Porter), and Wilkins. Fontane speaks of the cacophony of their voices as they addressed Macbeth, each having a kind of melody, like the cries of old and young ravens. Another critic writing many years later said that he could still remember vividly the grotesque intensity of malice conveyed by the face and voice of the first witch in the temptation scene.

Phelps's performance of the leading role was closely related to the staging, particularly to the new interpretation of the Weird Sisters. The most frequently mentioned characteristic of his Macbeth was its imposing strength, which now seemed the greater because the evil force he struggled against was more ominous, more universal, and more powerful. He suggested the force of Macbeth's character with his initial entrance in his martial stride and air of command, and he maintained it through the terrible rack of emotions until the final frantic courage of "Yet I will try the last."

By the time Phelps produced the original *Macbeth,* Mrs. Warner had left Sadler's Wells. Isabella Glyn had sufficient force to play the role impressively, but the audience did not like her stiff Kemble manner as much as the critics did. Fontane had high praise for Emma Atkinson, but most English critics called her competent rather than great, and Phelps himself preferred Mrs. Vezin, who was not primarily a tragic actress. Many of the performances of Macbeth at Sadler's Wells lacked an adequate Lady Macbeth, but as many critics said, general competence and harmony in the acting created a whole impression that satisfied the audience and perhaps gave them a better sense of Shakespeare's tragedy than two or three more prominent actors could have done.

In *A Midsummer Night's Dream,* Phelps fully expressed his concept of staging as interpretation. Giving up the usual tinsel wings, white muslin, glittering light, music, dancing, and stage machinery, he tried to create the poetic fantasy of Shakespeare's *Dream.* In the settings he sought the fluidity, insubstantiality, and silence of a dream. He avoided breaks between scenes by using a diorama and movable flats. In the fairy scenes he had a thin green gauze drawn up to mask the entire playing area of the stage from the floor to the borders and from the flat on one side to the flat on the other. The effect of these devices is described by Henry Morley in a well-known review:

> There is no ordinary scene-shifting; but, as in dreams, one scene is made to glide insensibly into another. We follow the lovers and the fairies through the wood from glade to glade, now among trees, now with a broad view of the sea and Athens in the distance, carefully but not at all obtrusively set forth. And not only do the scenes melt dream-like into one another, but over all the fairy portion of the play there is a haze thrown by a curtain of green gauze placed between the actors and audience, and maintained there during the whole of the second, third, and fourth acts. This gauze curtain is so well spread that there are very few parts of the house from which its presence can be detected, but its influence is everywhere felt; it subdues the flesh and blood of the actors into something more nearly resembling dream-figures, and incorporates more completely the actors with the scenes, throwing the same green fairy tinge, and the same mist over all.[56]

When the flats were changed during the performance, the movement was accomplished without sound, using the system of grooves in the floor. But the scenery had a simplicity that was designed to obviate the necessity of change. The views of the wood which had been painted on the moving back cloth were closely related, as if portraying the same area from different vantage points, and the flats which represented tree and foliage blended into the background even as it changed.

Light was also used to give variety to the scene, both by the use of mediums and by changes of intensity which suggested the progress of night and day during the action. The principles of camouflage were used in the costumes of the fairies, relating colors and design to the scenery. The invisible veil of gauze and the green light helped to blur definite outlines of the flats and to blend the actors more completely into the scenery. *Lloyd's Weekly* (October 23, 1853) described the setting thus:

> There is a misty transparency about the figures that gives them the appearance of flitting shadows more than of human beings. You fancy you can see the moon shining through them. . . . The different views of the wood were deliciously refreshing—just the cool, retired spots that the fairies would delight to dance in, on a warm midsummer's evening. There was no grand effect produced, but everything was natural and simple, and yet beautiful; precisely the impressive simplicity that one meets with in nature. . . . There are not more than three or four scenes in the whole play, and yet so artistically are the different changes of moonlight, fog, and sunrise produced, that you imagine you have been wandering through an entire forest, with a fresh prospect meeting you unexpectedly at every turn. The living figures are so dressed as to harmonize with the scenery, looking as if they were inseparable parts of the same picture; thus, the fairies, as they glide in and out of the trees and foliage, give you a notion that they have actually stepped out of them, as though the trunks and flowers were their natural abiding-places.

Staging, clearly, was an important aspect of this production. Many of the techniques, such as colored mediums, the gauze curtain, and costumes that blended with the scenery, had rarely been used before. Others, such as the diorama and variations of light, were employed in new ways. But once again, the innovations are less remarkable than the new concept of stage decoration which the production expressed. As in the *Macbeth* of 1847, the staging was used to define the underlying theme of the play and to create a mood which helped to interpret its meaning. The diorama did not call attention to itself, as it had in Macready's settings, but was used wholly for dramatic purposes: to give dreamlike fluidity and silence and to emphasize the theme of man's relation to nature which runs through the play.

In the acting of *A Midsummer Night's Dream* Phelps sought to convey the same atmosphere of dream and fantasy established by the setting. In the fairy scenes the poetry of the dialogue was given full prominence by skillful and unhurried reading, aided by the absence of all other sound and any distracting movement. When the lovers entered this natural fairyland, its mood infected them, as the gauze and green light blurred their physical outlines. Morley complained that the mood was broken by overly loud and comic acting in the parts of the quarreling lovers, particularly by Miss Cooper's Helena. It is possible that Fanny Cooper, who had played the role on the great stage of Covent Garden, did not wholly submit to Phelps's direction. She was at this time the most famous actress in the depleted company and immensely popular with the audience. In general the acting was not distinguished, since many of the actors were too young and untrained to create their individual parts with assurance and skill, but they had learned to read the poetry and to carry out the interpretation Phelps intended.

For the role of Puck, Phelps had carefully instructed a young boy, coaching him in speech and gestures so that he expressed Phelps's view of the role. Apparently Master F. Artis was able to add something of spontaneity to his memorized lesson, since Morley felt that he "secured for the character on the stage something of the same prominence that it has in the mind of closet readers of the play." In a later production Phelps had his boy Puck wear an outsize head—a grotesquerie that further emphasized the elfin quality and set him apart from the other fairies, while it drew a parallel with the ass's head. Phelps's interpretation of the play brought out the importance of Puck as a fairy who impinges upon the human world just as Bottom the Weaver invades the fairy world.

In his own acting of Bottom Phelps brought out the grotesque and dreamlike, subduing the human flesh in the fairy scenes and showing the remnants of the dream clinging to the workaday weaver as he puzzled over his recent experience:

> I have had a dream, past the wit of man to say what dream it was. Man is but an ass if he go about to expound this dream. Methought I was . . .

When Phelps produced *The Tempest,* he followed other managers, and particularly Macready, in making the scenery and costumes an important aspect of the performance. But even in his first production, when he simulated the shipwreck of the first scene, the gorgeous and elaborate scenery was dominated by his interpretation of the play. Once the characters were safely on the island he attempted to project the magic spell cast by Prospero to the audience as well as the shipwrecked nobles. Without wires or other stage machinery his Ariel remained a gentle spirit, appearing suddenly out of a fountain or sliding down sloping rocks with nimble grace. The *Athenaeum* (April 10, 1847) said that Phelps had solved the problems posed by the text with greater ingenuity and finesse than any previous stage manager.

In 1855 he produced his mature version of *The Tempest,* with a unity of concept and smoothness in execution that was entirely new. He restored Shakespeare's opening scene by making the stage itself the ship's deck, where the sailors ran about in terror.[57] The rolling of the ship was suggested by the simple device of a railing, which was constructed of canvas and elastic so that it moved up and down in the rhythm of heavy seas. Across the back of the stage stretched the cabin, richly decorated with gold, from which the courtiers descended to the deck. As the scene came to its climax, the gray light became darker until the deck faded out in blackness, while the noise of shouts and sea continued. The fade-out was again accomplished by the rising of the invisible gauzes, which gradually obscured the scene as the lights dimmed.

Then the noise itself faded into silence, and gradually a strip of land appeared in the foreground. Out of the darkness Prospero, in a brilliant costume of red and white, seemed to rise, and as the gauzes were withdrawn, the sea and rocky cliffs of the island appeared in full sunlight. According to the *Times* (September 21, 1855) this scene was less remarkable for its spectacular "effect" than for its presentation of the mood of the play:

> The same poetical feeling which seems to have guided the whole production is shown here by the manner in which all the roar and hurry of the storm and the storm-stricken seems to melt away like an unquiet dream, and leave the spectator in tranquil contemplation of the group formed by the aged magician and his docile child.

The rapid and unobtrusive change from the nightmare of the shipwreck to the quiet of the island is characteristic of the simple and flexible staging Phelps used. No time elapsed between the first and second scene.

Although there was sufficient splendor aided by ingenious device to give magical illusion to the rest of the play, it was carefully controlled to make the action move easily and to preserve a unity of impression similar to that of *A Midsummer Night's Dream*. The scenery is described by the *Times:*

> All the views are evidently from spots within a few yards of each other. Rocks of the same kind perpetually hem in the same blue waters; but nevertheless every variety that is within the reach of composition is produced, and, the natural objects generally being treated in a manner almost fantastic, the constant difference is as striking as the constant similarity.

The suggestive simplicity of this scenery—utterly foreign to the nineteenth-century theater—served the dual purpose of giving a dreamlike quality to the play and a flowing ease to the action.

The play was a good choice for the company of Sadler's Wells in 1855. Although Fontane felt that it did not use the theatre's greatest asset, Phelps's ability to hold an audience in the grip of intense emotion, he found Miss Eburne and Frederick Robinson completely satisfactory in the roles of Miranda and Ferdinand. He thought that they achieved the difficult task of avoiding both the ridiculous and the boring in acting the love scenes. English reviewers noted that Phelps presented a new interpretation of Prospero, giving him a "saint-like mildness" and an almost religious self-denial in his decision to give up his magical powers and return to life with those who had wronged him. English critics also found Phelps's Prospero more impressive as the years passed because few actors trained in the traditional school of elocution still remained on the stage. His reading of the poetry was unsurpassed. Barrett was the best possible replacement for Bennett in Caliban and used the same interpretation, combining the evidences of undeveloped intelligence with natural savagery. Lewis Ball and J. W. Ray followed their predecessors at Sadler's Wells in presenting Shakespeare's clowns with a comic spirit that owed nothing to buffoonery. Fontane placed the comedians of the company in the first rank of Shakespearean actors along with Phelps and Miss Atkinson. The only real weakness in the acting appeared in the fourth act, where the singing and dancing of Iris, Ceres, and Juno fell far short of the rest of the performance. Even the Ariel could not sing well enough to carry out the mood of magic and fantasy set by the rest of the play. This was the kind of inadequacy, usually forgiven by critics, which placed Sadler's Wells below the Princess's in the estimation of many playgoers. Phelps's failure to perfect such scenes was only partly owing to his lack of interest in singing and dancing. The high cost of good performers in an age of ballet and opera made it impossible for him to hire them at Sadler's Wells.

The staging of *Antony and Cleopatra* in 1849 was more lavish than any previous production at Sadler's Wells. Each of the principal characters appeared in four different costumes. There were thirty scenes decorated with sufficient magnificence to suggest the grandeur of royal palaces, and with careful regard for historical accuracy. Contemporary interest in classical history and archaeology made the staging particularly attractive to audiences, who were eager to be instructed in the recent discoveries of scholars. Their interest in seeing an authentically Roman banquet in the scene on board Pompey's galley is understandable, and Phelps's attempt to portray it was more justifiable than it would be today. Excessive realism had not yet taken possession of the theatre, and the moving picture camera had not made the spectacular commonplace.

Phelps gratified his audience's desire for splendor and historical interest in the setting, but he also used the staging to emphasize the contrast between Rome and Egypt, underlining a basic theme of Shakespeare's tragedy. After eliminating twelve of the original forty-two scenes, he was able to follow closely the indications of place and time given in the text, using his moving flats to change scenes quickly without lowering the curtain.

In one respect he departed from Shakespeare's intention. He did not use an elevated platform for the monument in which Cleopatra takes refuge; and therefore, he omitted the hoisting of the dying Antony up into the monument and the twenty-five lines which accompany that action. Such a scene would have risked appearing ludicrous on the nineteenth-century stage, and at Sadler's Wells it would have had the additional disadvantage of obscuring the final scene from the majority of the audience, who sat in the pit.

Despite the spectacular aspect of the production, interest centered in the acting and particularly in Isabella Glyn's performance of the demanding role of Cleopatra. No one doubted her ability to present the imperial dignity of Cleopatra, to give intensity to the expression of emotion, or to read the part intelligently; but few actresses with these talents can also suggest the sexual attractiveness, the caprice, and the vanity of Shakespeare's queen. Miss Glyn proved herself capable of this great variety, creating a Cleopatra that satisfied nearly all critics. Although even in her enticement of Antony, she did not allow her royal status to be completely forgotten, she played the lighter scenes with winning spontaneity and grace. She gave consistency to the characterization by linking all the various moods and poses with her underlying sense of pride. At her most frivolous she retained a suggestion of her capacity for the imperial grandeur she was to assume in her last scene. The death scene was a special triumph, both impressive and moving. In the words of the *Athenaeum* (October 27, 1849):

> The caprice, the grace, the pride of the character were exhibited with a power which exceeded expectation. . . . The whole portrait was thrown out with decision and force, and richly coloured.

Phelps was not entirely satisfactory as Antony, and Dickinson, new to the company, showed more energy than control as the youthful Augustus; but Marston was very good as Pompey, and Bennett made a superb Enobarbus, giving complete characterization to the bluntly honest soldier and satisfying importance to the descriptive poetry of his role. Full development of such minor characters as Lepidus, Eros, and the Clown realized on the stage the wide range and complexity of the tragedy.

Some critics had protested the revival of *Antony and Cleopatra,* and not all were converted to admiration after having seen it. The *Stage-Manager* of October 18 publicly advised Phelps not to attempt its performance and on November 22, after it had appeared, declared that it was a "long winded and certainly tedious tragedy." Most reviewers, however, like the audience, enjoyed this rare play with unqualified pleasure. Playgoers came from all parts of London, so that good houses kept it running for twenty-two nights. *Antony and Cleopatra* at Sadler's Wells was regarded as one of the most important productions of a theatrical generation, and certainly it must have been one of the most satisfying performances of the tragedy ever given. Although Miss Glyn continued to act her role of Cleopatra after she left Sadler's Wells, Phelps never again produced the play, probably for lack of a capable actress.

Timon of Athens had been passed over by actors for two centuries. Its only performance within living memory was Edmund Kean's assumption of the leading role in an adaptation that was played seven times in 1816. Phelps treated it as he had *Antony and Cleopatra*, investing 750 pounds in scenery and costuming, the largest sum he had yet spent on a single production. The sumptuous luxury of the early scenes and their careful imitation of ancient Greek life, based on archaeological discoveries, were interesting merely as a spectacle; but they also underlined the prodigality of Timon's generosity and the comfortable ease of his life. The cave scenes were as gloomy and stark as Timon's misanthropy, and reviewers noted that their darkness suggested the eclipse of light in Timon's soul. In every way the later scenes contrasted with the earlier and reinforced the effect of the catastrophe. A reviewer in the *Times* (October 13, 1856) said that the cave scene with the haggard figure of Timon in the foreground formed "one of the most effective combinations of desolation, mental and physical, ever presented on the stage."

In the last act a diorama, which was the most expensive and striking feature of the staging, was used to depict the march of Alcibiades' army toward Athens, ending at Timon's grave. Although this scenic device and the slight change in the discovering of the epitaph are open to the charge of being un-Shakespearean, they may be defended on other grounds than mere spectacle. On the proscenium stage, with its implied realism in setting, *Timon* seems to rush toward its conclusion with precipitate haste because modern audiences are not accustomed to the conventions that Shakespeare used to encompass imaginary time and space. Phelps's diorama served to bridge this gap and prepare his audience for the fact of Timon's death. In the same way Phelps's introduction of the tomb itself helped to heighten the effect of the epitaph, which for the Elizabethan audience could just as well be read from an imaginary wax impression as from an imaginary tomb.

Critics again noted that scenic decoration did not in any way eclipse the acting. In *Timon*, where the leading role dominates the play to a far greater extent than in most Shakespearean plays, Phelps's acting was the principal feature. It was the kind of character—sensitive, intelligent, and extreme in love and hate—that he was peculiarly able to make credible and impressive on the stage. But twenty-six other actors worked with him to make as complete a representation of the tragedy as possible, and reviewers said that its effectiveness on the stage derived from the total effect of the performance. The Poet and the Painter, played by J. W. Ray and Frederick Younge, captured the interest of the audience in the first scene, before Timon's appearance. Robinson, as one of the flattering lords, by careful delineation of his own part helped bring out the characterization of Timon. Graham's role as the faithful steward became one of the most effective on the stage. Marston was a gallant Alcibiades, with the strength and bluntness of a soldier, but no bluster. In this first production Bennett played Apemantus with perfect control in his use of irony and bitter force in his hatred. It is interesting that Marston playing Apemantus in the production of 1856 won equal praise for a different interpretation.[58] Twisting his face into an expression of malignity and carrying himself with a stoop and looseness of bearing that marked him as low born, he contrasted Apemantus with the noble Timon. His glance and voice betrayed spitefulness instead of the scorn in Timon's attitude. If this reading lost some of the irony Bennett had used so effectively, it added dimension to the character.

On the opening night, September 15, 1851, the theatre was crowded with playgoers who had come out of curiosity to see so rare a play. They found the performance, even with Phelps's first-night nervousness, unexpectedly moving; and reviewers were enthusiastic. Although some predicted that the magnificent setting would be the chief attraction, the *Athenaeum* (October 4, 1851) after a second visit reported that the audience appeared to be enjoying the poetry of the dialogue more than the spectacle. The play had a total run of thirty-one performances, surpassing all previous Shakespearean productions except that of *The Winter's Tale*. Phelps thought that this reception justified a second production with new staging in 1856, which reviewers said was even more splendid than the first. Although the second run was much shorter, its success at Sadler's Wells suggests that the neglect of *Timon of Athens* is a result of a mistaken estimate of its dramatic interest.

Of all Phelps's productions *Pericles* was the only one presented primarily as a spectacle—an excuse for the display of scenery, costumes, theatrical machinery, and even a ballet. It was his one venture into direct rivalry with the Princess's on Kean's own ground. The theatre was closed for a day in order to finish preparations for its opening, and the play ran more than seven weeks without interruption.

As in some of Macready's productions and many of Kean's, descriptions of the scenes were printed on the playbills, and on the opening night the scene painter, Fenton, was called before the curtain. Critics devoted a large part of their reviews to the scenery, and the *Theatrical Journal* (October 18, 1854) said that it deserved a separate notice of its own. A paragraph from the *Times* (October 16, 1854) summarizes the most striking "effects":

> Certainly, as a spectacle, the play of Pericles, as produced at Sadler's Wells, is a marvel. . . . When Pericles is thrown on the sands, it is with the very best of rolling seas, the waves advancing and receding as when governed by Mr. Macready, in Acis and Galatea, at Drury Lane. In the palace of Pentapolis he finds costumes of a kind with which we have been familiarized by Sardanapalus, at the Princess's. When the storm afterwards rocks his vessel, it rocks in real earnest, and spectators of delicate stomachs may have uneasy reminiscences of Folkestone and Boulogne. But all this is as nothing to the wonders that take place when Pericles has discovered his daughter, and sets sail for Ephesus. An admirably equipped Diana, with her car in the clouds, orders his course to her sacred city, to which he is conducted by a moving panorama of excellently-painted coast scenery. The interior of the temple, where the colossal figure of the many-breasted goddess stands in all its glory amid gorgeously-attired votaries, is the last "bang" of the general magnificence.

Phelps spent six months and nearly 1,000 pounds in preparing this setting.[59] Although the cost was only a third of Charles Kean's magnificent revivals, the *Athenaeum* (October 21, 1854) said that it might be compared with *Sardanapalus* at the Princess's. In the number and variety of scenes this *Pericles* exceeded other spectacles, but reviewers spoke of the admirable blending into one whole impression. The guiding theme of the fickleness of fortune was expressed in the instability of the sea. Even in this production *Lloyd's Weekly* (October 22, 1854) specifically exonerates Phelps from the charge that the play was smothered by its setting:

> Mr. Phelps is the best commentator of Shakespeare the people ever had— a commentator that, instead of obscuring the text as commentators generally do, throws a new light upon it.

Phelps as Pericles interpreted the character as a man who sees himself pursued by ill fortune. Even his joy at receiving Thaisa was tempered by doubt that such happiness could last. Morley says that Phelps presented his deepening despondency with "unostentatious truthfulness." [60] Until the last act the play offers little opportunity for impassioned acting, but in the recognition scene Phelps used his skill in showing the transition from despair to joy, accompanied by the conflicting emotions of hope and anxiety. Morley called it "one of the most effective displays of the power of an actor that the stage, as it now is, affords."

> They do not applaud rant at Sadler's Wells. The scene was presented truly by the actor and felt fully by his audience.

Whether or not playgoers came chiefly for the scenery may be debated, but it is certain that many came. *Pericles* was performed fifty-five times, a record run for Sadler's Wells. One rare visitor, the elderly Henry Crabb Robinson, who had once objected to the "coarse declamation" of the company, described the scene painting of this spectacle as "flimsy." [61] Such a comment calls into question the much vaunted magnificence of Victorian productions and hints that twentieth-century audiences, used to lavish films, would find them creaky and unconvincing. Phelps, himself, did not regard such scenic display as a necessary part of theatrical management, and even the success of *Pericles* did not tempt him to make another essay in this type of entertainment.

Gaiety, lightness, and elegance were the predominating characteristics of Phelps's production of *Love's Labour's Lost* in 1857. Reviewers praised the exquisite beauty of the scenery, consisting of wooded landscapes, painted by Phelps's new scene painter, C. S. James. Against this background the rich costumes of a medieval court were prettily displayed. The effect was sparkling and refreshingly simple, suggesting an unhurried ease that would allow time for wit and poetry.

The abundant wit was given full point by actors who were thoroughly familiar with the intricacies of Shakespearean dialogue. A particular instance of their talent is described by the *Times* (October 1, 1857) in speaking of Williams's Holofernes:

> The line, "Bone for bene. Priscian a little scratched; 'twill serve," he gives with marvellous effect, showing at once the magnitude of the crime committed by the ignorant curate and his own magnanimity in passing it over.

That two hours and fifty-five mintues of such intellectual pleasantry were enjoyed by the audience is sufficient evidence of the actors' skill in conveying subtlety of meaning. At Sadler's Wells, where the more casual modern idiom had not yet been adopted on the stage, Shakespeare's puns were delivered with courtly grace and received by the audience with a relish that showed comprehension.

A cast of twenty-one characters, who share almost equally the burden of carrying the play, was well filled by Phelps's company, which had grown stronger in comedy this season with the addition of Mrs. Charles Young and the return of Helen Fitzpatrick. They had a charm and grace, often lacking in actresses at Sadler's Wells, which furthered the illusion of an aristocratic milieu. Morley praised Phelps for "the lumbering helplessness of wit displayed by the great Spaniard when magnificently and heavily conversing with the tiny Moth." [62] Wealth of characterization combined with elaborate wit to make the play interesting.

Although the *Weekly Dispatch* (October 4, 1857) said that Phelps must have chosen this rare comedy "more as a sacrifice by the manager to the bard whom he loves so well and illustrates so ably than as a means of replenishing his treasury," *Love's Labour's Lost* attracted good houses for fourteen nights. We must agree with the *Athenaeum* (October 3, 1857) that such a run was "as much to the credit of the *habitués* in the pit as of the actors on the stage."

THE AUDIENCE

The character of the audience at Sadler's Wells was a major factor in determining the principles of Phelps's management. Although there is some conflicting evidence about the nature of this audience, the picture that emerges from the comments of reviewers over eighteen years is fairly clear.[63] At the opening of a new season in September, 1855, both the *Times* and the *Weekly Dispatch* made direct comments about the audience, describing the patrons as Islingtonians, not wealthy ("and burdened by a protracted war"), and as connoisseurs of serious drama. This description fits most of the evidence.

The Pentonville district surrounding the theatre was densely populated and shabby. Towse describes it thus:

It abounded in small shops, taverns, cheap lodging-houses and slums; and small tradesmen, mechanics, the commoner kind of clerks, peddlers, innumerable wage-earners of different kinds, with a plentiful sprinkling of degraded "sports" constituted the great bulk of the inhabitants.[64]

Most reviewers say that the audience came from this district, but Phelps's nephew asserts that the audience "came from the north and the south, from the east and the west" and that "it would consequently be erroneous to talk of audiences being for the most part local." [65] Phelps, himself, in the draft of a letter to Phipps, the Queen's Master of Revels, also once made this assertion:

> My theatre is (unfortunately for me) far removed from a central situation and surrounded by a non-theatrical population—the majority of my audience coming from a distance as a necessity. Therefore they (individually) come but seldom and are sooner exhausted than other houses in the "heart" of London—and I am compelled [to] produce a greater number of plays.[66]

But on another occasion Phelps, speaking to R. H. Horne, said that he had "only local audiences for the most part." [67] This statement accords with the unanimous testimony of reviewers. In 1857 Morley described the audience as "mainly composed of hard-working men, who crowd a sixpenny gallery and shilling pit." [68]

Perhaps it is chiefly a question of percentage. There is no doubt about the fact that playgoers from other parts of London attended Sadler's Wells. Westland Marston says that it was "a sort of pilgrim's shrine to the literary men of London, to the younger members of the Inns of Court, and to those denizens of the West in whom poetic taste still lingered." [69] Tom Taylor in one article speaks of "Sadler's Wells, with its public in great measure local, and its habitual, almost nightly, frequenters," and of "that larger public which . . . found in Sadler's Wells stronger and better served stage food . . . than they could find in any of the more aristocratic quarters of the town." [70] E. L. Blanchard commented on the "house full of *literati*" on the first night of *The City Madam*.[71] Perhaps Phelps thought of these visitors as the major part of his audience. In numbers they almost certainly did not equal the local frequenters, but they occupied the dress circle, where seats cost six times the price of a gallery seat and three times those in the pit. In financial terms their patronage was a high percentage of the house.

At the opening performance of the third season, *Lloyd's Weekly* (October 3, 1847) described a crowded audience as "an indiscriminate one, drawn from all classes of society, and representing the experiences of every condition of life." If this statement is modified with respect to the highest class of society—the fashionable aristocratic segment—it can be taken as a good description. *Punch* never tired of twitting the upper classes for their prejudice against traveling to Islington, based not on the distance but on its unfashionableness:

> There is a story of a swell, who being advised to go and see a play at Sadler's Wells, exclaimed "Aw—Sadlaw's Wells, wheaw's that?—aw—pwecious long way isn't it?—s'pose that one will have to change one's horses on the woad? [72]

To Fontane Sadler's Wells was a people's theatre, and this is the most important aspect of the audience, whatever the proportion of *literati* on some occasions.

Twentieth-century writers on the subject of the nineteenth-century theatre usually attribute the decline of legitimate drama to the influx of the lower classes into the patent theatres. There is some truth in this: the large national theatres built in the first decade of the century were meant to accommodate a larger and more popular audience. The O. P. riots which plagued Kemble indicate that prices were important to the customers of the pit. And there is no doubt that the huge size of the patent theatres coarsened acting techniques. To appreciate Edmund Kean playgoers had to leave their boxes and find seats in the pit.

But by the time Macready was playing under Bunn's management of Drury Lane, the pit was half empty. The lower classes came to the theatre, flooding the gallery and some of the pit, after the half-price at nine o'clock. For these patrons spectacle and opera were more attractive than serious plays. Macready attacked Bunn with physical violence, not because the truncation of *Richard the Third* (in Cibber's version) outraged his sense of devotion to Shakespeare, but because the tragedy was over before the half-price patrons arrived, and Macready hated to play to an empty house. Bunn knew that the half-price audience preferred opera, and he was manager of the theatre. During his own management Macready played to a half-filled pit except when he resorted to spectacle, opera, or the Queen's command.

Until Phelps's management of Sadler's Wells there was no popular Shakespearean theatre. The critics never ceased to be surprised at the kind of audience attracted to Sadler's Wells. This is good evidence that the lower-middle class had not been seen at serious dramatic performances within living memory. They found it even more remarkable that this audience, largely uneducated, learned to appreciate Shakespeare with a discriminating taste not found in any other theatre. One commentator called it "beyond comparison the most intellectual pit of any theatre in London." And a number of reviewers mention the fact that spectators in the pit and boxes brought texts to the theatre on the occasion of an unusual revival so that they could check the acting against printed copies of the play. Their preferences, reflected in the choice and style of Phelps's productions, testify to their good taste.

For this audience Phelps had to keep his prices low. In eighteen years the pit and gallery remained at the same shilling and sixpenny prices which had been in effect before he took over the theatre. And for this audience he had to use the repertory system, offering weekly variety in program that would keep regular patrons interested. He often had crowded houses, and several times each season critics speak of the difficulty of getting into the theatre, saying that hundreds of people were turned away. Early in his management the *Theatrical Journal* (December 6, 1845) expressed surprise that Phelps kept a strict repertory system in spite of a successful production:

> The public know how to appreciate the good taste and care with which it is produced, and we much wonder that, in consideration of the great success it received, it has only been played twice a week. But Mr. Phelps never had the fault (unfortunately but too common at larger theatres we could mention) of cramming pieces down people's throats.

The only larger theatres were the patent theatres, so the inference is clear.

Financial necessity forced Phelps to heed the preferences of his audience. Macready and Charles Kean could afford to ignore popular preference, since both had royal patronage, which was a potent social and economic force in the mid-nineteenth century, and private wealth, gained from star engagements and trips to the United States. A royal command at Drury Lane brought in more than a thousand pounds for Macready. A full house at Sadler's Wells brought in about 150 pounds. Both Macready and Charles Kean lost money by their managements, even with royal patronage and the support of wealthy individuals. Phelps made a comfortable profit year after year with no patronage.

This same financial necessity kept Phelps from following the road taken by Macready and Kean to expensive decoration and the resultant long run. Recent stage historians attribute the long run to increased population and better transportation in the midnineteenth century, but the practice began before it succeeded financially. Macready spent so much money on his productions that he had to "cram them down people's throats"—as many reviewers complained. And Kean, who frankly kept his lavish revivals on the stage after houses had dwindled, suffered serious financial loss. Kean invented the long run in the days when his audience still arrived at the theatre by private carriage.

The simplicity and economy of staging forced upon Phelps by the nature of his audience challenged him to produce plays in a way that earned the praise of critics while it kept his management financially successful. By avoiding complicated and expensive stage machinery and the inflexible box set, Phelps also avoided the necessity of cutting hundreds of lines out of Shakespeare's plays.

Charles Kean brought interest to Shakespeare by producing his plays with spectacular settings; Phelps had to bring Shakespeare to life, and he did it chiefly by the acting of his company. In view of the sharp contrast between these rival managements, it is strange that subsequent generations of actor-managers followed Kean's methods instead of Phelps's. Shakespeare staged with lavish realism and acted in the modern idiom has not proved any more successful in the last hundred years than it did at the Princess's.

Phelps first applied the principle of orchestral direction to Shakespearean plays, seeking harmony in all the parts and a consistent expression in acting and staging of his own interpretation of the poet's work.[73] The best theatrical critic of the time insisted that Phelps's methods of management would have made Shakespeare successful in the old legitimate theatres:

> It is not because of anything peculiar in the air of Islington, or because an audience at Pentonville is made of men differing in nature from those who would form an audience in the Strand, that Shakespeare is listened to at Sadler's Wells with reverence not shown elsewhere. What has been done at Islington could, if the same means were employed, be done at Drury Lane. But Shakespeare is not fairly heard when he is made to speak from behind masses of theatrical upholstery, or when it is assumed that there is but one character in any of his plays, and that the others may be acted as incompetent performers please.[74]

VI

Non-Shakespearean Drama at Sadler's Wells

Mᴏʀᴇ than half of the performances at Sadler's Wells during Phelps's eighteen years of management were not Shakespearean. A brief review of these productions is interesting for several reasons. The choice of repertory reveals the taste of the early Victorian period and how Phelps led it into some new areas. His methods of performance show how important acting was in keeping alive the old stock plays of English drama. His treatment of contemporary playwrights in the last years of the actors' theatre gives insight into Victorian drama before the advent of the modern play and the playwright's theatre.

ELIZABETHAN AND JACOBEAN PLAYS

The new reverence for Shakespeare expressed in Romantic criticism led writers to an interest in other Elizabethan and Jacobean playwrights, and Phelps followed them in his search for fresh dramatic material. An indication of the influence of literary criticism on Phelps's selection of plays is given by the playbills announcing *The Duchess of Malfi* on which are printed excerpts from the essays of Hazlitt, Lamb, and Charles Knight. Although Phelps's search revealed few plays that he considered suitable for presentation in his theatre and none that could be performed without revision, he produced those few with great care; and they attracted the attention of many playgoers.

Massinger's *The City Madam* was the first and one of the most suc-cesful of these neglected plays brought to the stage of Sadler's Wells. It had been performed only a few times in its two centuries of existence, and during the previous fifty years it had been seen only in a version called *Riches,* written by J. B. Burges for Edmund Kean. *Riches* had not been a success even with Kean's talent to support it. Phelps went back to the original play and made less drastic alteration than Burges.

In an effort to effect a compromise between Massinger's violence and Victorian sensitivity, he stopped Luke Frugal's cruelty before it reached the point of giving his sister-in-law to the American Indians for a ritual sacrifice to the devil, and made other similar adjustments of plot and character. He altered words and expressions to conform to the practices of the Lord Chamberlain. His most drastic change was in the ending, where he replaced the uncompromising bitterness of Massinger's "comedy" with the conversion of Luke from his evil ways. The result was an eminently actable play, preserving Massinger's language nearly intact, with a sentimental ending that provided a great scene of Luke's reconciliation with his niece.

Most critics felt that some revision of such a play was absolutely necessary. The *Weekly Dispatch,* for example, objected to Phelps's performance of *The Provoked Husband* because the "coarse language and broad innuendos" had not been omitted from his acting text. Nineteenth-century sensitivity was even more delicate than that of the highly moral audience who watched the puppet show of *The Provoked Husband* which Fielding's Tom Jones found "indeed a very grave and solemn entertainment, without any low wit or humor." Phelps's revision of *The City Madam* was generally approved, although the *Athenaeum* (November 16, 1844) called it a garbled version of the original and, characteristically, objected to new tamperings with classic plays in an age that had slowly been returning to the original Shakespearean texts.

Like the original, Phelps's version depended for its success upon imaginative acting. Massinger's satiric comedies do not attract audiences merely by wit or beauty of language. Tamely acted, the plots seem melodramatic and the characters absurd. At Sadler's Wells this play came to life in the acting, particularly in Phelps's brilliant portrayal of Luke. His ability to transform himself in bearing, facial expression, and gesture helped create a vivid portrait of an unnatural and exaggerated character. In the opening scenes he disguised his normally erect posture in a cringing servility which so perfectly suited the words and actions of the inhuman Luke that for the moment he became credible. And so, through all the violent changes Luke undergoes, he created suitable external forms that were sufficiently convincing to give him life on the stage. *Lloyd's Weekly*

(November 3, 1844), commenting that Massinger's character is rather a mask than a human being, felt that the actor lifted it to a new level:

> Mr. Phelps's performance of the part was excellent; he gave it an effect that did not belong to it, and raised it to assume an importance which it scarcely merited. Some of his transitions were as happy and as striking as we ever witnessed in any stage performance; the crawling, abject spirit and soft fellow-feeling of the humble petitioner were ably given. His delighted, dream-like amazement, when informed of Sir John's death, and that he had left him the whole of his fortune, was remarkably fine; and his triumph on finding Lady Frugal and her daughters entirely in his power was magnificent.

The appearance of this play during Phelps's first season of management created more interest in Sadler's Wells and brought critics who were rarely willing to travel as far as Islington in these early days. The *Times* (November 2, 1844) was impressed by Phelps's performance and by the appreciative attention of the audience:

> Phelps, who played Luke, shines in masculine pathos. No one can better convey the notion of a stern, rugged nature broken unwillingly into grief. The most orthodox venerator of original texts would scarcely fail to be moved at the genuine affection with which he embraced his niece; and the character generally was exceedingly well played. His reading is that of one who has carefully and judiciously studied the bearing of his words. His intercession for the poor debtors before his brother, Sir John Frugal, was an excellent specimen of eloquence. The house was quite full, and the audience was such an one as a dramatist ought to delight in. No hearers could be more attentive.

This production of *The City Madam,* with Mrs. Warner, Bennett, Marston, John Webster, and Fanny Cooper in the important roles, was performed sixteen times. The play was revived in four subsequent seasons.

The next year Phelps produced Massinger's *The Fatal Dowry,* another play rarely seen in the theatre. He used an acting version prepared for performance at Drury Lane in 1825, and again the *Athenaeum* objected to the alterations, asserting that they merely aggravated Massinger's faults and made the play "incoherent and stagey." It had the virtue of preserving the characters intact, thus allowing full importance to the unusual number of prominent roles; and it was this feature of *The Fatal*

Dowry—the sustained development of several interesting characters—that reviewers noted.

Marston played Charolais, the gentle and sensitive hero; Phelps, his friend Romont, an honest and reckless soldier; Bennett, Rochfort; and Miss Cooper, Beaumelle. Each was a notable performance. Critics found the characters convincing and the dialogue "full of glorious poetry and fervent passion." The *Theatrical Journal* (September 6, 1845) said that *The Fatal Dowry* had been produced "with an effect scarcely to be credited by those who have not witnessed the performance." This play also was revived in later seasons.

For Phelps the most important of Massinger's plays was *A New Way To Pay Old Debts*. The leading role of Sir Giles Overreach had attracted every important tragedian since John Philip Kemble, with the notable exception of Macready, and it had been one of Kean's masterpieces. Phelps had played it in the provinces, at the Haymarket, and a few times during his first season at Sadler's Wells. In 1849 he made it a specialty, and from that time on played the role frequently.

Sir Giles is an extreme portrayal of an avaricious and cruel man with no redeeming traits. To make such a monster credible on the stage an actor must be able to create a character without using natural human touches and without relying upon sympathetic understanding in the spectator. Kean did it by moments of brilliant insight and force; Phelps used completeness of characterization, with every tone and gesture adding something to the portrait. Both played with an intensity of feeling usually reserved for tragedy. A Dublin critic who saw Phelps as Sir Giles in 1852 records this impression:

> His anger towards the end was terrible; one felt keen pity mingled with horror; the quick changes from rage to rejoicing, and then the downfall, when there comes on that awful paralysis of soul, were thrilling. . . . I would scarcely wish to see it again; I felt almost as Byron did seeing Kean do it: the sight of wickedness so fearful, yet so painfully human, is not "good" for the thought.[1]

Of the three plays by Beaumont and Fletcher produced at Sadler's Wells, only *The Maid's Tragedy* in the revised form of *The Bridal* had lasting appeal. This was the play that Sheridan Knowles had adapted under Macready's supervision in 1837, when it became a major attraction at the Haymarket.

In its revised form the play was primarily a vehicle for the leading actor. The parts of Amintor and Aspatia had been severely cut, and Evadne reduced to secondary importance. Knowles had also changed the plot to suit nineteenth-century standards of decorum, which would have been outraged by the original. Indeed, the *Weekly Dispatch* (August 25, 1844) said that the original play was disgustingly coarse and "could not be publicly displayed or privately enjoyed at the present time." Knowles had added three new scenes, softening and blurring the nature of the relationship between Evadne and the King, and he had omitted the scene in which she murders him. Generally reviewers approved the Knowles-Macready version, but a dissenting voice in the *Theatrical Journal* (August 31, 1844) complained that the other characters had been cut "in order that Melantius (*ergo* Macready) may monopolize the whole and sole attention of the audience," and pronounced the result "a mere melodrama."

Melantius, with his forbidding exterior which masks a passionate soul, and his fierce devotion to the ideals of friendship and family honor, made a perfect Victorian hero. Macready had recognized his own affinity to the character and played it successfully for many years. At Sadler's Wells Phelps took up the role in his first season and had a similar success. The *Athenaeum* (August 24, 1844), noting that the part required "great physical energy, emphatic elocution, rapid action, and vehement passion," declared that "in all these points Mr. Phelps much exceeded our expectations." During the rest of his career he acted it more often than Macready had. Years later the *Theatrical Journal* (December 1, 1858) still considered it one of his best roles and noted that "we have nothing like it in any other actor of the present day."

At Sadler's Wells Mrs. Warner resumed the role of Evadne, which had brought her to the front rank of her profession, and again she scored a hit. She was especially good at creating the kind of larger-than-life portrait demanded by such a character. There was a majesty in her haughty contempt for the opinions and affairs of lesser beings and an awe-inspiring force in her passion that compelled the audience into belief. Even critics who disliked her style and complained of her lack of grace and gentleness in some characters found her Evadne impressive. One such critic said that as Evadne "she made sin beautiful." Dickens praised her "splendid and defiant" passion.[2]

When Phelps decided to produce *A King and No King* in his third season, the play was unknown in the theatre, the last performance, for one night only, having occurred sixty years before. In preparing his acting text he felt that it was necessary to soften the plot, since the main action springs from the passion of Arbaces for his supposed sister, Panthea. He spared the feelings of the audience by inserting several exclamations early in the play which hinted at the denouement, and he added several speeches in Panthea's role to make clear her horrified rejection of Arbaces. The question of how much a Victorian audience would tolerate in the discussion of incest may be debated. Whereas the *Theatrical Journal* refused even to summarize for its readers the plot of so indecent a play, the *Athenaeum* declared that the original text would have been perfectly successful.

In spite of the loss of suspense caused by Phelp's tampering, the play was effective. The torrents of emotional language that may seem excessive to a reader became on the stage a moving poetic expression of an overwhelming passion. A large audience, many of whom had come to the theatre out of a purely literary interest in Elizabethan drama, were surprized to find themselves held in the grip of the play and its language. Reviewers praised Phelps for giving credibility to an improbable character by the emotional force of his acting. *Douglas Jerrold's Weekly Newspaper* (January 16, 1847) found it remarkable:

> It is a greater and higher performance not only than any we have ever seen of Mr. Phelps's, but of any actor since *the* Kean. Without apparent effort, without stage artifice, it is a pure and powerful delineation of rapid and consuming passion, and places the enactor in the highest rank of his art.

Another in the series of Phelps's experiments with the neglected work of Shakespeare's contemporaries was *The Honest Man's Fortune* by Beaumont and Fletcher. Although he used a version by R. H. Horne which considerably remodeled the play, critics generally approved the adaptation. Some said that in modifying and softening a work which would not have been acceptable on the stage, Horne had also strengthened the plot and increased the play's interest. Even the *Athenaeum* (March 3, 1849) commented that the interpolations were written in a style so cleverly imitative of the original that they could not be detected in performance.

The best feature of *The Honest Man's Fortune,* variety of characterization, was skillfully exploited at Sadler's Wells. Bennett as La Poop, whose role had been enlarged by the revision, was the hit of the performance. He and Hoskins (Longueville) and Younge (Malicorn) played to each other with practiced dexterity. Phelps as Montague made the most of his great scene in the last act.

Fletcher's *Rule a Wife and Have a Wife* proved more successful than either of the two preceding plays. Phelps prepared his own acting text, staying as close as possible to the original. The *Athenaeum* admitted that his small alterations had been necessary in view of the "grossness of manners" in Fletcher's time.

Lively comedy and a variety of good roles, offering opportunity for creative acting, made the play attractive on the stage. Phelps had the difficult part of Leon, and reviewers said that he made credible his transformation from a simple-minded, duped husband to a hero of masculine forcefulness and dignity. Hoskins, often praised for his special talent in comedy, caught the swagger, charm, and effrontery of the Spanish captain, Perez—a part which Garrick had played. Fanny Cooper had the nominal lead, but Miss Huddart (Mrs. Warner's niece) was equally applauded for her portrayal of the attractive maid who proves as clever an opportunist as Perez. One critic noted that the success of such a play, which ran thirteen nights and was revived in four subsequent seasons, would not have been possible under the star system practiced at most theatres.

In the autumn of 1850 Phelps was looking for a play with a good part for Isabella Glyn and with sufficient interest that it could compete with Charles Kean's new management of the Princess's and Macready's farewell season at the Haymarket. Unexpectedly, the play appeared in the hands of R. H. Horne, who brought Phelps his rewriting of Webster's *The Duchess of Malfi*. Phelps decided at once that it could be successful, but he told Horne that the adaptation was worth more than Sadler's Wells could afford to pay and suggested that he try a theatre where higher prices of admission would provide a higher payment. Horne took it to Drury Lane, where Anderson was scheduled to open in January, but he was not interested. Phelps then bought the rights and made the play his most important production of the season.

In revising *The Duchess of Malfi,* Horne had gone beyond the usual process of making an acting version. His purpose, as stated in his introduction to the published edition, had been to eliminate contradictions, incongruities, and oversights; to tighten the construction; and to reduce both the length of the play and the number of scene changes required. In cutting he followed the usual method of removing short passages from every scene. By rewriting and interpolations he built up the characterization of Antonio, making him a man of action. He made more explicit the motivation of the Cardinal and of Duke Ferdinand. He prepared for the ultimate conversion of Bosola by emphasizing his good qualities early in the play. And he tried to connect the fifth act more closely with the rest of the play by inserting frequent mention of the death of the Duchess. In general it was not merely officious and gratuitous tampering. Considerable alteration was strictly necessary in order to get the play through the Lord Chamberlain's office and to make it endurable to a Victorian audience. His interpolations cleverly imitated Webster's style. The result was a powerful play, converted from a literary curiosity into the contemporary idiom. Nearly every critic, even the conservative reviewers for the *Athenaeum* and the *Times,* felt that Horne had done well.

Phelps was undoubtedly aware that the performance of *The Duchess of Malfi* would arouse widespread disapproval even though Horne had removed the language and situations most likely to provoke objections. In an attempt to disarm critics and to prepare his audience for Webster's violence of action and unrestrained language, he arranged to have a prologue read each evening justifying contemporary interest in the tragedy. Nevertheless, some critics insisted that the play should not be performed under any circumstances. The *Dramatic and Musical Review* (January 15, 1851) said, "We have before offered our objections to this class of drama—they were founded not upon its worthlessness, but upon its criminal tendency." George Henry Lewes, the playwright who had been unusually aggrieved by Phelps's rejection of his play, spoke of the mediocrity of Elizabethan dramatists and asserted that "the resuscitation of those dramatists has been a fatal obstruction to the progress of the drama." [3] The *Theatrical Journal* (January 9, 1851) found the incidents of the play "revolting to our nature," and the *Athenaeum* (November 23, 1850) declared that Webster should not be restored to the modern stage at all.

The audience, however, was not influenced by critical opinion. On the first night the spectators seemed to be totally absorbed in the play, which they applauded with unmistakable approval. During the next few weeks eager crowds filled the theatre whenever *The Duchess of Malfi* was performed. After Christmas Phelps announced the play for six nights a week, and it ran for most of January.

Critics were rather disconcerted by the unexpected appeal of Webster's tragedy. They were compelled to admit that it was attractive to the audience, or, as they carefully pointed out, to the pit. The *Athenaeum* said, "Though evidently somewhat puzzled by the horror of the situations, the beauties of the dialogue seemed to be appreciated by the pit." Since most of the audience sat in the pit, the implied distinction meant very little beyond a recognition that the opinion of the reviewers (who sat in the boxes) was not shared by the bulk of the audience. It is fortunate that the reaction of one member of the pit is preserved for us in the diary of Charles Rice, who made this entry on *The Duchess of Malfi*:

> Got up in the first style of excellence, and acted with wonderful effect. Phelps's Duke, Graham's Cardinal, Waller's Antonio, G. Bennett's Bosola fine studies; the latter highly finish'd.—Miss Glynn's Duchess painfully absorbing! If I mistake not, this lady will be the finest actress since Mrs. Siddons! [4]

Rice's comments summarize the important aspects of the production. Its staging was a main feature because of the splendid costuming and setting and the effective arrangement of scenes and stage business. The performance moved with an ease and smoothness from beginning to end that helped minimize the shocking nature of many incidents.

The center of interest was Isabella Glyn's portrayal of the Duchess. Except for her own Cleopatra, there had been no such piece of acting in the previous thirty years. The elevated style of the Kemble school, with its studied poses and chanting speech was well suited to the flamboyance of Webster, whose writing demands something more than naturalness in acting. Miss Glyn, reviewers said, caught the coquetry and liveliness of the early scenes and the majesty of the later ones with both grace and tragic force. The character was impressive and absorbingly interesting.

Bennett as Bosola had the most prominent male role of Horne's "reconstruction." The Kemble stiffness which limited his range in acting was not an impediment in this role. The *Athenaeum* said that he played Bosola with "that old feeling for the histrionic art which few modern professors seem to understand."

Phelps would have preferred to act Bosola, but he realized that the success of the play depended upon making Duke Ferdinand credible, both in his malignity and in his madness, and that this required a finesse which Bennett did not have. Although some reviewers were puzzled to find

Phelps in so unrewarding a role, the *Athenaeum* perceptively commented that Bosola had "very properly" been confided to Bennett, since the character of the Duke was made endurable only by Phelps's talent and judgment. His frenzy at the end of the second act and his raving madness in the fifth were played with a skill that kept to the fine line between underplaying (which would have failed to convey the force of Webster's conception) and exaggeration (which would have destroyed its credibility).

Phelps's bold venture in producing *The Duchess of Malfi,* which had not been seen on the stage since 1707, was a genuine success. Although most critics felt that the play was unsuitable for the nineteenth-century stage, the reviewer for *Lloyd's Weekly* (November 24, 1850) said, "It is a matter of regret that other managers, having pretensions to the 'legitimate' do not follow their example, instead of surfeiting us with melodramatic five-act dramas, void of poetry and every other requisite that characterize works of art." The audience agreed with this critic in preferring it to most of the contemporary plays Phelps introduced to the stage. He would certainly have revived it in later seasons except that he never again had a leading actress capable of playing the Duchess.

Miss Glyn later tried to repeat her success at the Surrey, but the production failed. D. W. Waller, the Antonio at Sadler's Wells, carried the adaptation to New York, where he used it for his wife's debut at the Broadway in 1858. Aside from William Poel's production of the original text in 1892, Phelps's was the only notable performance of Webster's play in two hundred years.

Rowley's *The New Wonder,* in a version made by J. R. Planché and called *A Woman Never Vext,* was performed six times in 1852. Although Phelps was not in the cast, reviewers detected his direction in the acting. One remarked that the comedy had far more interest on the stage than one might expect from reading it, but the play did not appear again.

RESTORATION AND EIGHTEENTH-CENTURY PLAYS

With a few exceptions the plays Phelps used from the Restoration period and the eighteenth century were well known in the theatre of his time. A few had not been acted since Kemble's managment. In 1844 all of them were new to that portion of the audience at Sadler's Wells who had not attended the legitimate theatres. By the end of his management his audience was the only one in London who knew most of these plays, since by 1862 the old repertory was no longer acted elsewhere.

The absence of Restoration comedy from this list is notable, but hardly surprising in view of the taste of the Victorian period. Colley Cibber is represented, with pruning. Otherwise, the repertory included a good selection of English comedy. Morley once noted that "Sadler's Wells has a reputation for its acting of old comedy, as well earned as its credit for fidelity to Shakespeare." [5] Frequently Phelps did not appear in the casts of the old comedies. Hoskins, Marston, Fanny Cooper, Helen Fitzpatrick, Mrs. Charles Young, Mrs. Marston, and sometimes Bennett played the important roles.

Phelps chose Colley Cibber's *She Would and She Would Not* so that Helen Fitzpatrick could play the dashing heroine. Even though the text had been carefully weeded of indecencies, the choice was considered daring, especially since the heroine appears dressed as a man. Hoskins had a gaiety and ease in his acting that made his Trappanti very good, and Julia St. George made an excellent Floria. Other members of the company were not entirely successful in catching the spirit of so unfamiliar a genre. Such an accomplished Shakespearean actor as Younge, according to the *Athenaeum* (September 29, 1849), failed to understand his role. The reviewer also complained of the bowdlerization, asserting that many jokes had been deprived of emphasis in deference to the taste of a prudish audience. In fact the audience enjoyed this play more than a number of sentimental comedies Phelps tried at Sadler's Wells.

Cibber's *Love Makes a Man* was performed only twice in the autumn of 1853 when Miss Fitzpatrick was not in the company. The *Theatrical Journal* said that it was "placed on the stage with great care," but it was not played again.

Mrs. Centlivre's *The Busy-Body* was performed only twice. *The Wonder* appeared half a dozen times. These plays were seldom seen on the well-mannered Victorian stage, and indeed the reviewer of *Lloyd's Weekly* took exception to any performance of Mrs. Centlivre's work on the grounds that "her dialogue is almost always indecorous, and not unfrequently inexcusably indecent." Nevertheless, the audience at Sadler's Wells appeared to enjoy them thoroughly when they occasionally appeared on the stage. Phelps himself twice played Don Felix in *The Wonder* for his benefit performances.

Several eighteenth-century comedies succeeded only when Helen Fitzpatrick or Mrs. Charles Young acted the leading role. Phelps put on the Vanburgh-Cibber *The Provoked Husband* in 1851 without success, but in 1858 it was praised by critics. Morley called it "an example of the finish with which a company well trained to work together may present a play demanding no little variety of talent" and noted that Phelps had chosen it not because it gave him a great role but because it brought out the force of his company.[6] Mrs. Charles Young played Lady Townley, and Phelps gave an interpretation of Lord Townley, basically different from Macready's, which Morley says added brilliancy to her role:

> Two renderings of the part of Lord Townley are possible: one, which is not the one selected, contains a display of restless uneasiness, breaking out here and there into passion, an effective and therefore a tempting version. In the other rendering, which Mr. Phelps has chosen, Lord Townley appears with all the dignity and self-command proper to a nobleman of the old school who had a warm, strong heart, but had learnt how to contain his passions. The repose and dignity thus given to the figure of the husband serve as an admirable foil to the wife's restless levity.

Mrs. Inchbald's comedy *Every One Has His Fault,* with Mrs. Warner and Henry Marston in the leading roles, appeared early in the second season of Phelps's management. Silence from reviewers and no further attempt at performing the comedy indicate that it was a failure. Similarly, Fielding's *The Miser,* adapted from Molière, in which Phelps played Lovegold in 1854, died after three performances. The *Athenaeum* (March 11, 1854) ranked Phelps's performance with his Bottom and Shallow, but apparently the audience did not like the play. Another adaptation of Molière, Arthur Murphy's *All in the Wrong,* was given two performances in 1849. According to a review in the *Stage-Manager* (April 28, 1849), the acting was excellent and a full audience enjoyed the play heartily, but it was an end-of-the-season novelty never repeated. Helen Fitzpatrick made her London debut as Letitia Hardy in *The Belle's Stratagem.* Reviews were excellent, and the *Athenaeum* (September 1, 1849) predicted a long run for the play, but Miss Fitzpatrick appeared in new roles the following week.

Isaac Bickerstaffe's *The Hypocrite* was a success in 1858, when Mrs. Charles Young was in the company. Although the play is a reworking of Molière's *Tartuffe,* through Cibber's *Non-Juror,* it has many virtues of its own, not the least of which is the character of Charlotte. Mrs. Young played the strong-minded heroine with sparkling vivacity, elegance, and delicacy.

Phelps had a new interpretation of Dr. Cantwell, the role made famous by Garrick and kept on the stage by Dowton and Farren. They had made him a shallow man, ridiculous in his unctuous piety, but Phelps made him a crafty imposter who deliberately used religion as a cloak for his villainy. This interpretation was closer to Molière and perhaps also to the nineteenth-century attitude toward religionists. It was also better suited to Phelps's comic style than the oily silkiness of the traditional interpretation. Some critics disliked it and found Phelps coarse.[7] But the *Weekly Dispatch* (November 21, 1858) liked his view:

> Mr. Phelps's is so very different, and yet so happy a conception, that it only affords another instance of how temperament and genius may place a character with equal justice in the most opposite points of view. The Cantwell of Dowton was one of those oily, smooth-faced, plenteous sons of heaven. . . . Mr. Phelps inclines to moisture rather than to substance. His Cantwell is a sniveller—a piece of pious drivel. . . . When not in tears he has a drawl of such slow and broken mournfulness that it threatens at every moment to give way to a gush. How indicative of the sufferer, and how provocative of sympathy! His face, too has a fixed dejection, quite in harmony with such endurance; his jaw a listless dropping, as though incapable of remonstrance; whilst his constant pressure of his heart, in averment of his sincerity, adopts a form that really looks like an involuntary confession. His fingers spread upon his breast till they resemble the claws of a wild beast.

Morley also liked Phelps's new interpretation and specifically mentioned the coarseness as a deliberate effect:

> The change, when he is unmasked, to a vulgar brutality of tone that without one touch of caricature expresses the lowness of his position among men and beasts; his coarse, excited triumph, and his miserable collapse when all his schemes have crumbled . . . are a few only of the points that attest the pains bestowed upon the study of this part by an accomplished actor.[8]

In the same review Morley mentions an aspect of the actor's art which is seldom spoken of in reviews of this period:

> The "make-up" of the character is wonderfully good, the actor has transformed his face, and a German critic might spend a chapter on discus-

sion of the artist's fine aesthetical treatment of his own nose. A couple of touches of black paint have given the effect of a true Cantwell pinch to the nostrils.

In December, 1858, another old comedy, Richard Cumberland's *Wheel of Fortune,* was produced at Sadler's Wells. Although described as a comedy, the play belongs to the sentimental genre that heralded the advent of Romanticism to the stage and has little resemblance to earlier eighteenth-century plays like *The Provoked Husband* and *The Hypocrite.* During the thirty years since its last performance it had been almost forgotten and was totally unknown to most of the Sadler's Wells audience. Reviews report that it was enthusiastically received. Although the *Examiner* (December 18, 1858) in adding "by a well-trained public" seems to hint that the audience was specially qualified to appreciate this play, the *Times* (December 11, 1858) noted that the frequenters of Sadler's Wells "deeply as they venerate Shakespeare, have not been trained in the traditions of the eighteenth century." Their training was rather in the appreciation of good acting than in specific knowledge of the genre, and it was the acting that gave the *Wheel of Fortune* fresh life. Henry Marston, Mrs. Charles Young, Frederick Robinson (recently returned to Sadler's Wells), and several minor actors displayed the company's talent for polite comedy.

Phelps played Penruddock, the role made famous by John Philip Kemble, and once again revised the traditional interpretation to suit his own talent and the temper of his time. Kemble had given the hero a classic elevation, embuing him with aristocratic pride, near insanity in his feelings of injury, and terrible force in his threatenings. In his hands a sentimental character had become almost tragic. Phelps, by contrast, played Penruddock with great restraint. He was more natural and rational, reducing his suffering to a quiet inner struggle and using his outbursts of anger as the temporary relief of internal feeling. In this case the elderly critic of the *Athenaeum,* who had disapproved of his Dr. Cantwell, preferred Phelps's new interpretation. He remembered Kemble's performance as showing "an insane excess of sentimentality" and found Phelps closer to the author's intention.[9] A similar opinion was expressed by the *Examiner,* which said that his performance was "marked with a taste that never by one coarse stroke invites attention from the audience." Perhaps the restraint of Phelps's style was closer to the spirit of sentimental comedy than the classic elevation which pervaded the theatre of Cumberland's day. In any case, the play after years of neglect was a success at Sadler's Wells, and the *Athenaeum* declared that when the stilts had been discarded Penruddock stood upon his own natural legs.

During the one season when both Mrs. Young and Helen Fitzpatrick were at Sadler's Wells, Phelps put on a number of pre-Romantic comedies. After notable productions of *Love's Labour's Lost* and *As You Like It,* he chose *The Clandestine Marriage* by George Colman the Elder and David Garrick. Although it had kept the stage for many years because of the effectiveness of the leading role in the hands of such a comedian as William Farren, its unsentimental and satiric tone did not generally appeal to Victorian taste. The *Athenaeum* (November 7, 1857) called it "a more onerous undertaking" than any previous comic revival.

At Sadler's Wells the play was seen as something more than a vehicle for the leading comic actor. Phelps, two excellent comediennes, and a number of lesser actors—even to Caroline Parkes as the chamber maid— gave a delicacy, artistic finish, and harmony to the acting that made it an appealing play. The *Athenaeum* found it full of dramatic interest, wrought up to a most effective climax, and remarkably rich in character.

Phelps played the old rake, Lord Ogleby, whose ridiculous affectation of youth is the chief object of the author's satire. The feeble voice, doddering step, and emaciated body contrasted with his assumption of the airs and graces of a young lover and with his conviction that he was irresistibly attractive to women. Phelps's comic genius was again evident in his realization of the humor without violating his consistency of characterization. He avoided the little tricks used by the traditional comedian, like Farren's device of putting his hair in curl papers to provoke laughter. Instead, he gave such a convincing portrait of Lord Ogleby's inner state of mind that the audience sympathized with him while they laughed at the outward absurdities of his behavior.

Some critics felt that Phelps's Lord Ogleby lacked sufficient gentility of manner—a criticism not infrequently made of his acting in polite comedy—but others said that the character displayed a magnanimity which compensated for any lack of courtliness. It was not a sentimental interpretation, since Lord Ogleby remained ludicrous, but it kept the sympathy of the audience for the old gentleman whose innate chivalry asserts itself in the last act.

The comedy ran for twenty-eight nights. Phelps revived it two seasons later, and in his later career often played Lord Ogleby, but no production had the appeal of the first one with its excellent cast working together in concert.

The same season, 1857–1858, saw a revival of Colman's *The Jealous Wife,* with Phelps as Mr. Oakley—a role Macready had played. The comedy had short runs in six seasons, whenever there was a leading actress capable of playing Mrs. Oakley.

Richard Sheridan's comedies were perennial favorites at Sadler's Wells. The cast of *The Rivals* varied from year to year (except that Mrs. Marston was always Mrs. Malaprop), but whether Younge, Marston, or Phelps played Sir Anthony Absolute seems to have mattered little to audience and critics. *The School for Scandal* was even more popular. In the early years George Bennett was the Sir Peter Teazle, but after he left the company, Phelps took the role and gave it a new reading. He followed neither of the traditional characterizations of Sir Peter—the foolish sexagenarian or the grotesque charlatan—but made him a good-natured old bachelor, sensible in everything but his marriage. Critics liked the performance, and Phelps played the role for many years.

Good acting kept Holcroft's *The Road to Ruin* on the stage of Sadler's Wells after it had disappeared from other theatres. Phelps's performance of Old Dornton was an important feature, but he did not make it a star part and always felt he needed a good cast to make the play successful.

By contrast, Macklin's *Man of the World* depends for its interest upon the acting of a single character, who is presented for the sake of a drastic and powerful satire upon the traits of meanness and self-interest. The plot exists for the sake of delineating Sir Pertinax Macsycophant, and the role itself contains no theatrical aids to help make a character effective on the stage. There are no striking situations, no touches of sentiment, no memorable lines. The man himself is entirely repulsive, unredeemed by virtue or charm. The role resembles that of Sir Giles Overreach in Massinger's *A New Way To Pay Old Debts* in its concentration upon the despicability of a single human being; but unlike Sir Giles, Macklin's character is a comic figure designed to provoke laughter from the audience. It is carefully drawn to give a creative actor the opportunity to develop his own characterization.

The name of one actor, George Frederick Cooke, was associated with the role. His brilliant impersonation of Macsycophant during the Kemble era was still remembered. Few other actors had been tempted to undertake a difficult role so closely related to the career of a famous actor. The Scottish dialect also deterred some; Edmund Kean had failed because he could not master it. Several comedians had used the role merely to show their mastery of the dialect and had failed to fill out the character. Phelps's assumption of the role in 1850 was unexpected and seemed to be a benefit-night stunt; but soon after the curtain rose the large audience, which had gathered to show respect for Greenwood, realized that Phelps's performance was one of the greatest achievements of his career.

When he came on the stage he was almost unrecognizable because of the complete transformation of his features and bearing. Henry Morley described the effect:

> Sir Pertinax Macsycophant . . . is represented by the actor even in what must pass for the repose of his face when on the stage. The features are cunningly hardened; the keen eyes, and a certain slight but frequent turn of the head, with its ready ear and fixed averted face, shrewdly suggests an intent, secret watchfulness.[10]

In his facile adjustment to the requirements of every situation characteristic of a man motivated solely by self-interest, he had the suppleness and hidden savagery of a cat. When he recounted the story of his climb to high position and wealth, the incongruity between the passionate intensity of his pursuit and the little meannesses of his methods made the scene irresistibly funny. The contrast was increased by the use of the Scottish dialect, which for Englishmen heightened the comic effect of his serious manner. Phelps was aided in this aspect of the character by his early mastery of the dialect. *Lloyd's Weekly* (November 30, 1851) said that "the Scotch accent had a depth and breadth in his pronunciation which we never heard in any other performer." The reviewer went on to describe his characterization:

> There was a matchless dissimulation in his sycophancy, and a stern impudence in his pride. His selfish sneer, the timid warmth of his ambition, . . . the inflexible coldness of his feelings, and the jealous caution of his worldly policy—and above everything, the over-acted cordiality, the uncandid smile, and boisterous insincerity of his laugh, the patient servility and the all-prevailing bow, are the distinctions of Mr. Phelps's Sir Pertinax, which make it stand alone, a finished piece of acting, not to be even imitated by any actor on the English stage.

The audience roared with laughter at the ridiculous pettiness of Sir Pertinax, but the devastating force of the satire left a deeper impression than pure comedy. Phelps's complete realization of the character made it an unforgettable performance. On May 10, 1850, after the first night the *Morning Advertiser* declared: "We never remember—though we remember the whole of the career of the elder Kean and of Miss O'Neill—to have seen a more perfect and more potent piece of acting." The *Dramatic and Musical Review* (February 1, 1852) echoed this opinion:

> Mr. Phelps' delineation we unhesitatingly pronounce to be a masterpiece: for a thoroughly artistic conception in all its details nothing like it has been seen for some time.

Because Phelps continued to act Sir Pertinax until the end of his career, after he had given up most tragic roles, many critics of a new generation remembered him for this role above all others. After Charles Fechter, Edwin Booth, Sir Henry Irving, and Johnston Forbes-Robertson had risen to fame in England, critics still spoke of Phelps's Sir Pertinax in superlatives. In 1915 the actor J. H. Barnes wrote:

> I have no kind of hesitation in stating that my very biggest memories are Ristori's Elizabeth and Phelps's Sir Pertinax Macsycophant.[11]

The American critic, J. R. Towse, writing in 1916, described it as "an impersonation to take rank with the greatest achievements of the stage." [12]

The tragedies from the Restoration period and the eighteenth century, with one exception, were far less successful at Sadler's Wells than the comedies. They were kept on the stage because of their traditional use as vehicles for aspiring young actors or actresses. The *jeunes premiers* of the company, Creswick, Dickinson, Robinson, Edmund Phelps, and Hermann Vezin, appeared in turn as the youthful heroes in Otway's *Venice Preserved*, Home's *Douglas*, and Southerne's *Isabella*. All of these, along with Rowe's *Jane Shore*, had good parts for young actresses. The audience, as conscientious as Phelps about training new actors, sat patiently through such a dull work as *Isabella* once every few years.

Phelps once tried an unfamiliar tragedy from this period, George Lillo's *Arden of Feversham*. At this the audience rebelled. Reviewers said that it was well acted but that no character except the murderers had any interest on the stage, and that the drama as a whole was "fearfully tedious." The audience gave it polite attention, but at the fall of the curtain condemned it by total silence.

The one popular tragedy was Edward Moore's *The Gamester,* which had furnished both Garrick and Macready with a successful role in Beverley, the hero, whose character and fortune are ruined by the vice of gambling. Phelps played Beverley in the second season at Sadler's Wells, when the play proved attractive to audiences. It was revived many times, but only for a few nights, either to provide novelty at the end of a season or to give a new actress the opportunity of playing Mrs. Beverley. A third prominent character, the villain Stukeley, was one of Bennett's best roles. The presence of three effective parts in a single play was a main reason for its frequent appearance at Sadler's Wells.

PLAYS OF THE ROMANTIC PERIOD

That the genius of the Romantic period did not lend itself to dramatic writing is clearly shown by the repertory at Sadler's Wells. The sentimental comedies of Thomas Morton and George Colman the Younger were performed as curiosities, sometimes winning favorable reviews; but except for Phelps's performance of Job Thornberry in *John Bull,* they did not draw large houses. The *Honey-Moon* by John Tobin, less sentimental and closer in spirit to the Elizabethan models, was successful. Except in a three-act version, the comedy had not often appeared until Phelps included it in his repertory. The *Athenaeum* called it "one of the most elegant and poetic comedies in our language"—a judgment with which the audiences apparently concurred.

Tragedies of the same period, with two notable exceptions, proved almost equally dull to Victorian audiences. Maturin's *Bertram* failed at Sadler's Wells. Several others succeeded only because of an important performance of the leading role. Milman's *Fazio* seemed old fashioned and heavy by 1850, but Miss Glyn wished to play Bianca in order to provoke comparison with Charlotte Cushman, who had recently displayed her tragic force in the heroine's intense emotions. Phelps played Edmund Kean's roles in Colman's *The Iron Chest* and Payne's *Brutus* with some success. A revival of *Brutus* in 1859 was loudly applauded because the expression of Roman patriotism awakened the audience's sympathy for the cause of Italian liberty.

Byron's *Werner,* in Macready's acting version, stands out as the single

English tragedy from the Romantic writers that achieved continuing popularity in the theatre. During his first season in Islington Phelps took up the role that Macready had made famous, and he continued to act it in nearly every season. One of the reasons he performed it so often is that the play offers a good variety of male parts and demands no strong leading actress.

Phelps had a special talent for a character like Werner, with his family pride and strong paternal love. He did not show the exasperation and restless vehemence of Macready's interpretation, nor did he sink into such utter misery; but his performance had its own virtues. Some critics felt that Phelps kept a more masculine and healthy tone throughout the play. He was moving in his expression of a father's love and anxiety, especially when he played with his own son in the role of Ulric. An Irish critic called Phelp's Werner "as noble a work of art as ever came from the mind of man," asserting that "it is no acting, it is perfect trans-formation." [13]

In an effort to find another such Romantic tragedy, Phelps seriously considered producing Shelley's *Cenci,* a play that had also suggested itself to Macready. A copy of the text with alterations that change Beatrice to Count Cenci's step-daughter is among Phelps's papers in the Harvard Theatre Collection. Rumor of his intention to produce the tragedy pro-voked a letter of fervent objection in the *Theatrical Journal* (October 11, 1849):

> I trust that if the manager of Sadler's Wells Theatre, does contemplate the representation of this fearful tragedy, that he will abandon the project. Count Cenci is a libel on humanity. . . . Every manager who produced it would be guilty of a serious offence against society.

Whether Phelps bowed to public opinion or whether he found the task of revision too difficult, he did abandon the project.

By far the most popular Romantic drama was one that barely achieved the status of tragedy. Thompson's *The Stranger,* translated from Kotzebue, was accepted into the canon of legitimate drama at the end of the eighteenth century; but like Sheridan's *Pizarro,* it resembles types of melodrama that were denied the status of tragedy in the nineteenth cen-tury. The distinction was important until 1843, and even after the repeal of the monopoly critics continued to draw a sharp line between legitimate drama and melodrama. Phelps only once produced a melodrama, Lewis's

Castle Spectre, and his audience objected; but they thronged to see *The Stranger.*

The great popularity of this work seems inexplicable today. The play presents the stereotypes of melodrama uttering sentimental ideas in undistinguished language. Nevertheless, its tale of a repentant adulteress who seeks her husband's forgiveness elicited sobs from the women and fervent concern from the men who watched it during an age that emphasized the primary importance of domestic honor. For a span of fifty years it was played frequently in England and the United States, although a number of critics found it immoral. The *Theatrical Journal,* always sensitive to moral implications, frequently censured playgoers for applauding *The Stranger* and found particularly distressing the fact that the full houses attracted to its performances consisted mostly of women:

> It is astonishing the anxiety of the softer sex to witness this play, which consists of four of the most disagreeable acts, to our ideas, ever put together.[14]

Queen Victoria, by having the play performed at Windsor Castle, showed herself considerably less prudish than this reviewer.

It is easy to see why *The Stranger* appealed to actors. Although it had the name of tragedy, it acted with the ease of melodrama. Few actors failed to win the sympathy of the audience in the roles of the Stranger and Mrs. Haller. Phelps enjoyed playing it, and so did Bennett.

PLAYS BY CONTEMPORARY AUTHORS

In choosing plays by contemporary authors, Phelps was influenced by two factors aside from his own judgment of their appeal to his audience. The first resulted from the artificial distinction between legitimate drama and minor drama, which grew out of the theatrical monopoly and lasted twenty years after its repeal. The second was the cost of new plays.

Phelps set out to make Sadler's Wells a serious playhouse, quite distinct from its former status as a "minor" theatre. In choosing contemporary plays, except for afterpieces, he was limited by a strong tradition to five-act verse drama. While the old theatrical monopoly was in force, critics as well as actors and managers had to maintain rigid distinctions between plays and other forms of entertainment, so that the legal drama could be clearly defined and the patent theatres protected from competition. Five acts and a poetic style were the hallmarks that

11. Portrait of Phelps drawn on stone by C. Baugniet. Courtesy Harvard Theatre Collection.

Sadlers' Wells
1862

Phelps as Macbeth

The Dagger Soliloquy

Henry Marston Macduff

Samuel Phelps

Miss Atkinson

"Enter Forces, marching"

"Last Scene of all"

Act 1st Scene 8. Phelps

Macbeth

12. Phelps and other actors in *Macbeth*. Drawn by M. Stretch, 1862. Courtesy Harvard Theatre Collection.

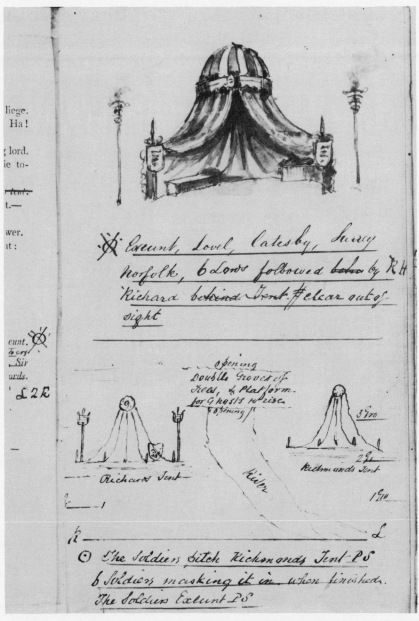

Exeunt, Lovel, Catesby, Surrey
Norfolk, 6 Lords followed tabes by R H
Richard behind Tent # clear out of
sight

Opening
Double Groves of
Reas, & Platform
for Ghosts to rise
to opening

Richards Tent

River

Richmands Tent

L

⊙ The Soldiers pitch Richmonds Tent PS
6 Soldiers masking it in when finished.
The Soldiers Exeunt PS

13. Sketch of stage arrangement for *Richard the Third,* act V, scene 3. From Phelps's prompt book of 1845. By permission of the Folger Shakespeare Library.

"Farewell—a long farewell—to all my greatness."

WOLSEY'S SPEECH.

ONE FARTHING REWARD,

The above will be paid to any Person discovering the

Sixty Members of the Garrick Club,

(*VIDE* PUBLIC PRESS).

forming the Grand Demonstration to put down Her Majesty and Mitchell, on Tuesday Evening, Jan. 19th, 1858.

VIVAT PHELPS!]   [NOT AN ORDER GIVEN.

14. Handbill on the controversy over the performance for the royal marriage of 1858. Courtesy Harvard Theatre Collection.

could be easily recognized when unlicensed theatres tried to perform plays.

While the monopoly had restricted the form of drama considered suitable for a legitimate theatre, it had also discouraged the growth of new forms by limiting professional dramatists to the kind of ephemeral entertainment that suited the taste of patrons of the minor theatres. Knowing that their work would probably not be taken seriously by managers, audiences, or critics, they constructed sensational melodrama, extravagant farce, and special types of characters that could be used as vehicles by popular actors. Until the advent of Mme. Vestris, minor drama was often carelessly produced and treated without respect.

After 1815 because the patent theatres were constantly in financial difficulties, a playwright could hardly hope to support himself by writing legitimate drama. With one notable exception—Sheridan Knowles— five-act plays were written by amateurs, men of private means, or writers with a reputation in other forms of literature. The traditional drama in isolated respectability slowly withered from lack of nourishment, while the new drama grew into maturity without the encouragement and correction of discriminating audiences, intelligent critics, or traditional actors.

By the time of the repeal of the monopoly the distinctions were too well established to be easily erased. Phelps's production of *Retribution*, George Bennett's romantic play, in 1850 was an attempt at cross-fertilization, and its success with the audience suggests that the history of Victorian drama might have been quite different if talented authors of minor drama with experience in the theatre had been encouraged to write for serious playgoers. But even this one attempt, suggested by the presence of the author in Phelps's company, was not welcomed by reviewers. Only Charles Kean among the tragedians of the time freely crossed the line between legitimate and melodrama, and he was severely criticized for the practice. His attitude helped to break down the distinction, but it did little to encourage English playwrights since he imported his romantic plays from the French stage. As late as 1862, when the *Times* first reviewed a three-act play as a serious dramatic work, the critic felt obliged to explain this departure from custom.[15]

There is some evidence that Phelps himself would not have been so rigid in observing the old distinction between a play and a "piece" if the policy of critics and taste of his audience had not been so conservative. In 1861 he put on a two-act play called *Doing for the Best,* in which he played the leading role, a carpenter named Stubbs; but according to his nephew, the audience objected to such a work as a featured production.[16] His nephew also apologizes for his putting on a play called *On the Jury* by Watts Phillips, when he acted at the Princess's Theatre in 1871, explaining that Phelps and the author were friends.[17] Because of such attitudes Phelps was limited, during his eighteen years of management, to a certain form of dramatic writing—one that proved unfruitful for contemporary writers.

Phelps also had to consider the price of a new play, since even the most successful productions could not bring in a large sum of money at the low prices of admission to his theatre. He could not afford the amount of money Benjamin Webster was willing to pay for new plays, but he was like Webster in treating playwrights fairly. Copyright laws and royalty agreements were just coming into use during the period of Phelps's management. A decade earlier Parliament had passed a bill guaranteeing sole rights of performance to English playwrights, but the pirating of Scott and Dickens to make melodramas in the minor theatres continued without legal interdict. Many theatres acquired their dramatic fare by translating French plays, which were not protected by copyright. Boucicault performed this service for Kean at the Princess's; Lewes, under the name of Slingsby Lawrence, did it for the Lyceum; and there were many others. Some English dramatic writers, like Bayle Bernard, Douglas Jerrold, John Oxenford, and Thomas Greenwood, scrupulously avoided such pirating. Since three of them were reviewers for important periodicals, they used their columns to castigate Charles Kean and other theatrical managers for this practice. They often praised Phelps for not "resorting to the French" in buying afterpieces.

In obtaining five-act plays for his stage Phelps had far greater difficulty than Macready, whose literary friends were eager to supply him with plays at very little cost. Bulwer-Lytton returned the check for 210 pounds which Macready paid him for the highly successful *Lady of Lyons.* With playwrights outside his social circle, Macready was notoriously stingy. He disliked paying authors anything beyond the initial flat sum, although the practice of adding a fixed sum per night was growing during the thirties and forties. He was annoyed when Knowles asked for 5 guineas per night during the run of *The Wife* in the spring of 1837, and he refused to give more than the initial flat sum to his pantomime writer.[18]

By the time of Phelps's management the practice of paying the author a fee for every performance had become established—partly through the influence of Dickens's insistence on a percentage of his publisher's profits. When Phelps produced Bulwer-Lytton's plays at Sadler's Wells, he sent the author (through John Forster) a sum of money for each night his work was acted, even though the plays had originally been sold to Macready.[19]

Phelps was willing to pay as much as he could afford for new plays, considering that a full house at Sadler's Wells brought in only 150 pounds, whereas Macready sometimes received more than 600 pounds at Drury Lane. For this reason Phelps told Horne to try the manager of Drury Lane with his revision of *The Duchess of Malfi*, but gladly bought it after it was rejected. Phelps sought a play from Bulwer-Lytton as early as 1846 and agreed to pay him 500 pounds for a reworking of the *Oedipus*.[20] The tragedy was never performed at Sadler's Wells because Bulwer-Lytton had designed the choruses for a musical setting, which proved a stumbling block. Mercadante was commissioned to write the music, but Phelps was unable to engage a full orchestra and chorus for a short term in the winter season for any reasonable price. Finally, Bulwer-Lytton took back the tragedy, requiring only that Phelps pay Mercadante for his musical composition.

Within the limitations of the genre he felt compelled to accept and the budget he had to work with, Phelps did all he could to find adequate contemporary plays. He read widely in published works to find unacted plays, and he gave careful attention to every manuscript sent to him. In his farewell address he said that he had paid as much as 400 pounds for a play. Tom Taylor describes him as a businesslike and unusually considerate manager:

> Phelps read my play with a promptness as gratifying as unusual. . . . He lost no time in satisfying himself, and me, that the piece would suit both him and his theatre, and that he would put it in rehearsal without delay. . . . I have no recollection of reading the play to the Sadler's Wells company. I rather think Phelps must have read it, but I may be mistaken; if he did read it, it is the only instance of managerial reading in my long experience of the theatre.[21]

Nevertheless, in his eighteen years of management Phelps produced no new play of lasting appeal.

The work of Sheridan Knowles and Bulwer-Lytton proved the most popular on the stage at Sadler's Wells. Macready first introduced these writers to the theatre, but Phelps performed more of their plays and more frequently than he had. His own performances of William Tell, Virginius, and Master Walter (in *The Hunchback*), of Claude Melnotte, Richelieu, and Evelyn were major attractions. *The Love-Chase* and *The Wife*, in which he did not appear, were also popular.

In 1855 Phelps opened his season with a new production of *The Hunchback*, in which he replaced Bennett as Master Walter. The *Times* (September 11, 1855) said that although the play had been worn threadbare at other theatres, at Sadler's Wells it appeared "with all its gloss on, as when new." Some of its sparkle came from a new interpretation of the hero, to whom Phelps gave a light playfulness which other actors had not found in the character. His dry humor pointed up an irony not recognized before, and critics were delighted with the new conception, which the *Athenaeum* (September 15, 1855) described as "much less theatrical than the usual mode." Although Phelps seldom had a leading lady who could play Julia with the grace and charm of Helen Faucit or Ellen Kean, the cast as a whole was excellent. Marston was noted for his Sir Thomas Clifford, especially in later years when his kind of gentlemanly grace and elocutionary skill had disappeared from other theatres.

Although *The Lady of Lyons* is today virtually unreadable because of its stilted language, outdated sentiments, and stereotyped characterization, it was one of the most admired plays of its time. Audiences seemed never to tire of the noble self-denial of the peasant hero, Claude Melnotte, who having tricked a haughty beauty into marriage, repents of his action and restores her to her family as he goes off to seek a heroic death in Napoleon's campaign. And they thoroughly enjoyed the happy denouement in which the humbled Pauline, confessing her love for her low-born husband, is rewarded by his return as a distinguished soldier. The announcement of the first performance of this play at Sadler's Wells brought such crowds to the theatre that the doors were forced open long before the time scheduled for the nightly rush to the pit.

Phelps was rapturously applauded in the role of Melnotte. Even Macready, generally regarded as neither handsome nor amiable, had received passionate declarations of love from women who witnessed his performance in this part. Neither actor normally felt at home in the role of a young lover, but Bulwer-Lytton had carefully tailored the character to suit Macready. The same outward reticence, troubled mind, and soldierly bearing fitted Phelps.

Each of the leading actresses at Sadler's Wells had her turn as Pauline. Mrs. Warner gave "a vast and commanding performance," eloquent, queenly, and beautiful in appearance. Laura Addison was charming and tender. The concerted effort of the whole cast gave life to minor characters and provided sufficient interest to carry the audience through long scenes in which the noble sentiments of the virtuous alternate with heartless schemes of the villains, unrelieved by dramatic incident.

Perhaps the moral of the play kept it perennially interesting to the audience at Sadler's Wells. In an age of emerging democracy the people of Islington must have welcomed the assertion that peasant and lady can be equals. Phelps himself did not like the play and once referred to it in a letter as "the eternal *Lady of Lyons*." In the later years of his management he was happy to give the part to younger actors.

Richelieu was also a favorite at Sadler's Wells. The old Cardinal, with his touches of irony and sarcasm, his moments of passionate force, and the sudden change from apparent defeat to victory at the end, suited Phelps as well as Macready. Phelps played the role with more humor and a relaxed manner, which was probably closer to the author's intention. Bulwer-Lytton, despite his tact, nearly quarreled with Macready in a vain effort to induce him to put more humor in his performance.[22] Phelps showed the highly intelligent mind at work behind a variety of outward poses while conveying the physical impotence of old age and the frustration felt by a once-powerful man become feeble. From his first appearance as Cardinal Richelieu in 1845 until his last in 1878, Phelps was admired in the role. The *Times* (June 19, 1845) said that there could not be a more perfect interpretation.

Bulwer-Lytton's *Money* was introduced in the second season of Phelps's management and often revived. He had less difficulty than Macready in assuming modern dress on the stage, and critics praised the easy grace of his Evelyn. Except for the leading actress, the cast at Sadler's Wells equaled the original at the Haymarket, so that the comedy remained attractive to audiences.

Phelps produced several contemporary plays that had failed in their initial performances at other theatres. Westland Marston's *The Patrician's Daughter* had not been seen since Macready's short run at Drury Lane, when Phelps introduced it for the debut of Laura Addison in 1846. Her youth and her sweet, unsophisticated manner made the title role particularly sympathetic. The author gives Phelps a large share of the credit for his play's success:

> Neither in respect of appearance nor of age was he well suited to the part of Mordaunt in *The Patrician's Daughter*. Nevertheless, he threw such reality into the pride, indignation, and repentance of the intentionally morbid hero, that my juvenile work became a stockpiece at his theatre.[23]

Another reason for the success of this tragedy at Sadler's Wells was the democratic sentiment (described once by the *Times* as "republican claptraps") expressed throughout.

Phelps gave Leigh Hunt's *The Legend of Florence* a second stage trial in 1850. Most critics felt that the play had not been fairly heard in its first production under Mme. Vestris' management of Covent Garden, because her company was not suited to poetic tragedy. Phelps gave the play a brilliant setting and provided a cast that could not have been surpassed in his day. He played Agolanti, Miss Glyn the patient Ginevra; Hoskins was Colonna; Anthony Younge, DaRiva; and Waller, Rondinelli. The opening night brought a full house including many of London's distinguished writers and critics, but the play was not applauded with enthusiasm by the regular frequenters of Sadler's Wells. The *Athenaeum*'s assertion that the play was a complete success was perhaps colored by the reviewer's admiration for Hunt's literary reputation. The *Theatrical Journal* pronounced it dull. Phelps continued performances for a second week, adding a new afterpiece, but houses were thin. After eight performances *The Legend of Florence* again disappeared from the stage. For Phelps it was an expensive failure.

In the same season a play called *The Cavalier* by Charles Whitehead was produced, with Bennett in the leading role. Its only previous production, some years before with Vandenhoff and Ellen Tree, had failed. Bennett's excellent performance in a showy part that gave him an opportunity for an emotional climax in every scene provoked rounds of applause and special comment in the *Athenaeum* (September 28, 1850):

> It is with more than common pleasure that we record this tribute to so old a servant of the stage—one who, it is generally felt, has deserved far greater fame than he has achieved. The stage of our day can show nothing greater than some of his performances.

The audience's enthusiasm was for Bennett and not for the play, which survived only two performances and went unnoticed by most reviewers.

With two plays by George Lovell and *Ingomar* by Mrs. Lovell, Phelps had better success. *The Provost of Bruges* was a play especially admired by critics, who declared that it had been neglected by contemporary actors. *Love's Sacrifice* drew better houses, and *Ingomar* was far more popular than either.

London Assurance had four performances in February, 1854. Perhaps the company did not capture the spirit of the play, which Mme. Vestris had successfully introduced, or perhaps the absence of Phelps from the cast lessened interest in the play. Whatever the cause, it did not hold the stage.

Browning's *A Blot in the 'Scutcheon* had not been acted since its three performances under Macready's management. Phelps prepared a new acting text, with fewer alterations than Macready had made, but with considerable shortening and some attempt at clarifying the plot. He was well aware of the difficulties he faced in trying to give dramatic interest to a play of such weak structure, lacking variety of characterization, and written in an elliptical and complex style. Hope for success depended upon subtle reading of the lines and a convincing portrayal of violent emotions, particularly in the long and difficult role of Lord Tresham.

Critics were unanimous in their praise of Phelps's performance. The *Athenaeum* (December 2, 1848) said that it had rare power and effectiveness. The *Dramatic and Musical Review* (January 1, 1849) called it unsurpassable. The *Theatrical Journal* (November 30, 1848) had this comment:

> Mr. Phelps was master of the author's meaning and gave it complete. His struggle between hope and fear, and the love he bore for the honour of his sister and his fame hereafter, was so forcibly acted that it became reality for the time being; but his fear and dread after he had slain the object of his sister's love, was wrought up in a way not describable by us. He rivetted the attention of the whole house, for it was as silent as the grave during this part of his acting.

Westland Marston, who did not place Phelps in the first rank of tragedians, felt that in this role he "went beyond himself":

> In the recoil of the rash brother from the dishonour of his house, he seemed as one *possessed* by passion. Pride raged in him like a demon;

his features were convulsed, his gestures wild, his voice charged with
sardonic hatred and scorn; while his despair, after slaying the betrayer of
his sister, was strangely moving by its heart-broken quietude. . . . He
rose into tragic passion and exaltation, as distinct from pathos and excited
feeling.[24]

Fanny Cooper played the sister, and Dickinson her lover. The revival
was considered a success, although it had only eight performances during
the season of 1848–1849 and was never again acted. Forster came to see it
twice—an indication of the interest shown by literary men in this production. Its failure to attract the wider public must be attributed to its lack
of dramatic interest. A play that depends so entirely upon the skill of one
actor can hardly compete with works of more diverse interest, particularly
in a theatre noted for the concerted playing of a large company.

Once, in his last season, Phelps "had recourse to the French"—a lapse
for which he apologized in his farewell address. The play was Casimir
Delavigne's *Louis the Eleventh,* which Charles Kean had found highly
successful in spite of critics' scorn for the "French melodrama," as they
termed it. It is another play in which the main character is the whole
interest, and in this case the character was drawn as a monster because
of the author's political thesis. Kean's success in the role was attributed to
his ability to intensify incredible passions. The *Weekly Dispatch* (September 29, 1861) described him thus:

Every aspect of the Royal culprit was expanded to the point of exhaustion.
If the King scolded a liege, he roared at him; if he seized a victim, he
foamed with fury; if he trembled under the dagger of an enemy, he
shrieked! It was the very excess of his expression which bestowed a sort
of naturalness on the forced creation of the writer.

Kean's interpretation carried melodrama to the very border of burlesque.
It was the same kind of art that fascinated audiences at the Olympic
when Robson carried burlesque to the border of tragedy.

Phelps could not have adopted Kean's technique. He tried instead to
make the character more human and credible. The *Morning Advertiser*
(September 23, 1861) contrasted the two approaches:

The grotesque, which occupied so conspicuous a portion of the persona-
tion at the Princess's, finds, very properly, no place in Mr. Phelps's delineation; but this very excellence will disappoint those who hunger after

perpetual points, and prefer the intensities of effect to the broader and truer delineation of character.

In Phelps's interpretation the King, though still a vicious man, was not a monster, but in his attempt to make the character more human and dignified—tragic instead of melodramatic—he had to struggle at every point with the author's obvious intention. Where Kean had increased the effectiveness of the play, Phelps brought out its glaring faults. Nevertheless, some critics felt that Phelps succeeded in his attempt. The *Weekly Dispatch* found him impressive:

> Its terrible grandeur has not been matched for many years. Altogether this is a performance so original and masterly that it cannot fail to become one of Mr. Phelps's best resources, and add another to the lengthened list of the great attractions at his house.

Even though he was praised for his acting, Phelps's own performance revealed the unsuitability of such plays for Sadler's Wells.

Phelps introduced to the stage fourteen previously unacted plays, out of the two thousand he read. They are nearly all five-act tragedies with pretensions to literary merit, and some were much admired by reviewers.

In his first season he put on *The Priest's Daughter* by Thomas J. Serle. It was an unfortunate choice, even in the dreariest period of dramatic writing. Serle, Macready's close associate, was the hack writer who had concocted the spectacle of Joan of Arc on a few days' notice to compete with Bunn's production of Balfe's opera *Joan of Arc*. His attempts at serious writing, although they utilized a thorough acquaintance with the theatre, had not been very successful. Macready performed his *Master Clarke* a few times at the Haymarket in 1840 without creating much interest. *The Priest's Daughter* had the virtue of some effective "situations"—the Victorian word for theatrical surprises; but it was an incongruous work, combining the emotional climate and stock characters of melodrama with the stilted poetic language of Shakespearean imitators. The *Athenaeum* called it a monstrosity. Only the high quality of the performance saved the play from failure.

In his second season Phelps introduced three new plays to the stage. The first, *The King's Friend* by Robert Sullivan (who later wrote *The Beggar on Horseback*), was a historical comedy with touches of humor that delighted the audience. The *Times* (May 23, 1845) described it as "neatly written" and "constructed with much skill." Although its blank verse was not distinguished, the plot was clear, and there was enough incident to hold the spectator's interest. The *Athenaeum* (May 24, 1845) remarked that its moderate success proved that a well-constructed story aided by good acting would create interest on the stage even in the absence of other qualities. It was performed eleven times during the early weeks of the season.

Before *The King's Friend* was withdrawn from the repertory, another new play was introduced. The production of two new plays on the stage of one theatre within two weeks was a rare occurrence in the old legitimate theatres. Phelps, clearly, was eager to find new sources of dramatic material. Unfortunately, the play was dull. The story was the tale of Fair Rosamond, set in a historical Italian setting and called *The Florentines*. The manuscript had been sent to Phelps anonymously. Many poets writing for the stage preferred not to divulge their names to the audience until after their work had passed the test of a first-night performance. The competence of the verse marked this work as the product of an experienced writer, later identified as E. L. A. Berwick, an Irish man of letters.

Reviewers made the complaints often heard of five-act verse plays in this period: the play lacked dramatic development, the characters were improbable, the ideas were commonplace, and the poetry was imitative. The *Athenaeum* called it "ephemeral mediocrity" and warned the management that it "must pursue another course if it would renew this season the success of the last." The play was not damned by the audience on the first night. Perhaps the acting and the attractive historical setting provided sufficient interest to win approval, or perhaps the evident effort of the management to give it a good production awakened a loyal response.

After the Easter recess there was another new play entitled *Judge Jeffreys* by Henry Spicer—probably the play Phelps had bought in 1843. It was an unpretentious work, which the *Athenaeum* called "sketchy," adding that it was admirably acted. The *Weekly Dispatch* (April 19, 1846) remarked upon the number of aristocrats, "real Westenders," who made the trip from St. James to Clerkenwell to see Spicer's play. He said that their unwonted effort was well repaid, but his own review dealt mostly with an interesting afterpiece starring Fanny Cooper.

In his third season Phelps finally found a new play that truly succeeded with audience and critics. For months he had been trying to get a play by James White, whose published but unacted *Earl of Gowrie* had attracted his attention in 1845. The author had refused Phelps permission to perform the play on the grounds that he was writing a new play for Macready to use at the Princess's and in deference to Macready's interests would not allow competition between two of his own plays. After Macready had successfully acted White's *King of the Commons* at the Princess's in the spring of 1846, the author offered Phelps a new, unpublished play called *Feudal Times*.

Unusual interest, aroused by the success of *King of the Commons*, greeted the production of White's second play; and its success was triumphant. Reviews praised the language of the play for its ease and poetic beauty. Some spoke of the intensely interesting plot and the appealing character of the hero. A few declared that *Feudal Times* would become one of the classics of the English theatre. The audience at Sadler's Wells found an additional reason for approval in the play's thesis that high birth does not determine a man's worth. So enthusiastic was its reception that Phelps announced the play for performance every night, abandoning for three weeks the usual alternation with other plays.

Justification for this rapturous reception is hard to find in reading it today. The plot, although based on a historical incident, barely gives excuse for the various situations that are used to set forth the admirable qualities of the two main characters, Walter Cochrane and Margaret Randolph. Aside from these two, who are frequently praised for their high thoughts as well as their exemplary conduct, the delineation of character is either sketchy or inconsistent. Lord Angus, the brave and stubbornly proud antagonist, is not convincing. King James III is weak; his lords are traitors; and they are all aware of their faults, which they do not hesitate to describe to the audience. The interest of the play lies in the saintly character of hero and heroine and their undeserved suffering, and in the poetic expression of commendable, if not original, ideas.

The acting of Phelps and Laura Addison in the leading roles was a primary reason for the success of *Feudal Times*. The *Theatrical Journal* (February 27, 1847) said that the part of Cochrane must have been written for Phelps because it gave him such excellent opportunities to show "that energy and manliness that Phelps has made peculiarly his own." Reviews also praised the manager for his large investment in the staging of an untried contemporary play, since they were often shabbily treated at other theatres. Phelps's concern for perfect historical accuracy in the setting can be seen from his correspondence with the author on such matters as broad-toed shoes and whether James III was the first to put the unicorn into the royal arms.[25]

Phelps produced a second of White's plays in November, 1847. It was called *John Savile of Haysted,* and like *Feudal Times* it was an immediate success. *Punch* (November 13, 1847), although rarely pleased by theatrical performances, had an enthusiastic review declaring that White was "a name henceforth to fill a pit." As in White's earlier plays, the language was considered a chief merit. According to *Punch* it had "the true dramatic sinew; quick, compact, with life pulsating in it," and in contrast to other contemporary dramatic poetry contained "no holiday, filagree sentences; but all is manly thinking, manly utterance."

The plot, however, was criticized as episodic and not skillfully managed. Character development and motivation were inadequate, so that the deaths of the two main characters in the last act were felt by some critics to be melodramatic rather than tragic. The acting apparently masked some of the play's faults. Phelps was able to make the title role interesting on the stage in spite of the dullness of the character. Bennett as a fanatic Irish soldier became the center of interest.

The setting and costuming, which were both splendid and historically interesting, added much to the appeal of the tragedy. *Punch* commented: "We can say nothing as to the manner in which the piece is produced, because nothing we can say will be praise enough." Douglas Jerrold, the dramatic critic of *Punch,* spoke feelingly of the production of *John Savile* because he belonged to that large group of would-be playwrights who had been unable to see their works acted. Although he is remembered now as the author of melodramas, he was vitally interested in more serious drama. Like many other writers, he laid the blame for the dearth of successful contemporary plays upon the policies of theatrical managers, who were afraid to risk the production of new plays except in the least expensive manner, and were unwilling to pay authors fair prices. "And now," he commented, "manager Phelps lays down his hundreds for fine five-act plays." *John Savile* was the fifth new play put on at Sadler's Wells in Phelps's three seasons of management, and each had been staged and acted with as much care as the classic dramas of the stock repertory. Their success, especially that of White's plays, both of which ran for twenty-five nights and were revived in later years, seemed to confirm the contention of these playwrights that with proper production their works could become popular in the theatre. Jerrold's feeling that he had been driven out of serious playwriting by the mistaken policies of theatrical managers is clear in his review of White's play:

The play was finely apprehended by the audience, finely received. It was a pleasant sight, in these days,—when five-act dramas are considered such evils that young dramatists ought to be inoculated against them . . . —to see the heathens of Islington, London, and the parts adjacent, so filling the house, that we believe it overflowed into the New River.

In November, 1847, Macready also produced a new play—Henry Taylor's *Philip Van Artevelde*—during his engagement at the Princess's Theatre. Macready had found the play already published, and his opinion of its worth had been confirmed by Dickens, Forster, White, Fox, and Stanfield. The play was a failure, perhaps because of the shabby staging and careless acting typical of Maddox's management.

The excitement aroused in London's most distinguished literary circle by White's second success at Sadler's Wells resulted in a renewal of the effort to bring Phelps into the group. Dickens wrote him a pressing note of invitation to his house.[26] Phelps refused but apparently after the successful opening agreed to attend a party at the author's house after the second performance—the only such invitation he ever accepted. It was a supper at which a large number of writers and critics were informally assembled to honor Phelps and express their gratitude. There can be no doubt that the guest of honor, who was a truly modest man and who distrusted self-congratulation as much as optimistic predictions about the success of a new venture, was thoroughly miserable.

Although Phelps asked White to write another play, none was forthcoming. Four years later he put on a reworking of his published play, now called *James the Sixth*; but it proved far less attractive and survived only eight performances.

In 1849 Boker's *Calaynos,* the play that had aroused controversy because its author was an American, had a good run at Sadler's Wells. Reviews spoke highly of its literary merit, and the *Theatrical Journal* (January 17, 1850) pronounced it "the best of our modern productions for some years."

Its plot was of the domestic kind that appealed to Victorian audiences: a Spanish nobleman trusts a false friend, who betrays him by stealing his wife, and in the last act after the wife returns repentant and dying, the nobleman redeems his honor in a fatal duel. Phelps as the high-minded Calaynos had the difficult task of setting forth the tenets of the philanthropic philosophy that motivates the hero's actions in the early scenes, but he was able to hold the audience's interest. His most effective scene was the discovery of his wife's elopement at the end of act four, where his sorrow and remorse reached tragic intensity. Fanny Cooper was praised for her delicacy and earnestness in the role of the wife. Marston's smoothness and gallantry gave the villain a superficial attractiveness that helped make the character credible. Dickinson was admired in the role of the faithful servant.

Boker was disturbed when he discovered, evidently from a review in the *Athenaeum,* that Phelps had rewritten much of the fifth act. Although this revision was chiefly to ease problems of staging, Phelps had apparently done it rather badly. The *Athenaeum* (May 12, 1849) said that while the early scenes of the play moved too slowly, the fifth act was hurried and ill managed. When Boker obtained a copy of the acting version used at Sadler's Wells, which he did not receive until August, 1850, his initial anger at the news of Phelps's tampering was modified by his realization that Phelps's idea had been a good one. He then rewrote the fifth act himself, using the denouement Phelps had invented, and sent a copy to the actor with the following letter:

Philadelphia
September 1st, 1850

Mr. Samuel Phelps
Dear Sir,

A few weeks ago I had the pleasure of receiving an acting copy of my tragedy of Calaynos, which you did me the honor of producing with such distinguished success at your theatre.

Upon reviewing the acting copy I was of course struck with the alterations which had been made at the conclusion of the play; but upon the whole think them very judicious for acting purposes. Within a few days the idea has occurred to me of re-writing the fifth act, at the same time preserving the *denouement* which you gave to it. Enclosed you will find the fruits of my labor, which you will be kind enough to use, if you should ever reproduce the play. . . .

I am sorry to have troubled you with all this matter about a play which you may have considered shelved long ago; but really I could not bear to see a play, supposed to have been written by me, with so much of another man's material in it. For my own satisfaction, the play, conclude as it may, must be in my language.

Have you seen my second play, Anne Boleyn, which has been published some months? It strikes me that it might be used with effect as a play for the holidays, being full of spectacle. You can probably procure a copy of John Chapman in the Strand.

My last play, The Betrothal, which I wrote entirely for the stage, has not been published, as we American authors lose all control over the production of our plays after they have been published.

If you should reproduce Calaynos with my alterations, will you be good enough to let me know of it?

> In the meantime, I remain,
> Your obedient servant,
> G. H. Boker[27]

Although Phelps apparently was not interested in *Anne Boleyn* or *The Betrothal,* he did produce *Calaynos* again in the following season; and evidently he used the author's revision, since the *Athenaeum* (January 19, 1850) commented that the new arrangement of the fifth act was an improvement. The sincerity of Boker's statement that he approved the central idea of Phelps's revision is shown by the fact that he followed it in preparing the text for a final edition of his collected works, which was not, however, published.[28] Phelps's denouement was also the one used in American productions of *Calaynos,* perhaps because Dickinson used the play for his first appearance in Philadelphia in 1851. Phelps's prompt discovery of Boker's first play, his effective revision, and his successful production were surely of great service to an unknown American playwright, whether or not he paid a nightly fee to the author.[29]

The two new plays produced in the following season, 1849–1850, make a contrast that is informative about Victorian critical standards. The first was *Garcia, or the Noble Error* by F. G. Tomlins, well-known dramatic critic and secretary of the Shakespeare Society. *Garcia* resembles other nineteenth-century tragedies in its imitation of Elizabethan form, use of blank verse, concern with domestic relationships, and oversimplified characterization. The hero is a young Spanish noble of the fifteenth century whose mother has been brought before the Inquisition for sheltering a Moor. He is persuaded by a friend that he can save his mother's life by murdering the Moor before the trial. After an agonized struggle with his conscience, he brings himself to murder, only to discover that his terrible act was unnecessary because the Countess had already been released. She dies of grief, and Garcia suffers great remorse before he is led off to execution. As usual, reviews recognized weaknesses in plot and structure but praised the ideas and moral tone of the play, in which they found the essence of tragedy.

On the stage interest centered in Garcia's conflicting emotions and the reactions of the major characters to his "noble error." Phelps was apparently successful in making his mental struggle seem real. He played the murder scene with a rigid intensity that conveyed his horror of the deed, and in the last act drew a convincing picture of a man overcome with remorse. Miss Glyn, as the Countess, was impressive in the courage with which she faced the terrors of the Inquisition and in the serenity of her death. A minor actor named Graham, who had served for six years in the lowest rank of the company as Utility Man until he made a hit with his fine performance of Eros in *Antony and Cleopatra,* was very effective as the Moor.

A crowded audience was attracted to the first night, applause was enthusiastic, and the reviews favorable. The following comments from the *Morning Chronicle* and the *Stage-Manager* are typical: "There is a fine moral tone throughout; and we could quote several passages of great power, concentrated thought, and beauty." The play "abounds in scenes of deepest sorrow, and speaks to the inward man in a language not to be misunderstood." In spite of this auspicious opening, *Garcia* suffered the same fate as most other Victorian tragedies. It was performed twelve times during the season and never played again.

An interesting contrast to Tomlins' tragedy is another new play called *Retribution,* which was also presented this season. Its author was George Bennett, the actor who had played many important roles at Sadler's Wells during Phelps's management. His play, frankly described as "a romantic play" to distinguish it from the traditional types of tragedy and comedy, was not formed on Elizabethan models. It was rather an attempt to raise to "legitimate" status a form of drama familiar to audiences of the minor theatres, in translations from French originals and adaptations of romantic novels. By giving five acts to a play which relied for its interest upon plot and incident and which made no attempt at profound psychological observation or poetic statement of important ideas, Bennett tried to break down the rigid distinction between legitimate drama and melodrama which had persisted after the repeal of the monopoly. Although many of the contemporary plays which Phelps had introduced to the stage may seem to the untrained twentieth-century reader indistinguishable from melodrama, critics of his day had no difficulty in recognizing them as legitimate plays even when they saw melodramatic elements in the writing. Tragedy and comedy remained the true types of drama, while the increasing quantity of two- and three-act plays were placed in another category and called by such names as melodrama, petite comedy, farce, or simply "piece."

Bennett's play was recognized immediately as outside the limits of legitimate drama. The *Athenaeum* (February 16, 1850) described it as a five-act melodrama interspersed with poetic illustrations. The *Weekly News* (February 16, 1850) carefully explained the basis of distinction between a play like *Retribution* and true drama:

> Of profound dramatic interest, either serious or comic, there is but little, Scott being, rather than Shakespeare, the model of the author. The superficies of character, rather than character itself, is given; and the language is rather happily descriptive of external events than indicative of those deep-seated emotions which characterize so peculiarly the old and true dramatist. In this respect it may be said to bear the same relation to the great drama that Rob Roy does to Richard III, or the Bride of Lammermoor to Hamlet. It is essentially of the melodramatic school, but then it is certainly of the *première qualité;* and is not without touches of the deeper and grander class of plays.

Thus critics dismissed the work as unworthy of serious attention, even though they admitted that it was in many respects superior to the poetic tragedies Phelps had produced. Bennett's professional knowledge of the stage and his actor's instinct for what is effective with the audience gave him an advantage over most Victorian playwrights. His plot was well constructed and full of incidents cleverly arranged to hold the interest of the audience. The characters were varied and had touches of individuality that actors could exploit on the stage. Even the *Weekly News* admitted that "we have not for a long time seen a play where so much interest is genuinely excited." It ran for twenty-one nights, in spite of critical disapproval.

The gulf that separated traditional acting from the new and more familiar style of melodrama was apparently still bridgeable in 1850. Reviews said that Bennett, Younge, and Dickinson were well cast and convincing in their roles. The *Theatrical Journal* (February 14, 1850) asserted

that "we never saw Mr. Phelps act with so much energy and self possession." Except for Isabella Glyn, whose heightened style was noticeably
out of place in the atmosphere of a popular romance, the actors were able
to adapt their acting to a more colloquial idiom.

In the remaining twelve years of his management Phelps produced
only four more new plays. One was another "romantic drama" sent to
him anonymously and called *Might and Right*. Critics quickly identified
it as a melodrama. The *Theatrical Journal* (December 15, 1852) also remarked, apparently without irony, that "the play is so carefully constructed that we fancy it must be a translation—perhaps from the German
or Danish stage." As in the case of *Retribution,* reviews warmly praised
the well-constructed plot and the intense interest of its action without accepting the work as true drama. The *Athenaeum* (December 11, 1852)
said that it had all the elements of a good play except for the language of
the dialogue, which lacked tone and color and was inadequate for the
actors. It ran for only eleven nights, in spite of the novelty of a Russian
setting with picturesque scenery and costumes.

In the autumn of 1855 Phelps featured a new historical play which was
safely in the category of true drama. It was called *Hamilton of Bothwell-
haugh* and was written by Angelo Slous, whose play *The Templar* had
been moderately successful at the Princess's. Phelps probably chose it because it required no strong leading actress and offered a prominent role
for Henry Marston as well as himself. This time critics said that the first
three acts were extremely tedious and that the blank verse was not really
poetic. Good scenery, costumes, and acting carried a heavy play through
its first-night test. The author was called to take a bow from his box.
After a slow start and without enthusiastic reviews, the play began to
draw audiences and ran for fifteen nights.

The thirteenth new play introduced at Sadler's Wells was by far the
most popular with audiences, and like Bennett's play it was closer to the
genre of melodrama than to classic English drama. The play, *The Fool's
Revenge* by Tom Taylor, cannot be called original without some qualifi-
cation, since it is a reworking of Victor Hugo's *Le Roi s'amuse,* which
was already familiar to English audiences through the opera *Rigoletto*.
Changes in plot and characterization, and the addition of some new material gave it the status of an original work in a period when French
drama was pirated without acknowledgment by many English dramatists. Taylor was already a successful writer of farces, melodramas, and

petite comedies, but this was his first attempt in the traditional five-act, blank verse drama.

The plot relies heavily upon coincidence, and except for the hero the characters are cast in the familiar molds of dissolute nobles, pure young lovers, and wronged avengers. The moral that desire for revenge is evil is didactically stated. The affectionate scenes between father and daughter, the emphasis upon domestic virtues, and the happy ending achieved suddenly after all hope is gone belong unmistakably to the melodramatic form. Morley asserts that Taylor "transformed the nightmare story . . . into a wholesome English-natured plot," but like other reviewers he refers to the work as a "piece" rather than a play.[30] The five-act, verse form which made it suitable for Sadler's Wells kept it from other stages so that it is the least known of Taylor's successful plays, but even critics who disliked the genre admitted that *The Fool's Revenge* was unusually good. Skillful workmanship in construction, careful development of the chief character, and the use of dramatic irony raise the play above the level of most melodramas. The *Weekly Dispatch* (October 23, 1859) called it "a melodrama of surprising merit" although the reviewer found that it had the fault of being painful and revolting as well as exciting. Another reviewer said, "We have not often made acquaintance with a drama better constructed, better written, better acted, and better put upon the stage than *The Fool's Revenge*.[31]

The great popularity of the play at Sadler's Wells, where it was performed forty-nine times in this season, can be attributed to Phelps's performance of Bertuccio, the court jester. This character, easily dominating a play peopled with superficially drawn figures, is certain to be effective on the stage, but for Phelps it held the additional advantage of being peculiarly suited to his talents. The jester's bitter humor and brooding soliloquies in the early scenes, his paternal affection suddenly revealed, and the swift alternation of strong emotions in the last act were played with a sincerity and power which belong to tragedy rather than melodrama. Morley describes Phelps's effectiveness in the role:

> A solidity of character is given to the Fool which accords perfectly with the genius of Mr. Phelps. While the lips gibe lightly, the hands clutch at the Fool's bauble as if it were a sword. It is the instrument of his revenge, and the actor tacitly suggests this by the manner of its handling. The dignity and tenderness of Bertuccio's relation as a father with his child, the struggle of his revengeful spirit with the counsels of her simple piety

and purity of heart, presently to be followed by the ferocity of exultation at what he believes to be the success of his relentless plotting, yield occasion for fine contrasts of dramatic color.

Tom Taylor was enthusiastic about Phelps's performance: "If ever actor satisfied author, Phelps satisfied me in Bertuccio. I have always thought it his most powerful impersonation." [32]

During his management of Sadler's Wells the problem of finding new plays plagued Phelps as much as any other difficulty. At the end of his management he complained of the lack of good original drama:

> Although I have given out of the limited means afforded by a small theater, demanding but moderate prices for admission, as much as £400 for a new play, I have been able to procure but few; yet in no one instance have I refused to purchase any drama, whatever its price or cost of production, which my judgment told me would succeed in acting. [33]

The failure of contemporary dramatists to write interesting plays in the old five-act, verse form laid upon them by the theatrical monopoly and convention was clearly the reason for Phelps's failure to produce good new plays. Competent dramatists were writing successful pieces for other London theatres during those two decades, but they had abandoned tragedy and comedy for the new types of drama which had been developing in the minor theatres. It was not until after the end of Phelps's management that Tom Robertson's comedies brought minor drama to maturity and won its acceptance as true drama.

VII

Return to the West End

WHEN Phelps left Sadler's Wells in November, 1862, he was offered an engagement by Charles Fechter, who had undertaken the management of the Lyceum. The terms of the contract required three performances a week for twelve months beginning on January 1, 1863 at a salary of 40 pounds a week.[1] Although Phelps's friends warned him that a long contract with a rival actor at such a low salary might not be made in good faith, he could not believe that Fechter was jealous and small minded. Only after the contract had been in force for three months without a single call for Phelps to appear on the stage did he realize that Fechter was paying 40 pounds a week to keep him from acting. Matters came to a head when Fechter finally assigned him the role of the Ghost in *Hamlet*. Both actors then agreed to submit their quarrel to the arbitration of Charles Dickens, who was a friend of both. Dickens decided that Phelps should be allowed to play prominent roles or else to cancel the engagement, and he suggested that Fechter play Iago to Phelps's Othello. This suggestion was not well received by the manager, who then released Phelps from his contract.

Fortunately, other offers were not slow in coming, and this time Phelps chose wisely. He engaged himself to Falconer and Chatterton, the lessees of Drury Lane, to play leading roles and to serve as director of dramatic productions at a salary of 80 pounds a week. Miss Atkinson, who had remained at Sadler's Wells until the end of Phelps's management, and Edmund Phelps were also engaged for the new company at Drury Lane, which included John Ryder, William Creswick, A. Raynor, Hermann Vezin, and Mrs. Vezin (the former Mrs. Charles Young).

With this group of competent Shakespearean actors the management proposed to reintroduce poetic drama to the stage of the great national theatre after an absence of twenty years. Their hope of success lay in the professional competence of the company and in the dearth of serious drama in London. It was the age of the "sensational" drama, when ephemeral works vied with each other in exciting the emotions of the audience by realistic stage effects, surprising incidents, and melodramatic situations. One reviewer described it as the drama of "the violent, the actual, and the frivolous." The old poetic drama was still remembered —by some as heavy, unnatural, and incomprehensible and by others as a vanished art—but it was virtually unknown to the most recent generation of playgoers.

Phelps's first production was the uncompromisingly poetic drama *Manfred*. Byron's play had never been in the standard repertory of acted plays, although its first appearance in 1834 had aroused considerable interest, and it seems a strange choice for the opening of the season. But the managers of Drury Lane and their new star proved to be right in their estimate of contemporary taste. According to the *Times* (October 13, 1864):

> There could not on Saturday night be a moment's doubt that the announcement of Lord Byron's Manfred, with Mr. Phelps in the principal character, had caused a fever of expectation and curiosity among that numerous class, in whose eyes "Old Drury" always has the prestige of nationality. Long before the commencement of the play, not only was every place occupied, but a train of disappointed persons might be seen returning from the doors unable to find room.

The same reviewer commented on the excitement caused by Phelps's appearance on the stage of the national theatre, not only because he was highly regarded as an actor but also because he was considered a champion of education for the masses and "one of the great benefactors of his age."

> We are, indeed, disposed to think that the anxiety to see Mr. Phelps in his new position was even more potent than the curiosity excited by the revival of Manfred, for scarcely ever was heard such a burst of applause as arose on Saturday when the curtain was drawn up, and discovered the tragedian alone upon the stage; the acclamations seemed to be all blended into one mighty voice, and that voice to express but one feeling.

A few days later the *Examiner* remarked upon the crammed houses which showed "the satisfaction of the public at seeing Mr. Phelps in his right place upon the boards of Drury Lane," and asserted that *Manfred* had brought the educated classes back into the theatre. The play ran for nearly a hundred nights in a house that seated more than three thousand spectators at prices of admission double those of the minor theatres, with no half-price admittance at nine o'clock. The event was a landmark in the history of the English stage.

The appeal of *Manfred* lay chiefly in Phelps's delivery of Byron's poetry. The title role, although it dominates the play, gives little opportunity for acting and offers no theatrical aids to expression of emotion. The *Examiner* carried two articles on the excellence of Phelps's elocution and cited the success of *Manfred* as evidence for the argument that poetic drama is really preferred by the public to "plays of French incident and intrigue, that have no words in them worth a good actor's speaking." The *Times* said that "the declamation of Mr. Phelps on Saturday could scarcely be surpassed, so true was his reading, so just, while so unobstrusive, was his discrimination of emotions." The production also inspired a pamphlet which praised Phelps's performance and suggested that he had chosen the play in order "to inaugurate a reaction against the too realistic tendencies of the day in matters theatrical" and "to restore some dignity and some elevation to the productions of the English stage." [2]

During the long run of *Manfred* Phelps occasionally performed Sir Pertinax Macsycophant to relieve the monotony of playing the same role night after night. After Easter *Henry the Fourth, Part One,* was produced with Phelps as Falstaff, Walter Montgomery as Hotspur, Walter Lacy as Prince Hal, and John Ryder as the King. Phelps's versatility as an actor surprised many who had never seen him before, and it was in this comic role that he began to establish himself as a Shakespearean actor on the boards of Drury Lane. That Sadler's Wells was generally regarded as totally outside the limits of London's theatrical world is indicated by Hollingshead's remark that Phelps was "received like a beloved Rip Van Winkle" when he appeared at Drury Lane.[3] To some members of fashionable society Phelps seemed tainted by his association with the suburban theatre. For example, Sir Theodore Martin, although he admired Phelps's reading of *Manfred,* remarked that, "It has done

Mr. Phelps little good, we fear, as an actor, to have been so long away from collision with performers and audiences of the first class." [4]

The attitude of the *haut monde* towards Phelps involved him in a serious controversy during the season of 1863–1864. Preparations for a festival to celebrate the tercentenary of Shakespeare's birth were begun by a committee of Stratford citizens in the autumn of 1863. On November 12 the committee wrote Phelps asking him to attend the festival and to serve as a vice-president on the occasion. On December 7 they wrote a second letter asking him to take part in the dramatic performances. Having received an affirmative reply, they wrote on January 16, 1864, asking him to play Iachimo in *Cymbeline*.[5] Phelps was, quite understandably, surprised that he should be asked to play such a minor role in a Shakespearean festival, since within the theatrical profession he had long been recognized as the foremost Shakespearean actor of his time, whatever the fashionable world might think of him.

It is possible that he might have agreed to play a secondary role had he not learned that Charles Fechter had been asked to play Hamlet at the same festival. As a leader of his profession he felt called to protest the choice of a French actor who had discarded all the traditions of the English stage as the chief impersonator of Shakespeare at a national festival. Phelps's personal distaste for a manager who would treat a rival as Fechter had treated him at the Lyceum may also have influenced him. He told the Stratford Committee that if Fechter played Hamlet, he would not participate in the festival.

Phelps's stand provoked some controversy, and there was a privately printed pamphlet by C. L. Kenney supporting his position against those who criticized him. It was the kind of affair that Phelps would have gone far to avoid, and he was thoroughly unhappy about it. On April 14 he wrote to a friend in Birmingham, "I have been so worried about the Stratford affair as to be really ill with it." [6] In the end Fechter did not appear at the festival. Phelps's only contribution to the celebration was the planting of an oak on Primrose Hill in the name of the workingmen of England. Thousands of workingmen were present to honor the poet and perhaps to express their esteem for the actor who was content to represent them. He had fought the committee for the sake of his profession, but he did not resent being asked to serve as a representative of the workingmen instead of the acting profession.

The successful first season under Falconer and Chatterton at Drury

Lane led to an expanded program of Shakespearean productions in 1864–1865. Playbills for the theatre announced proudly: "Open for the Season for the Performance of the Legitimate Drama." The company was strengthened by the addition of Helen Faucit and Henry Marston. Phelps set to work on a series of plays that would bring Shakespeare to life once again in the great national theatre. Directing the staging and acting with practiced skill, he aimed at a complete performance—not the kind of spectacular illustration developed by Macready and Charles Kean, but the carefully molded and harmonious interpretation he had sought at Sadler's Wells.

The season opened with a week's run of *Henry the Fourth, Part One,* in which Marston replaced Ryder in the role of the King. The *Examiner* commented on this improvement in the cast: "Mr. Ryder declaims very well, but he only declaims; Mr. Marston puts some of their life into the lines." On October 1, *Henry the Fourth, Part Two,* featured Phelps as both the King and Justice Shallow. On October 8, there was *Othello,* in which Creswick was the Iago, Miss Atkinson, Emilia, and Mrs. Vezin, Desdemona.

This production of *Othello* achieved some of that unity of interpretation and harmony in acting Phelps was seeking. The *Morning Advertiser* (October 10, 1864) noted this aspect of the performance:

> We have seen every actor of note from Edmund Kean in his earliest time, and we say with truth that we never saw the grand tragedy pass so swiftly and perfectly before the eyes of the audience. It was like a grand piece of music played flowingly, with all those gradations of effect that fine leading and perfection in the details produce. The entirety of the play was admirably displayed, and it left the effect of a complete and majestic work of art. We do not pretend to say that we have not seen greater actors in the secondary parts, but as the entire performance of a drama, magnificent and perfect in its gigantic proportions, it was completely performed.

Othello was followed by *Cymbeline,* with Helen Faucit as Imogen, Phelps as Leonatus Posthumus, and Creswick as Iachimo. *Macbeth* appeared on October 22 and ran four nights a week until Christmas. Phelps had always found Macbeth his most strenuous role, and now at sixty he felt the strain of this long run. Directing the play was also difficult, because Helen Faucit did not agree with his ideas of ensemble playing. She had learned from Macready, her tutor, how to make effective points, and she was not willing to change her way of acting the role—certainly not under the tutelage of an actor who had been assigned minor roles in Macready's company. The performance lacked the harmony and balance that had distinguished *Othello*. Phelps's Macbeth, which had always been more vigorous and martial than Macready's, seemed rugged next to Miss Faucit's ladylike and rather spiritless Lady Macbeth.

During the run of *Macbeth,* other actors were featured on the two "off nights" each week. Creswick and Miss Atkinson appeared in leading roles, sometimes also in *Macbeth*. Helen Faucit acted roles from her own repertory. During the second half of the season of 1864–1865, *King Henry the Eighth* and Bulwer-Lytton's *Richelieu* were produced, with Phelps alternating in performances of the two cardinals. These roles, which were far less strenuous than Macbeth and better suited to Phelps's age, proved attractive to audiences. The *Examiner* (February 25, 1865) noted the perfect ease and self-possession of Phelps's Wolsey and "the impression of busy power subtly given through a marked quietness of demeanor."

During the summer of 1865 Phelps played in the provinces. It was almost the last time his wife was able to go with him, and Phelps wrote generally cheerful letters to his children at home.[7] On July 24, he wrote his perennial complaint about small houses in Dublin, but two weeks later he said that he had made a great hit in *The Fool's Revenge*. He went on to Preston and Edinburgh, where he again played Sir Pertinax Macsycophant.

Back in London in the autumn of 1865 Phelps began his third season at Drury Lane. *King John,* well staged and carefully directed, was the major production. Phelps's impressive performance of the King was supported by a good cast. James Anderson, who had joined the company this season, was a competent Faulconbridge. Edmund Phelps, Emma Atkinson, and Mrs. H. Vandenhoff played the other prominent roles, and in the minor parts were several of the old Sadler's Wells company: A. Raynor, Barrett, Meagreson, and Lickfold.

For several weeks *Macbeth* was performed six nights a week, with Phelps and Anderson alternating in the leading role.[8] The jealousy of rivals which had marred Macready's management of Drury Lane was wholly absent from this company. Anderson says that there was "no ill-feeling, nothing but brotherly love," between the two tragedians.[9] They also played together as Brutus and Marc Antony and as Othello and Iago during the season.

The fourth season of Phelps's long stay at Drury Lane began in September, 1866, with another run of *King John*. The production was the same as the previous season except for two important changes in the cast: Barry Sullivan replaced James Anderson as Faulconbridge and Mrs. Vezin replaced Emma Atkinson as Queen Constance. Phelps's own comments on the opening night are preserved in a letter to his wife, who was away from London visiting their married daughter.[10] He is obviously trying to reassure his wife about his opening night, an occasion which she knew had been a strain for him without her presence:

> Every thing was right last night. The house was splendid. £50 more than any opening night yet. My reception lasted between two and three minutes. My voice was in fine condition and I never acted better. The Sadlers Wells lot were all there. "Bravoo" was in great force. Altogether it was one of our old enthusiastic first nights. Mrs. Young—or Vesin was a great improvement upon Atkinson and Sullivan upon Anderson.

This season Chatterton had become sole lessee of Drury Lane, bringing in a great emphasis upon spectacle. The most important production was an adaptation of Goethe's *Faust,* featuring elaborate scenery painted by William Beverly, mechanical stage effects, ballet, and music. The play itself was interesting as the first serious attempt to bring Goethe's version of the Faust story to the English stage. French versions were well known through Gounod's opera and Charles Kean's translation of Michael Carré, but the romantic German drama had not made its way into the English theatre. Bayle Bernard, who served as translator and adapter for this production, was a competent dramatist, and his work apparently showed both skill and a reverence for the original text. It was, however, a drastically cut version. Goethe's *Faust* would have been too long for the English theatre even without the spectacular adornments introduced by Chatterton.

The Drury Lane *Faust* gave Phelps the opportunity to create a new character on the stage. In English tradition Mephistopheles was a semi-comic and tangible demon; Phelps created a subtle and intellectual Mephistopheles, who was the evil shadow of Faust. He projected a sense of the supernatural by the contrast between the important ideas he expressed and the laughing sneer with which he uttered them. His light, careless tone was blood-chilling. The *Observer* (October 21, 1866) spoke of his thorough mastery of the role:

Mr. Phelps must have studied profoundly to produce so deep an impression as he does with the appearance of so much ease. Not the slightest inflection of meaning is lost.

The role required no such physical stamina as the great heroes of Shakespearean tragedy but offered opportunities for shades of facial expression and delicate emphasis in reading.

The play also gave Edmund Phelps a good role in Faust, where his earnestness, practiced elocution, and grace of movement made up for a lack of intensity and fire. Mrs. Vezin was a charming Margaret. Good acting combined with the appeal of the staging to make *Faust* a success.

After Easter, 1867, Phelps played a two-week engagement in Liverpool at the new Alexandra Theatre. Since Mrs. Phelps was too ill to accompany him on this trip, he wrote her daily of his experiences. The letters are interesting for their revelations of an old actor's reaction to a new kind of theatre and audience.[11] His first impression was highly favorable: the theatre was beautiful and the stage amazingly well equipped. But he found the settings for *A Midsummer Night's Dream* gaudy and inappropriate to his poetic interpretation of the play.[12] Over Easter weekend he worked hard at rehearsals to adjust the setting and give unity to the acting. On the opening night he had his first experience of a theatre without a pit. The orchestra was occupied by stalls (reserved seats) in which sat the upper-class audience he had been used to see only in the boxes. He found them stiff and unresponsive compared to the usual pit audience.

Well, my darling Wife, I have got the first night over. The house was very full—all rank and fashion, notwithstanding it was Easter Monday, and a wet night. It certainly looked splendid, but the audience are so infernally genteel that they seem to think it must be vulgar to laugh or applaud in the stalls (which is *all* the pit) and boxes—and the pit (which is above the boxes) and gallery people seem so overawed by the grandeur that they are dumb too. It was very depressing to me after what my "Bottom" has been used to. Still the managers tell me it was an uproarious audience to what they generally are. They certainly did smile a little in the last act—but altogether it put me in mind of Windsor Castle. Between the acts all the grandees go out to promenade in the magnificent crush room or go down to the refreshment department for coffee, etc. Five minutes before the acts commence the prompter strikes an electric apparatus which rings a bell in all the different rooms at once and that brings the swells back to their places. I fancy I shall be able to put a little life into them in a night or two as the managers tell me they were wonderfully pleased. The papers are loud in their praises . . . but they are "bosh."

The next day he wrote that "the audience were a *little* more lively. They even managed to get up a call at the end of one act and again at the finish." On Thursday he reported, "We had a great house last night and the audience *woke up* astonishingly." By Friday he was able to assure his wife of the success of his engagement:

We had a splendid house last night and *every seat* in the boxes and stalls is taken for to-night. The ladies dress so well that from the stage the house looks magnificent.

After Liverpool he went to Hull, where he found the theatre much deteriorated and the company wretched. He played Sir Pertinax to a small audience that was, nevertheless, larger than he had expected after first sight of the theatre. He was shocked at the performance of his colleagues:

Such an exhibition. Lord Lumbercourt, when he came on took my breath away! A little dirty scrub, with a rag tied about his neck—the whole dress not worth half-a-crown! & he knew *nothing about* it. Lady Rodolpha *knew less!* but looked very well. How I got through the second act I know not—the remembrance of it will be a future nightmare to me. Hamlet to-night. It has been played 4 or 5 times this season already by Kean, the manager, and one or two others to very bad houses. From what I see, the people must be disgusted. Kean did very badly and I fear I shall do ditto. I only wish I could get away. I shall be cautious how I engage for more than three or four nights for the future.

During the following week Phelps rehearsed the sad little company until he was very tired, but he was still disgusted by the performances. At Sheffield early in June he found an even worse company, and he refused to play *Hamlet* with them, confining his performance to plays which demanded little of the supporting cast.

During the summer of 1867 Mrs. Phelps died after her long illness. Although Phelps was not unprepared for the loss, a numbing sorrow remained with him for a long time. His mourning was increased by the death in November of his eldest son, who was only thirty-nine years old. William Phelps, chief justice of the island of St. Helena, happily married to the daughter of an old friend of Phelps, and father of several children, had been a source of pride to his father.

There remained five children besides the nephew May Phelps, whom Phelps had always treated as his own son. The oldest daughter, Eleanor, and the youngest, Esther, were unmarried and remained with their father to the end of his life. Sarah had been married some years before and was living in Preston with her husband and three children. Besides Edmund, the actor, who was married to a former member of the company at Sadler's Wells named Miss Hudspeth, there was a younger son, Samuel. Young Sam apparently led a wild life after his college years at Worthing, and within the year after his mother's death became so irresponsible that his sisters asked him to leave the house. In the Harvard Theatre Collection are a number of affectionate letters from Phelps to Sam, but one, written on black banded paper and beginning, "My wretched son," forbids him to re-enter the house or see his father again.

Soon after his wife's death Phelps moved his family from Islington to Camden Road, Holloway, where he had a comfortable home for the rest of his life. His management of Sadler's Wells had provided him with sufficient income to give him financial security, and his subsequent starring engagements paid well. He always lived as a gentleman, though without ostentation. His older sons had each spent three years studying at the university in Dresden, and his daughters had attended a private school in Kent. He had indulged his own taste for hunting and fishing by frequent vacations at Worthing, where he had excellent accommodations; and he continued to enjoy these sports to the end of his life.

In September, 1867, Phelps set out on another provincial tour. A letter to his children dated September 13 reports that he had good houses in Edinburgh and was going on to Glasgow for a week and then to Leeds.[13]

When he returned to London a few weeks later for his fifth season at Drury Lane he had a new role to study and a new production to direct. Chatterton had decided to produce Byron's *Marino Faliero* under the title *The Doge of Venice,* with Phelps as the Doge. Remembering Macready's failure with this play, Phelps worked hard on its production; but Chatterton's preference for spectacle and scorn for poetic drama allowed small scope to Phelps's talents. Later in the season he added another role to the series which had become his standard repertory at Drury Lane by playing Dr. Cantwell in *The Hypocrite.*

After Easter, 1868, he was again touring Edinburgh, Glasgow, Preston, Dublin, and Birmingham—this time under Chatterton's management. Although the schedule was strenuous, the terms of his contract and the quality of the theatres practically guaranteed him a salary of 100 pounds a week, the amount he had been receiving at Drury Lane. Moreover, the tour had been arranged so that his son Edmund was engaged to act with him.

The Edinburgh engagement went well. His letters to his daughters show contentment and optimism, and in one he says that he is considering an American tour.[14] But Dublin—a place he disliked from past experience—was worse than ever. He found that the local company had been playing to a house grossing only 4 pounds a night. Although his appearance brought better houses than expected, the receipts were too small to make his share a very large amount of money. He wrote his daughter for a blank check, "for things are so bad with business that I doubt if I shall have money enough to pay my expenses." Small audiences and the apathy he found in the theatre persuaded Phelps to perform only Sir Pertinax while he was in Dublin, without attempting to rehearse the company for more-demanding plays. Describing the city to his daughter, he wrote

> The fact is the place is *stagnant*. To mend the matter they have races this week, about 7 miles off—being so near half Dublin goes, so that amusements in town stand little chance. I am not sorry as it will certainly prevent my ever coming here again.

By the time he reached Birmingham at the end of May, Phelps was tired and discouraged. "I am so sick—heart sick of this knocking about," he wrote, "that I don't think any thing will ever induce me to do it again unless I get *certainly* well paid." Birmingham audiences were not much better than those in Dublin, and Phelps's share fell far short of the estimated 100 pounds per week.

After a summer vacation Phelps acted at Hull early in September, again under Chatterton's management. He returned to Drury Lane to open the season in a play called *King o' Scots,* an adaptation by Andrew Halliday of Scott's *The Fortunes of Nigel.* A reviewer described this production as "an elaborate spectacular drama, combining the scenic features of the realistic school with a certain amount of legitimate acting." Chatterton no longer pretended to maintain Drury Lane as the home of serious drama. His playbills described the theatre's offerings as

"Historical and Sensation Drama, Farce, and Grand Ballet Divertise-ment." For *King o' Scots* the playbills had a special paragraph on the scenery and stage effects. In this melodramatic spectacle Phelps played two roles, King James and Trapbois the miser. It was the kind of as-signment he could fill superbly. Towse says that the illusion of two dif-ferent actors was absolute.[15] Dutton Cook, who was not an admirer of traditional acting, found Phelps excellent in the two characters, remark-ing of his Trapbois that "so finished and forcible a picture of senile imbecility has seldom been seen on the modern stage." [16] The produc-tion drew large houses, and Chatterton advertised it as "the greatest suc-cess of any drama ever produced at this Theatre."

March, 1869, marked the end of Phelps's six consecutive seasons as leading actor at Drury Lane. The long engagement gave a generation of playgoers who had never seen Phelps at Sadler's Wells and were too young to remember Macready a glimpse of traditional legitimate drama. Although he was too old to play the most demanding Shakespearean roles with his full power—when he went to Drury Lane he was already older than Macready had been at his retirement—he could still give an impressive performance of Macbeth which displayed the traditional style. In the less-demanding roles that made up the repertory of his later years, he conveyed the full effect of his own genius and the traditions which he had inherited: Wolsey, Shylock, Falstaff, Bottom, Lord Ogleby, Sir Peter Teazle, Sir Pertinax Macsycophant, and Mr. Oakley. Some critics who knew Phelps only after he left Sadler's Wells described him later as the most impressive actor they had ever seen. Edward Stirling re-membered that he acted "with ability and correct judgment, with no straining after new readings or false interpretation" and that he gave "fair, smooth personations of character—*not points*." [17]

Still under Chatterton's management, although no longer at Drury Lane, Phelps toured the provinces during the season of 1869–1870, play-ing a variety of characters in short runs at many different theatres. The strain placed upon the sixty-five-year-old actor by the exhausting schedule Chatterton had arranged is shown in the following résumé in Phelps's hand, which is preserved in the Harvard Theatre Collection:

September	27th	Sadlers Wells	6 nights
October	4th	Leicester	3 "
" "	8th	Sadlers Wells	2 "
" "	11th	Nottingham	6 "

15. Phelps as Sir Pertinax Macsycophant. From a woodcut. Courtesy Harvard Theatre Collection. 16. Phelps as Falstaff at the Gaiety. Drawn by F. Barnard, engraved by Swain. From *Illustrated Sporting and Dramatic News,* January 30, 1875. Courtesy Harvard Theatre Collection.

Liverpool
Friday

My dearest Wife — I am
delighted that there is
a prospect of your getting
nicely down to Richmond
I only wish I were with
you — but never mind
I shan't be long from
you — We had a splendid
house last night and
every seat in the boxes
and stalls is taken
for to-night — The ladies
dress so well that from
the stage the house looks
magnificent — I went on
last night without a hand

17. Portion of a letter from Phelps to his wife, 1867. Courtesy Harvard
Theatre Collection.

18. Phelps as Henry IV. From an unidentified photograph. Courtesy Harvard Theatre Collection.

THE LATE MR. SAMUEL PHELPS.

"PEACE WITH HONOUR."

19. "The Late Mr. Samuel Phelps." Drawing by A. Bryan. From *Entr'acte,* November 16, 1878. Courtesy Harvard Theatre Collection.

"	"	18th	Derby	1	"
"	"	19	Lincoln	2	"
"	"	21	York	1	"
"	"	22	Huddersfield	2	"
"	"	25	Bradford	2	"
"	"	27	Leeds	4	"

Travell'd on Sunday

November 1st Newcastle 2 "

Taken ill—laid up. Came home and resumed on

11th Sunderland 3 "

Travell'd on Sunday

15th Manchester 12

29th Liverpool 18

Then ordered to Sadlers Wells for three nights—and thence to Belfast to act on the 27 Decr. Found myself unequal to the task of travelling etc. Did not go to Sadlers Wells but acted at Belfast for 12 nights—then ordered to Perth—finishing on Belfast on Saturday night, could not get away until 8 o'clock on Monday evening—sea voyage to Glasgow. Thence to Perth by rail, arriving on Tuesday evening to act on the four following nights—finishing on the Saturday. No travelling in Scotland on Sunday. Was ordered to Greenock to act on the Monday after travelling between 60 and 70 miles, and then to hold a rehearsal of the evening's performance. The following four nights to act Othello-Macbeth-Hamlet and Richelieu according to the managers programme, finishing at Greenock on Friday—having Saturday and Sunday to travel 300 miles more or less and act at Wolverhampton on Monday for 6 nights.

Even under this exacting schedule Phelps was able at times to capture the spontaneity and fire of his best performances. Two reviews from Manchester papers speak of the force of his acting in *Othello* and its electric effect on the audience so that "even the gods forgot to applaud" after some of the most thrilling passages.[18] One critic noted that "although his voice is not so flexible as it once was, it is still clear and resonant."

After such a winter, it is not surprising that Phelps left Chatterton's management early in the spring of 1870. In March he began a short engagement at Astley's with a good company including the Vezins. They played *Othello* with Hermann Vezin as Iago and his wife as Desdemona. On April 2, Phelps's son Edmund only 32 years old, died suddenly, leaving him doubly bereft, of a son and a professional colleague.

The following autumn he appeared as Bottom and Prospero at the

Queen's Theatre, Long Acre, under the management of Labouchere. During the rest of the season of 1870–1871 he had several provincial engagements without a strenuous touring schedule.

In September, 1871, Phelps went back to Drury Lane under Chatterton's management and played Isaac of York in Halliday's adaptation of *Ivanhoe* (entitled *Rebecca*). During the same season he was transferred to the Princess's, which was also under Chatterton's management (with Benjamin Webster as lessee and co-manager) and appeared there in a round of Shakespearean roles.

In 1872–1873 he was again at the Princess's. Here he played Hamlet and Macbeth for the last time. A young critic who saw him play Iago to Creswick's Othello in October remembered the performance forty years later as the best of the season:

> Phelps' Iago stood right out as of different rank to all else. . . . The touches of dry humor were quite splendid and the cold-blooded, deliberate slaughter of Roderigo unforgettable.[19]

One wintry night he caught cold and soon became so ill that he was confined to bed for many weeks. When he returned to the stage, it was evident that he had lost his former vigor. Although he continued to act for five more years, his voice was often weak and he showed the feebleness of age.

Choosing roles that were within his power Phelps undertook specific engagements for limited periods, and his performances continued to attract audiences. For several years he had short annual engagements at the Prince's Theatre in Manchester, where Charles Calvert was producing Shakespeare. In September, 1873, he played Malvolio in Calvert's *Twelfth Night*. Reviews were laudatory and noted the same features which had always marked Phelps's performances:

> It is scarcely possible to speak too highly of this masterpiece of genuine comedy—an impersonation carefully and profoundly studied, consistent in all its details, and wonderfully in harmony with the true rendering of the author.[20]

In 1874 he played Justice Shallow and King Henry in *Henry the Fourth, Part Two*. In 1875 he was Falstaff in *The Merry Wives of Windsor*. During these engagements he met Johnston Forbes-Robertson and renewed his friendship with Hermann Vezin. Wearing dressing gown and smoking cap Phelps joined the other actors of the company in the green room and conversed with them. Vezin found him "a great actor and a lovable man." [21]

Meanwhile, in London Phelps began his association with John Hollingshead, manager of the Gaiety. The Gaiety, built in 1868 on the Strand, was a new kind of theatre conceived by Hollingshead, who described himself in his autobiography as a "licensed dealer in legs, short skirts, French adaptations, Shakespeare, Taste, and the Musical Glasses." [22] A restaurant was attached to the theatre—an innovation which suggests the music hall and night club era. The theatre itself had two thousand seats, and the first five rows of the pit were divided into stalls which sold for 7 shillings each. Balcony stalls were 6 shillings. Even the stage was different, being cut off from the auditorium by the curtain with no projecting apron beyond the proscenium arch. The opening production featured Madge Robertson (later Dame Madge Kendal) in a burlesque, with music by W. S. Gilbert.

Into this unfamiliar milieu Phelps was introduced as a star for a short run between the end of the opera season and the beginning of the Christmas entertainments of 1873. Girls, music, and scenic wonders gave place to *The Hypocrite* with Phelps as Cantwell and J. L. Toole as Mawworm. On alternate nights *John Bull* appeared with Charles Mathews joining Phelps and Toole in the cast. Hollingshead later referred to this engagement as "the nine days' wonder" and congratulated himself on his correct estimate of the appeal which these famous old actors would have for London audiences. He later asserted that they brought in the largest receipts ever known at the Gaiety.[23]

After the success of the nine days' wonder, Hollingshead conceived the idea of Saturday matinee performances, another innovation to the English stage. A daytime performance suggested itself as a way of presenting a different kind of dramatic fare from that usually offered at his theatre, without interrupting the evening schedule. In practice, matinees proved to have other advantages. Actors could be hired from other theatres to fill out the cast of a traditional play which demanded many players possessing acting skills not found in most contemporary actors. Matinees also attracted a somewhat different audience, some of whom were not free to attend evening performances. In the latter class were actors, who availed themselves of Hollingshead's engagement of Phelps for Saturday afternoons as an opportunity to study Phelps's art. One critic remarked upon this unusual circumstance:

It was satisfactory to observe how many distinguished actors and actresses were present among the occupants of the stalls and boxes at the Gaiety on this occasion. For a young and ambitious performer there is no more instructive study than can be derived from observing closely the means by which Mr. Phelps in this part holds an easy command over the imaginations and the feelings of the audience.[24]

Among the plays produced in the spring of 1874 for Gaiety matinees were *The Hypocrite, Rob Roy,* and *The Clandestine Marriage.* Phelps's performance of Lord Ogleby, whom he portrayed as sufficiently ridiculous but with a courtliness and magnanimity which retained the sympathy of the audience, was especially interesting because few playgoers had seen it. Dutton Cook said that "his impersonation is as remarkable for its humour and force as for its artistic elaboration." [25]

In the following season, 1874–1875, Hollingshead interrupted his usual run of burlesques to present *The Merry Wives of Windsor* on an evening bill, with Phelps as Falstaff. The production featured music by Sullivan and a song by Swinburne, but the acting maintained its importance. Richard Dickins, who saw a performance on January 11, 1875, comments that "Phelps was splendidly humorous, and withal thoroughly sound and Shakespearean." [26] In the cast were Hermann Vezin and Johnston Forbes-Robertson, two actors in whom Phelps had special interest. For a time he tutored Forbes-Robertson in elocution with such lasting results that the effect of the training was noticed by critics to the end of his career.

In the green room of the Gaiety Phelps joined the younger actors of the regular company with a good-natured comradeliness which surprised some of them, particularly those who knew nothing of "legitimate" drama but its reputation. His reserved manner, erect bearing, and craggy face belied his modest and kindly disposition. Hollingshead records several anecdotes from this period, including one that tells of Phelps's cheerfully paying a fine for an alleged misquotation of Shakespeare, and gives the impression that Phelps was the pleasantest member of the company.[27] In earlier years his demanding work and his satisfaction with domestic life had kept Phelps from social entertainment, and even in his later years when he was on tour he kept a rigid schedule. Macqueen-Pope reports that when Phelps was in the provinces playing with Henry Irving, he had supper and went straight to bed after the performances, rising early in the morning.[28] Since Irving's habits were the opposite, they hardly saw each other except on the stage. But at the Gaiety when he was no longer responsible for stage management, and his home no longer offered real companionship, he enjoyed the social hours in the green room. He was even persuaded to join the Garrick Club, the resort of nearly all prominent actors.

During the rest of the season of 1874–1875, Phelps played only in Saturday matinees. In the summer of 1875 he went abroad with his two unmarried daughters, traveling in France, Switzerland, and Italy. He enjoyed the trip, especially a long stay in northern Italy, and returned home much refreshed by his five months' vacation.

In 1875–1876 he resumed the Gaiety matinees, playing Shylock, Wolsey, Malvolio, Sir Peter Teazle, Lord Ogleby, and the Stranger. Although the plays were put on in a haphazard fashion, with actors from many theatres hastily fitted into their parts, these matinees continued to draw full houses. The roles were well chosen to show Phelps's abilities without overstraining the physical power of a seventy-two-year-old actor, and the traditional elements in his acting were intensely interesting to a new generation of playgoers who had seen Shakespeare through Henry Irving's interpretation. George Gissing, for example, saw Phelps only in four roles during these last years and found him thoroughly satisfying:

> In each and all he was perfection, an excellent proof of which is, that whenever I take up a Shakespeare and read those parts, I fancy I hear and see the man before me, his every look and inflection of voice. His Malvolio was glorious.[29]

Percy Fitzgerald said, "Phelps was ever satisfactory; even in the latter days, when his voice was feeble, he always gave you a thoroughly enjoyable time of it." [30] Moy Thomas described the audience gathered to see Phelps's Wolsey in November, 1875:

> Never was an audience more closely packed, more attentive, or more enthusiastic than that which had gathered at the Gaiety on Saturday last.[31]

In September, 1876, Phelps went to the Queen's Theatre, Long Acre, to help initiate John Coleman's management. He was a friend of the young lessee. It was Phelps's suggestion that he play the fourth act of *Henry the Fourth, Part Two* as a prologue to Coleman's production of *Henry the Fifth,* but apparently nothing could have saved Coleman's *Henry the Fifth.* Joseph Knight said that it was as spectacular as a wax-

works exhibition, with gaudy ballets, and that Coleman was totally inadequate as the gallant King.[32] In spite of the failure of his management,
Coleman was grateful to Phelps for his aid and later wrote about him
in a well meaning but inaccurate manner.[33]

In October, 1876, Phelps was invited to attend a banquet given by
the Lord Mayor to the theatrical profession and to reply to the toast of
"The Shakespearean Drama." Overcoming his dislike of such affairs,
Phelps accepted in order that he might use the occasion to make public
a proposal which was close to his heart. His short speech was devoted
to the suggestion that the government subsidize a Shakespearean theatre
for popular audiences. Citing his own success in managing Sadler's Wells
for eighteen years, he argued that such a theatre could be made to pay
for itself:

> If that could be done by me as a humble individual, why could it not be
> done by the Government of this country? Why could not a subsidized
> theatre, upon a moderate scale of expense, be added to the late educational
> scheme, by which children are forced somehow or other into school? I
> maintain, from the experience of eighteen years, that the perpetual itera-
> tion of Shakespeare's words, if nothing more, going on daily for so many
> months in the year, must and would produce a great effect upon the pub-
> lic mind. . . . If I could find any member of Parliament (which I fear
> is hopeless), I would willingly devote what little of life remains to me,
> to point out the way in which this could be done, and I would willingly
> give evidence in the House of Commons to prove the truth of Shake-
> speare's educating powers.[34]

John Coleman seconded this plea for a people's theatre, but both actors
knew that there was little hope for such a venture in the near future.

Early in 1877 Phelps played farewell performances at Manchester,
Dublin, and Liverpool, acting Cardinal Wolsey, Richelieu, and Sir Peter
Teazle. A year later he had still not scheduled his farewell performances
in London. He was playing a limited engagement with performances
five nights a week at the Aquarium Theatre in London during February, 1878, when he caught cold. With characteristic determination to
fulfill his engagement, he continued to act for two weeks although he
was really ill, alternating Richelieu and Wolsey. On March 1, he played
Wolsey leaning on the arm of Norman Forbes-Robertson, his Cromwell,
faltered in the lines of the farewell speech, and was carried from the

stage. So well did he play his last part that the audience applauded his exit, unaware that he had succumbed to illness.

During the summer of 1878 under the care of his two daughters, he recovered his health sufficiently to plan his farewell performances at Drury Lane under Chatterton's management—fulfilling an old promise. But in the autumn he became ill again, and on November 6, 1878, he died at the age of seventy-four. At his funeral were George Bennett and Henry Marston among many younger actors and friends. He was buried next to his wife at Highgate cemetery.

In Phelps's death many critics recognized the end of the old stage traditions and the loss of an art practiced by generations of English actors. "His death would leave some ground for consolation," wrote Thomas, "if we could say that we have still upon our stage a performer of equal genius and variety of gifts who had been content to devote to his difficult art the careful study which contributed so powerfully to raise Mr. Phelps to the foremost rank in his profession." [35] Gissing expressed a similar opinion:

> We have none left like him. He had the interest of the legitimate drama at heart, and I can imagine with what scorn he thought of the trash which now occupies our boards. He had lived to see the days when "Our Boys" could run for 1,500 nights, and "Pink Dominoes" bid fair to run still longer.[36]

Percy Fitzgerald in 1895 lamented that "there is no one now on the stage his equal for giving weight and point to a sentence, which came out clean and emphatic, firm as from a mould." [37] An echo of the elocutionary art which was the basis of Phelps's style was still heard in the acting of his pupil Sir Johnston Forbes-Robertson, of whom Sir George Arthur wrote in 1936: "A quarter of a century has passed since Johnston Forbes-Robertson . . . has faced the public; but for purity of tone and perfection of phrasing . . . one has yet to look for his peer." [38]

Perhaps the best comment upon Phelps's death is that written by William Archer:

> Samuel Phelps was the last, and by no means the least, not only of a generation, but of a dynasty of actors,—the Shakespearean dynasty— founded by Burbage, and stretching in an unbroken line from Betterton downwards. For two hundred years the stage was at no time without its

two or three "legitimate" actors,—men who had been trained in the classic drama, who could move with ease and dignity through the whole poetic repertory; to whom the march of sonorous iambics was as little of a mystery as the modulations of the hexameters to the ancient rhapsodists. . . . Amid all their differences of method, the members of this dynasty passed on from generation to generation a great tradition and a great repertory. They all owned the same ideal; they all worked, in great measure, upon the same material. . . . Phelps, its last English scion, though he lived to see Mr. Irving almost in the plenitude of his power, would probably have been more at home with Burt and Mohun at the Cockpit than on the Lyceum stage. Betterton, Booth, Quin, Garrick, Kemble, Macready, Phelps,—so run the representative names, the last linked to the first by an unbroken chain of tradition. Phelps trod the stage in the buskin of Burbage; but to whom has he bequeathed it? [39]

APPENDICES, NOTES, BIBLIOGRAPHY, AND INDEX

Chart of Shakespearean Performances

	1844–45	1845–46	1846–47	1847–48	1848–49	1849–50	1850–51	1851–52
Macbeth	14	10		20		10	8	14
Othello	10	5	6			10	8	
Merchant of Venice	6	2	9			14	6	2
King John	21				16		6	
Hamlet	28	9		12			21	9
Richard III	24				14			
Henry VIII	1	3			12	9	2	7
King Lear		10		3				
Winter's Tale		45			20		11	4
Julius Caesar		1	9		6		2	4
Henry IV, 1			16			10		6
Romeo and Juliet			13					
Measure for Measure			15			6	2	
Tempest			22			17		
Cymbeline				19			10	
As You Like It				12				
Twelfth Night				16				
Merry Wives				12				
Coriolanus					16		6	
Much Ado					7		2	4
Antony and Cleopatra						22		
Timon of Athens								31
All's Well								
Henry V								
Henry IV, 2								
Midsummer Night's								
Pericles								
Comedy of Errors								
Taming of the Shrew								
Two Gentlemen								
Love's Labour's Lost								
Total Shakespeare	104	85	90	94	91	98	84	81
Non-Shakespearean	158	212	154	98	107	120	132	143
Total Nights*	262	296	244	192	198	218	216	224

* This chart was compiled from the weekly listings of theatrical performances in the *Theatrical Journal*. When the total number of nights for a season is less than the sum of the

1852-53	1853-54	1854-55	1855-56	1856-57	1857-58	1858-59	1859-60	1860-61	1861-62	Total
	6	7		11	8	6	5	7	7	133
5	4	6	6	4	10	7	7	8	3	99
6	8	6	7		4	1	5	2	3	81
			10			4		8		65
14	12	8	10	8	11	7	10	6	6	171
								14		52
		2		5		8	3		3	55
19	6		3		5		7	3	3	59
		13	9			15		12	8	137
				8	1	4				35
2				7				5		46
						5	10		4	32
				2						25
			28					13		80
		9			4			6		48
					13			7		32
14				9		3	3			45
				22	2				3	39
				5			1	7		35
2		3				2				20
										22
				10						41
11										11
39	9					8				56
8			3						12	23
	55		13						12	80
		55								55
			13	4	3	6	2			28
				10						10
				3						3
					14					14
120	100	109	102	108	75	76	53	84	78	1,632
63	84	53	55	54	83	86	106	76	74	1,860
183	184	162	153	160	158	152	156	160	152	3,472

Shakespearean and non-Shakespearean performances, two plays were given on a single night, as sometimes happened for benefit performances. Afterpieces are not included in the chart.

Non-Shakespearean Plays Performed at Sadler's Wells

Author Title (adapter)	Season and Number of Performances

ELIZABETHAN AND JACOBEAN PLAYS

Philip Massinger

The City Madam (Phelps)	1(16), 9(12), 10(3), 12(2), 18(1)
The Fatal Dowry (Sloan)	2(13), 5(7), 10(13), 14(4)
A New Way to Pay Old Debts	1(2), 6(6), 7(7), 8(5), 10(3), 12(3), 14(3), 16(3)

Beaumont and Fletcher

The Maid's Tragedy—The Bridal (Knowles, Macready)	1(21), 2(7), 4(11), 7(8), 11(6), 12(2), 15(4), 18(9)
A King and No King	3(12)
The Honest Man's Fortune (Horne)	5(10)

John Fletcher

Rule a Wife and Have a Wife	5(13), 7(3), 8(4), 9(4), 10(1), 16(1)

John Webster

The Duchess of Malfi (Horne)	7(22)

William Rowley

The New Wonder—A Woman Never Vext (Planché)	9(6)

RESTORATION AND EIGHTEENTH CENTURY PLAYS

Thomas Otway

Venice Preserved (1682)	2(2), 3(2), 5(3), 6(4), 7(2), 13(3)

Colley Cibber

Love Makes a Man (1700)	10(2)
She Would and She Would Not (1702)	6(7), 13(3), 15(2)

Author   Title   (adapter)   Season and Number of Performances

Vanbrugh-Cibber
    The Provoked Husband (1728)   1(8), 8(1), 15(5)
Mrs. S. Centlivre
    The Busybody (1709)   6(2)
    The Wonder (1714)   1(2), 4(1), 6(1), 17(3)
Henry Fielding
    The Miser (1733)   10(3)
Nicholas Rowe
    Jane Shore (1714)   2(6), 3(2), 5(5), 17(3)
John Home
    Douglas (1757)   2(2), 6(2), 9(2), 11(2)
George Lillo
    Arden of Feversham (1755)   9(2)
Edward Moore
    The Gamester (1753)   2(14), 3(7), 4(1), 5(3), 6(4), 7(3),
                                8(3), 9(2), 10(2), 13(2), 14(2),
                                16(3)
George Colman
    The Jealous Wife (1761)   1(2), 4(3), 11(3), 14(1), 15(3), 16(1)
Colman-Garrick
    The Clandestine Marriage   14(28), 16(9)
      (1766)
Thomas Southerne
    The Fatal Marriage—Isabella   2(7), 3(6), 4(2), 6(4), 7(3), 8(3)
      (Garrick)
Arthur Murphy
    All in the Wrong (1761)   5(2)
Isaac Bickerstaffe
    The Hypocrite (1768)   3(2), 10(2), 15(16), 17(3)
Oliver Goldsmith
    She Stoops to Conquer (1773)   6(2)
Richard Brinsley Sheridan
    The Rivals (1775)   1(10), 2(1), 3(2), 6(1), 8(1), 11(6),
                                 13(2), 14(2), 15(1), 17(2)
    The School for Scandal (1777)   1(7), 3(2), 6(1), 8(2), 10(11), 11(2),
                                 13(7), 14(3), 15(3)
    Pizarro (1799)   2(12), 18(9)
Charles Macklin
    Man of the World (1781)   8(20), 9(4), 10(6), 11(2), 13(2),
                                 14(3), 15(2), 17(3), 18(2)

Author   Title (adapter)   Season and Number of Performances

John O'Keeffe
  Wild Oats (1791)   1(3), 10(3), 11(1)
Thomas Holcroft
  The Road to Ruin (1792)   1(4), 3(3), 4(2), 8(4), 10(4), 11(1)
Mrs. H. Cowley
  The Belle's Stratagem (1792)   6(3)
Mrs. E. Inchbald
  Every One Has His Fault   2(3)
    (1793)
Richard Cumberland
  Wheel of Fortune (1795)   15(16)

PLAYS OF THE ROMANTIC PERIOD

George Colman, the younger
  The Mountaineers (1793)   6(1)
  The Iron Chest (1796)   1(3), 5(2), 12(1), 13(3)
  Heir-at-Law (1797)   4(2), 6(2), 7(1)
  The Poor Gentleman (1801)   4(2), 5(1)
  John Bull (1803)   3(1), 4(1), 6(2), 16(8), 17(7), 18(2)
Thomas Morton
  A Cure for the Heartache   14(1)
    (1797)
  Secrets Worth Knowing (1798)   8(2)
  Town and Country (1807)   3(4), 10(4)
Monk Lewis
  Castle Spectre (1797)   5(2)
Benjamin Thompson-Kotzebue
  The Stranger (1798)   1(7), 2(4), 3(7), 4(3), 5(4), 6(2),
                                      7(4), 8(4), 9(4), 10(6), 11(2),
                                      12(2), 13(1), 14(5), 15(8), 16(5),
                                      17(2), 18(2)

Andrew Cherry
  The Soldier's Daughter (1804)   1(3), 6(2)
John Tobin
  The Honeymoon (1805)   3(2), 4(4), 5(2), 6(2), 7(2), 8(2),
                                      10(2), 14(6), 17(4)
Charles Maturin
  Bertram (1816)   3(6)
Henry Hart Milman
  Fazio (1816)   4(2), 6(3), 7(7), 8(2), 13(3), 18(3)

Author Title (adapter)	Season and Number of Performances
John Howard Payne	
Brutus (1818)	2(6), 7(2), 15(1), 16(7)
Richard Sheil	
Evadne (1819)	2(4), 4(3), 6(2), 7(4)
J. Banim and Sheil	
Damon and Pythias (1821)	3(3), 5(2), 18(7)
Isack Pocock	
Rob Roy Macgregor (1818)	11(1), 12(3)
Samuel Beazley, Jr.	
The Steward (1819)	4(2)
J. R. Planché	
The Merchant's Wedding	9(4)
Lord Byron	
Werner (1830)	1(8), 2(3), 4(7), 6(4), 7(4), 8(4), 11(4), 13(2), 15(3), 16(1), 17(11)
Leigh Hunt	
A Legend of Florence (1840)	7(8)

PLAYS BY CONTEMPORARY WRITERS

Sheridan Knowles	
Virginius (1820)	1(4), 2(5), 3(4), 5(4), 7(4), 8(2), 10(4), 12(7), 13(5), 14(1), 15(2), 17(3)
William Tell (1825)	2(11), 6(9), 7(4), 9(6), 13(3), 17(1), 18(3)
The Hunchback (1832)	1(2), 2(2), 3(5), 4(2), 6(11), 7(5), 8(2), 9(2), 12(9), 13(1), 14(6), 16(5), 18(3)
The Wife (1833)	1(5), 3(3), 6(2), 7(1), 8(6), 9(3), 12(3), 13(2), 15(4), 17(9), 18(2)
The Love-Chase (1837)	6(5), 8(2), 10(2), 14(2), 15(7), 16(2)
Love (1839)	2(10), 4(2)
George W. Lovell	
The Provost of Bruges (1836)	3(1), 4(4), 11(7)
Love's Sacrifice (1842)	3(4), 5(2), 6(2), 7(2), 8(2), 13(2)
Sir Thomas N. Talfourd	
Ion (1836)	3(2), 8(4), 13(1), 18(3)
Charles Whitehead	
The Cavalier (1836)	7(2), 9(2)

Author Title (adapter)	Season and Number of Performances

Sir Edward Bulwer, Lord Lytton
The Lady of Lyons (1838) — 1(35), 2(14), 3(29), 4(6), 5(4), 6(2), 8(9), 9(4), 10(7), 11(3), 12(5), 14(1), 15(2), 16(6), 17(4), 18(4)

Richelieu (1839) — 2(39), 5(17), 7(9), 8(6), 9(4), 11(12), 13(7), 15(7), 16(4), 17(3), 18(3)

Money (1840) — 2(15), 3(10), 4(8), 5(5), 8(7), 13(1), 14(3)

Dion Boucicault
London Assurance (1841) — 10(4)

Westland Marston
The Patrician's Daughter (1842) — 3(13), 4(6), 14(5), 17(2)

Robert Browning
A Blot in the 'Scutcheon (1842) — 5(8)

Mrs. Maria Lovell
Ingomar (1851) — 8(25), 18(3)

Boucicault-Casimir Delavigne
Louis the Eleventh (1855) — 18(12)

NEW PLAYS

Thomas J. Serle
The Priest's Daughter — 1(8)

R. Sullivan
The King's Friend — 2(11)

E. L. A. Berwick
The Florentines — 2(9)

Henry Spicer
Judge Jeffreys — 2(7)

James White
Feudal Times — 3(25), 7(8)
John Savile of Haysted — 4(25), 8(7)
James the Sixth — 8(8)

George H. Boker
Calaynos — 5(9), 6(4)

George Bennett
Retribution — 6(21)

F. G. Tomlins
Garcia — 6(12)

Author Title (adapter)	Season and Number of Performances
Anonymous	
Might and Right	9(11)
Angelo R. Slous	
Hamilton of Bothwellhaugh	12(15)
Tom Taylor	
The Fool's Revenge	16(47), 17(9)
Rophino Lacy	
Doing for the Best	18(7)

Notes

I. THE TRAINING OF AN ACTOR

1. The incident is reported by John Forbes–Robertson in the Appendix to *The Life and Life–Work of Samuel Phelps*, W. May Phelps and John Forbes–Robertson (London, 1886). This accurate biography is the chief source of the facts of Phelp's early life given above. Hereafter it will be cited as *The Life*. Another biography, *Memoirs of Samuel Phelps*, John Coleman and Edward Coleman (London, 1886), contains so many errors that it cannot be relied upon.

2. A manuscript letter in the Harvard Theatre Collection, dated June 2, 1867.

3. A manuscript letter in the Harvard Theatre Collection.

4. *Plymouth, Devonport and Stonehouse Herald*, April 29, 1837.

5. *Western Luminary*, February 27, 1837, and *Flying Post*, March 16, 1837.

6. This correspondence is published in *The Life*, pp. 355–356. The manuscript letters written by Webster on July 20 and July 26 are preserved in the Harvard Theatre Collection.

7. Published in *The Life*, p. 356.

8. Published in *The Life*, p. 357.

9. Manuscript letter in the Harvard Theatre Collection.

10. Manuscript letter in the Harvard Theatre Collection, published in *The Life*, p. 43.

11. *The Diaries of William Charles Macready*, ed. William Toynbee, (New York, 1912), I, 405–406.

12. *The Life*, pp. 40–41.

13. The original document is in the Harvard Theatre Collection. The most interesting reviews from the eight-volume manuscript have been published by the Society for Theatre Research as *The London Theatre in the Eighteen-Thirties*, ed. A. C. Sprague and Bertram Shuttleworth (London, 1950). The review of Phelps's Shylock appears as Chapter XXXIII.

14. *Macready's Reminiscences, and Selections from His Diaries and Letters*, ed. Sir Frederick Pollock (New York, 1875), p. 414.

15. *The London Theatre in the Eighteen-Thirties*, Chapter XXXIV.

II. FROM ACTOR TO MANAGER

1. Macready's statement in his diary that he did not wish Forster to attack Forrest ("Wrote to Forster urging him to deal liberally and kindly by Forrest in his notice." [Ed. Toynbee, I, 350.]) must be understood in the light of Macready's strange lack of honesty in this supposedly private document. There was actually no reason for him to write Forster "to deal liberally and kindly" with an actor who was enjoying a great success in London. Macready had been angry because the *Times* had called Forrest "more spirited than any tragic actor now on the stage." Even Macready's good friend Dow, usually one of his comforters and referred to as "staunch old Dow," had infuriated him by calling Forrest a very good actor. Nothing in the diary indicates that Forster dissented from the general favorable opinion of Forrest until the remark about writing him to deal kindly with Forrest. Macready's real wishes were normally known to Forster, and indeed on the subject of Forrest, Macready indicated on several occasions that he considered praise of him an insult to himself. It is hard to escape the conclusion that his note to Forster was intended to produce unfavorable criticism of the American actor. On a later occasion when Macready records writing Forster "not to be severe on Ellen Tree," who was then enjoying her first London success, he found that Forster had taken his words too literally. (Cf. *Diaries,* ed. Toynbee, II, 24.)

2. Cf. *Diaries,* ed. Toynbee, I, 358.

3. Cf. Alan Downer, *The Eminent Tragedian, William Charles Macready* (Cambridge, Massachusetts, 1966), p. 104.

4. Mrs. C. Baron Wilson, *Our Actresses* (London, 1844), II, 16.

5. For Macready's opinions and his states of mind published portions of his diary have been used. Unless otherwise noted the quotations are taken from Toynbee's edition, but some of the information is taken from the edition of Sir Frederick Pollock, *Macready's Reminiscences and Selections from His Diaries and Letters.*

6. *The Life,* p. 50.

7. In his diary Macready asserts that Phelps withdrew from leading roles because he was afraid to act them. On November 20 he wrote: "Mr. Phelps refused the part of Exeter—is afraid to play the first and averse to take the second characters. I told Bartley to tell him I should shut the theatre if he did not play it." This entry shows the dishonesty and exaggeration into which Macready was led by anger. He may actually have told his stage manager to tell Phelps that he would close the theatre, but it is unlikely that he would have done so, especially since he had no immediate plans for producing *Henry the Fifth.* Certainly there had been nothing resembling fear in Phelps's eagerness to play Jaffier and Othello, nor in his protest against the withdrawal of these plays. Macready's description of Exeter as a "second character" is at the least an exaggeration. It is interesting to note that when *Henry the Fifth* was finally produced in the following season, Phelps was assigned an even more insignificant role, the "walking gentleman" part of the High Constable of France.

8. *The Life,* pp. 343–344.

9. Ed. Toynbee, I, 464.

10. James Anderson in his autobiography (*An Actor's Life* [London, 1902], p.

78) says that Macready took Covent Garden a second year because he had learned that his actors were planning to do it on shares, without him.

11. Ed. Toynbee, I, 440.

12. *Ibid.,* I, 461.

13. Macready innovated alphabetical listing of the members of the company. The customary playbill by the order of the names would have revealed the relative positions of actors in the company. Macready claimed credit with the public for adopting a more gentlemanly form and one which indicated the cooperative spirit in which they were banded together to save legitimate drama, without thought of individual position. It also enabled him to give private assurances to several actors, as he did to Phelps, that each would play "second leads." James Anderson reports (in *An Actor's Life,* p. 63) that Macready promised him "all the best parts after me which circumstances may allow me to offer." The actors were not long deceived. Anderson describes the method as "perfect Indian warfare—rank and file one long line, with Moccasin-Macready in front, and *he* took all the scalps." (p. 64.)

14. Ed. Toynbee, I, 258.

15. James Anderson says in his autobiography (p. 82) that a chief cause of the failure of Macready's management was his arbitrary withdrawing of successful plays and forcing of unpopular ones.

16. *Diaries,* ed. Toynbee, II, 13.

17. From the *Sunbeam,* quoted in *The Life,* p. 49.

18. Cf., p. 118.

19. Cf. Charles H. Shattuck, *Bulwer and Macready* (Urbana, 1958), pp. 156, 162.

20. Cf. *The Life,* p. 51.

21. *Ibid.,* p. 53.

22. *Ibid.,* p. 426.

23. Phelp's letter is published in *The Life,* p. 358.

24. Cf., p. 68.

25. Comments of reviewers are collected in Charles H. Shattuck, *William Charles Macready's* King John (Urbana, 1962), p. 50 ff.

26. Cf. Charles E. Pearce, *Madame Vestris and Her Times* (London, n.d.), p. 271. According to Pearce, Macready found out about her plans from Tom Cooke, who left her management for his in 1841.

27. *Diaries,* ed. Toynbee, II, 187.

28. *An Actor's Life,* p. 114.

29. Browning later believed that Macready had deliberately tried to discredit the play by giving it to Willmott. Cf. "Browning and Macready: the Final Quarrel," Joseph W. Reed, Jr., *PMLA,* LXXV (1960), 597–603. The only contrary evidence is a statement in Macready's diary (ed. Toynbee, II, 194) that Anderson had declined to read the play to the actors and had passed jokes on it during Willmott's reading. Macready's comment that this conduct was "not very decorous for an official" seems to indicate that he blamed Anderson for the entire incident, but Anderson was almost sycophantic in his support of Macready, often siding with the manager against the other actors. As stage manager he could hardly have refused to read a play to the company, since that was one of his official duties. It is far more

likely that he was carrying out what he believed to be Macready's wishes and follow-ing Willmott's lead in burlesquing the work. If Macready had not been satisfied with the reading, he would not have reported to Browning that the actors had laughed at his play. Browning's conviction that Macready had wished to discredit the play was founded on good evidence.

30. The manuscript and its revisions are described by Joseph W. Reed, Jr., *op. cit.*

31. Quoted in J. C. Trewin, *Mr. Macready* (London, 1955), p. 199.

32. Ed. Toynbee, II, 217.

33. These letters in Phelps's hand are now in the Harvard Theatre Collection. Many of them are undated, but in most cases I have been able to identify the en-gagement to which they refer and thus assign probable dates.

34. Reprinted in *The Life*, p. 60.

III. MANAGER OF SADLER'S WELLS

1. Cf. *Theatrical Journal* for December 21, 1839; March 12, 1842; June 10, 1843.

2. Cf. *The Life*, p. 12.

3. A copy of the handbill is preserved in the Harvard Theatre Collection.

4. Descriptions of the opening night can be found in the *Athenaeum*, June 1, 1844, the *Theatrical Journal*, June 1, 1844, and *The Theatre*, N.S. VIII (1886), 135.

5. The *Critic*, quoted in *The Life*, pp. 71–72.

6. *Observer*, December 8, 1844.

7. *The Critic*, quoted in *The Life*, p. 72.

8. Richard Lee in *The Theatre*, N.S., VIII (1886), 135.

9. *Theatrical Journal*, Sept. 19, 1846.

10. His house, at 8 Canonbury Square, still stands and is marked by a plaque as the residence of Samuel Phelps, tragedian.

11. September 14, 1844.

12. Cf. Sir Henry Irving in his address at the Perry Bar Institute on March 6, 1878, quoted in *Actors and Actresses of Great Britain and the United States,* ed. Brander Mathews and Laurence Hutton (New York, 1886), IV, 82; H. B. Baker in his *History of the London Stage* (London, 1904), p. 370; and Bernard Miles, *The British Theatre* (London, 1948), pp. 32–33.

13. The biography of the editor appears in the issue of June 25, 1862, and in the weeks following.

14. Cf. the transcript of the proceedings in *The Life*, pp. 250–251.

15. Both letters are published in *The Life*, p. 372 and p. 389.

16. Letters from Forster, Dickens, Bulwer-Lytton, White, and others are pub-lished in an appendix to *The Life*, pp. 355 ff.

17. Both this and the following letter are in the Harvard Theatre Collection.

18. A monthly which lasted only a few months in 1847. Edited by Thomas Marshall, it can be found in a bound volume entitled *Lives of the Most Celebrated Actors and Actresses*, London, (no date). The quotation above is on p. 127.

19. For Webster's view, cf. Margaret Webster, *The Same Only Different* (New York, 1969), pp. 52–53.

20. The letters are published in *The Life,* pp. 359–360.

21. *Lloyd's Weekly London Newspaper,* July 9, 1848.

22. Letters from Phelps to his daughters are in the Harvard Theatre Collection.

23. *The Theatre,* N. S. IX (1887), 189.

24. The course of the quarrel is dealt with at some length in Richard Moody's *The Astor Place Riot* (Bloomington, Indiana, 1958).

25. *Douglas Jerrold's Weekly Newspaper,* August 1, 1846.

26. *Macready's Reminiscences and Diaries,* ed. Pollock, p. 637.

27. *Theatrical Journal,* September 10, 1851.

28. Unidentified review in the volume of Sadler's Wells playbills in the Harvard Theatre Collection.

29. The *Post,* reprinted in *The Life,* p. 233.

30. H. Barton Baker, *History of the London Stage,* (London, 1904), II, 172.

31. From this review until the end of Phelp's management, the reviewer for the *Examiner* was Henry Morley, professor of English Literature in University College, London. Most of his reviews of Sadler's Wells are included in a book called *The Journal of a London Playgoer,* first published in 1866. My references are to a later edition (1891) published in London, indicated hereafter simply by *J.L.P.* The review of *A Midsummer Night's Dream, J.L.P.,* pp. 56–61, is also included in *Specimens of English Dramatic Criticism,* ed. A. C. Ward (Oxford, 1945), p. 123 ff.

32. *J.L.P.,* p. 138.

33. Address at the Perry Bar Institute, quoted in Mathews and Hutton, IV, 82.

34. *Examiner,* October 21, 1854, *J.L.P.,* p. 82.

35. John Coleman, *Players and Playwrights,* I, 182.

36. Published in *The Life,* p. 390.

37. *Ibid.,* p. 362.

38. *Ibid.,* pp. 362–367.

39. *Ibid.,* p. 148.

40. *Gesammelte Werke,* Zweite Serie, Band 8 (Berlin, [1908]), pp. 455–590.

41. *Ibid.,* p. 502.

42. *Ibid.,* p. 490.

43. *Ibid.,* p. 536.

44. *Ibid.,* p. 577.

45. Cf. *The Life,* pp. 244–253.

46. Reprinted *ibid.,* pp. 241–242.

47. *Gesammelte Werke,* Zweite Serie, VIII, 586. According to Ernest L. Stahl (*Das englische Theater im 19. Jahrhundert* [Munich and Berlin, 1914], p. 87) Prince Friedrich welcomed Phelps to Berlin because he had seen him play Macbeth at Her Majesty's during the marriage festivities of January, 1858.

48. *Ibid.,* p. 590. Through such criticism Phelps's principle of unity in production profoundly influenced the German theatre. The Duke of Saxe-Meiningen followed his methods in directing his court players, whose performances from 1874 to

1890 ushered in modern theatre practice. Cf., Ernst L. Stahl, *Shakespeare und das Deutsche Theater* (Stuttgart, 1947), p. 486.

49. A letter in the Harvard Theatre Collection dated "Hamburg, April 4." Phelps must have written the wrong month by mistake, since he played there early in May, 1859.

50. Letter to Dr. Swan in the Harvard Theatre Collection.

51. *An Actor's Life*, pp. 252–253.

52. The *Examiner*, September 22, 1860; *J.L.P.*, p. 214.

53. Cf. *Weekly Dispatch*, May 26; *Examiner*, June 1; *Theatrical Journal*, June 26, 1861.

54. *La Vie Moderne en Angleterre* (Paris, 1862), p. 95.

55. The *Dramatic Review*, I (1885), 292–293.

56. *Some London Theatres, Past and Present* (London, 1883), p. 22.

IV. PHELPS AND SHAKESPEARE: ACTOR

1. Herbert Steele, quoted in *The Life*, pp. 216–217.

2. *Gesammelte Werke*, Zweite Serie, VIII, 535–544.

3. Cf. Arthur Colby Sprague, *Shakespeare and the Actors* (Cambridge, Massachusetts, 1944), p. 154.

4. Cf. the *Weekly Dispatch*, August 4, 1844.

5. From a letter written by W. M. Whitney published in *The Life*, pp. 399–400.

6. *Sixty Years of the Theater* (New York and London, 1916), p. 40.

7. *Douglas Jerrold's Weekly Newspaper*, October 2, 1847.

8. J. R. Towse, *Sixty Years of the Theater*, p. 43.

9. *Our Recent Actors*, (Boston, 1888), II, 18–19.

10. Reprinted in *The Life*, p. 84.

11. *Sixty Years of the Theater*, p. 40.

12. *Morning Advertiser*, November 4, 1861. Cf. also the *Daily Telegraph* and the *Morning Herald* of the same date.

13. *Sixty Years of the Theater*, p. 43.

14. Reprinted in *The Life*, p. 324.

15. *The Life*, p. 238.

16. His attitude toward playing Romeo and Hotspur is clear from letters written to his wife during his Liverpool engagement of 1843–1844, which are in the Harvard Theatre Collection.

18. Cf. his discussion of Phelps as Falstaff, *Gesammelte Werke*, Zweite Serie, VIII, 549–556.

19. *An Actor's Life*, p. 253.

20. The description given here is based upon a number of reviews. One of the most famous is Morley's in the *Examiner*, January 24, 1857, *J.L.P.*, pp. 137–140.

21. Unidentified review dated November 27 in the volume of Sadler's Wells playbills in the Havard Theatre Collection.

22. *Our Recent Actors*, II, 29; the *Examiner*, October 15, 1853, *J.L.P.*, pp. 56–61.

23. Ms. letter in the Harvard Theatre Collection.

24. *Sixty Years of the Theater*, pp. 46–47.

25. *Manchester Courier*, September 30, 1874, reprinted in *The Life*, pp. 327–328.

26. *Our Recent Actors*, II, 31.

27. *Examiner*, December 6, 1856; *J.L.P.*, pp. 135–137.

28. Unpublished manuscript in the Harvard Theatre Collection.

29. *Our Recent Actors*, I, 227–228.

30. *Gesammelte Werke*, Zweite Serie, VIII, 589.

31. Quoted in *The Life*, p. 243.

32. *Gesammelte Werke*, Zweite Serie, VIII, 587.

33. *Examiner*, October 26, 1861; *J.L.P.*, pp. 227–232.

34. *Dramatic Reminiscences* (London, 1860), p. 309.

35. F. G. Tomlins in the *Morning Advertiser*, October 10, 1864, reprinted in *The Life*, pp. 295–298.

36. *Autobiographic Memoirs* (London, 1911), I, 339.

37. Cf. his nephew's statement in *The Life*, p. 15.

38. *Essays on the Drama* (London, 1874), p. 200. Sir Theodore was not an unprejudiced critic: his admiration for Helen Faucit, who became his wife, extended even to her step-father, William Farren, whose Justice Shallow he preferred to Phelps's.

39. *Theatrical Notes* (London, 1893), pp. 77–78. Cf. also Clement Scott, *The Drama of Yesterday and To-day* (London, 1899), I, 191; and Dutton Cook in *The World*, March 29, 1876.

40. *Sixty Years of the Theater*, pp. 44–45.

41. "Mr. Phelps as Cardinal Wolsey," in *The Academy*, VIII (1875), 563–564.

42. *Manchester Examiner and Times*, March 7, 1877, reprinted in *The Life*, pp. 329–332.

43. Review of March 6, 1877, reprinted in *The Life*, pp. 328–329.

44. Booth himself did not like being compared with Phelps. In a letter to L. Barrett, January 20, 1881, he complained of English critics: "Not one of them can look back beyond Phelps—a dear old pump of the 2nd class, to compare me with, which they consider the greatest compliment they can pay." Otis Skinner, *The Last Tragedian* (New York, 1939), p. 195.

45. Cf. E. J. West, "The American Stage, 1855–70," *Theater Survey*, I (1960), 43. On the subject of traditional vs. modern acting see West's "From a Player's to a Playwright's Theater," *Quarterly Journal of Speech*, XXVIII (1942), 430–436.

46. Michael Williams, *Some London Theatres, Past and Present*, p. 27.

V. PHELPS AND SHAKESPEARE: MANAGER

1. Cf. *Theatrical Journal*, August 2, 1845.

2. Cf. the *Sun*, August 22, 1844.

3. Described in a letter to his daughters written in September, 1848, preserved in the Harvard Theatre Collection.

4. *The Theatre,* N.S. I (1878), 341–342.

5. *The Theatre,* N.S. VIII (1886), 137. Cf. Lewis Ball's letter in Scott, *The Drama of Yesterday and To-day,* I, 198–201, and the testimony of Hermann Vezin in the *Dramatic Review* (June 6, 1885), Sir Johnston Forbes-Robertson, *A Player under Three Reigns* (Boston, 1925), pp. 68–69, and J. H. Barnes, *Forty Years on the Stage* (London, 1914), p. 68.

6. *Examiner,* October 18, 1856; *J.L.P.,* p. 130.

7. *Morning Post,* quoted in *The Life,* p. 235.

8. H. Barton Baker, *History of the London Stage,* II, 93.

9. *Household Words,* IV (1851), 27.

10. *Examiner,* October 18, 1856; *J.L.P.,* pp. 129–130.

11. Charles H. Shattuck, *Mr. Macready Produces* As You Like It (Urbana, 1962), p. 1.

12. Cf. Alan Downer, *The Eminent Tragedian,* pp. 224–234.

13. *Diaries,* ed. Toynbee, II, 17–18.

14. Cf. *Theatrical Journal,* August 19, 1857.

15. *The Theatre,* N. S. I (1878), 341.

16. Letter from W. M. Whitney, published in *The Life,* p. 400.

17. *The Theatre,* N.S. I (1878), 340–341.

18. *Examiner,* October 18, 1856; *J.L.P.,* p. 129.

19. *Gesammelte Werke,* Zweite Serie, VIII, 490 ff.

20. *Ibid.,* p. 562.

21. *Examiner,* October 21, 1854; *J.L.P.,* p. 83.

22. *Examiner,* October 15, 1853; *J.L.P.,* p. 57.

23. Letter dated "Sunday" in the Harvard Theatre Collection.

24. September 26, 1858, reprinted in *The Life,* pp. 227–230.

25. *Gesammelte Werke,* Zweite Serie, VIII, 484–485.

26. Cf. Charles Shattuck, *Mr. Macready Produces* As You Like It, Introduction and notes to the text.

27. The prompt book used in the production of 1845 can be identified by the names of the cast. It also contains the following inscription: "Time occupied in representation 2 hrs. 50 mins. Marked under the direction of W. C. Williams, T. R. S. Wells for S. Phelps Esqre."

28. Of the two Phelps prompt books for *Lear* in the Folger Library, one is clearly from 1845, although it has a second set of cuttings superimposed on the first.

29. Three of Phelps's prompt books for *Macbeth* are in the Folger Shakespeare Library. One, marked T R S W 1846, shows the version used in 1847 with subsequent revisions superimposed.

30. Phelps's prompt book is in the Folger Shakespeare Library.

31. *Ibid.*

32. *Ibid.*

33. *Examiner,* October 21, 1854; *J.L.P.,* p. 82.

34. Unidentified review dated September 2, 1852, in the volume of Sadler's Wells Playbills in the Harvard Theatre Collection.

35. Prompt book in the Folger Shakespeare Library.

36. *Ibid.*

37. Both prompt books in the Folger Shakespeare Library.

38. Prompt book in the Folger Shakespeare Library.

39. *Collected Works,* eds. Waller and Glover (London and New York, 1903), VIII, 276.

40. Prompt book in the Folger Shakespeare Library.

41. *Ibid.*

42. *Ibid.*

43. *Ibid.*

44. Prompt book in the Harvard Theatre Collection.

45. Prompt book in the Folger Shakespeare Library.

46. Cf. A. C. Sprague, *Shakespeare and the Actors,* p. 129.

47. Macready dimmed the stage lamps in *Macbeth* and *King John,* and he used blue mediums in front of lamps to create the effect of moonlight, but his stage was never really dark. The appearance of side illumination, as if light were streaming in through a window, was painted on the canvas background. Cf. Shattuck, *Macready's King John,* pp. 28 f. and Downer, *William Charles Macready,* pp. 318 f.

48. *Gesammelte Werke,* Zweite Serie, VIII, 535–544. For Phelps's acting and stage business, see above p. 168 f.

49. A sketch of the arrangement of this scene is given in the second of three prompt books in the Folger Shakespeare Library.

50. *Athenaeum,* March 1, 1845.

51. *Bell's Weekly Messenger* reprinted in *The Life,* p. 84.

52. An indication of the obscurity of Phelps's reputation today can be found in the fact that Dennis Bartholomeusz in his *Macbeth and the Players* (Cambridge, England, 1969) dismisses Phelp's productions of *Macbeth* in two pages while devoting twenty-five to Macready's.

53. *Gesammelte Werke,* Zweite Serie, VIII, 562–580. Cf. also Albert B. Weiner, "Samuel Phelps' Staging of Macbeth" in *Educational Theatre Journal,* XVI (1964), 122–133, which describes the production of 1857, using both Fontane and a prompt book in the Yale University Library.

54. Mr. Weiner describes the gauzes as descending from the flies, but Godfrey Turner's description (*The Theatre,* N. S. III (1884), 131) makes it clear that they were pulled up.

55. Cf. A. C. Sprague, *Shakespeare and the Actors,* pp. 251–264.

56. *Examiner,* October 15, 1853; *J.L.P.,* pp. 56–61; and in *Specimens of English Dramatic Criticism,* ed. A. C. Ward, pp. 123 f.

57. Described by Fontane, *Gesammelte Werke,* Zweite Serie, VIII, 544–549.

58. Reviews of *Timon* appeared in the *Theatrical Journal,* September 17, 1851; the *Athenaeum,* September 20, 1851; the *Morning Advertiser,* October 13, 1856; the *Times,* October 13, 1856; and the *Examiner,* October 18, 1856 (*J.L.P.,* 129–132).

59. Cf. *The Life,* pp. 204, 214.

60. *Examiner,* October 21, 1854; *J.L.P.,* pp. 78–84.

61. *The London Theatre, 1811–1866,* ed. Eluned Brown (London, 1966), p. 199.

62. *Examiner,* October 24, 1857; *J.L.P.,* pp. 165–167.

63. Cf. Chapter III above, *passim*.

64. *Sixty Years of the Theater*, p. 33.

65. *The Life*, p. 13.

66. Manuscript in the Harvard Theatre Collection.

67. Reported in *The Theatre*, N.S. I (1878), 437.

68. *Examiner*, January 24, 1857; *J.L.P.*, p. 138.

69. *Our Recent Actors*, II, 36.

70. *The Theatre*, N.S. I (1878), 342 and 344.

71. Clement Scott and Cecil Howard, *The Life and Reminiscences of E. L. Blanchard* (New York, 1891), I, 99.

72. XLI (October 5, 1861), 139.

73. Cf. Alfred Darbyshire, *The Art of the Victorian Stage* (London, 1907), p. 21: "I have called Charles Kean the pioneer of what we are pleased to call 'Revivals,' but Phelps was certainly the originator of what we understand by the word 'Productions.'"

74. Henry Morley, *Journal of A London Playgoer*, pp. 130–131.

VI. NON-SHAKESPEAREAN DRAMA AT SADLER'S WELLS

1. Herbert Steele, reprinted in *The Life*, p. 219.

2. Cf. Marston, *Our Recent Actors*, I, 282.

3. *Dramatic Essays by John Forster and George Henry Lewes*, ed. William Archer and R. W. Lowe (London, 1896), p. 119.

4. Dated Friday, November 22, 1850, in the unpublished manuscript in the Harvard Theatre Collection.

5. *Examiner*, September 25, 1858; *J. L.P.*, p. 188.

6. *Ibid*.

7. Cf. the *Athenaeum*, October 23, 1858; and Dutton Cook, *Nights at the Play* (London, 1883), I, 38–39.

8. *Examiner*, October 23, 1858; *J.L.P.*, p. 192.

9. December 18, 1858.

10. The *Examiner*, April 14, 1860; *J.L.P.*, p. 208.

11. *Forty Years on the Stage*, p. 137.

12. *Sixty Years of the Theater*, p. 55.

13. Herbert Steele, quoted in *The Life*, p. 219.

14. June 15, 1844.

15. *Supra*, p. 160.

16. *The Life*, p. 202.

17. *Ibid.*, p. 306.

18. Cf. *Diaries*, ed. Toynbee, I, 377; and II, 192.

19. Cf. *The Life*, p. 373.

20. Facts about this agreement and correspondence relating to it can be found in *The Life*, pp. 7–8, 396–397 and in letters in the Harvard Theatre Collection.

21. *The Theatre*, N.S. I (1878), 339–340.

22. Cf. Shattuck, *Bulwer and Macready*, p. 128.

23. *Our Recent Actors*, II, 22–23.

24. *Ibid.*, 17–18.

25. *The Life*, pp. 381–384.

26. *Ibid.*, p. 390.

27. The entire letter is published in *The Life*, pp. 397–399.

28. Cf. the article by A. H. Quinn in *P.M.L.A.*, N.S. XXV (1917), 234–238.

29. Cf. *supra*, p. 124.

30. *Examiner*, November 19, 1859; *J.L.P.*, pp. 200–201.

31. Unidentified review in the volume of Sadler's Wells playbills in the Harvard Theatre Collection.

32. *The Theatre*, N.S. I (1878), 342.

33. Farewell address, published in the *Morning Advertiser*, November 8, 1862, and reprinted in *The Life*, pp. 212–214.

VII. RETURN TO THE WEST END

1. Two letters written by Fechter to Phelps proposing the terms of his engagement came to light in 1939 upon the death of Phelps's friend Harry Plowman. The *Times* of April 11, 1939, reported the contents of the letters and commented upon Fechter's duplicity in the matter. The two letters are now in the Harvard Theatre Collection.

2. Cf. Samuel C. Chew, *Byron in England* (London, 1924), p. 106 n.

3. John Hollingshead, *Gaiety Chronicles* (Westminster, 1898), p. 73.

4. *Essays on the Drama*, p. 82.

5. These three letters are in the Folger Shakespeare Library.

6. Manuscript letter to Simmons in the Folger Shakespeare Library.

7. The manuscript letters are in the Harvard Theatre Collection.

8. One night when Phelps was acting, Tom Robertson and Joseph Jefferson (who was playing Rip Van Winkle at the Adelphi this season) visited Drury Lane to see his Macbeth. The incident is recorded in Jefferson's *Autobiography* (New York, 1889), p. 319.

9. *An Actor's Life*, p. 277.

10. A manuscript letter in the Harvard Theatre Collection, dated "Sunday Morn."

11. The letters are in the Harvard Theatre Collection.

12. Cf. *supra*, p. 213.

13. Manuscript letter in the Harvard Theatre Collection.

14. A series of manuscript letters addressed to Etty (Esther) in April and May, 1868, are in the Harvard Theatre Collection.

15. *Sixty Years of the Theater*, p. 58.

16. *Nights at the Play*, I, 84.

17. *Old Drury Lane* (London, 1881), II, 199.

18. From the *Sphinx* and the *Free Lance* of November 27, 1869, reprinted in *The Life*, pp. 322–326.

19. Richard Dickins, *Forty Years of Shakespeare on the English Stage* (London, c. 1907), p .15.

20. *Manchester Examiner and Times*, September 19, 1873, reprinted in *The Life*, pp. 326–327.

21. *The Dramatic Review*, June 6, 1885.

22. *Gaiety Chronicles*, p. 253.

23. *The Theatre*, N.S. I (1878), 352.

24. *The Academy*, VIII (1875), 564.

25. *Nights at the Play*, II, 27.

26. *Forty Years of Shakespeare on the English Stage*, p. 23.

27. *Gaiety Chronicles*, pp. 254–282.

28. *Gaiety, Theatre of Enchantment* (London, 1949), p. 152.

29. *Letters to Members of His Family*, ed. Algernon and Ellen Gissing, (Boston, 1927), p .35.

30. *Memoirs of an Author* (London, 1895), I, 348.

31. *The Academy*, VIII (1875), 564.

32. *Theatrical Notes*, p. 145.

33. *Memoirs of Samuel Phelps* (London, 1886) and *Players and Playwrights I Have Known* (London, 1888). These books contain more misinformation and unintentional misrepresentation than the usual actor's memoirs.

34. *The Life*, p. 335.

35. *The Academy*, XIV (1878), 485.

36. *Letters to Members of His Family*, p. 35.

37. *Memoirs of an Author*, I, 347.

38. *From Phelps to Gielgud* (London, 1936), p. 164.

39. *Actors and Actresses of Great Britain and the United States*, ed. Brander Mathews and Laurence Hutton, IV, 71–72.

A Selected Bibliography

I. BOOKS AND ARTICLES

Ackermann, R., *Microcosm of London,* 1809, reprinted 1904.

Allen, Percy, *The Stage Life of Mrs. Stirling,* London, 1922.

Allen, Shirley S., "Samuel Phelps, Last of a Dynasty," *Theatre Annual,* VIII (1950), 55–70.

Anderson, James R., *An Actor's Life,* London, 1902.

Archer, Frank, *An Actor's Notebooks,* London [after 1899].

Archer, William, and Robert W. Lowe, eds., *Dramatic Essays by John Forster and George Henry Lewes,* London, 1896.

Armstrong, Cecil F., *A Century of Great Actors, 1750–1850,* London, 1912.

Arthur, Sir George, *From Phelps to Gielgud,* London, 1936.

Arundell, Dennis, *The Story of Sadler's Wells,* London, 1965.

Baker, H. Barton, *The London Stage: Its History and Traditions,* London, 1889.

Ball, R. H., *The Amazing Career of Sir Giles Overreach,* Princeton, 1939.

Barnes, J. H., *Forty Years on the Stage,* New York, 1915.

Bartholomeusz, Dennis, *Macbeth and the Players,* Cambridge, England, 1969.

à Beckett, Arthur W., *Green-Room Recollections,* Bristol, 1896.

Belton, Fred, *Random Recollections of an Old Actor,* London, 1880.

Burton, E. J., *The British Theatre, 1100–1900,* London, 1961.

Calvert, Mrs. Charles, *Sixty-Eight Years on the Stage,* London, 1911.

Chew, Samuel C., *Byron in England,* London, 1924.

Coleman, John, *Players and Playwrights I Have Known,* London, 1888.

Coleman, John, and Edward Coleman, *Memoirs of Samuel Phelps,* London, 1886.

Cook, Dutton, *Hours with the Players,* London, 1881.

Cook, Dutton, *Nights at the Play,* London, 1883.

Cook, Dutton, *On the Stage,* London, 1883.

Cook, James, *The Actor's Notebook,* London, 1841.

334

Cumberland's British Theatre, London, 1826.

Darbyshire, Alfred, *The Art of the Victorian Stage,* London, 1907.

Day, M. C., and J. C. Trewin, *The Shakespeare Memorial Theatre,* London, 1932.

Dibdin, James C., *The Annals of the Edinburgh Stage,* Edinburgh, 1888.

Dickens, Charles, "Shakespeare and Newgate," *Household Words,* IV (1851), 25–27.

Dickins, Richard, *Forty Years of Shakespeare on the English Stage* [London, c. 1907].

Disher, Maurice W., *Blood and Thunder,* London, 1949.

Downer, Alan S., *The Eminent Tragedian William Charles Macready,* Cambridge, Massachusetts, 1966.

Faucit, Helena (Lady Martin), *On Some of Shakespeare's Female Characters,* Edinburgh and London, 1888.

Fitzgerald, Percy, *Memoirs of an Author,* London, 1895.

Fletcher, George, *Studies of Shakespeare,* London, 1847.

Fontane, Theodor, "Die Londoner Theater," *Gesammelte Werke,* Zweite Serie, Band VIII, Berlin [1908], 455–590.

Forbes-Robertson, Sir Johnston, *A Player under Three Reigns,* Boston, 1925.

Ganthony, Robert, *Random Recollections,* London, n.d.

Genest, J., *Some Account of the English Stage,* Bath, 1832.

Gissing, George, *Letters to Members of His Family,* ed. Algernon and Ellen Gissing, Boston, 1927.

Hackett, James H., *Shakespeare's Plays and Actors,* New York, 1863.

Harrison, Frederic, *Autobiographic Memoirs,* London, 1911.

Hazlitt, William, *Collected Works,* ed. Waller and Glover, London and New York, 1903, Vol. VIII.

Hollingshead, John, *Gaiety Chronicles,* Westminster, 1898.

Hollingshead, John, "Phelps at the Gaiety," *The Theatre,* N.S. I (1878), 352–354.

Horne, R. H., *John Webster,* Duchess of Malfi, London, 1851.

Jefferson, Joseph, *Autobiography,* New York, 1889.

Joseph, Bertram, *The Tragic Actor,* New York, 1959.

Kenney, Charles L., *Mr. Phelps and the Critics of His Correspondence with the Stratford Committee,* London, 1864.

Knight, Joseph, *Theatrical Notes,* London, 1893.

Lawrence, W. J., *The Life of Gustavus Vaughan Brooke,* Belfast, 1892.

Lee, Richard, "Samuel Phelps, a Biographical Sketch," *The Theatre,* N.S. VIII (1886), 59–69, 135–150.

Lee, Sidney, *Shakespeare and the Modern Stage,* New York, 1906.

Lewes, George H., *On Actors and the Art of Acting,* New York, 1878.

Lelyveld, Toby, *Shylock on the Stage,* London, 1861.

Lowe, R. W., *A Bibliographical Account of English Theatrical Literature*, London, 1888.

Ludlow, N. M., *Dramatic Life As I Found It*, St. Louis, 1880.

Macqueen-Pope, W., *Gaiety, Theatre of Enchantment*, London, 1949.

Macqueen-Pope, W., *Haymarket: Theatre of Perfection*, London, 1948.

Malot, Hector, *La Vie Moderne en Angleterre*, Paris, 1862.

Marshall, Thomas, *Lives of the Most Celebrated Actors and Actresses*, London [c. 1847].

Marston, Westland, *Our Recent Actors*, Boston, 1888.

Martin, Sir Theodore, *Essays on the Drama*, London, 1874.

Mathews, Brander, and Laurence Hutton, eds., *Actors and Actresses of Great Britain and the United States*, New York, 1886, Vol. IV.

Meeks, L. H., *Sheridan Knowles and the Theatre of His Time*, Bloomington, Indiana, 1933.

Merchant, Moelwyn, *Shakespeare and the Artist*, Oxford, 1959.

Miles, Bernard, *The British Theatre*, London, 1948.

Moody, Richard, *The Astor Place Riot*, Bloomington, Indiana, 1958.

Morley, Henry, *The Journal of a London Playgoer*, London, 1891.

Newton, H. Chance, *Cues and Curtain Calls*, London, 1927.

Nicholson, Watson, *The Struggle for a Free Stage in London*, Boston and New York, 1906.

Nicoll, Allardyce, *The English Theatre*, London, 1936.

Nicoll, Allardyce, *A History of English Drama*, 1660–1900, Cambridge, England, 1952–1959, Vols. IV, V, and VI.

Odell, George C. D., *Shakespeare from Betterton to Irving*, New York, 1920.

Pascoe, Charles E., *The Dramatic List*, London, 1880.

Pearce, Charles E., *Madame Vestris and Her Times*, London, n.d.

Pearson, Hesketh, *The Last Actor-Managers*, London, 1950.

Phelps, W. May, and John Forbes-Robertson, *The Life and Life-Work of Samuel Phelps*, London, 1886.

Planché, James R., *Recollections and Reflections*, London, 1872.

Pollock, Sir Frederick, ed., *Macready's Reminiscences and Selections from His Diaries and Letters*, New York, 1875.

Quinn, A. H., *A History of the American Drama*, 2nd. ed., New York, 1943.

Reed, Joseph W., Jr., "Browning and Macready: the Final Quarrel," *P.M.L.A.* LXXV (1960), 597–603.

Rice, Charles, *The London Theatre in the Eighteen-Thirties*, eds. A. C. Sprague and Bertram Shuttleworth, London, 1950.

Robinson, Henry Crabb, *The London Theatre, 1811–1866*, ed. Eluned Brown, London, 1966.

Rowell, George, *The Victorian Theatre*, Oxford, 1956.

Russell, W. Clark, *Representative Actors*, London and New York, 1888.

[Saintsbury, H. A.], *Letters of an Unsuccessful Actor,* Boston [1923].

Scott, Clement, "The Death of Mr. Phelps," *The Theatre,* N.S. I (1878), 325–329.

Scott, Clement, *The Drama of Yesterday and To-day,* London, 1899.

Scott, Clement, and Cecil Howard, *The Life and Reminiscences of E. L. Blanchard,* New York, 1891.

Shattuck, Charles H., *Bulwer and Macready,* Urbana, 1958.

Shattuck, Charles H., *Mr. Macready Produces* As You Like It, Urbana, 1962.

Shattuck, Charles H., *William Charles Macready's* King John, Urbana, 1962.

Sherson, Erroll, *London's Lost Theatres of the Nineteenth Century,* London, 1925.

Short, Ernest, *Sixty Years of the Theatre,* London, 1951.

Sillard, Robert M., *Barry Sullivan,* London, 1901.

Skinner, Otis, *The Last Tragedian,* New York, 1939.

Spencer, Hazelton, *Shakespeare Improved,* Cambridge, Massachusetts, 1927.

Sprague, Arthur C., *Shakespeare and the Actors,* Cambridge, Massachusetts, 1944.

Sprague, Arthur C., *Shakespearian Players and Performances,* Cambridge, Massachusetts, 1953.

Stahl, Ernst Leopold, *Das englische Theatre im 19 Jahrhundert,* Munich and Berlin, 1914.

Stahl, Ernst Leopold, *Shakespeare und das Deutsche Theatre,* Stuttgart, 1947.

Stirling, Edward, *Old Drury Lane,* London, 1881.

Tallis, John, *Drawing Room Table Book,* London and New York [1851].

Taylor, Tom, "Phelps and *The Fool's Revenge,*" *The Theatre,* N.S. I (1878), 338–344.

Thomas, Moy, "The Late Mr. Samuel Phelps," *The Academy,* XIV (1878), 485.

Thomas, Moy, "Mr. Phelps as Cardinal Wolsey," *The Academy,* VIII (1875), 563–564.

Tolles, Winton, *Tom Taylor and the Victorian Drama,* New York, 1940.

Towse, John Ranken, *Sixty Years of the Theater,* New York and London, 1916.

Toynbee, William, ed., *The Diaries of William Charles Macready,* New York, 1912.

Trewin, J. C., *Mr. Macready,* London, 1955.

Turner, Godfrey, "First Nights of My Young Days," *The Theatre,* N.S. IX (1887), 82–91, 187–193, 249–257, 297–304.

Turner, Godfrey, "Scenery, Dresses and Decoration," *The Theatre,* N.S. III (1884), 126–134.

Vandenhoff, George, *Dramatic Reminiscences,* London, 1860. (Apparently the same book as *Leaves from an Actor's Notebook.*)

Webster, Margaret, *The Same Only Different*, New York, 1969.

Weiner, Albert B., "Samuel Phelps' Staging of *Macbeth*," *Educational Theatre Journal*, XVI (1964), 122–133.

West, E. J., "The American Stage, 1855–1870," *Theatre Survey*, I (1960), 43–64.

West, E. J., "From a Player's to a Playwright's Theatre," *Quarterly Journal of Speech*, XXVIII (1942), 430–436.

West, E. J., "The Victorian Voice on the Stage," *Quarterly Journal of Speech*, XXXI (1945), 29–34.

Williams, Michael, *Some London Theatres, Past and Present*, London, 1883.

Wilson, Mrs. C. Baron, *Our Actresses*, London, 1844.

Whyte, Frederic, *Actors of the Century*, London, 1898.

Wyndham, Henry Saxe, *The Annals of Covent Garden Theatre*, London, 1906.

II. LONDON PERIODICALS*

The Athenaeum
Bell's Weekly Messenger
The Court Journal
The Daily News
The Daily Telegraph
Douglas Jerrold's Weekly Newspaper
The Dramatic and Musical Review
The Dramatic Review
The Era
The Examiner
The Globe
Lloyd's Weekly London Newspaper
The Morning Advertiser
The Morning Chronicle
The Morning Herald
The Morning Post
The Observer
Punch
The Spectator
The Stage
The Stage-Manager
The Sunday Times

* Many of the reviews quoted in the text are reprinted in W. May Phelps, *The Life;* but whenever the author has looked at the original review, she has made reference to the periodical only, for the sake of simplifying the footnotes.

Tallis's Dramatic Magazine
The Theatre
Theatre Notebook
The Theatrical Journal (*and Musical Intelligencer*)
The Theatrical Times
The Times
The Weekly Dispatch

III. PROVINCIAL NEWSPAPERS

Caledonian Mercury (Edinburgh)
Davenport Independent
Devonshire Chronicle and Exeter News (Exeter)
Edinburgh News
Edinburgh Observer
Evening Courant (Edinburgh)
Featherstone's Exeter Times
Manchester Examiner and Times
Manchester Guardian
Northern Whig (Belfast)
Plymouth, Devonport and Stonehouse Herald
Plymouth and Devonport Weekly Journal
Preston Chronicle
Preston Pilot
Sheffield Courant
Sheffield Independent
Trewman's Exeter Flying Post
Wakefield and Halifax Journal
Western Luminary (Exeter)
Western Times (Exeter)
Woolmer's Exeter and Plymouth Gazette
York Chronicle

IV. SPECIAL MATERIAL IN THE HARVARD THEATRE COLLECTION

Manuscript letters and papers in the Phelps collection.

Phelps's prompt books for *Henry the Fourth, Part Two,* and *Coriolanus.*

Playbills: Hull Theatre, Olympic Theatre, Drury Lane, Covent Garden, and Sadler's Wells.

Extra-illustrated edition of *Actors and Actresses of Great Britain and the United States,* ed. Brander Mathews and Laurence Hutton, Vol. IV.

Charles Rice, Dramatic Register (1835–1838) and Diary (1840–1850).

V. SPECIAL MATERIAL IN THE FOLGER MEMORIAL SHAKESPEARE LIBRARY
Manuscript letters and papers in the Phelps collection.
Collection of Phelps Prompt Books: *Antony and Cleopatra*; *As You Like It*
(2); *Comedy of Errors*; *Coriolanus* (3); *Henry the Fourth, Part One*;
Henry the Fifth; *Henry the Eighth*; *King John*; *Julius Caesar*; *King Lear*
(2); *Love's Labour's Lost*; *Macbeth* (3); *Measure for Measure*; *Midsummer Night's Dream* (2); *Pericles* (2); *Richard the Third* (3); *Romeo
and Juliet* (2); *Taming of the Shrew*; *The Tempest*; *Timon of Athens*;
Two Gentlemen of Verona; *Twelfth Night*; *The Winter's Tale*.

Bibliographical note: Kittredge's text has been used for numbering lines and
for comparison with texts of prompt books.

Index